British Encounters with Syrian-Mesopotamian Overland Routes to India, 1751–1795

I0901813

British Encounters with Syrian-Mesopotamian Overland Routes to India, 1751–1795

Rethinking Enlightenment Improvement

Mohammad Sakhnini

ANTHEM PRESS

Anthem Press
An imprint of Wimbledon Publishing Company
www.anthempress.com

This edition first published in UK and USA 2026
by ANTHEM PRESS
75–76 Blackfriars Road, London SE1 8HA, UK
or PO Box 9779, London SW19 7ZG, UK
and
244 Madison Ave #116, New York, NY 10016, USA

First published in the UK and USA by Anthem Press in 2023

British Library Cataloguing-in-Publication Data
A catalogue record for this book is available from the British Library.

Library of Congress Cataloging-in-Publication Data: 2026942760

ISBN-13: 978-1-80136-051-7 (Pbk)
ISBN-10: 1-80136-051-0 (Pbk)

Cover Credit: Yale Center for British Art, Paul Mellon Collection

This title is also available as an eBook.

CONTENTS

ACKNOWLEDGMENT

If one is given the choice to pick an image that reflects the efforts, space and time I spent on this project, then the picture of an eighteenth-century Middle Eastern commercial caravan marching in the desert comes to mind. During those days, the setting up of the caravan would often take a lot of time, and the people who would participate in it were usually from different social, religious and cultural affiliations and backgrounds (Muslim Arabs, Christian Arabs, Jews, Turks, Europeans and Indians); the march across the deserts was often hard and slow but nevertheless fruitful for those seeking to take the opportunity to improve themselves. It is in this spirit of improvement, a spirit of the Arab caravan, that I set up to write this book and, during the years of research and writing, I relished and benefitted from the experience of being in the company of many great teachers, mentors, colleagues, friends, family members and fellow travellers. When I set out to write this work, the extraordinary amount of material I found in libraries and archives made me despondent to the extent that I sometimes envisaged myself being a traveller in a rudderless caravan, but it was for the great support and mentorship of Professor Gerald MacLean that I was able to put myself back on track. Professor MacLean's immense scholarship and encouragement shaped my thinking about the relationship between improvement and cross-cultural encounters. Excellent conversations I also had with Professor Donna Landry about the British eighteenth century shaped my thinking about the historical context around the travel books I examined in this work. It is also because of the extraordinary support and encouragement I received from my mentors and teachers at the University of Exeter, Professor Regenia Gagnier and Dr. Paul Young, that I was able to think productively about the theoretical and methodological contexts around my work. Presenting my work about cross-cultural encounters in different venues in the United Kingdom, mainly at the Woolf Institute, Cambridge and UCL, London, allowed me to collaborate and interact with extraordinary people whose help, encouragements and conversations were among the kindest I have ever had in any academic setting: Dr. Esther-Miriam Wagner, Dunya Habash and Professor Haim Yacoubi. Also, I'd like to thank colleagues and friends whose conversations and collaboration on various projects enriched my thinking about the idea of a cross-cultural encounter between Britain and the Middle East: Sascha R. Klement, Mansour Nsasra, Lenora Hanson, Sarah Copsey Alsader, Mahmoud Shahin, Professor Mark Dressman, Kevin Garvey, and David Dalton. Special thanks should be directed to Sudha Narayanan, Venkat Perla Ramesh and Gomathy Ilammathe for overseeing the production and publication process. Finally, it is to my parents (Zakaria and Latifa) whose sheer stoicism in the midst of adversity has taught me how humility is essential to seeking knowledge and gaining improvement that I dedicate this book.

INTRODUCTION
PLURALISING THE ENLIGHTENMENT: IMPROVEMENT AND CROSS-CULTURAL ENCOUNTERS

Knowledge emerged from a practice.

—Henry Lefebvre, *The Production of Space* (1974)

In the Desert, as at sea, there is fellowship in every living thing.

—Thomas Skinner, *Adventures during a Journey Overland to India* (1863)

In the past 40 years, many scholars have debated the extent to which European literary, cultural and scientific traditions have been shaped by a rich history of encounter between Europe and the Ottoman-Arab region. In most of these studies, two methodological paradigms framed almost all scholarly engagements with the politics of encounter. The first paradigm I wish to call 'the hegemony paradigm'. This paradigm is shaped by a postcolonial reading of European literary and philosophical heritage of the past three hundred years.[1] Informed by Edward Said's *Orientalism*, which was first published in 1978, the scholarship in this paradigm has shown how many nineteenth- and twentieth-century European representations of the Orient shaped and were shaped by a systemic discourse of power and knowledge, what Said called 'the enormously systematic discipline by which European culture was able to manage-and even produce-the Orient politically, sociologically, militarily, ideologically, scientifically, and imaginatively during the post-Enlightenment period' (Said 2003: 3).[2] The second one I wish to call 'the displacement paradigm'. Informed by eminent anthropological and sociological works, such as those by Claude Lévi-Strauss (1955) and Clifford James Geertz (1997), studies in this paradigm showed how the act of 'speaking' about different cultures constitutes opportunities for negotiating and rethinking dominant debates in one's own culture.[3] Both paradigms differ on the question of agency, that is, the author, according to the first paradigm, speaks for the Other, whereas he or she, according to the second paradigm, uses the Other in an effort to speak to and on behalf of one's own culture. Despite the difference in the said approaches, both show how the Other embodies the values and manners which the Self wishes to negate about its own culture: despotism, religious excesses, misogyny and intolerant attitudes towards minorities. Despite their difference, both paradigms capture the moral tensions involving living in a world teeming with diverse cultural and value systems.

Scholars such as Billie Melman (1992, 2002), Gerald MacLean (2004), Geoffrey Nash (2005) and recently Katrina O'Loughlin (2018), among others, have complicated these paradigms by demonstrating how European writings about the Ottoman-Arab East revealed complex and diverse cross-cultural attitudes, showing how complex notions of class, gender and nation shaped and were shaped by encounters.[4] For all these scholars, Europeans' representations of other cultures expressed complex articulations of and reflections on political and social changes in Europe. In other words, writings about other cultures, in the words of Genevieve Lloyd, 'set the scene for a critical engagement with the author's own present' (Lloyd 2013: 22). The Orient in these articulations and reflections did not figure as a contrastive space, one of negation, but rather one of dislocation, a 'borderline' space, as Homi Bhabha termed it, where one feels empowered to ride on a mythical bandwagon of what Benedict Anderson called an 'imagined community' but while doing so he or she finds opportunities of dissent and critique, which complicates ideals of cultural purity and homogeneity.[5]

This book is a modest contribution to the recent scholarly efforts which complicated our understanding of cross-cultural encounter. The book shows how eighteenth-century British travels on the overland routes to India moulded the thinking of Britons with new perspectives and ideas that allowed them to rethink some popular debates in their own culture, mainly those relating to the meaning and value of growth and improvement.[6] Improvement, as a dominant practice and habit of thought in eighteenth-century Britain, mainly in the writings of the philosophers and historians of the Scottish Enlightenment, as Peter Womak argues, was a term charged with a 'narrowly economic' meaning (Womak 1989: 3). Improvement referred to the 'cultivation of an asset for purposes of making profits' (Womak 1989: 3). But it also, as Womak shows, infiltrated the realm of culture and acquired 'social, aesthetic, moral, juridical and religious applications' which informed responses to economic and political changes in modern British society now seeing itself as refined, civilised and polite (Womak 1989: 3). In academic and intellectual circles, improvement also shaped the philosophical discourses which explained the rise and progress of societies in stages. In these discourses, civility was seen as the trait distinguishing societies that managed to overcome barbarism, pastoralism and feudalism on their way to commercialism.[7] Eighteenth-century responses to improvement vacillated between cheerful optimism and repulsive pessimism. Many at the time held the position that certain societies often distance themselves from, but also yearn to, a set of moral, political and religious virtues that are no longer workable in modern times.[8]

These responses, as this book shows, shaped British travel writings about the Arabs and Muslims. Travellers and travel writers who visited and wrote about Arabs and Muslim land in the eighteenth century were not radical believers in improvement. Nor did their travel experiences indicate that all British travellers in the Ottoman-Arab land expressed dissenting voices critiquing modern enchantments in Britain with what the late eighteenth-century English philosopher William Godwin called the 'perfectibility of man' (Godwin 1793: I, 43). Yet their concerns about the changing social, political and moral landscape of their nation – one redolent with voices normalising corruption, poverty, avarice and luxury as indicators of a modern, improved and commercial society – were highlighted and also negotiated in their accounts of a region and culture that the proponents of improvement in Britain often associated with barbarism and primitivism. The eighteenth century, as this book argues, was an important period in the annals of British encounters with the Arab-Ottoman world mainly because it was a transitional period between an early-modern age in which Europeans feared Islam and the Ottoman Empire and a nineteenth-century era in which British commentators on the region, as historian Kathryn Tidrick wrote, 'believed in' Britain's 'rights to interfere in the affairs of others' (1989: 159). As this book shows, travellers in the overland routes to India did not act as, in the words of Adriana Craciun and Mary Terrall, 'history's mobile agents of global change' (2019: 7). They were rather the knowledge brokers between East and West. Their encounters with the Middle East provided them with new insights on how to negotiate cultural difference in a modern age dominated by what the English philosopher Bernard Williams called the habit of 'reflectiveness', that is, the consciousness among many in modern Europe that up to a certain point there was an 'integrated, concrete, familiar and community life' shattered by radical political and social changes that many in Britain associated with improvement (1985: 163).

Historical and Political Context

In the second half of the eighteenth century, mainly in the period between the Seven Years War (1756) and the French occupation of Egypt (1798–1801), many in Britain and India, mainly the officials associated with the East India Company (EIC), were immensely interested in securing safe passages for British dispatches, merchants, military officers and servants who flocked in great numbers on the Syrian and Mesopotamian overland routes to India. An example showing how this route was immensely important for the EIC officials is the story of a dispatch sent from London to India in 1756. In his *British Interests in the Persian Gulf* (1967), Abdul Amir Amin reported how a dispatch carrying news about the declaration of war between Britain and France was sent by the EIC across Syria to India (Amin 1967: 60). The war was announced in May 1756 and the letter reached India in November of that year. The letter took six months on the road between England and India, whereas a copy of the same letter took nine months to reach India by the Cape of Good Hope.[9] The Syrian-Mesopotamian overland routes included the region circling Latakia and Iskenderun on the Mediterranean Sea and Basra and Bandar Abbas on the Persian Gulf [Figure 1]. Some Britons reached India by travelling across shorter Middle Eastern routes to India such as those connecting El Qoseir on the Red Sea with Alexandria on the Mediterranean. But the political instability that beset Egypt throughout the eighteenth century made these routes impractical for many British travellers.

The Cape of Good Hope route remained the principal commercial transit between Europe and India throughout the eighteenth century. But travelling to and from India across Syria and Mesopotamia by many Britons, including those 'officers on furlough' who wished to make a 'speedy communication between Great Britain and India', was seen as less expensive, speedier and more convenient than that across the Cape route (Taylor 1799: II, 1). Robert T. Harrison has recently stated that routes across Syria and Mesopotamia were seen by many in the EIC as 'the lynchpin and lifeline of' the

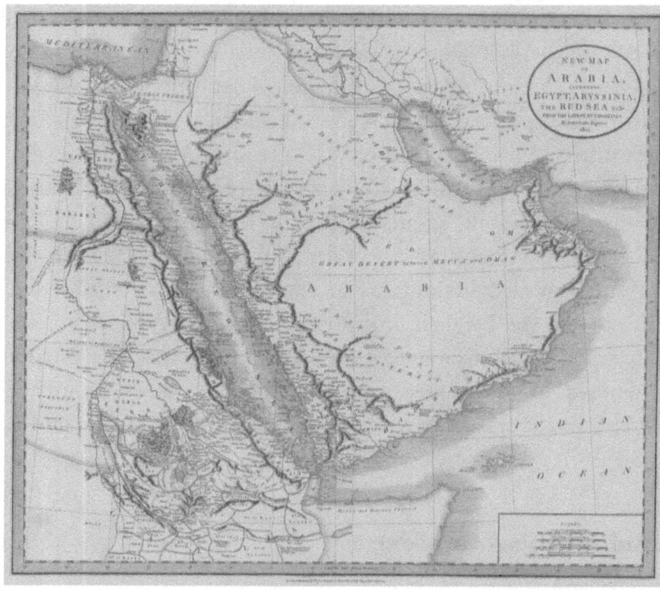

Figure 1 John Cary (circa 1754–1835), a new map of Arabia, including Egypt, Abyssinia and the Red Sea, from the latest authorities. Courtesy: Qatar National Library.

British 'empire' (Harrison 2016: x). Additionally, as the English traveller Samuel Evers in 1784 recalled, these routes were seen as safer and cheaper than 'the longer and more tedious one by' the Cape of Good Hope (Evers 1784: vii). The English journalist and travel writer Perceval Landen, who toured Syria and Iraq in the early part of the twentieth century, explained why these routes were seen by early-modern Britons as the most convenient: 'in those days it was easier to obtain protection at a price from a land chieftain than to secure immunity from the pirates who swarmed at sea' (Landen 1915: 508).

Realising the importance of these routes, British merchants and consuls stationed in Aleppo, Basra and Baghdad and the successive British ambassadors who served in Istanbul popularised two objectives in their efforts to protect British access to Levantine routes to India: (a) they sought to develop amicable relations with local rulers and (b) they aimed to stem the tide of rising French commercial and political influence in the Levant.[10] British consuls stationed in the region followed these objectives to the letter. The East India and Levant Companies, with the help of British ambassadors in the Ottoman capital (Sir James Porter, John Murray and Sir Robert Ainslie), often lobbied the Porte with the aim of securing protection for British merchants and travellers in the Syrian-Mesopotamian routes to India.[11] But the great efforts exerted during the period to secure British travels in the region were those by British consuls and residents who served in major cities located on the Syrian-Mesopotamian routes to India. For many years, John Abbott in Aleppo and William La Touche in Basra helped to improve British relations with the governors and tribal chiefs of the region by cultivating friendships and distributing gifts.[12] None of these Britons imagined that their country should militarily interfere in the region to secure British interests. The EIC sometimes used its military power to help Ottoman rulers of Baghdad and Basra to stem the tide of piracy in the Persian Gulf.[13] However, Britain was far from being a bullish political and commercial player in the region.[14] As the English historian and diplomat John Gordon Lorimer put it, the various challenges Britain faced at home and in the colonies, mainly the wars with the French, the Americans and Indian rulers (First and Second Mysore Wars) contributed to making British policy in the Arab-Ottoman region 'wanting in strength and decision' (Lorimer 1915: I, 149). Indeed, Britain's presence in the Middle East in the two centuries after the formation of the Levant and East India Companies, as Robert Harrison showed, was 'characterised by weakness' and 'bare-knuckle survival' (Harrison 2016: 6–7). The only British military expedition in the Middle East in the early-modern period took place in 1622. It was not directed against the locals. Rather it mainly aimed to drive away the Portuguese, who had dominated the Persian Gulf and the Indian Ocean trade for more than a century, from the coasts of Oman and Persia. The Persian ruler at the time, Shah Abbas, cooperated with the British, aiming to remove the Portuguese and thus establish himself as the dominant power in the Gulf.[15]

Overland travels between Britain and India go back to the sixteenth century when Queen Elizbeth I set out to improve British commerce and navigation in the hope of competing with England's Catholic enemies, the Spanish and Portuguese, who were ahead of the English in the trade and navigation of the Indian Ocean (Rowse 1955: 161). Roused by the influx of wealth into Portugal by means of trade with the East Indies, British travellers in the service of the Levant and East India Companies began to flock across Syria and Mesopotamia with the aim of opening new trade routes to India and further afield to China. John Newbery, John Eldred and Ralph Fitch, supported by Queen Elizabeth I, were the first Britons who travelled across the Syrian-Mesopotamian routes in 1583. They set out with the hope of establishing regular trade links between Britain and the commercial El Dorado of the early-modern world: India.[16] In 1599, two English merchants, John Cartwright and John Mildenhall, passed through the desert routes with the aim of expanding British trade with India. Cartwright's description of the regions in which he and Mildenhall travelled were published in his *Preacher's Travels* (1611) in the same year in which one intrepid British mercantile traveller, Sir Anthony Shirley, crossed the Syrian deserts onto Persia where he met the Persian monarch, Shah Abbas, who was keen on expanding trade with England. Shirley's account of his journey across the Syrian-Mesopotamian desert was published in *Sir Anthony Shirley: His Relation of His Travels into Persia* (1613).[17] Shirley and other early-modern Britons many years ago, Ram Chandra Prasad argued, 'were not the real architects' of British imperial and commercial expansion in the East. Nevertheless, he continued, their travels revealed 'the onerous task of exploration and reconnaissance'; they showed 'the proper road to wealth' and mapped out 'the markets where trade could yield prosperity to the English nation' (Prasad 1965: 23).

The Britons mentioned here were not the only Europeans who travelled and wrote accounts about Levantine routes to India. In fact, the first European who crossed the

Syrian-Mesopotamian desert routes was Anthony Terrniec. In 1528, Terrniec was commissioned by the Portuguese governor of Hormoz at the time, Mendoza, to deliver dispatches and news about Portuguese settlements and wars in Asia to the imperial government in Lisbon.[18] As the news of Terrniec's journey across the deserts spread among Europeans, many followed his footsteps.[19] The venetian traveller and merchant Caesar Federici followed the footsteps of Terrniec in 1563 to reach India. His travel book first appeared in Italy in 1587; a year later it was published in England.[20]

Portuguese and Italian travellers had crossed these routes before the English and the French did. On his way back from India to Europe, the Portuguese explorer Pedro Teixeira reached Basra in 1604 where he joined a local caravan to Aleppo and then Scanderoon where he sailed to Europe. The narrative of his journey was published in a book titled *Relaciones de Pedro Teixeira d'el origen, descendencia y succession de los Reyes de Persia* (1610). Twelve years after Teixeira crossed these routes, another European, the Italian man of letters Pietro Della Valle, reached the Holy Land before he travelled to Mesopotamia and Persia where he was received in the court of Shah Abbas; in 1624 he left Persia for Europe, passing through Basra, Baghdad, Aleppo and Scanderoon where he joined a Flemish ship sailing to Europe. His *Viaggi di Pietro della Valle il Pellegrino* (1650) details the conditions of travelling in these routes in an age in which the Ottomans were fiercely battling the Persians over the control of frontier cities like Baghdad and Basra.[21] Not only the Portuguese, the Italians and the English travelled across these routes. The French were also keen on cultivating overland channels of trade and travels with Persia and India. Barthélemy Carré, a French priest, crossed the overland routes in May 1672 with the hope of reaching India to report back to France's first minister Jean Baptiste Colbert who had sent him to spy on French and European commercial and military activities in the East Indies. In his *Voyage des Indes orientales* (1699), Carré recorded how he passed as a 'Frankish doctor' among the Arabs he encountered in the Syrian deserts (Carré 1947: I, 84).

In the early-modern period, Syrian-Mesopotamian routes to India were mostly popular among Italians and Portuguese travellers. Indeed, for a century after Terrniec had travelled in these routes, Portugal was the single most powerful trading and military power in the Persian Gulf, and the Italians were the most successful European merchants in the Levant; indeed, Italian was the lingua franca in the Levant before the English and French arrived in the region.[22] In the eighteenth century, however, the Italian and Portuguese commercial interests in the East were at their lowest ebb, which explains the scarcity of Italian and Portuguese travel accounts about the overland routes to India. The French and English, as the number of English and French travel books of the period reveal, continued to flock across these routes at a time when their imperial outposts in India continued to expand.[23] The French developed amicable relations with the Beys of Egypt, who were semi-independent from the Ottoman Empire for most part of the eighteenth century. In so doing, they were keen on opening Egyptian overland routes for French merchants and travellers stationed in India. The British, through the efforts of the EIC official in Cairo, George Baldwin, sought to block French efforts to access Egyptian markets and routes to India, but the British government and the Levant Company were reluctant to revive Egyptian trade routes to India at the expense of the Syrian-Mesopotamian routes. One explanation for this was that Egyptian Beys were less accountable to the Ottoman sultan than the pashas of Syria and Mesopotamia, which deterred the EIC from investing considerable political, financial and diplomatic capital in the efforts to facilitate British travels between India and Europe across Egypt.[24]

Syrian and Mesopotamian routes to India, thus, remained at the centre of British diplomacy in the Levant. Many Britons travelled and recorded their observations of these routes.[25] In their travel books, they showed how these routes, as one intrepid English traveller put it, were 'pregnant with danger and fatigue' but nonetheless were useful channels of communication with India (Taylor 1799: I, 1). The experiences across these routes, which involved encountering many cultural, political, social and moral differences, improved British knowledge about the region. But they also allowed British travellers to reflect on their own traditions and culture. Those who wrote their travel accounts about these routes drew on Enlightenment traditions of universalism and cosmopolitanism, showing that there is nothing a European traveller encounters abroad, whether in civilised or non-civilised cultures, that does not contribute to the improvement of the Self. Major John Taylor, who was involved in Britain's heavy-weight commercial and military activities in India, believed that travel in the Levant brought many benefits to the traveller and his nation: even 'contention of zealots' as the crusaders, Taylor wrote, 'brought back with them from Syria and Palestine [...] a knowledge of policy and refinement, and a taste for the fine arts, which intercourse with the inhabitants of those parts had contributed to inspire' (Taylor 1799: I, 7). The crusaders were humiliated in their wars with Muslims, Taylor stated, but the encounter between Christians and Muslims was immensely beneficial for Europe. 'To this cause', he concluded, 'is to be ascribed the return of learning and science into Europe, the rise of progressive discovery in the West' (Taylor 1799: I, 7). Taylor, like the travel writers examined in this study, wrote from the perspective of an Enlightenment cosmopolitan who found in the encounter with others an opportunity not only to negotiate the distance of his culture from religious and confessional wars many in modern Britain would associate with primitive times but also to showcase the enriching experience of the encounter.

Enlightenment and 'the Imperative to Develop'

The terms 'enlightenment' and 'Enlightenment' in this study are used cautiously.[26] Following the lead of Clifford Siskin and William Warner, I use the word 'Enlightenment' to refer to a historical event and intellectual phenomenon in post-Renaissance Europe that emphasised 'the imperative to develop', the propensity in 'men' to advance their knowledge of the world in a post-metaphysical, post-theological age (Siskin and Warner 2010: 2). But I also use it to refer to the social relations and networks within which ideas about the value of progress and growth were debated, negotiated and complicated. In so doing, I follow the lead of the scholars who rethought the old paradigm in Enlightenment studies which abstracted the

Enlightenment from its social, lived conditions and its global reach and who mostly focused on philosophical arguments and debates which took place in literary salons in France and scientific societies and universities of Britain and to a lesser extent the Netherlands. Enlightenment in this study is seen in the efforts of travellers to replace a theological view with a materialist view of the world, revealing a developmental mindset that defines European (man-made) progress through the lens of cultural difference. Enlightenment is also seen in the social relations and exchanges of opinions between 'men' from different social and cultural backgrounds, what Thomas Ahnert and Susan Manning called 'the process of socialisation' which produces improved and enlightened selves (Ahnert and Manning 2016: 2).[27]

In eighteenth-century Britain, the imperative to develop was an established code in a culture which started to view the period before 1688 (before the Glorious Revolution) with suspicion: the past is one of religious intolerance, enthusiasm and primitivism. The origin of this prevailing code goes back to late seventeenth century when John Lock set out to examine the position of man in a cosmological order, what was known then as the Great Chain of Being. For John Locke, in his *An Essay Concerning Human Understanding* (1689), the duty of man is to improve the material context in which he lives and in so doing he is expected 'to magnify the bountiful author of our being, for that proportion and degree of knowledge he has bestowed on us, so far above all the rest of the inhabitants of this our mansion' (Locke 1836: 2). Locke's imperative to develop rose from the ashes of the Reformation and the Civil War. The old tyranny of the court and ecclesiastics gave way to new mental and moral views, new patterns of taste, new ways to think about human nature.[28] With Locke, that is, the pursuit of improvement was driven from the cabinet into the field and instituted man as superior to non-human animals.[29] Although Locke acknowledged the humble status of man in a larger cosmological order orchestrated by God, this does not mean that man, as Arthur Lovejoy argues, was 'intended to occupy forever the *same* place' because 'the scale' in Lockean views of human progress 'is literally a ladder to be ascended, not only by the imagination but in fact' (Lovejoy 1936: 205). The Lockean imperative to develop influenced the travel writers in this study.

Another influence was the idea of improvement popularised by the Scottish Enlightenment philosophers such as Adam Smith, Lord Kames, David Hume, John Millar and William Robertson for whom, as Allan Ramsey in his poem 'The Prospect of Plenty: A Poem on the North Sea' (1721) put it, 'universal Plenty shall produce/ Strength to the State, and Arts for Joy and Use' (Ramsey 1797: I, 134). In his *Lectures on Jurisprudence* and *The Wealth of Nations*, Adam Smith was the first Scottish philosopher who produced a theoretical model explaining the rise and progress of nations: the closer a society gets to commercialism, Smith argued, the more developed it becomes.[30] This developmental tradition in Scottish thought social scientists and historians call stadial theory.[31] Stadial theory is the branch of philosophical history – that also had an impact on political economy and moral philosophy – which, as the Scottish philosopher Dugald Stewart wrote, invites philosophers to compare 'our intellectual requirements, our opinions, manners, institutions, with those which prevail among rude tribes', a comparison which 'cannot fail to occur to us an interesting question, by what gradual steps the transition has been made from the first simple efforts of uncultivated nature, to a state of things so wonderfully artificial and complicated' (Stewart 1853 :xxxiv).[32] In broader terms, this philosophical tradition in Scottish thought divided societies into commercial (civilised) and primitive (non-civilised).[33]

In their efforts to produce a history of the species rooted in this tradition of developmentalism, David Hume, Adam Smith, John Millar and Adam Ferguson were aware of the cultural, linguistic and physical pluralities of the modern world. But this did not stop them from producing a fixed set of natural laws that were seen as applicable to all societies that live in similar economic, social and political conditions. Their philosophical investigations, Silvia Sebastiani argues, introduced 'a grid', 'a natural history', and 'a system for classifying and describing creation, but it also indicated the natural course of the development of societies: the process of civilization, as it came to be known in the second half of the eighteenth century' (Sebastiani 2013: 8). Kathleen Wilson has reminded us that this stadial movement of societies produced some irreducible categories of difference which 'located' nations and civilisations 'in a relatively fixed spatial and cultural terrain that was conceived of geographically and ethnographically (as well as ethnocentrically)' (Wilson 2003: 7).[34] While many non-European societies lived in nascent stages of development, Europe emerged into 'Light', as David Hume articulated the rapid economic and scientific changes which he saw in the Europe of his lifetime. But how did Hume and other Enlightenment philosophers come to know about non-European nations and cultures? Instead of mainly relying on the biblical explanation of human diversity, Scottish philosophers collected their information about ancient societies by reading the Bible and classical historians and about modern non-European societies by reading modern travel writers. In an Enlightenment age which 'valorised the senses', Nigel Leask observes, travel writing was granted a special status in 'the epistemology of the eighteenth century, particularly in the intellectual crucible of the Scottish Enlightenment' (2009: 276). Smith owned around 56 titles of books on North America, 7 titles on Arabia, 7 titles on China, around 36 titles on India (East) and around 10 titles on the Ottoman Empire.[35] Smith's friend David Hume was also an avid reader of travel literature. In 1727, he wrote a letter to the Scottish publisher William Strahan in which he recommended the publication of his friend Patrick Brydon's travel observations about Malta and Sicily.[36] Eighteenth-century travel writers shaped and were shaped by the tradition of developmentalism in the Scottish Enlightenment. Both genres, that is, Enlightenment philosophical histories and travel writings, however, should not be considered as identical in their approach towards non-European societies and interpretations of cultural difference.

Systematic Improvement

Stadial philosophers' attempts to cover the entire history of societies back to primitive stages made sufficient evidence needed for such confirmation hard to come by with respect to non-European societies. To that end, Scottish philosophers often relied on travel writings in their efforts to trace different stages of development in different societies. In so doing, they found the material that helped them to give credence to their philosophical speculations. As William C. Lehman observes, 'the hard facts of experience and observations' of travellers 'were rarely left to stand unrelated to a larger theoretical and philosophical frame of reference' (Lehman 1960: 94). In his *Observations Concerning the Distinction of Ranks in Society* (1771), John Millar noted how 'relations of traveller' constituted an important source for the philosopher who aims to collect information about non-European societies, but he also accepted that these 'relations' should not be blindly followed: it is difficult, he wrote, to account for 'relations of travellers whose characters and situation in life, neither set them above the suspicion of being easily deceived, nor of endeavouring to misrepresent the facts which they have related' (1771: 12). For Millar, this dilemma cannot be simply alleviated by accepting everything travellers report, but the 'veracity of the traveller' can be thrown 'out of the question', he argued, once the philosopher read travel reports with a certain theoretical model in mind. When 'facts' reported by travellers confirm a general principle in the four-stage theory of progress, he wrote, then travellers' reports are bound to be trusted. Those 'extraordinary facts', however, that do not elucidate a general principle or hypothesis within that theory should be ignored. 'We cannot refuse our assent' to such method, added Millar, 'without falling into a degree of scepticism by which the credibility of all historical testimony would be in a great measure destroyed' (Millar 1771: 13). Miller's explanation illustrates the method which the Scottish philosophers of progress often used in their reading of travel books: they selected 'from a great number' of travel texts 'a few' observations which fulfilled a certain function in their theory (Millar 1771: 12).

In eighteenth-century Britain, Adam Smith was the master of this method. In his *Lectures on Jurisprudence*, Smith explained how Arabs and Tartars (Turkic inhabitants of the Russian Empire) live in a pastoral stage. They do not labour, own private property, form a regular government and establish complex laws. The absence of private property and regular government and the prevalence of a nomadic mode of subsistence among them explain the absence of a peaceful and prosperous life in their societies. Politeness, civility and respect of the law existed in commercial, not pastoral, society. 'In a nation of shepherds', Smith stated, 'everyone without distinction goes to war. This was the case amongst the Children of Israel and is so at present amongst the Arabians[...]' (Smith 1982: 229). However, selfish manners, individualism and excess, traits widely popular in opulent society, do not exist among nations of shepherds. In *The Wealth of Nations* (1776), Smith found in Richard Pococke's *Description of the East and Some Other Countries* (1743–1745) this general principle of his stadial theory: that is, hospitality 'seems to be common in all nations to whom commerce and manufactures are little known' (Smith 1776: I, 496). It may have been the case that Smith, while completing his graduate studies at Baliol College, Oxford, came to know Pococke's two volumes about his journey in the East, published in 1743 and 1745.[37] Pococke himself read law at Oxford before leaving England for Egypt, Palestine and Syria (he was in the Levant between 1737 and 1741).[38] Both might have met in England before Smith returned to Scotland to take up a teaching position at the University of Glasgow in 1745. Yet both wrote about Arabs from two different perspectives. In *The Wealth of Nations*, Adam Smith quotes Pococke:

> ‘I have seen’, says Doctor Pocock, ‘an Arabian chief dine in the streets of a town where he had come to sell his cattle, and invite all passengers, even common beggars, to sit down with him and partake of his banquet’. (Smith 1776: I, 496)

In Pococke’s travel account, the scene took a different course:

> And an Arab Prince will often dine in the street, before his door, and call to all that pass, even beggars, in the usual expression, Bisimillah, that is, In the name of God; who come and sit down, and when they have done, give their Hamdellilah, that is, God be praised. For the Arabs are great levellers, put every body on a footing with them; and it is by such generosity and hospitality that they maintain their interest; but the middling people among them, and the Coptis, live but poorly. (1743: I, 138)

Pococke’s admiration of the levelling-up nature of Arab society might have been shaped by his Christian piety, one in which all humans were seen to possess equal dignity in the eye of God. In the preceding passage, Pococke’s middle-class background made him sympathise with ‘the middling people among them’ who ‘live but poorly’. Indeed, what the passage above shows is Pococke’s view of Arab society is more complex than that offered by Smith. Pococke did not follow a theoretical frame which placed Arabs in a lower rank of development, a people with no property, no government, no refinement and in constant war with settled people from outside their tribe. Rather Arabs in his account appeared as both nomadic and settled, ‘good’ and ‘bad’, lawless thieves in deserts who ‘love plunder’ and settled ‘honest people’ in villages, ‘especially in upper Egypt’, where he saw them ‘mostly employed in tilling the ground’ (1743: I, 177-8). Pococke recalled how he ‘often sat down with them’ over meals and coffee, offering his readers a nuanced narrative about Arabs which does not figure in Smith’s account (Pococke 1743: I, 183).

Pococke certainly was not an Arabophile: his Bible always reminded him that the land in which he travelled had a Christian story, one of fertility and prosperity, before the ‘despotic’ Turks and the ‘plundering’ Arabs invaded it. However, the experience of meeting, conversing and breaking bread with Arabs allowed Pococke to develop a complex set of views that cannot be simply reduced to a collection of laws which Smith and his fellow Scottish *literati* considered as valid for explaining the diversity of manners and morals across the globe. Pococke did not use the image of the hospitable Arab to invalidate a theoretical frame of reference explaining the rise and progress of nations from barbarism to civility. The claim in *The Wealth of Nations* that the Arabs are still cherishing traditions now extinct in Britain shows how Smith, by using the character of a primitive but hospitable Arab, mainly aimed to prove that Britain, in modern time, has now crossed into the shores of modernity. It will be unfair to Smith and his fellow Enlightenment literati, however, to be accused of adopting in their philosophical projects a binary opposition between East and West, Europeans and Arabs. For Smith lived in an age in which his fellow Scots in the Highlands of Scotland were often called primitive and barbaric in mainstream English discourse. But Smith and other Scottish philosophers used the nomadic and lawless character of the Arabs as a thought experiment in the wake of the Jacobite Rebellion, an age in which the middle and upper classes in Scotland were prepared to rethink ancient freedoms, manners and mores in the hope of attaining modern prosperity which the union with England promised.[39]

One writer who understood this change well was Adam Ferguson, the only Gaelic-speaking philosopher of the Scottish Enlightenment. In his *An Essay on the History of Civil Society* (1767), first titled *A Treatise of Refinement,* Ferguson admired the military valour of the Arabs. 'When roused by the prospect of conquest, or disposed to act on a plan', he wrote, 'they spread their dominion, and their system of imagination, over mighty tracts of the earth' (Ferguson 1776: 169).[40] For Ferguson, who served as a chaplain for the Black Watch regiment that fought on the side of the British government in the Battle of Fontenoy, the military valour of Arabs did not bode well with the idea of living in a commercial polity. A society whose members are in a constant state of war cannot be one of peace, prosperity and civility. It cannot develop complex laws, establish a regular government and exhibit polished manners: this explains why Arabs 'carry to the rest of mankind aspects of banditti and robbers' (Ferguson 1776: 232). Ferguson wrote about the freedom and military valour of the Arabs, but he might have had in mind the Scots of pre-modern times. Ferguson, like Smith, was aware of how the union between England and Scotland secured his country immense economic growth, but, unlike Smith, he considered economic development a threat to civic virtue. The dilemma of yearning for freedom while living in a prosperous society, one heavily regulated and redolent with political and moral corruptions, serves to illustrate the function of the image of the Arab warrior in Ferguson's theory of progress.[41]

Ferguson learned about the manners of the Arabs from what he called D' Arvieux's *History of the Wild Arabs.* Laurent d'Arvieux, a diplomat, traveller and a scholar from Marseilles, wrote a travel book about his observations of the government, tribes and society of Syria among whom he lived for many years in the seventeenth century.[42] But his book was never titled a 'History of Wild Arabs'. The 1718 English translation was titled *The Travels of the Chevalier D'Arvieux in Arabia the Desart; Written by Himself and Published by Mr De. La roque.* Although 'wild' did not appear in the English title, Ferguson used it to make a wider point about the primitive stage to which he thinks the Arabs belong. In Samuel Johnson's *Dictionary of the English Language,* the word 'Wild' carried certain meanings that confirm the primitive stage that Ferguson throughout his account associated with non-commercial society: 'not tame', 'not domestick', 'savage, uncivilized', 'turbulent; tempestuous; irregular', 'licentious, ungoverned', 'inconstant, mutable; fickle', 'inordinate; loose', and 'uncouth; strange'.[43] None of these formulations figured in D'Arvieux's account about the Arabs. Before he travelled through the Levant and North Africa between 1654 and 1686, he developed, as the French traveller Jean de la Roque wrote, 'a predominant inclination for the Languages and Travels of the Levant' (D'Arvieux 1718: iv). While living in Saida for 12 years (between 1653 and 1665), D'Arvieux became fluent in 'the Oriental tongues'. He spoke 'the Hebrew, the Syriac, the Arabic, and the Turkish and the Persian', de la Roque stressed, 'the three later of which he spoke with so much Certainty and readiness, that the Skillfullest in those Languages thought he could not possibly have learnt any other than what they heard him talking' (D'Arvieux 1718: v). In his travel book, D'Arvieux appeared greatly sympathetic to Arab traditions and manners. He responded to 'the false notions' in Europe 'given us' by travellers who [...]

> never met with anything but their Robberies, and from their showing them to us, in their Relations, only to the worst advantage, not daring to venture an inquiry after what is good and commendable amongst them, nor to stay long enough with People they are always mistrustful of, and whose Language and Customs they are utter strangers of. (D'Arvieux 1718: 94–95)

Although D'Arvieux repeated the famous trope in Europe which associated Bedouin Arabs with Ishmael of the Bible, he did not see all Arabs, as Ferguson did, as 'enemies to the rest of mankind'. Rather, like all societies, Arabs had good and bad qualities. D'Arvieux noted how European merchants in Alexandria employed 'young Bedouins' in their houses as 'Domesticks' and 'Interpreters' (D'Arvieux 1718: 102). These Arabs 'are honest' and speak 'the Provence dialect of the French language very well' (D'Arvieux 1718: 102). This image about Arabs being honest, hardworking and peaceful towards people from different cultures did not figure in Ferguson's account. Ferguson was mostly interested in finding in D'Arvieux's book the evidence that supported his theory, that is, the civilisational status of any nation is shaped by their stage of economic development. In so doing, Ferguson mainly focused on general principles rather than particularities of societies. As a philosopher of history, Ferguson only cared about general rules that treat variables as, in the words of John Gray, 'ephemeral, or at least developmental, phases in the history of the species' (Gray 2007: 187).

The same strategy of reading travel books was applied by another celebrity philosopher and historian of the Scottish Enlightenment, David Hume, who, like his fellow Scottish philosophers, was an avid reader of travel accounts. In his essay 'Of Polygamy and Divorces', Hume used Joseph Pitton de Tournefort's *Relation d'un voyage du Levant* (1717) to give credence to his argument that polygamy in non-civilised societies eliminates equal relations between men and women. 'Tournefort tells us', Hume wrote [...]

> that when he was brought into the grand signior's seraglio as a physician, he was not a little surprised, in looking along a gallery, to see a great number of naked arms, standing out from the side of the room. He could not imagine what this could mean; till he was told, that those arms belonged to bodies, which he must cure, without knowing any more about them, than what he could learn from the arms. He was not allowed to ask a question of the patient, or even of her attendants, lest he might find it necessary to enquire concerning circumstances, which the delicacy of the seraglio allows not to be revealed. (Hume 1753: I, 261)

Barbara Taylor has argued that '[w]omen, British Enlightenment thinkers all agreed, were primary bearers of the "affections", meaning not just love of family and other intimates but the "social sympathies" on which civilised progress depended, since it was through feminine influence that men, that bellicose and uncivil sex, became "softened" into social beings' (Taylor 2005: 37). Seen in this context, the reference in Hume's passage to the practice of imprisoning women in *harems,* which existed 'all over the east', as Hume's reading of Tournefort taught him, confirmed a principle in his developmental theory: the absence of the freedom of association between men and women in any society is a signifier of its level of backwardness.[44]

Tournefort's views of Muslim society is more complicated than that of Hume's. Although he confirmed the despotic behaviour of elite men in the Ottoman court, Tournefort did not argue that this phenomenon exists all over the East, nor did he care to interpret what he saw in the Ottoman Empire from a progressivist frame like the one shown in Hume's essay mentioned earlier. As a physician schooled in the traditions of Hippocrates, Tournefort, who travelled across the Ottoman Empire between 1700 and 1702 for purposes of expanding his botanical and medical knowledge about the region, valorised seeing rather than reading about Muslims. As he proposed at the start of his journey, the idea of 'personally studying Nature and Men' offers 'a much surer foundation' for the expansion of knowledge 'than by reading in one's closet' (Tournefort 1718: I, 2). As his *A Voyage into the Levant* shows, Tournefort saw travelling among and socialising with people from different social and religious backgrounds an opportunity to produce new ideas and information that complicate previous accounts written by those who never made it outside Europe. Such an approach to travelling and travel writing made Tournefort much more nuanced than Hume in his views of Muslims. For example, from the same city in which he saw Muslim women being oppressed by Muslim men from elite backgrounds, he, while observing the manners of people from lower social backgrounds, reported how '[t]oo much constraints make them [women] sometimes seek divorce', a reference to the idea that Muslim women were not often powerless as Hume argued (Tournefort 1718: 68). For Tournefort, women sometimes pushed back against oppression. Tournefort mentioned how 'the Alcoran requires them [women] to be treated well', showing a nuanced approach to the difference between religious and cultural practices in Islamic society (Tournefort 1718: 70). He added that female spaces in the Ottoman Empire were not protected from a culture of 'intrigue' which was broadly associated in Hume's essays with polite and commercial nations. In big cities like Constantinople, Tournefort noted, 'women know how to manage their intrigues so well' despite strict morals and manners of the Turks, and if a husband accuses his wife of 'adultery' without 'being able to prove it', he 'shall be condemned to twenty and four Strokes of the Batoon' (Tournefort 1718: 73). But if the husband insists that his wife cheated on him, 'there must be Witnesses' and the husband shall 'swear four times before the judge that he speaks the truth and, and protest five times, that he desires to be accused of God and Men if he lyes' (Tournefort 1718: 73). While the husband's testimony might be considered in court, Tournefort maintained, '[t]he woman laughs in her heart, for she is believed upon her Oath, provided she prays to God five times that she may perish, if what her Husband says is true' (Tournefort 1718: 73). In Tournefort's account, the culture of intrigue in Istanbul seems to have been described with a Parisian slant. However, his descriptions of the relations between males and females in Islamic society complicate the prevailing discourse in Europe, to which Hume participated, which attributed the rise of moral corruptions and the culture of intrigue to civilised and commercial nations.

Hume's philosophical inquiry fixed some universal laws and principles which glossed over the diverse traditions, manners, laws and morals of Islamic societies. What did encourage Hume and other Scots to adopt such an ambitious task in which they set out to fix laws about, in Hume's phrasing, 'Every emergence of Human life' (Human 1748: 6)?[45] For John Marriott, the idea of improvement in Scottish philosophical history 'served to consolidate the self-identity of the West, in part and increasingly by the exclusion both of subordinates and non-Western people as lower others' (Marriot 2003: 27–28). Alasdair Macintyre associated the idea of 'universal human nature' in Scottish Enlightenment thought, particularly in the wirings of David Hume, with what he called 'the prejudices of the Hanoverian ruling elite' (Macintyre 2007: 231). Other scholars like Jennifer Pitts attributed this phenomenon to what she called European 'parochialism'. '[D]espite Enlightenment historians' aspirations to universalist impartiality', Pitts wrote, 'scientific and scholarly attention to global phenomena was in part driven by, and can be said to have contributed to, European parochialism, as Europe came to be figured as, at the same time, unique and a model for the rest of the world' (Pitts 2014: 192). The binarism which appeared in Marriot and Pitt's views of the Enlightenment was rethought by historians of eighteenth-century Scotland. Murray Pittock, for example, argues that the Scottish philosophers were intrigued with primitivism in an age in which, after the Battle of Culloden (1746), many Scots looked forward to a future of commercial prosperity (2003: 266).[46] The thrust of Pittock's argument is that Scottish philosophers' celebrations of and anxieties about modern commercial life encouraged them to examine the mores, manners and traditions of pastoral societies, a pursuit at the heart of which was a developmentalist view of the world in which disparate societies share common desires to advance but are nevertheless located in different socio-economic temporalities. What this argument shows is that while the Enlightenment philosophers, as Anthony Pagden argues, hoped for the perfectibility of European laws, governments and societies, their aspirations were partly shaped by a desire to know about non-Europeans.[47] To that end, it is the contention of this book that Enlightenment is a cross-cultural process at its inception was the idea of learning about and from cultural differences despite the efforts of some scholars to nationalise it, 'Westernise' it and demonise it.

Enlightenment and Encounter

During the age of steam, many Europeans understood civilisation as a discourse of 'diffusionism', in James Blaut's words; prior to this, there was the age of encounter in which British travellers in the Ottoman-Arab region considered their experiences abroad as opportunities of learning about and from those among whom they spent a considerable amount of time travelling on routes between India and Europe.[48] I use the word 'encounter' and 'encountering' here advisedly, drawing on the recent scholarship in travel writing in which we find examples of travellers setting out with 'exotic fantasies', as Catherine Mee shows, which proved too fragile to hold their ground once the traveller finds herself embroiled with the 'practicalities of interacting and negotiating' with different people and cultures; in an encounter, fantasies tend to 'dissolve' (Mee 2014: 3).[49] Sara Ahmed, in her *Strange Encounters: Embodied Others in Post-coloniality* (2000), has written emphatically about the impact of 'close encounter' on managing the boundaries of the Self: encounter, she argues, 'fleshes out' national, cultural and racial boundaries around 'aliens', but encounter with strangers – an opportunity which includes hospitality, surprise and conflict – also impels the Self to cultivate social relations in which it becomes necessary to turn 'alien to gain access to alien worlds previously uncharted by other humans' (Ahmed 2000: 2). Encounter, Ahmed suggests, involves 'both fixations, and the impossibility of fixation' (Ahmed 2000: 8). Ahmed's idea of fixation and the impossibility of fixation guides the argument in this book. This study shows how in their encounters with different people, British travellers often found themselves in situations in which, even if they were keen on policing boundaries between 'us' and 'them', they often failed to predict the outcome. Encounter 'facilitated', as Kathleen Wilson observed, 'the formation of identities that resulted in pluralities and contradictions as well as unities and coherences' (Wilson 2000: 159).[50] Encounter involves a great deal of surprises which require a great degree of modification of preconceived notions about different cultures. This process has a profound impact on our understanding of contact zones in which, as Bernard Williams put it, 'Cultures [...] constantly meet one another and exchange and modify practices and attitudes' (Williams 1985: 158).

Encounter is redolent with opportunities of critique and dissent. Encounter helps us to read travel literature against the Orientalist grain. It allows us to see culture, identity and nation as constructs imagined during meetings between strangers.[51] But encounter also has its own limitation. Rachel Finnegan has recently argued that European travel accounts about the Ottoman Empire often draw impenetrable boundaries between Self and Other and East and West. Such boundaries are drawn once the traveller defines her own 'familiar' culture in the context of encountering 'unfamiliar' cultures, traditions, values and attitudes. Visitors to the Ottoman Empire, as Finnegan observed:

> [...] often commented on the less positive aspects of eastern life, such as the neglect and misuse of classical monuments, the squalor of the cities and what they perceived to be the inequities of the social and political system [...] [These travellers] failed to recognise in Turkish society the familiar virtues of their own country. (Finnegan 2019: 24)

Encounter, as the preceding passage shows, produces failed attempts to understand different cultures beyond existing notions in Europe framing the debate about what makes a culture improved, modern, refined, just and polite. This encounter does not indicate an opportunity of critique and dissent; that is, it does not allow the Self to turn 'alien', in Sara Ahmed's words, so that it could understand an 'alien' culture. Finnegan's reading tends to settle for the triumph of the familiar over the unfamiliar- 'We' over 'them' – which undermines the power of encounter to unsettle barriers between Self and Other. The argument here which shows how encounter could be a limiting practice also appeared in many studies of European travels in and travel writings about the Middle East, studies in which the European traveller seemed devoid of a sense of particularity; it acted as a cog in the machine of collective discourse.[52]

Social and political complexities of encounter help us to see Enlightenment – the period in the intellectual history of Europe that many associate with the rise of a materialist and rationalist understanding of human progress – in a different light. Throughout the eighteenth century, the philosophical investigations which set out to explain how different stages of development exist in different societies invested vast intellectual capital in creating what David Hume in the introduction to his *Treatise of Human Nature* called 'the science of man', on in which, as Fabian argues, 'religious and metaphysical searches for mankind's origin and destiny were to give place to a radically immanent vision of humanity at home in the entire world and at all times' (Hume 1878: xx; Fabian 1983: 7). This radical vision aimed to replace theology with observable laws explaining the rise and progress of societies – a rise from 'Obscurity' to 'Light', as David Hume put it – to the extent that the editor of *Berlinische Monatschrift* in 1784 required clarification with a direct question: What is Enlightenment? (Hume 1748: 10). One powerful response to the question came from the Prussian city of Konigsberg. In his essay 'An Answer to a Question: What Is Enlightenment?', published in the *Berlinische Monatschrift* in 1784, Immanuel Kant defined 'enlightening' as the public use of one's reason: the ability of people to collectively depart from being told what to think into thinking for themselves. This 'exit' or 'way out', in Michel Foucault's formulation, is what Kant called a departure from 'nonage' or 'immaturity': a transition from ignorance to light (Foucault 1984: 34; Kant 1996: 58). This transition Kant found in Fredrick's Prussia, but he had no illusions that 'enlightening' was complete. As John Robertson writes, enlightening for Kant was not 'a finite phenomenon or period carrying the definite article' (Robertson 2015: 20).

Kant, as Michael Foucault argues, did not aim to relate the present to 'a totality or future achievement'; rather he was 'looking for a difference': for him the main question was, 'What does today introduce with respect to yesterday?' (Foucault 1984: 34). This idea which associated the Enlightenment with a 'way out', a transition from ignorance to reason, has appeared in works by eminent scholars who, nonetheless, regarded the Enlightenment, as John Robertson put it, as 'a finite phenomenon and period carrying the definite article' (Robertson 2015: 20). Emerging from the shadow of World War II, Adorno and Horkheimer, in 1944, for example, argued that the Enlightenment 'program' should be 'understood in the widest sense as the advance of thought' which 'has always aimed at liberating human beings from fear and installing them as masters' (Adorno and Horkheimer 2002: 1). By replacing God with man, the Enlightenment gave a nod for the improvement of knowledge, but it also unlocked a mine of human disasters such as Nazism.[53] In the 1960s, however, a more optimistic view of the Enlightenment emerged in North America, but it did not depart from what Adorno and Horkheimer proposed about the systemacity and uniformity of the Enlightenment. For Peter Gay, 'there were many philosphes in the eighteenth century but there was only one Enlightenment' (Gay 1966: I, 3).

The Frankfort School's and Gay's interpretations of the Enlightenment have been rethought by scholars who located different Enlightenments in different national and religious contexts. John. G. Pococke's term 'family of Enlightenments', David Sorkin's 'religious Enlightenment', Jonathan Israel's 'radical and moderate Enlightenments', Isaiah Berlin's 'counter-Enlightenment' and Darrin McMahon's 'enemies of the Enlightenment' complicate previous studies that spoke of the unity of the Enlightenment and its radical progressivism.[54] What these new directions in Enlightenment studies reveal is that we are no longer able to think of the Enlightenment as one phenomenon, one project and, as Peter Gay puts it, 'a single army with a single banner' (Gay 1966: I, 7–8). Instead, eighteenth-century Europe, the recent scholarship argues, saw diverse Enlightenments that thrived side by side; they sometimes jostled each other with the result that sometimes one tradition overshadowed another but overall, each tradition emerged in a different historical and political context which made it difficult to speak of a single Enlightenment.[55]

While offering nuanced interpretations of Enlightenment, the aforementioned works have mostly considered it as an intellectual, philosophical and bourgeoise phenomenon in modern Europe. Other directions in Enlightenment studies such as the one championed by Robert Darnton in the 1970s took issue with the idea that the Enlightenment was mainly intellectual, philosophical and a provenance of high culture. Darnton argued that the business of publishing books in France 'represented the diffusion of the Enlightenment on a massive scale' with the result that the old cosmology of the Catholic Church and the authority of the monarchy were increasingly challenged by an expanding republic of letters (Darnton 1979: 6). This approach founded on the diffusion of Enlightenment beyond the exclusive circle of philosophers was adopted by recent studies which focused on enlightening practices in broader, more complex historical and social contexts than had previously been appreciated. Historians such as Dorinda Outram, in her *The Enlightenment* (1995), have expanded the geographical range of Enlightenment by showing how the circulation of global commodities, slaves and travel stories in Europe complicated some important eighteenth-century debates about human diversity and cultural particularism.[56] In her *The Republic of Letters: A Cultural History of the French Enlightenment* (1996), Dena Goodman has investigated the effective roles women played in the eighteenth-century French 'republic of letters' where social relations between both genders 'substituted reciprocity and equality for hierarchy' (Goodman 1994: 5). Murray Pittock's *Enlightenment in a Smart City: Edinburgh's Civil Development 1660-1750* (2019) examined the causes of change in Enlightenment Edinburgh; he found in the city's diverse communities – the 'strong immigration, population movement, population clustering, strong relationships and intersections between clubs and societies' – the expression of what he called the 'associational life' that helped to unleash innovation and improvements, two important enlightening catchwords (Pittock 2019: 29).

These scholarly works are diverse in scope and content, but they share one common feature: that is, they took Enlightenment studies into uncharted territories in which previous interpretations of the Enlightenment (which posited it as mainly philosophical, European, bourgeoise and male) were no longer satisfactory. While doing so, these scholars nuanced our understanding of the Enlightenment by welcoming to the field new voices, regions and identities historically excluded from the scholarship.[57] In the past decade, a range of novel and illuminating works in the fields of literary studies and intellectual history helped to expand traditional cultural and geographical boundaries of Enlightenment. For example, in his *Enlightenment Orientalism: Resisting the Rise of the Novel* (2012), Srinivas Arvamudan showed how Oriental tales – a less regarded genre in eighteenth-century Europe – smuggled critiques and promoted values we traditionally associate with the Enlightenment. 'The oriental tale', Arvamudan argues, 'is a simulacrum of traditional forms, with a highly misunderstood yet crucial function in relation to the public culture of the Enlightenment and political modernity' (Arvamudan 2012: 17). In his *The Republic of Arabic Letters: Islam and the European Enlightenment* (2018), Alexander Bevilacqua studied the Orientalist scholarship among eighteenth-century 'community of scholars' whose works produced 'an Enlightenment now largely lost from view in which Europeans learned Arabic and read Islamic manuscripts' (Bevilacqua 2018: 1;3). For Bevilacqua, the works of these scholars show how major Enlightenment intellectual and scientific developments – such as natural history and secular historicism – were shaped by Arabic manuscripts and translations whose entry to the European republic of letters was not then seen as alien but rather as part of the efforts of the human family in East and West to improve the human condition.

Studies like those by Arvamudan and Bevilacqua helped to unsettle cultural and geographical boundaries traditionally drawn around the Enlightenment. In so doing, they showed how European modernity was constituted by its global connections. Nonetheless, a cross-cultural Enlightenment in these works broadly emerged as the provenance of an eighteenth-century 'republic of letters' whose members had no or little contacts with the East, never travelled in the East and never met and conversed with Indians, Persians, Chinese and Arabs. Arvamudan's non-Eurocentric Enlightenment was an Orientalised and exoticised fictional alternative to a rational, national and sober narrative of modernity propped up by an eighteenth-century literary genre known as the novel. Bevilacqua's non-Eurocentric Enlightenment appeared mainly in the academic, clerical and highly educated circles in which sympathetic ideas towards Islamic cultures were shown but proved unable to repel the tide of progress and secularisation in Europe after 1750 which saw the rise of tropes about the superiority of Europeans to the world of Islam. As he argues, this period saw economic and scientific improvements in Europe that helped to produce new attitudes which 'in turn lowered interests in Islam' and began to view it as a backward 'force holding Muslims back' (Bevilacqua 2018: 200).

As this book argues, Enlightenment did not necessarily produce an exotic Orient antithetical to rationalist Europe nor was it an academic fad which came to an end around 1750. Enlightenment in this study is rather a collection of practices that included eighteenth-century face-to-face encounters, conversations and exchanges of polite words and gifts between Europeans and Muslims: practices that displaced social, cultural and geographical boundaries and, in Anthony Pagden's phrasing, generated 'a belief, measured and at times sceptical, in progress and in the general human capacity for self-improvement' (Pagden 2013: 1). In posing Enlightenment as a collection of practices, this study draws on the scholarship of Janet Starkey whose study of Alexander and Patrick Russells's writings revealed how tropes of improvement in Scottish Enlightenment culture shaped and were shaped by Scottish encounters with the East. Starkey's reading of the Enlightenment as 'a constellation of practices' – a term which she borrowed from Jonathan Sheehan's *The Enlightenment Bible: Translation, Scholarship, Culture* (2005) – bears resemblance to Outram's two useful terms in her magisterial book *Panorama of the Enlightenment* (2006): 'Sociable' and 'Global' Enlightenments.[58] Outram's term 'Sociable Enlightenment' refers to social relations in 'broad-based popular culture' in which people participate in 'reading and writing and the sociable experience of conversing and corresponding, of listening to music and viewing pictures' (Outram 2006: 56). Outram traced these sociable activities in gentlemanly clubs, scientific institutions, coffeehouses and masonic lodges in Europe, showing that some of these social spaces were open for people from upper classes and 'the middling sorts' who afforded to pay an entry fee. Despite the attempt in Outram's study to pluralise our thinking of Enlightenment culture, she said nothing about the possibility that similar social practices could have taken place in the context of encounter between Europeans and non-Europeans. The kind of Enlightenment that Outram found in European encounters with non-Europeans is mainly based on colonial relations. For European encounters with non-Europeans, Outram used the term 'Global Enlightenment' [...]

> a world drama of cross-cultural contact, a theatre of exploration and exchange in previously unknown worlds where the Enlightenment was to work out its own meaning as much as it did in the Berlin competition. For indigenous peoples, contact with Europeans often destroyed their societies. For Europeans, such encounter supplied data used in important debates about the nature of variety and difference, and about the possibility of a common human history. Disturbingly for eighteenth-century people, knowledge of other cultures also posed the problem of relativism. Were there absolute standards as they were human societies? These concerns are still with us in the shape of multiculturalism. Should European values be universal standard, or should there be a plurality of values systems and meanings? These very current questions were first posed during the globalization of the Enlightenment world. (Outram 2006: 134–135)

Concurring with Outram's proposition that the Enlightenment was not the exclusive territory of men in Berlin, this study broadens the sociocultural scholarship on Enlightenment by showing how enlightening practices also took place in encounters between Britons and Muslims from different social backgrounds. The only quarrel this study has with Outram's thesis is when she recalls that the 'Sociable Enlightenment' mostly took place in bourgeoise spaces in Europe and when she argues that European encounters with non-Europeans 'destroyed' indigenous 'societies': maybe this is true in European encounters with the South Pacific, as Outram shows, but in the Arab-Ottoman world of the eighteenth century, such a gloomy image of encounter is far from what the travel writers in this book inform us.

The Scope of the Book

One common feature among all the writers whose travel books this study sets out to examine is that they all lived and worked in the East for many years: Henry Abbott (Chapter four) and Eyles Irwin (Chapter five) were born in the East, the former in Istanbul and the latter in Calcutta; John Carmichael (Chapter one) and Donald Campbell (Chapter six) were in the military service; Edward Ives (Chapter two) was in the Royal Navy; and Abraham Parsons (Chapter three) worked for the Levant Company. Another common feature among all these writers is the idea that travelling abroad was an opportunity of improvement, a feature which eighteenth-century reviewers of their books highlighted. For *The Gentleman's Magazine*, John Carmichael's travel account 'manifests a great degree of accuracy and perseverance': accuracy in the method of reporting about desert routes and Carmichael's perseverance while crossing the land known in Europe for being mysterious (1792: 145). *The Analytical Review*, in 1796, argued that Donald Campbell's account of his overland journey from Aleppo to India, 'through a distance of 1400 miles [...] render this part of the narrative in many respects original' (1795: 361). Reviewing Abraham Parsons' *Travels in Asia and Africa*, *The Eclectic Review* in 1808 observed that 'to many readers a large proportion of it will be new, and to all we can recommend it as authentic' (1808: 924). Another feature noted by reviewers is the cosmopolitanism travellers showed towards the people among whom they travelled. Campbell, *The Analytical Review* acclaimed, offered an extremely positive image of Muslims: 'he points out many particulars' of Islamic 'customs, manners, religion, and government' which 'compared with Europeans, the balance is in their favour' (1796: 359). *The Critical Review* in 1773 captured an attitude of cosmopolitanism in Edward Ives's travel account in which 'particulars relative to the Turks [...] contradict the commonly received notion of their cruelty [...]' (1773: 210). A seemingly balanced report on Arab manners and traditions was also captured by *The Critical Review* in its essay on Eyles Irwin's travel book. Irwin was just in his views of the Arabs: he described their 'ignorance and cunning' and their 'wisdom and generosity' (1780: 408). In eighteenth-century readings of travel books about the overland routes to India, another commonplace trope emerged: it is the idea that Britons abroad faced many dangers, but their heroic characters allowed them to overcome all troubles – they bore the pain of facing the chilling breeze of the desert in winter, the scorching heat of the sand in the summer and the danger of robbers all year around. *The Analytical Review* recalled how 'Mr C (Campbell) having experienced a variety of extraordinary incidents before he arrived in safety at Madras' (1796: 355). *The Critical Review* further noted how Irwin 'met many hair-breadth escapes, and braved innumerable dangers among a set of unlettered, barbarous, and perfidious savages, through dangerous and cultivated deserts, hitherto unknown to the European traveller' (1780: 405). The image of British heroism abroad serves to illustrate how the practice of travelling along Arabian deserts was often seen by contemporary commentators on travel writing as a masculine enterprise.[59] This was amply confirmed by the fact that not until Lady Anne Blunt visited and wrote about the deserts of Syria and Iraq in the last two decades of the nineteenth century can we find a travel book authored by a British female traveller in the region. Lady Blunt did not travel in the deserts on her own. She was accompanied by her husband, Wilfred Scawan Blunt, who edited and co-authored *The Bedouin Tribes of the Euphrates*, a book in which, as Wilfred wrote in the preface, the chapters which produced serious knowledge about the geography and politics of the region were composed by himself, the only experienced geographer and political thinker in the book, rather than his wife who was rather, as he reported, 'the first *bona fide* tourist who has taken the Euphrates road' (Blunt 1879: I, viii).[60]

The masculine and heroic enterprise in the reports of travellers who passed through the Arabian deserts was glorified in the eighteenth-century English press. But nowhere do we find there any association between British travels on the overland routes and British political and imperial influence in the Arab-Ottoman region. Scholars who read these books, however, preferred to view British travels across these routes as a manifestation of British imperial expansion and dominance in India and the Arab-Ottoman region. For Douglass Carruthers, who edited *The Desert Route to India: Being the Journal of Four Travellers by The Great Desert Caravan Route between Aleppo and Basra 1745-1751* (1729), British travels along the Indo-Syrian routes were 'typical' of 'a great age in the annals of British rule in India' (1929: xxiii). William Beawes, an East India official who travelled along the Syrian deserts in 1745, Carruthers recalled, 'was the first representative of this new Power which had established itself in India [...]' (1929: xxiii). Nine years after Carruthers's book was published, Christina Phelps Grant published a geographical and historical study of the Syrian deserts, *The Syrian Desert: Caravan, Travel and Exploration*, in which, like Carruthers, she referred to the British heroic efforts to open a route of communication between India and Britain. 'When the desert bridge finally came back into use', Grant observed, 'it was always completely monopolized by Englishmen, servants of the East India Company [...]' (1937: 102). The Scots and the Irishmen who crossed this desert bridge were counted by Grant as 'Englishmen'. In 2016, one scholar similarly saw eighteenth-century British desert travels as documentary evidence of Britain's rising power in the Middle East. Eva Johanna Holmberg in her essay in *The Routledge Companion to Travel Writing* (2016) recalled that 'In the mid-eighteenth century, the British started to dominate the area, with William Beawes, Gaylard Roberts, Bartholomew Plaisted and John Carmichael all describing the route' (Holmberg 2016: 377). While it is true that many Britons travelled in the region in the second half of the eighteenth century, they, as this book will show, never 'dominated the area', nor their travel books show any reference to British triumphalism over the Ottoman-Arab region. Britain was not then an imperial power in the region, and all these Britons that Homberg, relying on Carruthers's account, considered as a dominant force in the 'area' were actually men of sociability and cosmopolitanism in the Syrian deserts.[61] As the Frenchman Pierre Marie Francois Pages, who visited Basra on the way back from India in 1770, observed, Britons in the Ottoman-Arab region 'have discovered the good policy of appearing open and liberal' to the locals (1791: II, 83).[62]

Chapter one examines the travel narrative of John Carmichael, a Scotsman, who found in ruins and barren deserts an opportunity to reflect on fears and hopes in his native Scotland regarding the benefits and drawbacks of living in an age in which everything was measured by its material worth. Travelling in lands known in the past for being fertile but now barren and littered with ruins made Carmichael reflect on what he called the instability of the human condition, an idea which also stimulated the minds of many Enlightenment philosophers who otherwise were confident about the perfectibility of man and the unbounded progression of human knowledge. Chapter two examines the travel book of an English surgeon, Edward Ives, whose encounters with Arabs and Muslims allowed him to offer himself to his reader as a refined gentleman different from those surgeons many in England associated with low social class, men of rough manners acquired by the kind of work in their profession. Additionally, Ives aimed to rethink contemporary attitudes in Britain towards

Britons serving in the East, most notably those affiliated with the India Company who, like himself, came from humble backgrounds but were able to ascend the social ladder despite many in Britain accused them of corruption. Chapter three examines a travel book by another English merchant, Abraham Parsons, whose encounters with the world of Turks and Arabs taught him how commerce is a good force in life but also one which causes greed, war and violence. Chapter four examines a travel book and an unpublished autobiography written by an English merchant, Henry Abbott, whose encounters with Arabs and Turks allowed him to reflect on the meaning of Englishness in modern times: his social life in the Levant shows how his definition of Englishness was contingent on the social context within which he lived. Abbott showed how travels not only created cosmopolitan opportunities but also revealed the limitation of cosmopolitanism. For Eyles Irwin, in Chapter five, descriptions of the landscape of the overland routes to India and the kind of political rule in the region allowed him to confirm and rethink commonplace discourse in Enlightenment Britain that associated material improvement with political stability. In Chapter six, we look into a travel narrative written by a man from an aristocratic background in Scotland and a military officer in the EIC, Donald Campbell, for whom showing sympathy towards those whom he encountered was meant to critique radical voices at home who in their efforts to change the established political order posited the Ottoman Empire and its subjects as a medley of despots and slaves. Despite the different social backgrounds and experiences of these travellers, they shared a common thread on two aspects which will appear in more than one place in this book: first, Britons abroad were polite to those they encountered, particularly those they met along routes they considered immensely important to their country's settlements in India; second, they did not consider the Arab and Muslim cultures and communities living in lands many in Europe traced to pre-modern, ancient and biblical times as inferior to those in Europe – rather they showed how these cultures and communities retained many virtues, traits, habits, crafts and manners which aroused European travellers to reflect on the corruptions and excesses of modern and civilised nations of Europe.

In the conclusion, I aim to close this study by briefly examining *The Travels of Abu Taleb Mirza Khan in Asia, Africa and Europe* (originally published in Persian and was translated into English in 1810–1814). Abu Taleb Khan was a Shi'a Muslim from an Indo-Persian background. He travelled along the overland routes to India in 1803 as a pilgrim on his way back from England. Throughout the journey, Abu Taleb Khan was confronted with some of the pressing concerns that the European travellers discussed in this book also faced: issues of religious toleration, hospitality to strangers, politeness and identity were negotiated and contested in the context of encountering fellow Muslims (from Shia and Sunni communities) and European residents in the region. The book concludes with one thought: celebrating and contesting modernity – its promises and failings – was not a unique European way of thinking. Nor was the practice of sociability something of unique import to Europeans. If we agree that the Enlightenment was a global phenomenon which took place in Europe as well as the deserts of Syria, as this book persistently argues, then we can appreciate the extent to which encountering different cultures created the modern world. We will be able to understand how the Enlightenment context of improvement was cherished and contested among eighteenth-century travelling (Muslim and European) 'selves' who belonged to different social and cultural backgrounds but shared similar hopes and concerns. This *Discordia Concordia* phenomenon of the age of the Enlightenment, as we might call it, was the result of an expanding volume of East-West travel accounts to which European and Muslim travellers contributed and myriad encounters in which they participated.

Notes

1 Two important studies influenced the pattern of scholarship of European encounters with non-Europeans in the period between World War II and the publication of Edward Said's *Orientalism* (1978). The first was Theodore W. Adorno and Max Horkheimer's *Dialektik der Aufklärung*, first published in 1947 and translated into English in 1972 under the title *Dialectic of Enlightenment*. The second important study which influenced the field is Michel Foucault's *Discipline and Punish: The Birth of the Prison* (1975). Both studies cited above showed how in modern European thought, mainly that of the age of the Enlightenment, the instrumentalisation of knowledge was mainly aimed to hegemonise over the objects and people studied. Such a thesis also influenced Edward Said's main argument in *Orientalism*. A good discussion of the interdependent relationship between Orientalism and the hegemonic component of knowledge production processes, see Jane Hiddleston's *Understanding Postcolonialism* (Stockfield: Acumen, 2009); see particularly the third chapter about 'Foucault and Said: Colonial Discourse and Orientalism'.

2 Studies which belong to this paradigm include Rana Kabbani, *Europe Myths of Orient: Devise and Rule* (London: Macmillan, 1986); Lisa Lowe, *Critical Terrains: British and French Orientalisms* (Ithaca and London: Cornell University Press, 1999). Derek Gregory, 'Scripting Egypt: Orientalism and the cultures of travel' in *Rites of Passage: Reading Travel Writings*, ed. Derek Gregory and James Duncan (London: Routledge, 1999). For a good explanation of this paradigm, see Stuart Hall's essay 'The West and the Rest: Discourse and Power' in *Essential Essays: Identity and Diaspora*, ed. David Morley (Durham and London: Duke University Press, 2019), 141–184.

3 For example, see Paul Gilroy, *The Black Atlantic: Modernity and Double Consciousness* (London: Verso, 1993); Nicholas Thomas, *Entangled Objects: Exchange, Material Culture and Colonialism in the Pacific*. (Massachusetts: Harvard University Press, 1991); Vanessa Smith's *Intimate Strangers: Friendship, Exchange and Pacific Encounter* (Cambridge: Cambridge University Press, 2010). The displacement paradigm also influenced studies that examined European writings about the 'Orient'. See for example, Ros Ballaster's *Fabulous Orient: Fictions of the East in England 1662–1785* (Oxford: Oxford University Press, 2005); see also chapter two in Genevieve Lloyd's *Enlightenment Shadows* (Oxford: Oxford University Press, 2013).

4 Geoffrey Nash, *From Empire to Orient* (London: I.B Tauris, 2005); Billie Melman, *Women's Orients: English Women and the Middle East, 1718–1918* (Basingstoke: Macmillan, 1992); 'The Middle East/Arabia: 'The Cradle of Islam'' in *The Cambridge Companion to Travel Writing*, ed. Peter Hulme and Tim Young (Cambridge: Cambridge University Press, 2002), 105–119. Katrina O'Loughlin, *Women Writing and Travel in the Eighteenth Century* (Cambridge: Cambridge University Press, 2018). Gerald MacLean, *The Rise of Oriental Travel: English Visitors to the Ottoman Empire, 1580–1722* (New York: Palgrave, 2004).

5 Homi K. Bhabha, *The Location of Culture* (London and New York: Routledge, 1994), 2. Benedict Anderson, *Imagined Communities: Reflections on the Origin and Spread of Nationalism* (London: Verso, 1983).

6 On the traditions of improvement in travelling and writing travels in the eighteenth century, see Judith Adler, 'Origins of Sightseeing', *Annals of Tourism Research*, 16 (1989), 7–29; James Buzard, 'The Grand Tour and After (1660–1840)' in *The Cambridge Companion to Travel Writing*, ed. Peter Hulme and Tim Youngs (Cambridge: Cambridge University Press, 2002), 37–52. For a good account about the Enlightenment period debate about improvement, see J. B.

Bury's *The Idea of Progress*. (New York: Dover, 1932). See also the essays in *Turgot on Progress: Sociology and Economics: A Philosophical Review of the Successive Advances of the Human Mind*, ed. Ronald L. Meek (New York: Cambridge University Press, 1973). Also see Georg G. Iggers, 'The Idea of Progress in Historiography and Social Thought Since the Enlightenment' in *Progress and Its Discontents*, ed. Gabriel A. Almond, Marvin Chodorow and Roy Harvey Pearce (Berkley, Los Angeles, London: University of California Press), 44. Michael Allen Gillespie, *The Theological Origin of Modernity* (Chicago: The University of Chicago Press, 2008), 257.

7 Christopher Berry, *The Social Theory of the Scottish Enlightenment* (Edinburgh: Edinburgh University Press, 1997), and *The idea of Commercial Society in the Scottish Enlightenment* (Edinburgh: Edinburgh University Press, 2013); Alexander Broadie, *The Scottish Enlightenment* (Edinburgh: Berlinn, 2007). Richard Sher, *The Enlightenment and the Book: Scottish Authors and Their Publishers in Eighteenth-Century Britain, Ireland and America* (Chicago: The University of Chicago Press, 2006).

8 On the tension between the Christian notion of virtue and modern espousals of individualism in capitalist societies in Europe, see chapter five in Alasdair Macintyre's *After Virtue: A Study in Moral Theory* (1981; Indiana: The University of Notre Dame Press, 2007). On the classical conception of virtue, see Quentin Skinner, *Visions and Politics: Renaissance Virtues* (Cambridge: Cambridge University Press, 2002); on tension between faith and reason, see Terry Eagleton's *Culture and the Death of God* (New Haven and London: Yale University Press, 2014), 5.

9 Abdul Amir Amin, *British Interests in the Persian Gulf* (Leiden: Brill, 1967), 60.

10 These foreign policy objectives appeared in an East India Company letter sent to the newly appointed British Resident in Baghdad, Harford Jones, in 1798. The letter was published in John Gordon Lorimer's *Gazetteer of the Persian Gulf, Oman and Central Arabia*, 2 vols (Calcutta: Superintendent Government Printing), Vol I, 1620–1621. See also Arnold Wilson's 'A Periplus of the Arabia Gulf' in *The Geographical Journal* 69:3 (1927), 235–255l; particularly page 342. On British spying activities in the region, see the correspondence between John Abbott, the Levant Company Consul in Aleppo, William Digges Latouche, the East India Company Resident in Basra, in which Abbott spotted a Frenchman passing through Aleppo in 1781 whom he suspected to be an army officer sent by the French to help French forces in their wars against the English in India: The British Library, India Office Records and Private Papers, IOR/R/15/1/4, ff 8v-9; see pages 15–16. French vessels in the Mediterranean were often on the lookout for British travellers and dispatches passing through Italy, Malta, Egypt, Syria and India. See 'Captain Mark Wood's Narrative of his Overland Journey, 1779–1780', The British Library, India Office Records and Private Papers: IOR/L/MAR/C/570, ff 12–55; see page 15. Captain Richard Scott who crossed the Syrian deserts on his way to India was told by one Arab Sheikh: 'an Englishman pays double for everything abroad than any other person'; see Scott's 'Letter on the Passage Over the Isthmus of Suez and Project of a New Route to India, 1780' in East India Company, the Board of Control, the India Office, or other British Government Department, IOR/L/MAR/C/570, ff 56–84; see pages 135.

11 Most of the academic studies on Ottoman-British diplomatic relations during the eighteenth century emphasise the point that what British ambassadors mostly worried about in their interactions with the Ottomans was the idea of stopping the French from gaining commercial and political influence in the region and reviving a dying British trade in the Levant. See Geoff Berridge's *British Diplomacy in Turkey, 1583 to the Present: A Study in the Evolution of a Resident Embassy* (Leiden: Martinus Nijhoff Publishers, 2009). Michael Talbot's *British-Ottoman Relations, 1661–1807: Commerce and Diplomatic Practice in Eighteenth-Century Istanbul* (Woodbridge: Boydell & Brewer, 2017); 'Gifts of time: Watches and Clocks in British-Ottoman Diplomacy, 1693–1803', *Jahrbuch für Europäische Geschichte* 17 (2016), 55–79. 'Petitions of the Supplicant Ambassador: British Commercial Representations to the Ottoman State in the Eighteenth Century', *Osmanli Arastirmalari / The Journal of Ottoman Studies* 46 (2015), 163–191.

12 Arnold Talbot Wilson, *A Précis of the Relations of the British Government with the Tribes and Shaikhs of Arabistan* (Calcutta: Superintendent Government Printing, 1912), 5. British Library: IOR/L/PS/20/E96.

13 Ibid,1.

14 For most parts of the eighteenth century, Jerome Antony Saldanha wrote, the East India Company's 'policy was to make every endeavour to prevent their being embroiled in the

troubles' of the region, mainly in the Persian-Ottoman wars, *Précis of Turkish Arabia Affairs. 1801–1905* (Simla: Government Central Press,1906), 4.

15 Arnold Wilson, *The Persian Gulf* (Oxford: The Clarendon Press, 1928), 144–145.

16 Fitch's, Newberry's and Eldred's travelling observations and correspondences were first collected by Richard Hakluyt who published them in his *The Principal Navigations, Voyages, Traffiques, and Discoveries of the English Nation.* (London, 1599) Vol II, 245–271. A good account of Fitch and Mildenhall's travels is Ram Chandra Prasad's *Early English Travellers in India* (Delhi: Motilal, 1965); see chapter two and three. On Fitch and other early-modern travellers on the overland routes to India, see also J. Horton Ryley's *Ralph Fitch: England's Pioneer to India and Burma, His Companions and Contemporaries, His Remarkable Narrative Told in His Own Words* (London: T. Fisher Unwin, 1899).

17 During the period in which he stayed in Aleppo (total six weeks), Shirley, with the help of the English consul and merchants in the city, was able to find a secure way to cross the route between Aleppo and Baghdad. He accompanied two Ottoman officials, 'the Tafterdall, which is the Treasurer, and the great Cady, which is, as it were, the Lord chiefe Justice of Babylon', *Sir Anthony Shirley: His Relation of His Travels into Persia* (London: Printed for Nathaniell Butter 1613), 18.

18 Taylor, Vol 1, 17.

19 Nathaniel William Wraxall, *The History of France* (London, 1814), Vol I, 278.

20 *Viaggio di M. Cesare de Fedrici, nell' India orientale.* (Venice: Apresso Andrea Muschio, 1587); *The Voyage and trauaile of M. Caesar Frederick, merchant of Venice, into the East Indies* (London: Printed by Richard Iones and Edward White, 1588).

21 Pietro Della Valle, *Viaggi di Pietro della Valle il Pellegrino* (Roma, 1650).

22 Harrison, 3.

23 14 travel books about the overland routes appeared in print in Britain in the period between 1748 and 1798; these books were first counted and briefly examined by Mohamed Ali Hachicho in his article' English Travel Books about the Arab Near East in the Eighteenth Century', *Die Welt Des Islam*, 9:1 (Brill, 1964), 1–206. Less travel books in French appeared on these routes throughout the period, but two French travel accounts stand out: François Pagès, in his *Voyages autour du monde et vers les deux pôles, par terre et par mer, pendant les années 1767 à 1776* (Paris, 1782) told us that he, on his way back from India to Europe, crossed the overland routes between Basra and Aleppo in 1770. This book was translated into English, *Travels round the world, in the years 1767, 1768, 1769, 1770, 1771 by Monsieur de Pagès*, in 1791. Towards the end of the eighteenth century, Pierre François Henry published his travel observations of both Egyptian and Syrian overland routes to India in *Route de l'Inde, ou Description geographique de l'Egypte, la Syrie, l'Arabie* (Paris, 1799). An indication of how the French were interested in improving their knowledge about Levantine overland routes to India is the translation into French of the travel books of two Englishmen who crossed the Syrian and Egyptian deserts on their ways back from India in the second half of the eighteenth century. Thomas Howel and James Capper's descriptions of their journeys appeared in *Voyage en retour de l'Inde, par terre, et par une route en partie inconnue jusqu'ici, par Thomas Howel; suivi d'Observations sur le passage dans l'Inde par l'Egypte et le grand désert, par James Capper* (Paris, 1796), just three years before Napoleon set up a military campaign aiming to threaten British interests and settlements in the region.

24 An excellent study of European travels across Egyptian overland routes to India, see H. L. Hoskins' *British Routes to India* (London: Frank& Cass, 1966).

25 George Baldwin, the East India Company consul in Egypt in the last three decades of the eighteenth century, recalled how Egyptian overland routes were important for British communications with India: 'I had the satisfaction also to convey [across the overland routes] the first advice of the war in 1778 to the East Indies; by means of which we were enabled to the astonishment of all England, when the news arrived, to expel the French from India, before the succour could reach them, and to add their possessions to our own', *Political Reflections Relating to Egypt* (London: Printed for H. Baldwin and Son; New Bridge Street, 1801), 6–7. On the importance of the Syrian overland routes to Britain, see chapter five in Christina Phelps Grant's *The Syrian Desert: Caravan, Travel and Exploration* (London: A. & C. Black LTD, 1937). See also Douglas Carruthers' introduction to *The Desert Route to India: Being the Journal of Four Travellers by the Great Desert Caravan Route between Aleppo and Basra*

1745–1751, ed. Douglass Carruthers (London: Hakluyt Society, 1929). On the importance of the Egyptian overland routes to Britain, see chapter one in Hoskins's *British Routes to India*.

26 The term 'enlightenment' was first used in English in 1865 by James Hutchinson Stirling in his *Secret Of Hegel* (1856). Stirling associated eighteenth-century dissenting movements and ideas, such as deism, atheism and pantheism, in England with the rise of a culture of free thinking, what he called 'Enlightenment', in which 'Spiritualism seems dying out in England, and that more and more numerous voices daily cry hail to the new God, Matter [...]' (Vol I, xxxii). In 1898, Edward Caird similarly referred to 'the age of the Enlightenment' in his *The Critical Philosophy of Kant* (1898) as 'the age of Individualism, Secularism, even, in a sense, of Atheism' (44). As these two scholars' works have shown, the Enlightenment was an age of disenchantment. Hutchinson and Caird's view of the Enlightenment age in Europe as one of complete de-sacralisation was re-iterated by Theodore Adorno and Max Horkheimer's *The Dialectic of the Enlightenment* (1944), Peter Gay's *The Enlightenment: An Interpretation: The Rise of Modern Paganism* (1966) and *The Enlightenment: An Interpretation: Science of Freedom* (1969), and John Gray's *Enlightenment's Wake Politics and Culture at the Close of the Modern Age*.

27 Michael Losonsky, *Enlightenment and Action From Descartes to Kant: Passionate Thought* (Cambridge: Cambridge University Press, 2003), 2. Michel de Certeau, *The Practice of Everyday Life*, trans., Steven Rendall (Los Angeles and London: The University of California Press, 1984), 47–48.

28 Eagleton, *Culture and the Death of God*, 2–3. Roy Porter, *The Creation of the Modern World: The Untold Story of the British Enlightenment* (New York: W.W Norton, 2000), 445. Dennis. C Rasmussen, *The Pragmatic Enlightenment* (Cambridge: Cambridge University Press, 2014), 193.

29 On how early modern British culture saw attempts to move knowledge away from the direction of the medieval scholastic tradition, see Judy A. Hayden's essay 'Intersections and Cross-Fertilization' in *Travel Narratives, The New Science, and Literary Discourse 1569–1750* (Farnham: Ashgate, 2012), 3–4.

30 Adam Smith, *Lectures on Jurisprudence*, ed. R.L Meek, D.D Raphael, and P.G Stein (Indianapolis, 1982); *An Inquiry Into the Nature and Causes of the Wealth of Nations*, 2 vols (London: Printed for W. Strahan).

31 *See* Ronald l. Meek, *Social science and The Ignoble Savage* (Cambridge: Cambridge University Press, 1976), 5.

32 There are many studies about the Scottish tradition of theorising progress in stages. But one excellent explanation of how this tradition came into being can be found in Frank Palmeri's introduction to *State of Nature, Stages of Society: Enlightenment Conjectural History and Modern Social Discourse* (Columbia: Columbia University Press, 2015).

33 H. M Höpfl, 'From savage to Scotsman: conjectural history in the Scottish Enlightenment', *The Journal of British Studies* 17 (1978), 19–40.

34 Onni Gust has recently argued that racialised tropes played an important role in the production of civility and progress in Scottish Enlightenment thought; see the first chapter in *Unhomely Empire: Whiteness and Belonging, 1760–1830* (London: Bloomsbury, 2021).

35 Shinji Nohara, *Commerce and Strangers in Adam Smith* (Singapore: Springer, 2018), 23.

36 David Fate Norton and Mary Norton, *The David Hume Library* (Edinburgh: Edinburgh Bibliographical Society, 1996), 14.

37 For a good account on Smith's life, see Chapter five in Alan Macfarlane's *The Riddle of the Modern World: Of Liberty, Wealth and Equality* (New York: Palgrave, 2000).

38 A good account about Pococke's life in Britain and travels in the East can be found in chapters three and six in Richard Finnegan's *English Explorers in the East (1738–1745): The Travels of Thomas Shaw, Charles Perry and Richard Pococke* (Leiden: Brill, 2019).

39 John Dwyer, *Virtuous Discourse: Sensibility and Community in Late Eighteenth Century Scotland* (Edinburgh: John Donald Published Ltd, 1987), 2.

40 One reason why Ferguson was interested in the military character of Arabs was because, as Fania Oz-Salzberger observed, his background. He is from the Highlands of Scotland. He was served as a soldier in British military campaign in Flanders during the War of the Austrian Succession (1740–1748). As Oz-Salzberger noted, 'He remained in the British army for some nine years [...] More than any other thinker of the Scottish Enlightenment, Ferguson was to insist on military valour as a cornerstone of civic virtue' (x).

41 Ferguson's fascination with the military valour of Arabs in the context of rise and progress of nations was also shaped by his readings of the rise and fall of the Roman Empire, a topic about which he wrote *The History of the Progress and Termination of the Roman Republic.* 3 vols (London: Printed for W. Strahan, 1783). On how Ferguson's Scottish experience informed his views of rise and progress of nations, see Ian McDaniel's *Adam Ferguson in the Scottish Enlightenment* (Massachusetts: Harvard, 2013).

42 A good account of d'Arvieux's life and travels in the Levant is Elizabeth Sirriyeh's 'The Memoires of a French Gentleman in Syria: Chevalier Laurent d'Arvieux (1635–1702)', *Bulletin (British Society for Middle Eastern Studies)*, 11: 2 (1984), 125–139.

43 Samuel Johnson, A *Dictionary of the English Language,* 4th edn (London: W. Strahan, 1773).

44 See Karen O'Brien's *Women and Enlightenment in Eighteenth-Century Britain* (Cambridge: Cambridge University Press, 2009), 2.

45 Many years ago, Gladys Bryson commented on how many Scottish literati gained improvements in their travels. She did not specify where these literati travelled, but the implication is that they were knowledgeable with the intellectual life and philosophy of the continent, mainly France. *Man and Society: The Scottish Inquiry of the Eighteenth Century* (Princeton: Princeton University Press, 1945), 5.

46 On the celebrating of and fears about commercialism in Enlightenment Scotland, see Chapter eleven in Nicholas Philipson's *Adam Smith: An Enlightened Life* (London: Penguin, 2010).

47 *The Enlightenment: And Why it Still Matters* (Oxford: Oxford University Press, 2013), 2.

48 On nineteenth-century Eurocentric discourses about the responsibility of Europeans towards primitive societies, see James Morris Blaut's *The Colonizer's Model of the World: Geographical Diffusionism and Eurocentric History* (New York: Guilford Press, 1993). As far as the Middle East is concerned, Jonathan Parry has recently argued that one important staple in nineteenth-century British policies and attitudes towards the Arabs was that the British undertook the responsibility of civilising them: 'Britain had to think seriously about how to manage and cultivate... [Middle Eastern] inhabitants, which meant mainly the Arabs', *Promised Land: the British and the Ottoman Middle East* (Princeton: Princeton University Press, 2022), 3.

49 See the collection of essays in *Curious Encounters: Voyage Collecting and Making Knowledge in the Long Eighteenth Century*, ed. Adriana Craciun and Mary Terrall (Toronto: The University of Toronto Press Toronto 2019). Fariba Zarinebaf, *Mediterranean Encounters: Trade and Pluralism in Early Modern Galata* (California: University of California Press, 2018). Daniel O'Quinn, *Engaging the Ottoman Empire: Vexed Mediations, 1690–1815* (Pennsylvania: The University of Pennsylvania Press, 2019).

50 Felicity A. Nussbaum, Jonathan Lamb, Nigel Leask, in their different ways, showed how Edward Said's conception of Orientalism which associated European writings about the Middle East with hegemonic colonial relations was revealing but not the only model available to scholars. They showed how complex social and material encounters between Europeans and non-Europeans helped to constitute complex European identities whose articulation of human and cultural differences were shaped by shifting notions of class, gender, and race in eighteenth-century Europe. This study draws on these important works: Nigel Leask, *Curiosity and Aesthetics of Travel Writing: 1770–1840: From an Antique Land (*Oxford: Oxford University Press, 2002). Jonathan Lamb, *Preserving the Self in the South Seas, 1680–1840* (Chicago: University of Chicago Press, 2001). Also, the collection of essays in *The Global Eighteenth Century*, ed. Felicity Nussbaum (Maryland: The John Hopkins University Press, 2003), and the essays in *A New Imperial History: Culture, identity and Modernity in Britain and the Empire, 1600–1840*, ed. Kathleen Wilson (Cambridge: Cambridge University Press, 2004).

51 Nadia Atia, 'A Relic of its own past: Mesopotamia in British Imagination: 1900–14', Memory Studies 2 (3), 232–241.

52 Important studies in the field include James Canton's *from Cairo to Baghdad* (London: Bloomsbury, 2011). Sara Mills's *Discourse of Difference: An Analysis of Women Travel Writing and Colonialism* (London: Routledge, 1991); See also Saree Makdisi and Felicity Nussbaum's introduction to *The Arabian Nights in Historical Context Between East and West* (Oxford: Oxford University Press, 2008), 9–11. See chapter one in Lisa Lowe's *Critical Terrains: French and British Orientalisms* (Ithaca and London: Cornell University Press, 1991). Recently the Saidian

model which dominated earlier studies of European encounters with the Middle East have been rethought in the scholarship of Alexander Bevilacqua, in his *The Republic of Arabic Letters: Islam and the European Enlightenment* (Belknap Press: Cambridge, Massachusetts, 2018) and Humberto Garcia's *Islam and the English Enlightenment.*

53 As Srinivas Arvamudan commented on Theodore Adorno and Max Horkheimer's *Dialectic of the Enlightenment* (1944): 'According to the Frankfurt School, the Enlightenment instrumentalised knowledge in a manner that led to fascism and the death camps of the Holocaust', *Enlightenment Orientalism: Resisting the Rise of the Novel* (Chicago: Chicago University Press, 2012), 2.

54 J. G. A. Pocock, *Barbarism and Religion: The Enlightenments of Edward Gibbon 1737–1746,* Vol I (Cambridge: Cambridge University Press, 2004), 9. David Sorkin, *The Religious Enlightenment: Protestants, Jews, and Catholics from London to Vienna* (Princeton and Oxford: Princeton University Press, 2008); Jonathan Israel, *The Revolution of the Mind: Radical Enlightenment and the Intellectual Origin of Modern Democracy* (Princeton and Oxford: Princeton University Press, 2010). Isaiah Berlin, 'The Counter Enlightenment', *Against the Current: Essays in the History of Ideas,* ed. Henry Hardy (Princeton and Oxford: Princeton University Press, 2013); Darrin McMahon, *Enemies of the Enlightenment: The French Counter-Enlightenment and the Making of Modernity* (Oxford: Oxford University Press, 2002).

55 For an excellent account about these directions in Enlightenment studies, see chapter one in John Robertson's *The Case for the Enlightenment: Scotland and Naples 1680–1760* (Cambridge: Cambridge University Press, 2005).

56 Dorinda Outram, *The Enlightenment* (Cambridge: Cambridge University Press, 1995), 8.

57 The case for a heterogenous Enlightenment can be found in the collection of essays in *The Enlightenment World,* ed. Martin Fitzpatrick, Peter Jones, Christa Knellwolf and Iain McCalman (Abingdon and New York, 2004).

58 Janet Starkey, *The Scottish Enlightenment Abroad: The Russells of Aleppo and Bradshaw* (Amsterdam: Brill, 2018).

59 Even those women travellers who published their narratives throughout the period were not taken seriously by reviewers and the public. They mostly wrote their travel observations in the form of private letters to family and friends, a form considered suitable for the domestic, private space to which women belonged. See Susan Pickford, 'The Page as Private/Public Space in Mariana Starke's Travel Writings on Italy' in *Travel Writing, Form and Empire,* ed. Julia Kuehn and Paul Smethurst (London: Routledge, 2009), 64. Carl Thompson also argues that fewer women travellers and travel writers published travel accounts because of 'the prevalence of' a 'patriarchal ideology' which 'has [...] created the reality it purports to describe, imposing numerous constraints and limitations on any woman who wished to travel', *Travel Writing* (London: Routledge, 2011), 169.

60 Julia Kuehn, *Female Poetics of Empire: From Eliot to Woolf* (London: Routledge, 2014), 94.

61 Indeed, only after Napoleon invaded Egypt in 1798, that British travellers and travel writers began to advocate direct military intervention in the region. In this context, British understanding of progress began to adopt, in the word of the historian James Blaut, diffusionist rhetoric. Therefore, in 1801, in the year that Napoleon left Egypt, we find George Baldwin, the British consul in Egypt, advocating 'retaining Egypt under the control of Great Britain' in the name of improving commerce between Britain and Egypt; see Baldwin's *Political Recollections,* 16. Also, in the deserts of Syria in 1835, Captain Francis Rawdon Chesney in Syria commanded a small expedition (two British streamers in the Euphrates) in the hope to establish a regular route of communication between Syria and India. The account of this expedition was published in *The Expedition for the Survey of the Rivers Euphrates and Tigris.* Carried on by order of the British Government in the years 1835, 1836, 1837 [...]. Vol I and II (London : Longman, Brown, Green, and Longmans, 1850). On the association between nineteenth-century European conceptions of progress and the expansion of empire, see Blaut's *The Colonizer's Model of the World.*

62 British residents and consuls in the Levant were highly respected by locals. Eyles Irwin who visited Aleppo in 1777 recalled in a poem he wrote in 1784 and titled 'Epitaph' how John Abbott, who held the position of a consul of the Levant Company from 1770 until his death in 1783, was a hospitable and friendly Briton in the Levant: 'That form of Hospitality pourtray/Bowe'd, like a mourner, o'er her Abbott's clay! / The stranger's spirit at thy board

to raise/ And, from the Arab bear his local praise/', *The Poetical Register* (London, 1814,), 206. James Capper in 1787 noted how the 'Arab inhabitants' of Basra 'showed great respect to Mr Latouche,' the East India Company resident in Basra, 'on account of his generosity and humanity towards them and his countrymen', *Observations on the Passage to India Through Egypt, and Across the Great Desert with Occasional Remarks on the adjacent Countries, and also Sketches of the different Routes* (London, 1783), 86.

Chapter One

IMPROVEMENT OF KNOWLEDGE: JOHN CARMICHAEL'S *A JOURNEY FROM ALEPPO TO BUSSERAH, OVER THE DESERT* (1772)

Plac'd in this isthmus of a middle state,
A being darkly wise and rudely great,
With too much knowledge for the sceptic side,
With too much weakness for the stoic pride.

—Alexander Pope, *An Essay on Man (1733)*

John Henry Grose's *Voyage to the East Indies* (1757) offered 'a faithful recital of facts' collected during the many years of his service at the East India Company's (EIC) military station in Bombay.[1] Grose's book enjoyed a brief period of popularity immediately upon its publication. Indeed, many eighteenth-century travel writers and authorities on travel and exploration praised the book for its detached and scientific style, which was important for informing the public about British wars and imperial expansions abroad.[2] But the spontaneous style of Grose's book – the fact that he reported on what he observed in a forensic manner without necessarily showing that he had background knowledge of the region – was little appreciated by some. The *Monthly Review* (1757), for example, accused Grose of exploring Oriental 'theology' without showing any expertise on the topic (1757: 302). The *Critical Review* in 1758 did not 'recommend' the book because 'the stile is stiff and labored' and 'in some parts of the performance absolutely unintelligible' (1758: 319). Yet, all agreed, as the *Critical Review* affirmed, that Grose's book offered valuable information relating to 'the interests of England' in the East Indies (1758: 319). After all, the book was published during a period in which the EIC was battling the French and their Indian allies in the Carnatic region.[3] This view of travel writing as a valuable means to promote 'the interests of England' appeared in an age of rapid British imperial expansion in the East, which encouraged Grose to add to the 1772 edition of his book a short travel narrative titled *A Journey from Aleppo to Busserah*, written by the Scotsman John Carmichael, who travelled along the overland routes between Europe and India in 1751. Norbert Schürer argued that despite the hostile treatment it received in the press, the *Voyage* showed a hospitable view of Islam in contrast to Carmichael's hostile views of Islam and Prophet Muhammad in his short narrative: 'it is somewhat surprising that Grose included Carmichael's "Journal" in his *Voyage*' (Schürer 2019: 304). James Rennell, a leading English geographer and cartographer, however, did not find it surprising at all that

Grose included Carmichael's narrative in his book. In his *On the Rate of Travelling as Performed by Camels and Its Application, as a Scale, to the Purposes of Geography* (1791), Rennell, extolled Carmichael and other explorers who travelled on the overland routes – men such as Robert Hunter, James Capper and Eyles Irwin. He made it clear in his essay that the efforts of those who set out to explore the Syrian-Mesopotamian desert routes should encourage other Britons to seek to improve British knowledge of Africa. Rennell expressed his disappointment that in modern times few British travellers managed to explore the interior parts of Africa – only the eccentric Scotsman James Bruce was able to reach northern Abyssinia in the late 1760s, but his travel account was widely ridiculed in Britain for being an extraordinary collection of lies.[4] Rennell's critique of the lack of serious efforts in Britain to explore Africa expressed the hopes of the African Association, to which he was an advisor at the time, to expand British knowledge about a continent many in Britain saw as an important source of material and human capital to the British Empire. Such was the view of Henry Beaufoy, the secretary to the African Association, in *The Proceedings of the Association Promoting the Discovery of the Interior Parts of Africa* (1790), who regretted how 'almost the whole of Africa' is now 'unvisited' and is currently 'unknown' (Beaufoy 1790: 3).[5]

Rennell's description of Britain's daring explorers in Arabia aimed to address this problem: his praise of Arabian travels, including Carmichael's, perhaps encouraged the Scottish explorer Mungo Park to undertake an arduous journey to West Africa in 1794.[6] Upon his return, Park approached Rennell, an advisor to the African Association at the time, who praised his report and helped him to prepare his travel book for the press: the illustrations and the map in Park's *Travels in the Interior Districts of Africa* (1797) were supplied by Rennell.[7] Rennell found Carmichael's narrative immensely important not only for encouraging Britons to explore the inland districts of Africa but also for improving British knowledge of overland routes between Europe and India, those routes located in a region which many saw as extremely valuable for the safety and security of British possessions in India.[8] For Rennell, Carmichael in the deserts of Syria and Mesopotamia followed a method of exploration which showed exceptional British perseverance, ingenuity and heroism. Rennell admired Carmichael's effort 'to keep a register of the course by a compass, and to compute, comparatively, if not absolutely, the intermediate distance on each course; by computing the steps of the camel on which he rode, during a certain interval of time; and afterwards measuring a number of them on the ground' (Rennell 1791: 131). Such method is not necessarily reliable, Rennell wrote, but 'his process has furnished others with the means of ascertaining the whole distance in the aggregate, and of proportioning the parts throughout' (Rennell 1791: 132).

Rennell was correct in his estimation of the importance of Carmichael's efforts to measure distances in the deserts. In the wake of Carmichael's journey, most British travellers on the overland routes started to calculate distances between major towns and cities they passed through by using simple methods such as counting the steps of their camels, which they later converted into miles. Many added to their travel accounts tables showing the different stages of their journeys in miles, inviting their readers to appreciate the serious efforts they exerted while using simple methods and tools.[9] Calculating the steps of a camel, however, was proven useless in 1836 by Francis Rawdon Chesney who led a well-funded and well-equipped expedition across Syrian-Mesopotamian routes accompanied by, as Chesney wrote in his *Narrative of the Euphrates Expedition* (1868), 'engineers who made a most careful survey' of the region (Chesney 1868: ix).[10]

Despite the simple method of exploration in Carmichael's book, Rennell could not but praise its rigour during a period in which Britain was concerned about growing political influence of the French in Ottoman-Arab land, an influence which harmed British easy access to India through Egypt and Syria.[11] But Rennell ignored the fact that Carmichael's experience in Syrian routes to India included moments of extreme vulnerability that complicated the image of British heroism and perseverance abroad. The camel which Rennell saw as a docile animal used as an instrument for calculating distances between major landmarks on the road appeared in Carmichael's account as a companion upon whom he depended for his survival across parched and inhospitable deserts. In addition, Carmichael, riding a camel for the first time, knew that to be precise and exact in one's calculations of distances is impossible. 'The motion of my camel', he wrote, 'would not admit of that exactness I could have wished, in estimating our course by the compass' (Carmichael 1772: 50). Rennell was aware that Carmichael's method was 'governed' by the motion, 'economy' and certain 'circumstances' of the Arab caravan, thus showing a sense of frustration that British knowledge of overland routes to India cannot be seen as complete (Carmichael 1772: 123). But the reader of his account is left with the impression that expanding British knowledge in the field of geography mainly depended on heroic and innovative character of the British improver/traveller/explorer in the field, one whose modest skills in geography and reliance on few tools (camels, a compass, telescope and watch) could not stop him from improving British knowledge of Arabia.

This chapter sets out to complicate the story of British heroism abroad which appeared in Rennell's views of Carmichael's exploration work. As this chapter argues, a journey in the overland routes is an attempt to uncover, unpack and reconcile the possibilities and impossibilities, successes and failures that the modern travelling experience entails. It was one which not only allowed the traveller to see the self as being of service to the nation but also gave him an opportunity to vent frustrations about its fragmented situation. In the wake of the failure of the Jacobite Rebellion (1745), one fronted by Charles Edward Stuart and his Scottish supporters who set out to take over the British throne, Carmichael's country, Scotland, was successfully annexed into an English capitalist system whose champions were optimistic about changing pastoral and traditional communities to a commercial nation concerned about improving their material life.[12] Ambivalences accompanying this radical vision were negotiated by Carmichael while travelling in barren deserts and among tribal people. As this chapter shows, a journey in Arabian deserts was an opportunity to unpack this change. If there is a drama in this chapter, it concerns the making of the modern British self, one whose encounters with ruins and tribal society, to recall Walter Benjamin, flashed up a memory of a brilliant past at a moment of an extreme anxiety of change in the present.[13]

Caravan Sociability

According to Grose, Carmichael served in the EIC military station in Bombay and Anjengo for many years before the Company decided to dismiss him in 1751 for his insolent behaviour. Carmichael left the EIC after some 'disputes [he had in Bombay] with the Governor and Council' (Grose 1772: 10). He went back to London in the hope of seeking redress. After arriving in London, '[h]is conduct was so much disapproved', added Grose, 'that, instead of meeting with redress, he was dismissed [from] the service; and on his application for leave to go back, in order to settle his affairs, was refused a passage on board any of the Company's ships' (Grose 1772: 10). The hero of Rennell, thus, while falling from grace of the EIC, preferred to trek back to India across Syria and Mesopotamia. Carmichael did not mention why he chose to go back to India across Syrian routes. Further, unlike most English and Scottish travellers who often recalled how the British residents in Aleppo, Baghdad and Basra accommodated and welcomed them in their houses and among their families, he did not mention whether the British community living in cities on the overland routes to India entertained him.[14] In Aleppo, Carmichael called Alexander Russell, the physician for the Levant Company between 1745 and 1755, 'my friend'. But he said nothing about whether Russell entertained him in his house in Aleppo or not. Probably Carmichael, now unemployed and short of enough cash to fund his travels, chose to travel back to India across the Syrian routes because they were known for being viable and shorter in comparison to those of the Cape of Good Hope. '[M]y finances not being in the best order', Carmichael wrote in his diary (Carmichael 1772: 31).

Immediately after arriving in Aleppo, Carmichael joined a merchant caravan travelling to Basra on 22 October 1751.[15] The caravan in which he travelled was multicultural and multireligious: it 'consisted of thirty-three Christians, merchants and passengers, seven Jews, and about twenty Turks', he wrote, 'with Sheikh Mahauson [an Arab], our conductor' (Carmichael 1772: 4). More people of non-Islamic backgrounds than Muslims were in the caravan, Carmichael noted. Not only was Carmichael fascinated by the diversity of the caravan. He was also surprised when discovering that half of the camels and goods in the caravan belonged to Jewish and Christian merchants: 'twelve hundred camels, six hundreds of which were laden with merchandize, chiefly belonging to the Christians and Jews, amounting in value to near three hundred thousand pounds sterling [...]' (Carmichael 1772: 4). In the caravan, Carmichael did not appear to have been a traveller of the first rate: that is, he did not mention that he paid for a local dress, riding tools such *mahafa* (a box fixed on the back of the camel) and *takhtirwan* (camel litter), interpreters, servants and guides.[16] While European travellers in the region, men of scholarly and artistic backgrounds such as Robert Wood, James Dawkins, John Bouverie and the Italian artist Giovanni Battista Borra, purchased some relevant history and travel books, mathematical instruments and presents to local rulers and caravan guides, Carmichael had little money even to spend on hiring a horse.[17]

Carmichael was a man of modest means across the desert, which explains why he was sociable among his fellow travellers. He mentioned how a European traveller in the Arabian deserts often faces a raft of problems which require a great deal of patience to handle: problems like the inclemency of the weather, scarcity of water and looming danger of scores of robbers, all of which required a full cooperation with the natives.[18] On the way to Basra, Carmichael, for example, recalled how once 'my handkerchief was conveyed away, and this evening they [the Arabs] stole my blanket':

> Having suffered much last night (which was very cold) from the want of my blanket, I thought of the following stratagem to recover it. I entered into conversation with the Arabs on the subject of my loss, and took occasion to show how they were celebrated by travellers for their honesty; which made me conclude that my blanket had been taken away by some mistake, and would be returned as soon as the error was discovered. This had the desired effect; the Arabs who had it fearful for their national honour, returned it, pretending he had found it on a camel. On the recovery of my property, I complimented the thief on his not deviating from the integrity of his countrymen. (Carmichael 1772: 5)

The tension in the above passage between 'national honour' and individual practices reveals an important line of thought in almost all British travel writings about Arabs which praised their hospitality but decried their violent raids of travellers and caravans. The above passage, moreover, reveals that Carmichael was aware of the discourse in Europe about Arabia being a haven of lawlessness and chaos, a discourse which is rooted in European hostile views towards the biblical Ishmael, whom European Christians considered as the father of the Arabs and an embodiment of violence and barbarism in comparison to the covenanted Issac (more on this point in Chapters four and five).[19]

But Carmichael also belonged to a generation of British travellers in Arabia for whom encounter involved performative practices, such as initiating conversations and sharing compliments, which helped to facilitate safe journeys across the deserts and allowed travellers to rethink some dominant tropes in Europe about Arab violence and barbarism. One such incidence occurred when Carmichael offered to examine the medical condition of an Arab Sheikh in the deserts, 'a great fat fellow, a Sheik' who 'came to our tent in search of a doctor' (Carmichael 1772: 16). Carmichael, in the manner of an eighteenth-century quack, volunteered to examine his medical condition: he 'felt his pulse, and finding it feverish, prescribed bleeding' (Carmichael 1772: 16). Carmichael, however, did not dare to do the operation because, as he wrote, he had no 'lancet' with him (16). The Arab barber who volunteered to do the operation, Carmichael regretted, used a 'rusty razor' and 'made a large orifice, or rather a hole, which with great difficulty was afterwards closed' (Carmichael 1772: 16). Before the Arab man's medical condition improved, Carmichael found himself in an extremely vulnerable position. If this Arab Sheikh died, he would have been held accountable. Carmichael was relieved when he found that '[a]fter the operation', the Sheikh 'slept for about three hours, got up, broke wind, eat a large dish of pillaw, and found himself perfectly recovered' (Carmichael 1772: 16).

For contemporary readers of European travel books about Arabia, such a story does not seem completely unbelievable: many travellers throughout the seventeenth and eighteenth centuries, as Chapter two shows, boasted of their medical skills in the company of Arabs and Turks despite most of them had little knowledge of medicine. The French spy in India the Abbe Carré in 1673 reported how assuming the character of a physician in Arabia secures the European traveller a respectable status among Arab tribes. But other travellers, such as the physician Thomas Howell, warned European travellers in the Arab-Ottoman land of the danger of prescribing violent methods of treatments because in case their patients happen to die in the process, the relatives of the patients will take revenge against the European physician.[20]

Carmichael drew on this tradition in European writings about Arabs, showing how he, assuming the character of a physician, enjoyed a special privilege among them. 'Had my friend Dr. Russell seen him [the Sheikh] eat', Carmichael added, 'I am persuaded he would admit my knowledge in therapeuticks' (Carmichael 1772: 16). Carmichael knew that Alexander Russell was a respected medical man in Syria: in Aleppo, Russell treated men of wealth and power in the city; his medical professions allowed him to frequent the social circles of the elite.[21] It is likely the case that Carmichael will be called by Russell, a university-trained physician, a practising doctor in London and Aleppo and a member of the Royal Society, a quack if both happened to converse about such medical adventure in the Arabian desert. However, both Russel and Carmichael belonged to an age in which many surgeons and quacks with no medical degrees were free to practise despite the efforts of many physicians in Britain to improve the medical field by turning it into a scientific discipline, one with professional licences and affiliations; quackery, as the next chapter will discuss, enabled many during the period to make enormous wealth; it also earned them the privilege of entering social circles of high society. Carmichael's quackery in the deserts helped him to make Arab friends and secured him a safe passage across spaces many in Britain feared and associated with barbarism.

Recalling Past Virtues

More than two hundred years after Rennell's praise of Carmichael was recorded, another intrepid English explorer expressed her admiration of Carmichael's exploration work in the Syrian-Mesopotamian deserts. Gertrude Bell lived and travelled extensively in the Middle East in the first decade of the twentieth century. She was a typical Victorian traveller who often wedded the idea of imperial service to that of exploring new places and sites. She was educated at Oxford University and widely versed in the history of the Arabs.[22] She was also an avid reader of previous European and British travel books about the Middle East. In *Amurath to Amurath* (1911), a diary which *The Times* described as 'a serious contribution to Mesopotamian exploration', Bell wrote about her travels in the Syrian deserts and 'along the banks of the Euphrates', what she called 'the leisurely course of Oriental travel' where she encountered the ancient site of Ukhaidir, a famous Mesopotamian palace located in the southwest region of Baghdad (Bell 1911: vii).[23] She recalled the names of the European travellers who previously visited the place, but she emphasised that 'Neither to M. Massignon [a French Orientalist who also visited the palace in 1908, only one year before she was in the region] nor to me belongs the honour of discovery'. Rather it was Carmichael, 'an unknown Englishman' who first 'visited the palace in the eighteenth century' (Bell 1911: 148). It is important here to note that Bell in 1911 did not mention that she read Carmichael's travel diary. Rather she knew about it from reading the travel account of the eighteenth-century German explorer in Arabia, Carsten Niebuhr. Niebuhr, in his *Reisebeschreibung nach Arabien und andern umliegenden Ländern* (1778), recalled having 'found in the journal of an Englishman' a reference to a site called 'El Khader'.[24] It is this note which introduced Bell to the work of Carmichael, that 'nameless Englishman', who she considered the first European who visited and wrote about the Ukhaidir castle (Bell 1911: 148).

In 1911, Bell visited the site for the second time; it was a short trip during which she photographed and measured what remained from the palace.[25] Three years later, she published detailed descriptions of the site in her *Palace and Mosque at Ukhaidir: A Study in Early Mohammadan Architecture* (1914). In this book, the name Carmichael appears again as one of the early discoverers of the Ukhaidir Palace. 'This Englishman', Bell wrote in *Palace and Mosque*, 'I conjecture to have been Mr. Carmichael, whose route is shown in a map published by Ives and there called the common route of the caravans from Aleppo to Bassora over the great desert of Arabia, as described in a journal kept by Mr. Carmichael in the year 1751' (Bell 1914: x). In addition to reading Niebuhr's book and Ives's map of the desert [Figure 2], in which Carmichael's route was traced, Bell did not recall that she read Carmichael's account. All that interested her in the history of European exploration in the region was the idea that the site of Ukhaidir was first discovered by 'an Englishman'; Bell did not even refer to the Scottishness of Carmichael.

In all counts, Bell was wrong to mention that Carmichael was the first European who visited and discovered the site. The French merchant and traveller Jean Baptise Tavernier, in 1638, was the first European who recorded his observation of the palace. In his travel account, Tavernier showed no interest in the history of the palace. All that he cared to record was the idea that Arabs little appreciate the importance of antiquities and that the deserts around the palace were previously cultivated simply because 'the

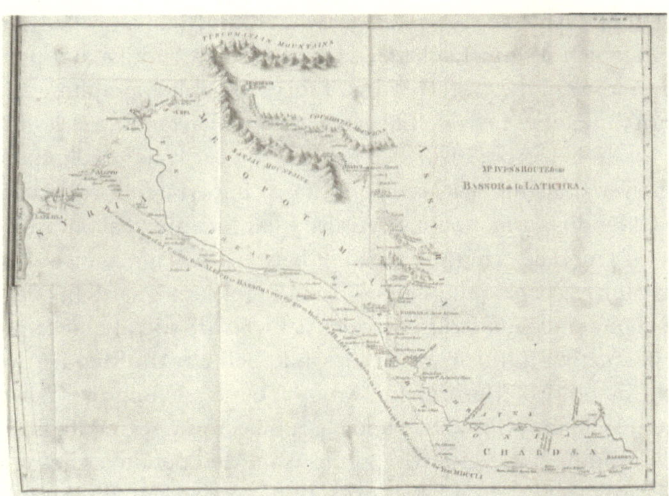

Figure 2 Edward Ives's route across the Syrian-Mesopotamian overland routes. *Travels from Persia to England* (1773). Courtesy: The British Library.

Bricks had been burnt with the Straw' (Tavernier 1684: 62). Tavernier used his observations to confirm the craftsmanship and industriousness of the people who lived in these deserts in the past. Little did he bother to reflect on the religion, cultures and ethnicity of the people who built the palace.

For Bell, however, architecture appeared as a historical metaphor of the rise and fall of civilisations. In *Palace and Mosque* (1914), the book in which Bell recorded her observations of the palace of Ukhaidir, she started from the proposition that Arabs and Muslims could not build magnificent palaces in their deserts and despite that the remnants of great architectural past in their region, sites like 'the rock-cut tombs of Madain Salih' and 'Petra' embody 'a higher order of artistic impulse', she wrote, 'it is an impulse which borrowed its power from without, from Hellenized Egypt and Hellenized Syria'(Bell 1914: vii). Arab and Islamic architecture, for Bell, should not be considered the achievement of a nomadic people.[26] Some Arab conquerors encouraged building palaces, but in so doing they mainly relied on the expertise and knowledge of the sophisticated civilisations they managed to conquer at the time: the Persians in the East and the Greeks and Romans in the West. 'The Mohammadan invaders', wrote Bell in *Palace and Mosque*, 'were essentially nomadic; their dwelling was the black tent, their grave the desert sands. The inhabitants of the rare oases of western and central Arabia were content, as they are today, with a rude architecture of sun-dried brick and palm-trunks, unadorned by any intricate device of the imagination, and unsuited to any but the simplest needs' (vii). Bell doubted that the palace of Ukhaidir could have been built by Arabs, the people she posited as static and unable to achieve material progress for most of their history.[27] 'The palaces of the conquerors were planned, constructed, and adorned', Bell wrote, 'by those whom they had conquered; their learning and their civilization were borrowed from them; even the ritual of their faith was shaped by contact with older forms of worship [...] . Greek and Persian builders created an architectural type which governed the whole Mohammadan world' (vii-viii). For Bell, whose approach to antiquities was shaped by the imperial ideology of progress, what Billie Melman called 'a new imperial world order' in which new technologies such as cameras, trains and planes reshaped British understanding of the past, the idea of surveying, photographing and excavating Middle Eastern antiquities became the gateway to understanding Britain's new rule as a modern, civilisational force (2020: 4). Therefore, an excavator and imperial agent like Bell, now empowered by this new vision of Britain's imperial role, ruled confidently that the palace of Ukhaidir was not built by Arabs: what Johannes Fabian called 'the denial of coevalness' was mobilised in the encounter between Bell and a piece of rock for purposes of marshalling new meanings about Britain's role as a guardian of architecture of ancient civilisations and a moderniser of societies who are still unable to progress in the present. It is fascinating in this regard that while Bell was drafting her work in which she recalled the inability of Muslims and Arabs to build and improve their material life, her countryman William Willcocks, a notable engineer who served in different imperial outposts in the empire, led engineering projects in Mesopotamia aiming to utilise the waters of the Tygris and Euphrates for agricultural purposes. In his lecture to the Royal Society delivered in January 1910, Willcocks recalled how his Mesopotamian irrigation projects aimed to turn the Arabian desert into a garden.[28]

Many decades before Bell was in Iraq, Carmichael visited the palace and named it 'Alcander', 'a large and antient fort', as he wrote (Carmichael 1772: 29). Carmichael used the word 'fort' instead of a palace, focusing on the defences built on this site. In so doing, Carmichael, as a soldier, viewed architecture from the point of view of a military man rather than a historian of the rise and fall of civilisations. Carmichael knew nothing about the history of Arabic, 'Mohammadan', Persian and Greek architecture. Unlike Bell, he did not have the previous education and knowledge allowing him to speculate about previous empires and civilisations that ruled the region. Rather Carmichael learned about the history of the palace from conversing with his fellow Arab travellers who told him a story about a Christian queen who decided to build a palace on this site but was not able to find enough stones to complete the project. She relied on Arab tribes inhabiting the region who supplied the queen with plenty of stones at a time of 'scarcity of stones' in the deserts. The queen promised the Arabs one load of gold for each load of stone they bring to the site. Many Arabs believed her and brought more than what the queen needed. The queen, however, only offered to pay for one load: 'her promise extended only to one load, and that no more than that quantity [of stone] was wanted' (Carmichael 1772: 29). The result was that 'rather than return with their burdens, [the Arabs] threw them down, by which she became possessed of more than sufficient for the completion of the fortress' (Carmichael 1772: 29). This dishonourable treatment angered the Arabs who considered the queen as an exploitative and unprincipled ruler and then determined to occupy the 'fort' by pursuing 'the following contrivance':

> The Arabs having first privately lodged a number of men near the fort, ordered a small caravan slightly guarded to pass by, consisting of a number of camels, each carrying two armed men enclosed in baskets, disguised like bales of goods; the Christians sallied out, and seizing the supported booty, carried it into the fort. At this instant the Arab party discovering themselves, seemed to prepare for an assault, when all the garrison running to the walls, gave the men hid in the baskets time to disengage themselves; which they instantly did, and seizing one of the gates, let in their comrades. Could it be supposed that the Arabs had ever read Virgil, I should have imagined they had formed the plan of this stratagem, from that of the Trojan horse. (Carmichael 1772: 30)

In the passage above, the image of the Arabs as an independent and free people appeared in the backdrop of a period in which the EIC was immensely concerned about protecting its possession from attacks by local Indian, Dutch and French powers. As Jeremy Black showed, the EIC during the period went out of its way to build and expand walls, forts and docks around its acquired settlements.[29] But the dialectic of freedom, heroism and conquest in the passage indicates a larger concern by Carmichael in the wake of the Jacobite Rebellion. While land enclosures were increasingly gaining momentum in Scotland, many feared the loss of freedom and virtue in an increasingly commercialised Britain, an idea which occupied the minds of many Scottish historians and philosophers during the age of the Enlightenment.[30] Like his countryman Adam Ferguson, Carmichael in the passage above flirted with the idea that heroism is the trait of non-commercial people unburdened with the fear of protecting their private property and uncorrupted and unenervated by a life of luxury.

Moreover, the reference to Virgil's *Aeneid* in the passage above is quite revealing: many eighteenth-century British travellers mentioned how being in Arabia was like entering the gates of history. Ancient Roman and Greek manners and traditions were often recalled the moment travellers set foot in Egypt, Palestine and Syria. The classical writer in England Robert Wood tells his reader in the preface to *An Essay on the Original Genius and Writing of Homer* (1775) how his journey in the Levant in 1751 was performed with the aim of reading classical Greek and Roman writers on the spot where ancient heroes lived, fought and died [Figure 3]. For Wood, as well as Carmichael, the Arabs, like the heroes of ancient times, are the remnants of primitive ages known for heroism and liberty. Although Wood praised Arab freedom, he also posited them as violent: a people whose life is mostly dedicated to pillage rather than to 'agriculture' and 'architecture' (Wood 1775: 150). Wood went to Oxford University and was close to corridors of power in the British state: he envisaged modern Britain as the guardian of past Greek and Roman virtues, his excursions in lands where virtues were held in the past but no longer in the present helped him to gain the experience that paved his entrance to the civil service in the British state.[31] Carmichael, like Wood and Bell, could not escape seeing the region he visited as a hub of history, but, unlike Bell and Wood, he did not interpret the history of Middle Eastern ruins in a language in which Arabs were seen as aliens in the lands in which they lived.[32] Carmichael as a Scotsman, whose Gaelic roots cherished liberty and poetry, was fascinated with tribal heroism and conquest.

Figure 3 James Dawkins and Robert Wood discovering the ruins of Palmyra. By Gavin Hamilton (1758). Source: The National Gallery, London.

Ruins and Improvement

In the past two decades, scholars of European encounters with the Levant have shown how European fascination with antiquities of the region revealed three traits which shaped the field: first, antiquarianism created the character of a man of taste and science for whom travelling, collecting relics and sketching ruins helped to forge the image of a gentleman who, as the *Monthly Review* in 1776 put it, is 'fond of some of the polite arts in which he was not deeply conversant; particularly drawing, painting sculpture, and architecture' (1776: 379). Although, as the *Monthly Review* here hints, antiquarians were subjected to ridicules for being purposeless and pedantic, that is, for being collectors of 'objects with no discrimination and no higher purpose of intellectual enlightenment in mind', in Rosemary Sweet's words, the act of collecting and writing about antiquities mostly helped to elucidate and digest evidence from the past for purposes of finding useful knowledge that would enrich thinking about troubled political and social events of present times (Sweet 2004: 9). To that end, the travelling antiquarian pursues what Samuel Johnson recommended in his 1760 essay for *The Idler*: 'He only is a useful Traveller who brings home something by which his country may be benefited; who procures some supply of Want, or some Mitigation of Evil, which may enable his readers to compare their conditions with that of others, to improve it whenever it is worse, and whenever it is better to enjoy it' (1825: 665). Second, European curiosity about antiquities, as scholars have shown, that is, writing about and sketching Levantine antiquities – prior to the period when the field turned into a profession and science – influenced and was influenced by a cosmopolitan republic of letters in which many set out to collect historical traces confirming the convergence rather than divergence of the human family.[33] Third, the efforts to acquire antiquities and also collect relics from famous architectural sites were shaped by outward-looking, imperial nations looking to expand in the East. European monarchs such as Louis XIV, George III and Fredrik V collected Eastern paraphernalia, including manuscripts, medals, relics and drawings, showing how their reigns saw the efforts to expand not only trade and empire but also European knowledge.[34]

For many British and European travellers who described their experiences in famous architectural sites, encounter with ruin helped them to further bonds with their nation while showing their distance from it. In the eighteenth century, educated and philosophical travellers viewed ruins as, in Johannes Fabian's phrasing, 'temporal devices' that signalled 'difference as distance', that is, an escape into a historical locale radically different from modern Europe (16). But recently Billie Melman in her *The Culture of History: English Uses of the Past 1800-1935* has offered a nuanced reading of the encounter with the past, what she called our 'uses of the past', which ruins somewhat represent (Melman 2006: 4). She examined what she called 'the circulation of history' in different genres in post-Enlightenment Britain and found that individual and collective interpretation of history is a complex process that included social practices, that is, 'social lives and meanings given to' historical objects such as relics and sketches of ruins. It also included, Melman added, 'fantasy and imagination' (Melman 2006: 4). Based on Melman's materialist understanding of history, it becomes clear that the encounter with ruins in Carmichael's book was a social act that makes use of the past (which ruins represent) for purposes of making sense of modern changes in Britain. This circulation of history process helps a traveller to imagine new ways to address and plaster wounds of distance and estrangement between Self and its own nation and culture.[35] One can here find many examples from seventeenth- and eighteenth-century writings about Middle Eastern antiquities that illustrate the complex social and political process involved in making meanings of ruins. But the few examples I prefer to analyse below represent a dominant habit of thought and structure of feeling among eighteenth-century British travel writers who considered the experience of seeing and writing about ruins as an enabling exercise that helped them to rethink the meaning of progress in modern nations.

It is difficult to make any meaningful argument about early modern fascinations with Levantine ruins without recalling a well-known travel writer who visited the region in the seventeenth century. George Sandys, an Englishman of letters known in England for his translation of Ovid, visited the Middle East in 1610. He published his observations in an account titled *A Relation of a Journey* (1615). In the preface of this book, he compared the ancient and present conditions of these lands: 'goodly cities made desolate; sumptuous buildings become ruins; glorious Temples either subverted, prostituted to impietie; true religion discountenanced and oppressed; all Nobility extinguished; no light of learning permitted, nor Virtue cherished. [...]' (Sandys 1615: viii). The idea that England was going through a period of religious strife in which voices of dissent from mainstream Calvinist theology were suppressed meant that Middle Eastern ruins, for a dissenting voice like Sandys, could offer 'the rest of the world [...] threatening instructions' (Sandys 1615: viii).[36] Ruins are perfect reminders of the discontinuity of the past from the present, and, in that sense, they offer people a moral lesson about 'the frailty of man, and mutability of what so ever is worldly; and assurance that as there is nothing unchangeable saving God, so nothing stable but by his grace, and protection' (Sandys 1615: viii).

In an early modern cosmic order in which Man has not yet replaced God as the driver of human happiness, ruins represented a tension between mutable 'worldly' desires and an immutable deity. In the eighteenth century, the metaphor of ruins in European travel writings reflected a new understanding of the human condition. The idea that ruins recalled a memory of an ideal religious Utopia was not something that most eighteenth-century travellers would have accepted: after all, the eighteenth century was an age when, in David Hume's words, 'religion' is 'scarcely [able to] support itself'.[37] Instead, for eighteenth-century travellers ruins represented, in Sabrina Ferri's phrasing, 'revelatory metaphors' offering lessons about past 'glory' and 'reminders that any path of progress is ultimately a path towards decadence' (4). This shift was illustrated in Carmichael's account of monuments and relics he encountered on the road between Aleppo and Basra.

Basra, Carmichael wrote, was 'a place of great trade, and the one seaport for Assyria and a great part of Arabia; it carries on besides a considerable commerce with Syria, by means of caravans, from Aleppo and Damascus' (Carmichael 1772: 52). But 'should any vicissitude of fortune at this time depopulate Busserah', Carmichael added, 'its situation in a few ages would nowhere be traced; as its ruins would soon be levelled by the rain, and covered with sand from the desert, which possibly was the fate of those ancient cities before mentioned' (Carmichael 1772: 53). The choice of term here – 'vicissitude of fortune' – hints at the reluctance of Carmichael to wrap causes and effects in a theological cover: that is, to speak directly about God's punishment of sinners. But, at the same time, it reveals a lack of trust in the ability of humans to control their own destiny, to continue to improve with no fear of fall. Encounter with ruins elucidates this bind. Indeed, Carmichael expressed these concerns about the futility of human endeavours in 1751, one year after London suffered an earthquake which brought terrible scenes of destruction and misery to the heart of the British metropolis. Many sermons, tracts and books about the causes and consequences of the earthquakes were published during the period, but what emerged from these publications was the idea that God's revenge against sinners was the main reason for the earthquake.[38] Carmichael, although he constantly referred to biblical prophesies to make sense of why the deserts were barren, did not recall the idea of God's revenge against sinners.

Rather Carmichael associated barren deserts with the lack of a culture of improvement among those who live on the land. For example, Carmichael, on the road to Basra, recalled how he passed through 'Issabier [...] a mean Arab town, consisting of many houses or rather huts, containing about six or seven hundred inhabitants, and appears a most dirty and wretched place' (Carmichael 1772: 47). For Carmichael, Arabs fail to control nature and thus were bound to live in primitive, unimproved conditions. In Cabesee, a village in the desert, the caravan stopped for refreshments. Carmichael took the opportunity to stroll around this site. He found a 'deep aqueduct, cut in the rock thro' the hill' (Carmichael 1772: 26). This aqueduct, although ancient, was still useful. Carmichael found that in this aqueduct 'there is a run of water sufficient to work a mill'. Local inhabitants were not doing enough work to utilise the water properly: 'before it reaches the town, it is much ameliorated by the earth and air' (Carmichael 1772: 26). Amid ruins, Carmichael not only mused about a glorious past but also the decadent present. Ruins, as temporal devices, generated hope that the future will be better than the present, as the above image suggests (aqueducts could still be improved).

But such a vision of improvement can only make sense if one contrasts primitive conditions of the land with their glorious past.[39] The primitive conditions of the land and its inhabitants defined the modernity of the Enlightenment traveller. For many Britons who went to the Levant in an age in which modern Britain was imagined as the heir to the glorious ancient civilisations of the Romans and Greeks, modern inhabitants of the region appeared as destroyers of ancient monuments rather than preservers and improvers of these past gains. Richard Pococke, known in polite circles in England as an Oxford bishop, a man of letter and a traveller, toured the Levant between 1737 and 1741. He published his travelling observations in two volumes, *A Description of the East and Some Other Countries*. The first volume was published in 1743 and was mostly about his observations of Egypt; the second volume was published in 1745 and was about Palestine, Syria and Mesopotamia. In the second volume, Pococke appeared mostly fascinated with the past of Syria and Mesopotamia more than with their present conditions: 'the history of which we have delivered down to us from the earliest times, as they were inhabited by the patriarchs and afterwards became the renowned scenes of action of the Persians of Alexander the great and of the Macedonian kings' (Pococke 1745: II, iii). Reminded of the glory of the Roman civilisation in the famous site of Balbec, Pococke recalled how 'it is a melancholy thing to see how the barbarous people of these countries destroy such magnificent buildings, in order to make use of the stone; they privately chip in pillars in order to undermine them, and when they fall, the stones are so large that they can carry away but very few of them' (Pococke 1745: II, 109–110). For a bishop who was also versed in the classics, the past or evidence of its glory should not be destroyed but preserved.

Carmichael, a military man whose career revolves around building fortifications, however, considered ruins as historical treasures that can be improved: in other words, the past for Carmichael should not be seen as untouchable but rather as an inspiration of change in the present. Michel Baridon reminds us that encounter with ruins is 'indeed an essential element of the landscape of [modern] sensibility' because ruins are often 'identified with the modernity of an age whose pride was innovation' (Baridon 1985: 84). It is true that ruins inspired travellers like Carmichael to celebrate the capacity of the modern man to change his material condition, but it also reminded others of ancient communities whose virtues the moderns should learn about, imitate and revive in their lives.

A few years before Carmichael travelled in the region, the Scottish diplomat and merchant, Alexander Drummond, travelled overland from Europe to Syria, before taking up the post of a consul to the Levant Company in Aleppo in 1751. He published his observations in an account titled *Travels through the Different Countries of Germany, Italy, Greece, and Parts of Asia Minor, as far as the Euphrates, with an Account of What Is Remarkable in Their Present State and Their Monuments of Antiquity* (1754). Like Pococke, Drummond was fascinated with ruins. He collected many medals and inscriptions. He sent some of them to his patron in Scotland, the Duke of Argyll. Maurits van den Boogert reminds us that 'Drummond's dispatch of antiquities to the Duke of Argyll was not only an attempt to secure the duke's continued patronage, but it also shows that he participated in the intellectual fashion of his day of collecting and describing antiquities' (Drummond 1754: 118). In examining ruins and collecting remnants of the Syrian past, moreover, Drummond, like Wood and Pococke, aimed to elucidate and digest historical facts for purposes of improving the moderns. In his letters, he recalled how a local grandee named Chirdgee Ogle visited his tent pitched outside Aleppo in order to invite him to his house. Drummond refused the invitation, since 'our intention was to visit ruins, not men, we declined the proffered honour, and he dispensed with our compliance' (Drummond 1754: 199). Drummond often used words like 'savages', 'brutes 'and 'barbarians' to describe the people he encountered in the vicinity of sites of ruins, showing how the land and its inhabitants in modern time contrast with those who lived there in the past (Drummond 1754: 187, 193, 194). But among ruins, Drummond also found a connection with the past, one of heroism and military virtue now lamented and derided among supporters of modern commercialism; among the remains of what he believed the ancient city of Cyrrus in Northern Syria, Drummond inspected some stones shaped like 'a theatre' which 'appears to have been built in a good taste' (Drummond 1754:

201). These ruins reminded a classically minded traveller like Drummond of a past age of heroism now forgotten in modern Britain: the moment he saw these ruins, he imagined 'gladiators' entering and leaving a theatre (Drummond 1754: 201).

Enlightenment travellers who visited ruins and described their experiences often faced the question of how the past can benefit those who live in the present. Robert Wood, in *The Ruins of Palmyra Otherwise Tedmor in the Desert* (1753), appeared mostly concerned about the ancient history of the land rather than its present. 'But however, we might each of us have some favourite curiosity to indulge', he wrote, 'what engaged our greatest attention was rather their antient than present state' (Wood 1753: 2). Wood, like Drummond and Pococke, cared little about what the Arab and Muslims might have written about the history of these cities. Instead, what mattered for him was how a desert city like Palmyra has acquired such an illustrious reputation in the past and how the trade with India influenced the prosperity and security of the city. At a time when the EIC was struggling to make headway in the East (in the period before the battle of Plassey in 1757), Wood mentioned how ancient channels of trade between Syria and India secured Palmyra impeccable wealth. Wood recalls how Palmyra's rulers Odaenathus and Zenobia were great leaders whose military characters brought prosperity to their state: Palmyra served as the central government of Syria, Mesopotamia and Egypt, and its inhabitants were 'rich, free and trading people' (Wood 1753: 4).

But glorious days are bound to be followed by a moment of fall: a strong and prosperous nation is bound to be subject of enemy attacks. 'So quick a transition from long enjoyed liberty to a state of slavery, is apt to suggest desperate measures. The inhabitants cut off the Roman garrison', Wood lamented. 'Aurelian [Roman general]' led an 'uncommon expedition' against Palmyra: he 'took and destroyed the town, putting to death most of the inhabitants, without regard to age or sex' (Wood 1753: 13). Such a position which shows Wood lamenting the fall of Palmyra, its freedom and prosperity and the transformation of its people into slavery is slightly disingenuous, particularly if we recall that Woods's expedition in Syria was entirely funded by his friend James Dawkins, a son of a sugar-plantation owner in Jamaica.[40] But it is understandable that Wood expressed his anxiety about this idea of the fall of strong, commercial states like Palmyra at a time when Britain, in the period preceding the Seven Years War, was rattled about a rising French power in India and North America.[41]

Recalling the travel observations of the Frenchman Constantine Volney, the *Monthly Review* states that for almost all eighteenth-century travellers in the Levant, the encounter with ruins 'turned their thoughts to passed times' and 'raised' in their 'minds serious and solemn ideas' about the present (1791: 548). In their different ways, Carmichael, Woods, Pococke and Drummond found that visiting and sketching ruins generated the idea that deepened their knowledge of ancient history, which in a way helped reduce contemporary anxieties about war and loss of age-old virtues. Still, taking a broader look at Wood and other travellers' accounts, including Carmichael's, and reading their narratives against their own grain, as it were, we find that that the dislocation of these travellers from their own cultures was enabled and revived by a sense of cooperation with local Arab tribes, Ottoman governors and caravan leaders who helped them to secure a moment of calm and reflection among ruins. Carmichael was always cautious about the idea of strolling alone in the deserts without his Arab companions. Pococke carried a letter from the British consul in Tripoli to the Ottoman governor of Balbec, asking for his protection to see antiquities: 'When I asked his leave to see the antiquities, he told me I might go where I pleased, and called for a janizary to attend me' (Pococke 1745: II, 122). Drummond entertained two Kurdish chieftains, Hussein Aga and Aligoura Aga, in his tent near the town of Afrin in northern Syria, which indicates how his curiosity could not be quenched without appeasing local rulers. Similarly, Robert Wood and his companions would not be able to reach Palmyra without the help of the Ottoman governor of Hassia 'whose jurisdiction extends as far as Palmyra' (Wood 1753: 33).

Textual Universe

Like all European travellers in Syria, Carmichael was aware that he was travelling in a region of huge importance to the Christian imagination. He was troubled by the deserts because they contradict what the Bible mentioned regarding the fertility of Syria and Mesopotamia. But he also found in the Bible what allowed him to make sense of the radical change these lands went thorough throughout their history. He constantly referred to Isiah and Jeremiah's prophecies in which the Holy Land and Babylon were meant to be destroyed. But Carmichael was not keen on using his observations on the ground to offer a historically and theologically informed justification of the authenticity of the Bible.[42] To that end, he resembles one seventeenth-century traveller who confirmed what the Bible mentioned about the land in which he travelled without displaying a line of doubt. John Cartwright, who wrote a diary about his journey across the Syrian and Mesopotamian routes to India, mentioned how the Tigris and Euphrates were 'two great rivers which watered Paradice [Paradise]' (Cartwright 1611: 716). Other travellers in the region, however, were troubled with the biblical geography of the Garden of Eden. The Englishman Charles Thompson considered the banks of the Tygris and Euphrates in Mesopotamia as the site of the biblical paradise, whereas the French naturalist Joseph de Pitton Tournefort associated it with the plains of Armenia.[43] Indeed, the idea that paradise, according to the Bible, was founded on the banks of the Tigris and Euphrates occupied the minds of many seventeenth- and eighteenth-century European travellers in the region, with some doubting and others confirming it.[44] Travellers who used their travel books to examine the authenticity of the Bible were ridiculed by the *Critical Review* in 1759: they 'who shall go a hundred mile to admire a mountain, only because it was spoken of in scripture' (1759: 505).

Carmichael was one of these travellers who could not let go of the fact that he was treading on scripture ground: 'Indeed this country affords a melancholy proof of the instability of human affairs', Carmichael wrote, 'when it is remembered, that of the part adjacent to the river Euphrates, and within the compass of thirty miles there were formerly not less than three hundred and fifty cities, towns, and villages, of whose ruins scarce a single trace at this time remains' (Carmichael 1772: 12).[45] But Carmichael's line was not meant to prove the credibility of the Bible.[46] Nor does the confirmation about the fall of these lands from grace in his account show any sign of what Zur Shalev called 'devout curiosity', that is, a medieval and early modern confessional framework shaped by travelling in, writing about and mapping the Holy Land.[47] Rather Carmichael belongs to an Enlightenment tradition in which the Bible – with all its narratives, heroes and villains – was transformed into a historical document in which the modern reader can find moral lessons which serve to alleviate anxieties about the danger of avarice, luxury and despotism of the modern age.[48] Constantine Volney illustrated this point clearly in Palmyra in the 1780s when he recalled the biblical reference to Ophir (the city of gold), showing how the pursuit of wealth, whether in Solomon's days or in modern times, shaped the imagination of avaricious rulers who do not hesitate to go to wars for the sake of wealth, trade and empire.[49]

Carmichael's main frame of reference about the region was the Bible. But he also read one important book about Christian and classical history of the region: an account of one controversial figure in early eighteenth-century Britain, Humphrey Prideaux (1648–1724), the dean of Norwich, known for his fierce battles in print with English deists.[50] Prideaux, in *The Old and New Testament Connected in the History of the Jews and Neighbouring Nations* (1715–1717), subjected the Bible to a modern method of historical and textual analysis, aiming to dispel late seventeenth and early eighteenth-century doubts over the historicity and credibility of that religious document.[51] To that end, Prideaux showed how biblical accounts of places like Babylon and Seleucia confirm rather than contradict writings by ancient, non-Christian historians such as Pliney and Strabo and medieval and early modern travellers in the region such as Benjamin Tudela, Pedro Teixeira and Leonhard Rauwolf.[52] In an earlier work, Prideaux offered himself to an increasingly expanding constituency of sceptics as a scholarly churchman who was committed to an orthodox and Anglican form of Christianity. In his *The True Nature of Imposture Fully Displayed in the Life of Mahomet* (1697), Prideaux defended Christianity against the charges of the deists and sceptics by arguing that 'Mahomet' was a false prophet who 'drew up a Scheme of that Imposture [...] which being a Medley made up of Judaism, the several Heresies of the Christians then in the East, and the old Pagan Rites of the Arabs, with an indulgence to all Sensual Delights, it did too well answer his Design, in drawing Men of all sorts to the embracing of it' (Prideaux 1696: 11).

Despite the fascination of Rennell with the rigour of Carmichael's method of exploration, it is clear from his travel account that Carmichael lived up to the expectation of Prideaux by showing how his findings on the spot confirm rather than contradict the Bible. Carmichael, while proving the truth of the Bible, concluded that Prophet Mahomet was an 'imposture', thus showing another influence of Prideaux on his description of the region. 'Mahomet', Carmichael noted, 'pretended to affirm by inspiration that the Haran where Abraham dwelt was the very spot where the temple of Mecca now stands, and which the Mahometans still call Haran' (Carmichael 1772: 24–25). 'It must be remembered', Carmichael continued, that

> [...] Mecca lies six hindered miles south from Canaan. Therefore I may safely conclude Mahomet very boldly asserted a falsehood, and was influenced by a different spirit from Moses; but as this imposter generally enforced, his assertion by club eloquence, few cared to oppose such forcible argument. (Carmichael 1772: 25)

Carmichael could not escape Europe's discourse about Islam in which the trope of 'Mahomet' being 'an imposter' played an important role in the intellectual battle between the deists and Anglican polemicists in the late seventeenth- and early eighteenth-century Britain.[53] We have no evidence that Carmichael entered this battle during the period, but Carmichael's knowledge of the region was shaped by a textual universe previously charted by Prideaux, and Carmichael's encounters in the region and his observations on the spot did not entirely shake off this predisposition.

Carmichael's entrenchment with this textual universe was critiqued by one cosmopolitan English traveller in the Syrian desert. In his *Journal with Occasional Remarks Made on a Trip from Aleppo to Bussora Across the Grand Desert of Arabia* (1789), Henry Abbott, an English traveller in the Levant in 1784, regretted that 'Mr. Carmichael in particular, represents the inhabitants of Mahshed Aly as the most barbarous and inveterate enemies to the name of a Christian' although he 'never was near the town' (Abbott 1789: 71). Abbott, about whom I will say more in Chapter four, was familiar with the nuances of Islam and Islamic cultures. As reported in his unpublished memoir, Abbott was born in Istanbul and educated in Aleppo before he left Syria for India where he set up his own business.[54] While travelling between Aleppo and Basra, as his *Journal* showed, Abbott stopped at the famous city of Najaf in central Iraq, where, as many Muslims believe, the famous cousin of Prophet Muhammad, Ali Ibn Abi Talib, was buried. Abbott socialised with the people in the city and found them of 'great civility' (Abbott 1789: 66). He knew that Imam Ali was 'Mahommed's son in law' while he objected that Carmichael erroneously called him 'the Persian prophet'.

Unlike Abbott, Carmichael did not have sufficient knowledge about Shi'a and Sunni Islam. Carmichael knew much about the inhabitants of Najaf from reading the account of a British 'gentleman', as he wrote in his narrative, whose name he did not mention: this 'gentleman' was probably Captain William Beawes, whose caravan stopped at Meshed Ali in 1745, six years before Carmichael had been there.[55] 'I would fain have gone for the sake of personally examining the truth of his description', Carmichael wrote after his caravan stopped near the city,

> [...] but was dissuaded, on account of the great risqué I should have run of being murdered, or at least ill-treated, by the guardians of the prophet's tomb, who are reported the most abandoned miscreants on earth; and, like their masters, declared inveterate enemies to the Christians, from whom this country was conquered, under the conduct of Ali and his son. (Carmichael 1772: 40)

The word 'miscreant' in the above passage is illustrative of how Carmichael viewed Muslims. The word 'Miscreant' in Samuel Johnson's *Dictionary of the English Language* (1755) referred to a person who holds 'false faith' and believes in 'false gods' (Johnson 1756: 73).[56] To that end, Carmichael posited Islam as a false religion, thus repeating an old trope in Europe which also appeared in Prideaux's work. However, Carmichael's prejudiced views towards Islam and the Prophet did not stop him from appreciating Islamic architecture: 'it is in the tomb of Ali that the eastern magnificence is more particularly manifested, which, according to an account I have seen written by a gentleman who visited it, is of exquisite workmanship, and set with jewels with immense value, altogether making a most dazzling appearance' (Carmichael 1772: 40).

The Mosque of Ali, he added, was 'lately repaired and adorned, at a vast expense, by Nader Shaw, the sophy of Persia' (40). The arch-rival of the Ottomans at the time, Nadir Shah, who tried to capture Iraq from the Ottoman three times between 1733 and 1743, was known in Europe as a cruel ruler and brutal despot, but Carmichael considered him as a patron of magnificent architecture.[57] While serving in India, Carmichael must have learned about the efforts of Nadir Shah to turn Persia into an imperial power. Nadir Shah invaded Delhi in 1739 and sought to control the navigation of the Persian Gulf. He bought two ships from the EIC, *The Northumberland* and *The Cowan*, and devised a plan to transport timber from the Caspian Sea region to the Persian Gulf coast to build a fleet to compete with the English ships dominating navigation in the Persian Gulf at the time.[58] His imperial designs, however, did not see the light of day as Persia was embroiled with internal and external wars for several decades of the eighteenth century.

Carmichael was hostile to Islam, but he was an admirer of Nadir Shah. Carmichael learned about the history of the Mosque of Ali from Beawes's *A Journey from Aleppo to Basra in 1745*. 'The mosque has also minoretts [minarets] on each side', Beawes wrote,

> [...] which are curiously wrought, and as well these as the whole fabric are entirely covered with plates of copper thickly gilt and are neatly laid on, and all the doors, windows, galleries &c., beautifully decorated with fret work, azure borders with inscriptions of gold ideas after the Eastern manner; making together, it is most certain, a grand appearance and must have cost an infinite sum. [...] (Carmichael 1772: 23)

Carmichael travelled hundreds of miles with many Muslims, which allowed him to develop friendships with fellow caravan travellers, but this does not mean that he was prepared to move beyond the old prejudices against Islam. Carmichael was a product of his age, an age in which 'Mahomet' was still being viewed in England as an imposter, a false prophet, especially by those Orthodox Christians, such as Prideaux, who railed against emerging deistic voices which contrasted the monotheism, egalitarianism and rationalism of Islam with what they considered an institutionalised Christianity burdened with powerful and corrupt clerical elites.[59] Carmichael did not necessarily participate in the debate in Britain between Unitarian deists and Protestant Anglicans, the debate in which Islam appeared as a screen upon which many projections and critical reflections were cast.[60] But Carmichael's position on the errors of 'Mahomet' and the false message of the Prophet confirmed his sympathies with the conservative Christian voices of his age. The reference to the false message of 'Mahomet' in comparison to the true one of Moses and Jesus in his text attests to how he was committed to his Judeo-Christian heritage. But Carmichael did not show any sign of superiority to those Arabs and Muslims with whom he travelled, as the incident mentioned above about Carmichael's interaction with the Arab Sheikh shows. Although Carmichael lamented the primitive conditions of the land, that is, the idea that Arabs do not improve the barren land in which they live, he admired Islamic architecture as his description of the Mosque of Ali indicates.

Conclusion

Towards the end of the journey, Carmichael offered his fellow Britons who wished to travel the region some advice on how to undertake a successful journey in the desert. He suggested that travelling in the caravan would allow the British traveller, whom he called 'our people', to save money and further provide a social network which is immensely important in barren and parched spaces. It is only by joining a caravan that a traveller could feel safe. 'There is no danger of being ill-treated by them [the Arabs] in the caravan', Carmichael noted, 'farther than a few insolent freedoms they think themselves justified in taking, on the strength of being Mahomet's countrymen, on which account they conclude themselves superior to the rest of mankind' (Carmichael 1772: 52). As Chapter four shows, many eighteenth-century European travellers in the region recalled how Arabs often view the desert as an asset inherited from their ancestors, Ishmael and 'Mahomet', which explains why they often collected taxes from caravans passing through the desert. Carmichael suggested that Arabs feel empowered in their deserts ('superior to the rest of mankind'), but Arabs are friendly to Europeans, he added; indeed, they were 'better than the commonality of Egypt and Turkey' (Carmichael 1772: 52). Carmichael did not mention that he travelled through Egypt and other parts of the Ottoman Empire before he went to Syria. But the reference in his text to the good characters of the Bedouin – in comparison to that of 'the Turks' – indicates that Carmichael was aware of a common trope in eighteenth-century European travel writing about the region: that is, the 'Turks' – who live in cities – are superstitious and inured to despotism in comparison to the Bedouin Arabs who are free and autonomous in their deserts. Another British traveller, Edward Ives, as the next chapter shows, found similar opportunities of encounter in the region through which he improved his knowledge of the people living there, but the idea in Carmichael's text that Arabs of the deserts are hospitable and free in contrast to those who live in urban regions indicates that he had an ambivalent relationship with the Enlightenment obsession with improvement: Could it be that Carmichael saw in the Arab manners and culture the remnants of the Highlanders' traditions that English commercialism, in the wake of the Battle of Culloden, then set out to change in the name of improvement? In any case, Carmichael enjoyed travelling in the deserts. An Englishman from a city known for being home to the Royal Navy, Hampshire, however, associated the Syrian-Mesopotamian desert with diseases and risks. It is to Edward Ives's travel text that we should now turn.

Notes

1 *The Critical Review or Annals of Literature* (London: Printed for A. Hamilton, 1757), 439–445. See page 439.

2 Ibid., 439–445. On how scientific and exploration institutions in Britain like the Royal Society emphasised this use of scientific and detached style in reporting travels, see Paul Smethurst, *Travel Writing and the Natural World, 1768–1840* (Basingstoke: Macmillan, 2019), 23.

3 On how the genre of travel writing during the eighteenth and nineteenth centuries was shaped by popular directives in the print scene in Britain, which included associating travel books with gathering knowledge, which was meant to be of service to Britain's expanding empire, see the introduction and chapter two in Innes M. Keighren, Charles Withers, Bill Bell's

Travels into Print: Exploration, Writing and Publishing with John Murray 1773–1859 (Chicago: The University of Chicago Press, 2015).

4 A good account of the controversies around Bruce's travel report can be found in Percy Adam's *Travellers and Travel Liars 1660–1800* (New York: Dover Publication, 1980), 210–222.

5 On the modern European encounters with Africa, see Ib Friis's 'Travelling Among Fellow Christians (1768–1833): James Bruce, Henry Salt and Eduard Rüppell' in *Abyssinia in Early Scientific Expeditions and Local Encounters*, ed. Id Friis, Michael Harbsmeier and Jörgen Baek Simonsen (Copenhagen: Royal Danish Academy, 2013), 161–194.

6 In the preface to his travel book, Park praised Rennell's 'superior knowledge' and 'distinguished accuracy in geographical researches'. Rennell supplied Park with two maps of West Africa, which appeared in Park's book. Park also added in the appendix to his book a section written by Rennell titled 'Geographical Illustrations of Park's Journey'; in this section Rennell praised Park's extensive exploration efforts in Senegal, Gambia and Niger. Rennell considered Park' travel narrative as a new addition in the annals of Western exploration of Africa because it supplied moderns Europeans with new 'facts' about 'Western Africa' that none of 'former travelers' had ever mentioned and also helped the modern to confirm 'some points of facts, both of geography and natural history, which have appeared in ancient author, but to which our own want of knowledge has denied credit', *Travels in the Interior Districts of Africa* (London: Printed by W. Bulmer, 1799); the quotes above are taken from the preface (viii and ix) and the appendix (iii and iv).
illustrate ancient accounts of West Africa.

7 On Rennell's important contribution in expanding British knowledge of the interior parts of Africa, see chapter seven in Clements R. Markham's *Major James Rennell and the Rise of Modern English Geography* (London: Cassell and Company, 1795).

8 On the rapid expansion of the economic and military presence of the British in India during the eighteenth century, see K. N. Chaudhuri's *The Trading World of Asia and the English East India Company 1660–1760* (Cambridge: Cambridge University Press, 1978). Also see Barbara Harlow and Mia Carter, ed., *Imperialism and Colonialism: A Documentary Source Book* (Massachusetts: Blackwell, 1990). 4–5.

9 James Howel, *A Journal of the Passage from India* (London, 1791), 159–169. Ives's *A Journey from Persia to England* (London, 1737), 373. James Capper, 'Supplement Containing the List of Stages in the Different Routes from England to Bussora' in *Observations on the Passage to India* (London: Printed for W. Faden, 1785). Taylor, *Travels from England to India*, Vol II, 19–22.

10 Captain Francis Rawdon Chesney in Syria commanded a small expedition (two British streamers in the Euphrates) in the hope to establish a regular route of communication between Syria and India. The descriptions of the countries that the expedition surveyed were published in *The Expedition for the Survey of the Rivers Euphrates and Tigris. Carried on by Order of the British Government in the Years 1835, 1836, 1837*, Vol I and II (London: Longman, Brown, Green, and Longmans, 1850). The narrative of Chesney and his companions' journey across Syria, Palestine, Mesopotamia and Turkey was published in *Narrative of the Euphrates Expedition: Carried on by Order of the British Government in 1835, 1836 and 1837* (London: 1868).

11 Despite the efforts of the British, Austrian and Russian ambassadors in Istanbul to drive a wedge between the Ottoman Porte and the new regime in France in the wake of the Revolution, the Ottoman Empire did not let go of its strategic political and commercial relations with France, not until Napoleon invaded Egypt in 1798. On Ottoman-French relations during the period, see Pascal Figres's *French Revolutionaries in the Ottoman Empire, 1792–1789* (Oxford: Oxford University Press, 2017).

12 Gust's *Unhomely Empire*, 79.

13 Walter Benjamin, *Illuminations* (New York: Harcourt, 2007), 255.

14 In his diary of an overland journey he undertook between India and Aleppo in 1780, Sir Eye Coote recalled how in Aleppo '[t]he pro-consul and the gentlemen of the British nation there, came out to a village about 3 miles from the city to congratulate [him] on his save arrival', 'Diary of a Journey with Sir Eyre Coote from Bussora to Aleppo in 1780, from the Original MS', *The Journal of the Royal Geographical Society of London*, 30 (1860), 98–211; 211. Another Briton, James Silk Buckingham, in 1816 wrote how he was welcomed by Claudius James Rich, the British resident in Baghdad: 'I was fortunate in finding, in the ancient city of the Caliphs, all the comforts of an English home, in the house of the British Resident, Mr Rich,

and the society of his amiable family', *Travels in Assyria, Media and Persia* (London: Henry Colburn, 1829), 1.

15 Carmichael said nothing about whether his countrymen in Aleppo had helped him to obtain a safe and secure passage across the deserts. Apart from recalling his connection with Dr Russell, the Scottish doctor in Aleppo who worked for the Levant Company at the time, Carmichael mentioned nothing about his Aleppo experience. Many British travellers in the region reported about how British consuls in Aleppo and Basra often helped them to hire caravan leaders, interpreters and servants before setting out across the deserts. They also mentioned how consuls helped their countrymen to obtain letters of recommendations from powerful Ottoman governors. One good example of a spirited public servant in Aleppo was the English consul John Abbott who lived in Aleppo between 1770 and 1783. Eyles Irwin, the East India Company servant who visited Aleppo in 1777, wrote an 'Epitaph' about the hospitable character of Abbott; it was published in *The Poetical Register And Repository for Fugitive Poetry for 1810–1811* (London: Printed for F.C And J. Rivington), 206.

16 These were important items of desert travel. But the most important one was the local dress. Many English travelers in the Arabian deserts have powerfully written about the importance of wearing the local dress while travelling in a region whose inhabitants often considered foreigners wearing their native dress as respectful people. The local dress also offered European travelers in the Arabian desert a tool for disguising themselves from local bandits. In 1799, one English traveller in the deserts, Henry Jackson, observed how the safety and security of travellers in the region demanded the traveller to buy the following articles of clothing: '1 Arab cameline or riding cloak. 2 Under coats. 2 Pairs of drawers. 2 Shirts. 1 Cumberland. 1 Turban. 1 Woollen cap; and 1 Pair of yellow slippers', *Journey from India Towards England, in the Year 1797* (London: Printed for T. Cadell, 1799), 138. Henry Abbot in 1789 recalled how he wore 'A complete Arab dress' while travelling between Aleppo and Basra, *A Journey on a Trip from Aleppo to Bussora* (Calcutta, 1789), 109. The merchant Abraham Parsons in 1774 mentioned how the strong wind in the deserts encouraged him to place 'a gauze handkerchief under my turban…', *Travels in Asia and Africa Including a Journey from Scanderoon to Aleppo, and over the Desert to Bagdad and Bussora (*London, 1808), 101.

17 Most European travellers who crossed desert routes in the fall, spring and winter seasons preferred to do this on the back of a horse. Abraham Parsons (Chapter three) and Donald Campbell (Chapter six) were two prominent examples during the period. Others who crossed the deserts between May and October did so on the back of a camel: Irwin (Chapter five), Ives (Chapter two), Abbott (Chapter four).

18 Travelling in the Syrian deserts routes at the time was mostly safe, as many British travellers recalled, and Arab tribes were on good terms with the English merchants then operating in big cities such as Aleppo, but this does not mean that travellers faced no problems on the road. The idea that there were many robbers in the region, as the English doctor Edward Ives, who travelled in an Arab caravan between Basra and Aleppo in 1773, wrote, 'alarmed us all to a great degree, and threw a damp over those flattering hopes which we had lately entertained of being in ten or twelve days blessed with the sight and conversation of our countrymen at Aleppo', *Journey* , 343. Besides the presence of robbers, other habits in the deserts such as riding on the back of the camel during the summer season and drinking stagnated water also alarmed British travellers. See 'A Journey from Aleppo to Basra in 1745' in *The Desert Route to India: Being the Journals of Four Travellers by the Great Desert Caravan Route Between Aleppo and Basra 1745–1751*, ed. Douglass Carruthers (London: Hakluyt Society, 1929), 16.

19 For a detailed discussion about eighteenth-century European views of Arabs as the modern Ishmaelites, see my article 'Improving Experiences: Eighteenth Century European Encounters with Arabs, *Journal of Intercultural Studies* 43: 1 (2021), 1–17.

20 Howel, 48–49.

21 Janet Starkey mentioned the financial rewards the English levant company doctors enjoyed in Aleppo: 'In Aleppo, physicians could charge subscription fees for each patient allowing any number of consultations. The rate was then about £30 p.a. (equivalent to c. £3500 in 2016), with extra charges for medicines', *The Scottish Enlightenment Abroad*, 44. Another good account of the Russell brothers in Aleppo is Christine Laidlaw's *The British in the Levant: Trade and Perceptions of the Ottoman Empire in the Eighteenth Century* (London: I.B Tauris, 2010).

22 Nowadays, Bell is mostly known in the Arab world as the imperial engineer of the borders Britain concocted between Iraq, Jordan, and Turkey. Bell studied history at Oxford University. Then she joined the intelligence and imperial office in Cairo and Baghdad. But before this, Bell travelled in the region and developed passion for archaeology. On the association between empire and travel in Bell's career and writing, see Julia Emberley, 'Gertrude Lowthian Bell in Mesopotamia' in *Writing Travel and Empire: Colonial Narratives of Other Cultures*, ed. Peter Hulme and Russell McDougall (London: I.B Tauris, 2009), 119–146. On the life and achievement of Bell, see Georgian Howell's *Queen of the Desert: The Extraordinary Life of Gertrude Bell* (London: Macmillan, 2006).

23 This quote is taken from Janet Wallach's *Desert Queen: The Extraordinary Life of Gertrude Bell, Adventurer, Advisor to Kings and Ally of Laurence of Arabia* (New York: Anchor Books, 1996), 140.

24 This noted is translated by Douglass Carruthers in his 'Prefatory Notes' about Carmichael's journal. See his *The Desert Route to India Being Journals of Four Travellers*, 133.

25 For more details about Bell's fascination with the site of Ukhaidir, see chapter three in Lisa Cooper's *In Search of King's and Conquerors: Gertrude Bell and the Archelogy of the Middle East* (London: I.B Tauris, 2016).

26 There are two suggestions that the Arabs might have built the palace. The Iraqi historian Shukry Aloussy argued that one Christian Arab named Ukhaidir built the palace after he was expelled from Arabia in 632 AD; another suggestion is that the palace was built by Isa Bin Musa, a nephew of the Abbasid Caliph Almansour. Isa built the palace as a retreat after he was estranged from the Abbasid court. For an exploration of these two suggestions, see Geoff Han, Karen Dabrowska, Tina Townsend-Greaves, *Iraq: Ancient Sites & Iraqi Kurdistan*, (2002; Guilford: Bradt Travel Guides Ltd, 2015), 264.

27 Bell's views of the inability of Muslims to progress appeared in a period in which Britain was the colonial ruler of Iraq, Palestine, Jordan and Egypt. As the English traveller and artist Donald Maxwell wrote after visiting Iraq in 1914, 'Now that the British are in occupation of the land instead of the Turk, the natural assumption of every patriotic Briton is that the desert will immediately blossom as the rose and the waste places become inhabited……Our army of occupation includes irrigation officers and gradually the work of watering the country is extending', *A Dweller in Mesopotamia, being the adventures of an Official Artist in the Garden of Eden*, (London: John Lane, 1921), 101.

28 William Willcocks, 'Mesopotamia: Past, Present, and Future', *The Geographical Journal*, 35: 1 (1910), 1–15; particularly, see page 15. Willocks composed several works about engineering projects he led in the Levant including *Egyptian Irrigation* (1889) and *The Irrigation of Mesopotamia* (1911). On Willocks's career in the east, see Michael Ledger-Lomas and David Grange's 'Introduction' in *Cities of God: The Bible and Archaeology in Nineteenth-Century Britain*, ed. Michael Ledger-Lomas and David Gange (Cambridge: Cambridge University Press, 2013), 1.

29 Jeremy Black, *Fortifications and Siegecraft: Defense and Attack through the Ages* (Rowman & Littlefield: Maryland, 2018), 152.

30 A good analysis of how many in eighteenth-century Scotland were concerned about the impact of commerce and luxury on individual liberties, virtue and freedom, see Berry's *The idea of Commercial Society*.

31 He served as a Under Secretary of State to Lord Chatham during three administrations. On Wood's life and career, see *The Critical Review* (London, 1793), Vol VIII, 91–92.

32 Eva-Maria Troelenberg, '"that we trusted not to Arab notions of archaeology": *Reading the Grand Narrative Against the Grain' in Antiquarianisms: Contact, Conflict, Comparison*, ed. Benjamin Anderson and Felipe Rojas (Oxbow: Oxford, 2017), 166.

33 Zur Chalev, 'The Travel Notebook of John Greaves' in *The Republic of Letters and the Levant*, ed. Alastair Hamilton, Maurits H. Van Den Boogert and Bart Westerweel (Leiden: Brill, 2005), 77–102. See also chapters four in Simon Mills's *A Commerce of Knowledge: Trade, Religion, and Scholarship Between England and the Ottoman Empire 1600–1760* (Oxford: Oxford University Press, 2020).

34 The French monarch, Louis XIV, sponsored Johann Michael Wanseleben's antiquarian expedition in the Levant in 1671; for details about French Orientalism during the seventeenth and eighteenth centuries, see the introduction to *Johann Michael Wansleben's Travels in the Levant, 1671–1674*, ed. Alastair Hamilton (Leiden: Brill, 2018); see also Nicholas Dew's

Orientalism in Louis XIV's France (Oxford: Oxford University Press, 2018). In Denmark, Orientalism was supported by the court of Fredrick V. The Danish monarch funded an expedition in Arabia (1760–1763) headed by Carsten Niebuhr. On the history of this expedition, see Lawrence J. Baack, *Undying Curiosity: Carsten Niebuhr and the Royal Danish Expedition to Arabia* (1761–1767) (Stuttgart: Franz Steiner Verlag, 2014). The famous Scottish explorer of Abyssinia James Bruce presented his drawings of Syrian and North African architecture to King George III in 1774: the drawings are now held in the Royal Collection at Windsor Castle. On Bruce's travels, see Miles Bredin's *The Pale Abyssinian: The Life of James Bruce, African Explorer and Adventurer* (London: Harper Press, 2012).

35 The idea of using antiquities to address a raft of moral, political and social anxieties appeared in many studies: see Rosemary Sweet's *Antiquaries: The Discovery of the Past in Eighteenth-Century Britain* (London: Hambledon and London, 2004).

36 See chapter two in James Ellison's *George Sandys: Travel, Colonialism, and Tolerance in the Seventeenth Century* (Cambridge: D. S Brewer, 2000).

37 David Hume, *Essays and Treatises on Several Subjects*, 4 vols (London, 1753), Vol 1, 75.

38 Thomas Sherlock, *A Letter to the Clergy and People of London and Westminster On Occasion of the Late Earthquake* (London, 1750); Philip Doddridge's *The Guilt and Doom of Capernaum, Seriously Recommended to the Consideration of the Inhabitants of London* (London, 1750); Samuel Hull's *The Fluctuating Condition of Human Life: And the Absolute Necessity of a Preparation for the Eternal World* (London, 1750).

39 Samuel Evers, an East India Company man of a military training, travelled in the deserts of Syria in 1779. He always showed in his diary how he was interested in the great past that scattered ruins across the deserts represented. To that end, he lamented how 'those curious relicts of ancient architectural grandeur, are hid in a veil of obscurity, the result of modern Eastern ignorance, and want of literature', *A Journal Kept on A Journey from Bussora to Bagdad…* (Horsham: Printed by Arthur Lee, 1784), 79.

40 Olga Zoller, 'Crossing Borders: The Pioneering Role of the Architect- Engineer Giovanni Battista Borra between Piedmont and Britain' in *Turin and the British in the Age of the Grand Tour*, ed. Paola Bianchi and Karin Wolfe (Cambridge: Cambridge University Press, 2017), 264.

41 The fascination of Wood with Palmyra as an emporium of trade was captured by Constantine Volney who visited Syria in the 1780s. France, like England throughout the eighteenth century, was ambitious about the prospect of expanding its trade channels with the Levant and the East Indies, which explains why Voleny, who read Wood's book, speculated, in his travel book, on how Palmyra's wealth in the past could teach modern readers lessons about trade and improvement. See Volney's *Travels Through Syria and Egypt*, 2vols (London, 1788), Vol II, 291–294.

42 A popular tradition in the intellectual quarrel between the sceptics and their enemies in late seventeenth- and early eighteenth-century Europe was the use of non-literary evidence such as coins, medals, relics and inscriptions to cast doubt or alternatively to confirm the authenticity of the Bible; Arnaldo Momigliano, 'Ancient History and the Antiquarian', *Journal of the Warburg and Courtauld Institutes* 13 (1950): 285–315.

43 Charles Thompson, *Travels Through Turkey in Asia, the Holy Land, Arabia, Egypt and Other Parts of the World*, 2 vols (London: Printed for J. Newberry, 1758), 150–160. Joseph Pitton de Tournefort, *A Voyage into the Levant*, 3 vols (London: Printed for D. Midwinter, 1741), 160.

44 Jean Delumeau, *History of Paradise: The Garden of Eden in Myth and Tradition* (New York: Continuum, 1995). See also Alessandro Scafi's *Mapping Paradise: A History of Heaven on Earth* (Chicago: University of Chicago, 2006); 'Mapping Eden: Cartographies of the Earthly Paradise,' in *Mappings*, ed. Denis Cosgrove, 50–70 (London: Reaktion Books, 1999).

45 Indeed, many travellers who encountered ruins in the Levant did not escape thinking about the idea of doom and destruction, especially when comparing the past of these lands with its present conditions. The British traveller William Beawes recalled how 'time and other circumstances have produced a scene which only serves at present to excite a melancholy reflection of the instability of human things', 14. Although Carmichael and Beawes wrote about two difference places in the deserts, both shared the same trope about 'the instability of human things', reminding their readers that they were travelling in lands of past prosperity but now lost to ruins. In 1785, the British marine officer Francis Vernon arrived in Alexandria where he was struck with the radical difference between the glorious past of the

city, which he read about in the accounts of classical historians, and its modern, decadent present. He wrote: 'The intermediate spaces present an awful picture of the instability of earthly grandeur which formerly this city eminently possessed being built by Alexander the Great, on account of the convenience of its harbours, the only good ones along the coast of Egypt; and thereby becoming the staple for merchandize, arrived to a great degree of consequence', *Voyages and Travels of A Sea Officer* (London: Printed for the Author, 1792), 129.

46 Not until Francis Rawdon Chesney surveyed the Euphrates and Tygris rivers in 1832 do we find views in British travel writings which refute the Biblical narrative about the Garden of Eden. See Chesney's *The Expedition for the Survey of the Rivers,* 266–267.

47 Zur Shalev, *Sacred Words and Worlds: Geography, Religion and Scholarship, 1500–1700* (Leiden: Brill, 2017), 12.

48 Jonathan Sheehan, *The Enlightenment Bible: Translation, Scholarship, Culture* (Princeton: Princeton University Press, 2005), chapter two.

49 Volney's *Travels Through Syria and Egypt*, Vol II, 291–294. The search for the biblical Ophir has occupied the minds of many European explorers since the days of Columbus. In the early-modern period, when European colonial projects mostly focused on North and Central America, explorers associated Ophir with Peru. In the eighteenth century, the actual location of Ophir was associated with Southeast Asia, India and Indonesia. Ports located on the Persian Gulf and the Red Sea were seen as the stations which facilitated the movement of the wealth of Ophir to Solomon's Palmyra and Judea. On how the Biblical Ophir shaped European geographical and political imaginings, see Steven Weitzman, *Solomon: The Lure of Wisdom* (New Haven: Yale University Press, 2011). In the nineteenth-century, Ophir continued to shape European imperial imaginings. As Timothy Alborn shows, Europeans associated the gold mines in Southern Africa with the Ophir of the Old Testament, showing how the Bible 'informed their imperial hopes and dreams', 'King Solomon's Gold: Ophir in an Age of Empire,' *Journal of Victorian Culture*, 20:4 (2015), 491–508; the quote is from page 492. In eighteenth-century Britain, James Bruce, who travelled in the Levant and Abyssinia between 1763–1773, was the first Briton who located Ophir on the coast of Mozambique, *Travels to Discover the Source of the Nile*, 6 vols, (Dublin, 1791), Vol II, 70–74. Richard Sullivan, who served in the East India Company in the 1770s, located Ophir in Sumatra: see *Philosophical Rhapsodies: Fragments of Akbur of Betlis*, 3 vols (London: 1784), Vol 1, 240–242. The Levant traveller Charles Thompson mentioned how the ports in Southern Arabia and the Red Sea were central to the transportation of the wealth of Ophir into Jerusalem during the days of Solomon and David. In modern days, he added, the wealth of Ophir, which he located in India, was transported to Europe by the Dutch and the English through the Cape of God Hope, *Travels Through Turkey in Asia*, 2 vols (London: 1767), Vol II, 224–232.

50 S. J Barnett, *The Enlightenment and Religion: The Myths of Modernity* (Manchester: Manchester University Press, 2003), 68–69.

51 Sheehan, *The Enlightenment Bible,* chapter two.

52 Humphrey Prideaux, *The Old and New Testaments connected in the history of Jews and neighbouring nations*, 2 vols (1716; New York: 1842), Vol I, 420–423.

53 A good discussion of this battle, see *Mythologies of the Prophet Muhammad in Early Modern English Culture* (Cambridge: Cambridge University Press, 2013).

54 *Memoire and Diary of Henry Abbott.* The British Library, India Office Select Material MSS EUR B412 (A), 9.

55 Beawes's travel journal, alongside Carmichael's, was edited by Carruthers in 1929 for the Hakluyt Society; see his 'A Journey from Aleppo to Basra in 1745'.

56 Johnson, *A dictionary of the English language: in which the words are deduced from their originals and explained in their different meanings* (London: Printed for J. Knapton; C. Hitch and L. Hawes; A Miller; R and J Dodsley and M and T. Longman, 1756), Vol 2.

57 Nader Shah ruled Iran between 1736 and 1747; he invaded Delhi in 1737 and fought the Ottoman Empire for a good part of his life. In 1742, the East India Company factor in Surat James Frazer published the first account in England about Nader Shah, *The History of Nadir Shah Formerly Called Thamas Kuli Khan, Present Emperor of Persia* (London: Printed by W. Strahan for the Author, 1742). In 1773, William Jones produced another account about Nadir Shah, *The History of the Life of Nader Shah, King of Persia. Extracted from an Eastern Manuscript, which was translated into French by Order of His Majesty the King of Denmark.* (London: Printed by J.

Richardson, 1773). But the first account in England in which the character, life and manners of Nader Shah was examined in an Enlightenment fashion of writing history in which actions of fallen tyrants offer readers moral lessons about the futility of seeking power through the 'light of fire and sword' was Jonas Hanaway's *An Historical Account of the British Trade over the Caspian Sea ... To which are added, The Revolutions of Persia during the present century,* 4 vols (1753). Hanway was an English merchant in the British Russian Company: he travelled in Persia in 1743 on a mission to assess the state of British trade and navigation in the Caspian Sea. The reference to Nadir Shah above is taken from Hanaway's third edition, *The Revolutions of Persia* (London, 1762), Vol II, 436.

58 Willem Floor, 'The Iranian Navy in the Gulf during the Eighteenth Century', *Iranian Studies,* 20:1 (1987), 31–53. Hanway,1, 192; Laurence Lockhart, *Nadir Shah: A Critical Study based Upon Contemporary Sources* (London: Luzac & Co, 1938), 78; 213–214; 220–229; 285–286. See also his article 'Nadir Shah's Campaigns in Oman, 1737–1744', *Bulletin of the School of Oriental Studies* 8:1 (1835), 157–171.

59 Prideaux's *A Life of Mahomet* (1697) was preceded by his *A Letter to the Deists* (1696).

60 On how Islam and 'Mahomet' became useful material for both the orthodox and dissenting voices of the period in their pamphlet wars, see the first and second chapters in Humberto Garcia's *Islam and the English Enlightenment 1670–1840* (Baltimore: The John Hopkins University Press, 2012).

Chapter Two

POLITE ENGLISHMAN IN THE EAST: EDWARD IVES'S *JOURNEY FROM PERSIA TO ENGLAND* (1773)

The extensive intercourse, which is now kept up between nation and nation, has enlarged and expanded the human heart to a degree unknown before, even under all the advantages of which Philosophy so proudly boasted.

—Samuel Evers, *A Journal Kept on a Journey from Bassora to Baghdad over the Little Desert* (1779)

Edward Ives's *A Voyage from England to India* (1773), as we shall see, is the first English travel book about the overland routes in which we find an Englishman from a humble background, a surgeon by profession, telling his readers how Ottoman governors in different cities in Syria and Mesopotamia highly respected English travellers in their land. He reported how he and his companions enjoyed the hospitality of Muslim rulers, showing how the English were highly respected for their polite manners and accommodating behaviour towards non-Europeans. Travelling in the East, as this chapter shows, offered Ives opportunities to reinvent the Self abroad as one of improvement, respectability and politeness; the idea of being among others – a manifestation of a 'relational' condition in the making of the modern self, one 'outwardly' and 'socially turned' as Dror Wharman has argued – allowed Ives to reimagine the old regime of identity in England in which boundaries were strictly demarcated by fixed markers in contrast to the modern age known for mutability and transience, what Marshall Berman in 1982, via Karl Marx's *The Communist Manifesto*, called, 'all that is solid melts into air'.[1] Before he set out to the East, Ives was one of those 'rambling mind[s] and a fortune too narrow to allow' one 'to travel like a gentleman', as Alexander Hamilton in 1739 put it (Hamilton 1739: xxvi). But the idea of joining the Royal Navy as a surgeon gave Ives many opportunities to rub shoulders with people, European and non-Europeans, from different social and economic backgrounds, which enabled him to perform the character of a modern gentleman whose manners and appearance rather than his lineage, family background and religious piety defined his identity. In his travel book, Ives used polite performances and the ethos of improvement well known among the upwardly mobile middling ranks of eighteenth-century Britain to negotiate the freedoms and challenges of modernity. On the one hand, living in a society dominated by the economic ethos of progress allows for experiences of self-improvement, an opportunity to assert the uniqueness of the self, but it also entails a fear of loss of what Charles Taylor in 1989 called a sense of 'orientation', that is, the substantiality and stability once known in a traditional society shaped by religious and civic 'frameworks' defining the good of the community, nation and family.[2]

While travelling among Muslims and Arabs, Ives, a surgeon by profession, produced the values of improvement typical of an eighteenth-century bourgeoise culture in which, as Paul Lanford argues, 'It was easier to progress from rags to riches' if one chose his profession carefully (Langford 1989: 72).[3] It is in this society dominated by values of industriousness and self-improvement that the old social hierarchy, rooted in the division of wealth and power between Court and Country, was challenged. This challenge was undertaken by a new class for whom newly acquired riches allowed them to seek to, as Issac Kramnick's argues, break 'the hierarchical political ideal of Christian and aristocratic Europe', namely the idea of God's Chain of Being (Kramnick 1990: 5). These industrious men were Bolingbroke's 'upstarts and moneymen' and Edmund Burke's 'calculators and economists' and Alexander Pope's 'prideful' men who 'quit their place' and broke 'the chain alike'.[4] Like the experience of Tobias Smollett's intrepid surgeon, Rodrick, in *The Adventures of Rodrick Random*, for whom travelling was an addiction, Ives's travels in the Ottoman-Arab world fashioned him with opportunities that helped him to elevate the social position of a self-made man, 'the bred' rather than the 'born gentleman', in Daniel Defoe's formulation (Smollett 1784: I, x).[5]

Who Is Ives?

I could not find substantial sources about Ives's early life before he joined the Royal Navy, but historians have argued that surgeons of the Royal Navy were mostly men of humble backgrounds.[6] Ives was born in 1719 in Hampshire. Ives's village of Titchfield was not far from the town of Gosport, which during the eighteenth century was known for being home to many families of those who served in the Royal Navy, including the Alms family with whom Ives developed a friendship through Captain James Alms (1728–1791) who served in India with Ives and who was Ives's companion on the way back to Europe in 1758.[7] Ives might have developed connections with the Royal Navy through his acquaintances in Gosport. Historians have written about the reasons why young surgeons joined the Royal Navy at the time but perhaps five reasons stand out as the most relevant to what the *Voyage* tells us about the character of the author. As we learn from reading the book, Ives joined the Royal Navy to gain experience in the field of medicine, see more of the world, serve his king and country, develop contacts with influential men in the Royal Navy and the East India Company and, finally, secure a stable income.[8]

Ives's first experience in the sea was in 1741 when he joined HMS *Folkstone* commanded by Commodore Curtis Barnett who cruised the Mediterranean during the War of Austrian Succession (1740–1748). Barnett's intention was to destroy Spanish ships which were sent to the Caribbean to defend Spanish settlements against British incursions. During what was known as the War of Jenkin's Ears, Barnett, while on the lookout for Spanish ships, ended up clashing with four French ships on their way back from Martinique.[9] This military exchange happened off the coast of Cadiz where Ives, as he wrote in the *Voyage*, was charged with dressing wounds and 'amputating limbs' of injured 'seamen' (Ives 1773: 451). Such an experience, Ives recalled, was tough for a young surgeon operating in a small cabin. Recalling the horror of British naval wars in the eighteenth century, the Royal Navy officer and historian Sir Herbert William Richmond stated that 'seven were killed and eight were wounded' during this naval engagement in which Ives was serving as a surgeon (Richmond 1920: 162).

But this bruising experience did not deter Ives from joining another Royal Navy engagement in places far more dangerous than the one he had in the Mediterranean. In 1749, he joined Admiral Charles Watson in his expedition to the East Indies. He served as a chief surgeon aboard the HMS *Kent*, an armed frigate with '70 guns' (Ives 1773: 2). Ives reported that the main reason why the squadron sailed to the East Indies was to assist the East India Company in its war against the French and their local 'auxiliaries' (Ives 1773: 2). In India, Ives's work mainly focused on treating wounded soldiers who fought with Admiral Watson and Robert Clive in Plassey (1757) against the Nawab of Bengal, a remarkable event that laid the foundation for British rule in India.[10] In the preface to his travel book, he tells us that:

> Admiral Watson on the part of his majesty, entered into a written contract with me, for the establishing of an hospital in the several settlements of India, into which I was to receive the sick and hurt of the squadron, and providing them with medicinal and surgical assistance, and also with provisions, nurses, &c. (Ibid., 177: 18)

Returning from India, perhaps after a lucrative career, Ives cultivated social relations with members of England's prestigious circles such as the Royal Society and the Royal Colleges of Physicians. He developed friendships with Charles Morton (1716–1791), a physician and a librarian of the British Museum, and James Lind (1716–1994), one of the great authorities on naval medicine and hygiene in eighteenth-century Britain.[11]

After serving in the Royal Navy for nine years, Lind was appointed as a physician in the Royal Hospital at Haslar near Portsmouth and elected a fellow in the Royal College of Physicians. His name rose in the medical world of London upon the publication of his *The Treatise on the Scurvy* (1753) and *On the Most Effectual Means of Preserving the Health of Seamen* (1757), works which were widely celebrated in Britain because, in the words of the *Monthly Review* in 1757, Lind's work was 'calculated to prevent and lessen the many diseases to which that brave part of our fellow subjects, the sea-faring people were exposed' (1757: 90). Ives was a friend of Lind: he, in his travel account, called him 'my dear friend'. Ives's observation of the diseases in European settlements in India, which he published as an appendix to his travel account of 1773, first appeared in Lind's *An Essay on Diseases Incidental to Europeans in Hot Climate*s (1768). In a period in which Britain was heavily involved in the business of war, naval physicians and writers on naval diseases were considered immensely important for the nation.[12]

Outside the field of medicine, Ives also cultivated relations with the wealthiest nabob in England, Robert Clive, with whom he served in Plassey.[13] Clive was one of the most reviled people in England because of what was then considered as his role in opening the door of corruption for British officials in India.[14] For Ives, however, Clive was a hero whose achievements in Plassey saved the British Empire. '[S]ome persons have taken the great pains to misrepresent it [Plassey]', Ives wrote, 'with a view to tarnish the glory of Colonel Clive on that important victory. [...]' (Ives 1773: 153). They should know, Ives continued, that Clive was a man of 'magnanimity and good fortune' (Ives 1773: 93).

Ives was a friend of another member of the elite during the period. He was in close contact with Sir Charles Watson, who was awarded a baronetcy by King George II at the age of eight because of his father's long service to the Royal Navy.[15] '[I]f what I have written of your excellent Father', wrote Ives addressing Sir Charles, 'and other deserving Officer under him, or the Religion, Customs, and Manners of Foreign Countries shall contribute to your improvement, and set you forward in the paths of virtue, I then shall be beyond measure happy' (Ives 1773: 4). Virtue here was offered in a civic humanist frame in which the health of the nation mainly depends on the improvement of the aristocracy.[16] Ives here appears, as Stephen Copley has recently found in the works of Defoe and Steele, as a bourgeoise Englishman who knew his place in the social hierarchy of England, for whom 'the value of an aristocratic governing elite in society remains unquestioned' (Ives 1773: 6–7). But Ives was also an ardent middle-class progressivist for whom bourgeoise values of hard work and industriousness are vital for the improvement of Self and Nation. Surgeons, as many eighteenth-century commentators noted, showed middle-class values of self-improvement and industriousness; they were the people who often showed a desire which 'comes with us from the womb, and never leaves us till we go into the grave', as Adam Smith wrote, that is, the desire to change one's social and material conditions in life (Ives 1773: 415).[17] Ives yearned for social virtues from the past – active service and selfless patriotism – which the characters of Admiral Watson and his aristocratic son embodied, but he also knew that modern England is dominated by men like himself and Lord Clive, men from non-aristocratic backgrounds whose values of hard work, individualism and the pursuit of wealth substituted improvement with virtue.

Medical Encounters

On Saturday, 19 November 1757, Ives, with his English companions (six in total), left Calcutta for the Persian Gulf. They carried some letters and dispatches 'of importance from Admiral Pocock', the man who replaced Admiral Watson in India, 'to one of the Secretaries of State, and to the Secretary of the Lords of the Admiralty' in London (187). They joined an East India Company frigate, *The Revenge*, which carried goods destined for the port of Bandar Abbas on the Persian Gulf. The ship arrived at the port on the 11th of March 1758.

'Gambaroon' (as Europeans called the Persian city of Bandar Abbas during the seventeenth and eighteenth centuries) boasted a prosperous trade when the French merchant and traveller Jean Chardin was in the Persian Gulf in March 1676. Chardin found many merchants from diverse backgrounds – English, French, Dutch and Indian – residing in one place. 'The houses are computed at 14 or 1500, one-third of which are Indian Gentoos or Idolators, a few Jews; the greatest part are Persians, and the rest are English, French and Dutch, belonging to their respective Companies' (Chardin 1760: 16). Carsten Niebuhr (1733–1815) who visited the port in 1766 on his way to India recalled how the city 'was famous through all the last century, and in the beginning of the present, as the port of Shiraz, and of all the south of Persia. Its trade was, at that time, very extensive' (Niebuhr 1792: II, 141). However, by the time he was there in 1766, there was no 'single European counting house in the city' (Niebuhr 1792: II, 141). 'This decline', Niebuhr added, 'has occasioned by the domestic disturbances in Persia, and the wars and disputes between the French and the English. The Dutch for a while continued to carry trade here. But since they formed a settlement in the isle of Karek, they have entirely deserted Gambron' (Niebuhr 1792: II, 141).

Ives, who was in Gambroon eight years before Niebuhr visited the city, noted how the Dutch used its port to sell their Surinam sugar to the Persians.[18] However, despite the efforts of the Dutch to revive European trade in the region, Ives regretted, trade in the Persian Gulf was in a state of steep decline because of the diversion of most Anglo-Indian trade towards the Cape of Good Hope route, the devastating civil wars in Persia and the thriving piracy in the Persian Gulf. 'The two factory houses [the English and French] are the only buildings remaining of any importance', Ives in 1758 noted, and 'the whole city besides is almost one entire scene of ruins, which served indeed to convince us of its once flourishing state; but the constant wars carried on in this country, and their attendant confusion and anarchy, have deprived the English of almost all their commercial advantages [...]' (Ives 1773: 198). The East India Company, however, continued to use the port for transporting English 'broad cloth' for Persian markets.[19] The port was also important for shipping Caramania wool into the British settlements in India. One year after Ives left Gambroon, the French (in 1759), during the Seven Year Wars, attacked and destroyed the English factory.[20] Although he enjoyed the company of the Dutch and English residents of Gambroon, Ives, while recalling the changeable condition of the city, was sensitive to the transient nature of prosperity.

Despite their commercial significance, Gambaroon [Figure 4] and other port towns on the Persian Gulf were known among British residents and visitors for their unhealthy air and malignant fevers. The reason for this was, as Captain John Wainwright of the East India Company, who visited the region in 1809–1810, remarked, 'the free circulation of air' which brings along with it a dreadful disease known as the plague.[21] Just a few months after Ives left Gambaroon, the English physician in the factory John Parker was 'attacked with violent and inflammatory fever' (102). Unable to continue to serve in Gambroon, Parker wrote to the East India Company presidency in Bombay asking for 'their permission to return to the presidency to establish my former health' (102). 'The Persians themselves fly from it', Ives confirmed, [...]

> in the bad season, and few of our factory escape the putrid and intermitting fevers which principally rage in the months of May and September and though they sometimes recover, yet it generally happens that their constitutions are much impaired; they lose the European complexion, become pale, and enervated, and their diseases terminate in obstruction of the liver, and adhesion of it to peritonaeum. (Ives 1773: 198)

Figure 4 View of the city of Gambroon (1740). Courtesy: Koninklijke Bibliotheek.

The idea that Ives included the above medical remarks in his travel book testifies to the important role played by medical professionals who cared to expand their country's knowledge of its vital commercial centres in the East.[22] But the passage above displays Ives's anxiety about the extent to which the pursuit of trade and wealth in the East not only compromises the body's medical condition but also alters a well-established tradition in Europeans' conception of their difference from non-Europeans: 'the European complexion'.[23]

If an encounter with difference causes radical changes in one's medical condition and alters the 'the European complexion', it could also be a drive for improvement. In an age when Britons were expanding their trade and settlements in all corners of the globe, British medical reports about the Levant, Arabia, India and Persia were immensely important for advancing British medical culture in an age in which Britain's medical education was considered by many beneath that of the Dutch and the Italians: the University of Leiden and Padua, not Oxford or Cambridge, remained the prime destination for Europe's medical students throughout the eighteenth century.[24]

To that end, in Ives's account, the idea of reporting about the medical scene in the Persian Gulf was particularly important because Britain's gateway to India (Gambroon, Basra, Cairo, Aleppo) were often seen as exporters of a violent disease, the plague, which many European trading centres in the region were concerned to prevent its arrival on European shores. Throughout the seventeenth and eighteenth centuries, many consulates and trading posts shut their gates for many months for fear of exporting the disease to Europe. The plague which hit the Levant regularly throughout the period was a thorn in the back of European trading posts in the Ottoman Empire and Persia.[25]

Ives wrote his remarks about the medical condition of Gambroon after inspecting the 'impaired constitutions' of his fellow countrymen in the region. But Ives's remarks were shaped by those of Patrick Oliphant, a Scottish naval surgeon and physician to the English factory in Gambroon between 1729 and 1740. In the appendix to his *A Voyage*, Ives printed the observations of Patrick Oliphant under the title 'An Account of the DISEASES incident to Gombroon, contained in a letter from an ingenious Physician who resided several years in that settlement', a short treatise in which Oliphant explained the differences between various fevers and different methods of treating them. What stands out in this treatise is the idea that Oliphant administered methods of treatments which show how he relied on both the European and Eastern *materia medica* in his work. He used common medicines in Europe for treating fevers; he applied different barks and spirits of vitriol known as 'Gas Sulphuris', but he also mixed Senna, an Arabian plant commonly known as a purge, with an 'elixir of vitriol' (Ives 1773: 505).[26]

Oliphant's observations were first published in the first volume of *Medical Observations and Enquiries* (1758), a London pamphlet published by a group of physicians (The Society of Physicians) whose main aim, as the editor of the first volume recalled, was to advance the English medical scene by collecting observations of Britons who served and travelled in different parts of the world.[27] To that end, many Britons who traded and served abroad began to put in print medical remarks about diseases, medical practices and nostrums of regions in which they lived and travelled. In addition, many physicians and surgeons who served in the Royal Navy, the Levant and the East India Companies published accounts which subsequently became major reading material in Britain's medical arena: James Lind's *Treatise on the Scurvy* (1753) and Patrick Russell's *Treatise of the Plague* (1791) are well-known examples.

Reporting about the medical culture of foreign nations, thus, was an attempt by Oliphant and Ives to improve the medical dispensation of their own countries. In an age in which medicine was mostly seen in Britain as a private enterprise open for profiteers and quacks, foreign herbs and plants were often seen as immensely important for advancing Britain's medical culture.[28] The Levant and Arabia ranked the highest on the list of suppliers of drugs and plants to Britain: famed nostrums in Britain imported from drugstores in Aleppo, Cairo and Constantinople included the balsam of Mecca, olibanum, myrrh and senna.[29] In the appendix to Ives's travel book, we find a list of names of Indian trees and plants which eighteenth-century Indian and European physicians used in their medical work. In the same section, Ives mentioned how he constantly conversed with Indian physicians (whom he called 'black doctors'), about different diseases in India. He reported how one Mr Thomas, an English surgeon who served in HMS *Salisbury* before residing in Bombay, owned many drugs imported from Arabia: 'Gum Arabic, Myrrh, Olibanum and Senna' (Ives 1773: 44). In Gambroon, he examined the plants in the gardens of East India Company factory and found a tree, 'Gum Arabic' [Figure 5] which 'the gentlemen of our factory seemed quite unacquainted with [...]' (Ives 1773: 198). We do not know whether the English were planting Gum Arabic trees on the coast of Persia for purposes of exporting them to India and Europe, but Ives was clearly aware of the medical benefits of such a plant whose fame travelled East to India and West to Europe.[30]

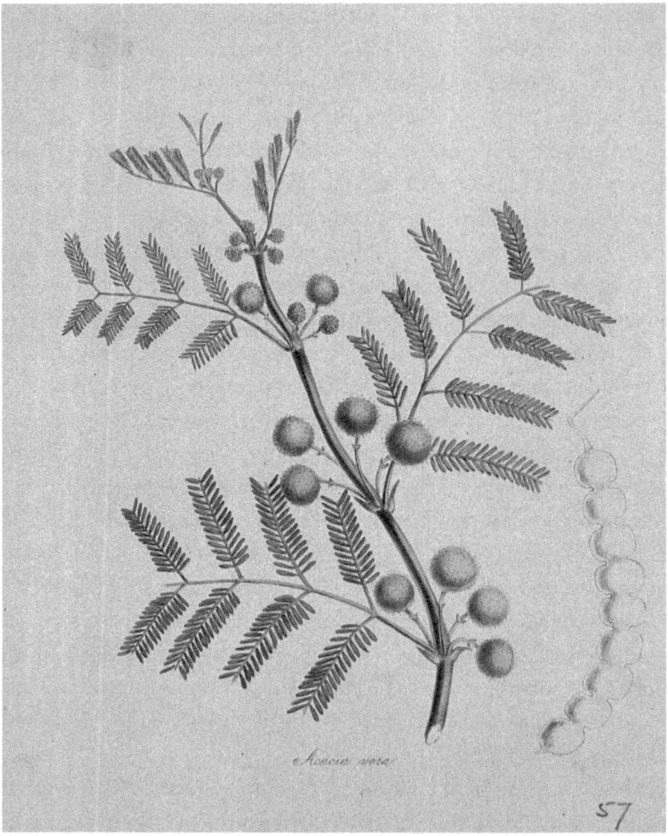

Figure 5 Egyptian gum arabic (*Acacia nilotica*): flowering stem with separate seed pod. Coloured lithograph after M. A. Burnett, c. 1842. Courtesy: The Wellcome Library.

The medical virtues of the aforementioned Arabian plants, drugs and herbs were well known to European physicians, particularly those versed with the writings of ancient physicians such as Pedanius Discorides and Galen.[31] But the first European researcher who reported about the benefit of Gum Arabic while residing and practising in the region was the Italian physician Prosper Alpinus. In *De plantis Aegypti* (1592), Alpinus recalled how the Egyptians used Gum Arabic for treating haemorrhages (1592: 6). In the eighteenth century, it was the Swedish traveller and physician Hasselquist who suggested the 'nutritive virtue of Gum Arabic' while observing how travellers across Egyptian deserts often ate this plant when their food ran out. 'Gum Arabic', he wrote, 'is gelatinous, and undoubtedly contains some nourishing particles' (Hasselquist 1766: 298).[32] In eighteenth-century England, 'Gum Arabic' was imported by the Levant and East India Companies and was 'of frequent use in medicine'. According to the physician John Hill in *The History* of *Materia Medica* (1751), it was a drug used in treating 'the

Acrimony of the Humours', and in 'Stranguries, in Coughs and in Spitting of Blood' (Hill 1751: 742).[33]

Ives was aware of this culture of exchange between the Middle East and Europe in the field of medicine. But this is where his medical knowledge *in* and *of* the region stops. A close reading of Ives's text will make it clear to the reader that Ives was uneasy about the idea that he travelled in the Levant as a medical professional. He knew that many great medical authorities visited the region and wrote about its plants, medical practices and diseases in great detail: for example, when he briefly spoke about the plague in Syria, he referred his reader to the work of the Scottish physician Alexander Russell whose work *The Natural History of Aleppo* was widely received both in the Levant and Europe. But unlike Russell, Ives added no new knowledge about the plague. In addition, unlike most medical men who wrote about the region during his lifetime, men such as Joseph Pitton de Tournefort in France and Peter Forsskål in Sweden, Ives did not have the academic knowledge in botany and medical theory that often encouraged medical travellers to explore and build on the systems of knowledge previously introduced by Galen (of the ancients) and Carl Linnaeus (of the moderns).[34]

Travellers and physicians who visited the region before Ives, such as Prospero Alpini (1553–1613), Leonhard Rauwolf (1535–1596), Joseph Pitton de Tournefort (1656–1708), Fredrick Hasselquist (1722–1752), Peter Forsskål (1732–1763), Alexander (1727–1805) and Patrick Russell, were all familiar with classical medical theories and writings about medicine. That is, they were, unlike Ives, widely versed in *botany* and *physick* beyond just the realm of practice and observation; however, they claimed that it was the idea of observing plants and people on the spot rather than reading about them in books which mostly encouraged them to travel and write their travel experiences about the Levant.

Moreover, unlike Leonhard Rauwolf and Alexander and Patrick Russell, Ives did not mention that he bought any medical manuscript in the region or even read medical books and treatises well known in the Islamic world such as those by Ibn Sina, Al-Zahrawi and Al-Razi.[35] The idea that Ives ignored examining the medical culture in the Levant did not necessarily indicate the superiority of the European traveller in the Islamic world. Rather, it was a sign of the anxiety of a surgeon who had modest grasp of the field beyond just dressing wounds, amputating limbs and prescribing purges. Ives's medical knowledge was purely practical.

An example of Ives's anxiety about the idea of being a medical man in the region was his brief encounter with Patrick Russell in Aleppo. Ives's encounter with Patrick Russell did not go beyond exchanging polite words upon meeting each other. He did not recall that he spoke with Patrick about the plague which reached Syria in milder forms in the 1750s; while Patrick was busy running around in the city treating local patients and recording his notes which later appeared in his magisterial book *Treatise of the Plague* (1791), Ives spent most of his time in Aleppo socialising with his fellow countrymen.

There is another reason which explains why Ives showed little interest in the local medical culture in the Levant and Arabia. Ives, unlike many medical (and no-medical) European travellers in the region, avoided speaking with locals about medicine and medical knowledge because in so doing, as he told us, he avoided the hassle of being constantly stopped on the road by locals and their rulers who often thought that all Europeans were skilled in the practice of medicine. From his conversation with a Catholic missionary who worked as a physician to a local governor in Mesopotamia, Ives learned that Hussein Pasha of Mosul employed an Italian physician who accepted the Pasha's offer as 'a post of honour, which besides protecting him and his brethren, makes him of some consequence in the country' (Ives 1773: 322). But Ives also learned that local rulers did not offer generous payments to physicians. Padre Francisco's role as a physician in the Pasha's palace, Ives recalled, 'produces very little pecuniary profits' because Hussein Pasha, 'like the rest of great men in Turkey, being not only very covetous, but also is of opinion, that any person is amply rewarded by having the honour of admittance into his presence, without receiving any other emoluments for his service' (Ibid., 1773: 322). As this anecdote shows, Ives viewed the medical profession as a route to prestige and, most importantly, an opportunity of making money like the London-based physician, Dr Lavement, in Smollett's *The Adventures of Roderick Random*.[36] But the fear in Ives's narrative of the idea of being a physician in the Levant is understandable given that he passed through the region in times of extreme fears of the plague, constant famines and excruciating poverty. This explains why his account lacked substantial knowledge about the medical culture of the region.

Ives's reading of Leonhard Rauwolff's travel account, published after the German physician returned to Europe from the Levant in 1575, probably encouraged him to hide his true profession while interacting with locals. In his travel diary, Rauwolff, a physician and botanist from Augsburg, recalled how in Baghdad one notable merchant, a Christian, 'proffered of his own accord to recommend me to the Bashaw who was then sick, and his very good friend, to be his Physician' (192). Rauwolf politely refused the offer. 'I would not undertake it, fearing I should have the same measure, and instead of a Reward have my liberty taken away from me [...]' (Rauwolf 1693: 192–193). Rauwolff was an ardent Protestant who travelled in the Ottoman Levant during a period known for religious tensions in Europe between Protestants and Catholics; this age was known as the Reformation. To that end, the idea of working in an Ottoman court scared him and made him imagine the possibility of losing his faith while interacting with people from other religions. Ives, however, had nothing to say about the fear of losing one's faith while practising among Muslim elites and governors. He mostly concerned with the lack of financial rewards in lieu of working for what he called 'covetous' Muslim rulers.

Ives might have also learned from the Frenchman Jean de Thevenot (1633–1667), whose travel book he was familiar with, how the Levant 'was no Country for Physicians to get Estates in, because [...] they are subject to few Diseases, and besides are but very bad Paymasters to those who Cure them: and if the Physicians should prove unsuccessful, and the Patient Die, they are so far from Paying them, that they put them many times to Trouble, and sometimes to Charges, accusing them of having Killed the Patient: as if the Life and Death of Men were in the hands of Physicians, and not God' (Thevenot 1687: 37). This position was later confirmed by the French botanist Charles Sonnini (1751–1812) who, while he was in Egypt in the 1770s, found the people appreciative of European medical skills but warned that '[if] the physician has the misfortune to be sent for by a man of power, that which would, in our country, be the source of satisfaction, consequence and riches, is here a source of perpetual inquietude and danger'(Sonnini 1800: 529). For Thevenot and Sonnini, as well as for Ives, the medical profession in Europe was more profitable than it was in the Arab-Ottoman region.[37] But they were certainly wrong that Europeans respected the character of the physicians more than it was the case in Ottoman-Arab land.[38] 'Though the Turks are predestinarians', Alexander Russell in *The Natural History of Aleppo* wrote, 'they are taught however to believe that tho' God has afflicted mankind with diseases; yet he has sent them also the remedies, and they are therefore to use the proper means for their recovery: so that practitioners in physic are here [in Aleppo] well esteemed' (Russell 1756: 79).

Meanwhile, in Britain, the image of the cruel, profiteering and heartless physician became a fashionable subject of critique in the print scene of the period. Roy Porter has shown how 'the Georgian medical elite grew more fashionable, more prestigious, more well-to-do than its Stuart equivalent' but the majority of English physicians 'remained sitting targets for satire and censure, being presented as living fossils, clinging to obsolete learning' (Porter 1995: 34; 39). A cursory look at the representations of surgeons and physicians in eighteenth-century British literature and culture reveals how the medical profession was perceived as a replenished repository of quackery, fraud, deceit and cruelty.[39] In Tobias Smollett's novel *The Adventures of Roderick Random* (1748), the main character Roderick was a naval surgeon in the Royal Navy. In the different expeditions he was engaged in, we were told, he was disliked by his mates, not only because he was a Scotsman but also because he was a surgeon; as the commander of the West India ship in which he worked observed, surgeons are 'unnecessary animals on board of a ship': they are good for nothing but for sealing the death of the injured rather than curing them (Smollett 1748: II, 2). Smollett himself was trained as a physician, but as a writer he could not escape the cruel jokes about physicians and surgeons which circulated in British culture.

In Smollett's eyes, the nature of Ives's profession would have made him a cruel physician. Ives, unlike other European physicians and botanists who travelled in the Levant throughout the eighteenth century, did not use any of the medicines known in the region. He rather prescribed to his fellow English travellers an English medicine, a strong chemical emetic known in Britain as Dr James's Powder, a drug that many in Britain associated with 'violence'.[40] In eighteenth-century Europe where many medical professionals often recommended the use of 'potent drugs' and 'surgical interventions', as Dorothy and Roy Porter wrote, Ottoman medical practices and drugs were often admired for being less painful (Porter 1989: 60). Also, chances of death for those who used them were quite low in comparison to those in Europe. Mary Montagu, who campaigned against older methods of treating the smallpox disease, recommended an Ottoman method because, unlike the European methods of treatment, she said, it causes zero fatality.[41] Dr William Rowley, an English physician who travelled in Europe, confirmed the violent method of treatment 'in France, Holland, Flanders [and] Italy'. In these countries, he stated, 'the application of bleeding, refrigeratory medicine of nitre' causes 'an enormous fatality' (Rowley 1804: 116).

In contrast to what Rowley found in Europe, many eighteenth-century European commentators on the medical culture of the Levant noted the softer method of treatment among local Muslim physicians. In so doing, they mounted a subtle critique of

European heavy medicines and rough methods of treatment. Carsten Niebuhr noted how in the period before he visited Cairo the main 'Mouritan', hospital in the city, 'formerly provided' the patients 'with everything that tend to sooth their distress, not excepting even music' (Niebuhr 1792: I, 62). As Niebuhr remarked on this softer method of treatment, 'Over all the East the power of sympathy in curing diseases is firmly believed' (Niebuhr 1792: II, 277). This observation was confirmed by Alexander Russell who was also a critic of European medical practices, which included antiseptics, excision, amputation, dissection and, to a large extent, bloodletting.[42]

Ives, as a surgeon who often applied violent treatments throughout his career in the Royal Navy, was silent about the extent to which Arab and Ottoman medicines and medical practices were less violent than the European ones. But despite that Ives did not bother about collecting and writing about medical herbs, plants and practices of local physicians in the Levant, as other European and British travellers in the region certainly did, he tried one herb that many in the region saw as medically beneficial: tobacco. In the Levant, tobacco was considered an effective emetic cure and a good solution for soaring body temperature. In *Al-ṣulḥ bayn al-ikhwān fī ḥukm ibāḥat al-dukhkhān* ('Making peace between brothers on the issue of legalizing smoking'), the Damascus Jurist Abdul Ghani Al-Nabulsi (1641–1731) defended smoking on legal and medical grounds in an age in which tobacco smoking was viewed by many in Istanbul and Damascus as anti-Islamic, foreign and a symbol of hellfire.[43] His manuscript first appeared in 1682, but it continued to circulate in the region in the first half of the century. Like Al-Nabulsi, Tournefort recalled the medical benefit of tobacco in his *Materia Medica* (1708).

Ives, unlike Tournefort and Al-Nabulsi, was keen on the recreational rather than the medical value of tobacco. Ives reported he smoked the Persian pipe [Figure 6] at least twice en route to Syria: in Gambroon he smoked the '*Calloon*' and 'Kerim Can [Khan]', as the pipes were then called, in the company of a Dutch couple 'in whose garden we passed some hours very agreeably' (224). He did not hesitate to smoke the '*Calloon*' because it was 'used by the gentlemen here' (224). The historian James Grehan observes that one main difference between Ottoman and Persian tobacco cultures was that the water pipe in Persia, which Ives smoked in Gambroon, was often linked to the upper classes, whereas in the Arab land, where tobacco was produced locally and thus was cheap, smoking pipes were spread across all sections of society.[44] The nineteenth-century English traveller Edward William Lane noted how in Egypt 'the Persian pipe, in which the smoke passes through water [...] [is] [...] commonly used by the persons of the higher classes [...]' (Lane 1836: I, 167). Ives, while smoking the Persian hookah which people from the upper ranks in Aleppo adopted, cut a figure of a gentleman.[45] Smoking for Ives was mostly a recreational and sociable activity like playing cards or drinking ale in England. But the fact that he, as a medical professional, was keen on smoking '*Calloon*' in the Persian Gulf and Syria might indicate that he was aware of the medical benefits attached to tobacco both in the region and in England.[46]

To conclude, Ives belongs to an age in which many in Europe advanced the opinion that a European *material medica* is far superior to a non-European one, but the age also saw many voices which admired Arab and Ottoman medical traditions. Thevenot recalled how '[t]he Turks are long lived, little subject to diseases, and we have many

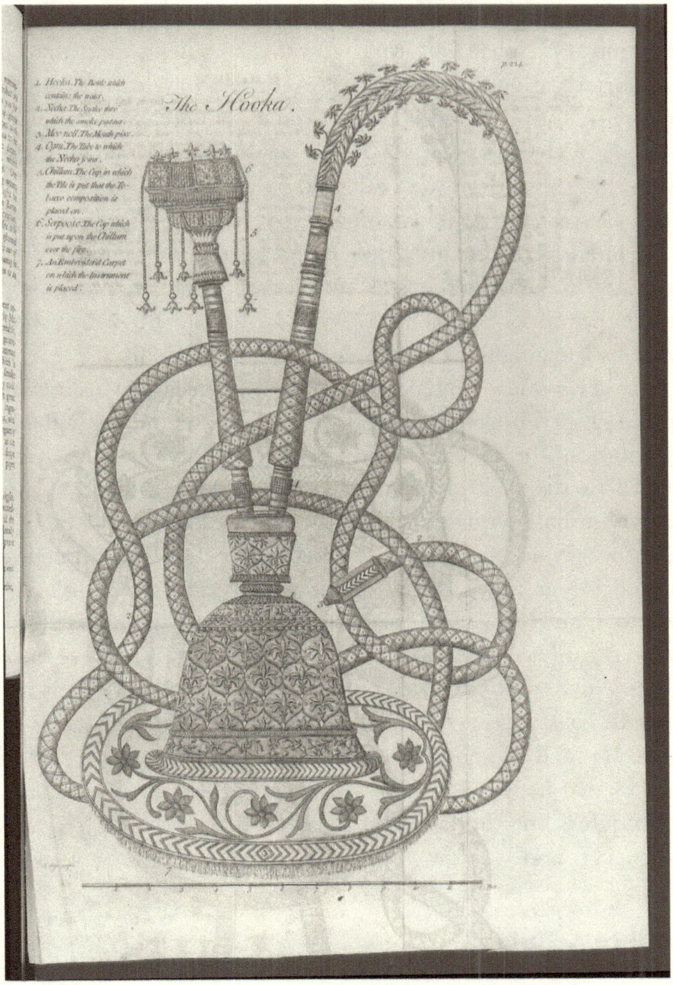

Figure 6 A Persian hookah in Ives's *Travels from Persia to England* (1773). Courtesy: The British Library.

dangerous distempers that are not known amongst them; as the Stone, and many more' (Thevenot 1687: 37). Thevenot attributed the 'healthfulness' of the 'Turks' to their 'frequent Bathings' and 'temperance in eating and drinking' (Thevenot 1687: 37). Unlike Christians, he concluded, 'they make no Debauches in wine and use exercise'; it is because of this that 'they have no Physicians' (Thevenot 1687: 37). The French naturalist and traveller in Egypt Charles Sonnini recalled how in line with the common belief in Egypt many French 'sailors from Provence were so firmly persuaded of' the 'prolific virtues' of the Nile water 'that if they touched in Egypt [...] they never failed to fill a cask [...] and carry it home to their wives as the most effectual means of obtaining a numerous progeny' (Sonnini 1800: 251). Not only the commoners of

Provence who happened to work as sailors admired the 'virtues' of the Nile water. Sonnini himself drank 'immoderate quantities' and found that 'it never did me any harm: on the contrary, I observed it passed off very quickly, and that, consequently, it was very salubrious' (Sonnini 1800: 252). A British physician who travelled in the Ottoman Empire in 1775 recalled how 'the women of Circassia, and likewise those of Turkey [...] devote a considerable part of the day to dancing among themselves; and I sincerely wish that the custom were adopted by the British ladies' (Anon 1770: 158). Among 'genteel' classes in Britain, dancing takes place once a week in 'assembly-rooms' (1770: 157). The 'method of dancing a little daily', he added, would be of immense value to 'health especially in the winter season when ladies often complain of such ailments as dancing would either cure or prevent' (1770: 158). The health of British women would greatly improve by learning from the Ottoman dancing culture.

Such a rich archive of encounters between Europeans and Muslims did not appear in Ives's medical observations on the region. And this is understandable. When Ives arrived in Gambroon, the region was in a state of panic due to the plague. Ives, for example, noted how the state of health in Aleppo was in a deplorable position: 'this dreadful calamity' usually visits the city 'once in 12 or 13 years' (Ives 1773: 372). Each day Aleppo buries around 200 people. He further recalled how 'there is a little difference between the present malignant fever and what is commonly called the plague'. In the city, his companion Henry Doidge fell ill. Ives 'ordered him an emetic' which helped him to relieve to regain his appetite (Ives 1773: 372). Apart from these medical observations and others which mostly focused on the plague, which he mostly borrowed from Alexander Russell's *The Natural History of Aleppo*, Ives had little to say about the plants, cures and medical practices and diets of the region. As the next section will show, Ives preferred to show that he was a man of taste and polite manners, a collector of antiquities, rather than just 'the surgeon' that many in Britain would have associated with modest social background.

A Gentleman in Arabia

After they left Gambroon, Ives and his companions arrived in Basra on 22 April. William Shaw, the East India Company resident in the city, welcomed his countrymen. He 'received us with the greatest politeness and hospitality', Ives wrote, 'and provided lodgings for us under his own roof' (Ives 1773: 232). In Basra, Ives, like Carmichael, marvelled at the prosperous commercial scene in the city. 'Much trade is carried on here, through a navigable canal which is cut into the river', Ives noted, and 'there is a daily intercourse with Baghdad by water, on the two great rivers, Euphrates and Tygris' (Ives 1773: 231–232). The ruler of Basra at the time was Solyman Pasha Abu Layla (Abu Layla in Arabic means 'the father of the night', a name given to him because of the campaigns against rebellious tribes which he often led at night).[47] Before he became the governor of Basra, he was a slave to Ahmad Pasha, the ruler who governed Baghdad between 1704 and 1723. Solyman rose into prominence after he saved his master from a lion attack (this is the reason why Baghdadis call him Solyman the Lion).[48] This magnificent feat 'was immediately repaid by the promise of Achmed's [Ahmad] eldest daughter for his wife [...]', the traveller William Heude in 1817 wrote (146). '[This] was the means of raising him progressively, from an inferior employment to those of higher dignities, which placed him ultimately in the possession of the honours of Pashalik', Heude added (Heude 1817: 146).

Under the government of Solyman, the English were encouraged to live and trade in the city, but trade in Basra would not be profitable without a secure caravan route to Aleppo, the economic metropolis of Syria throughout the period and an important centre for dispatching the East India Company letters to Europe. In a letter to the English resident in Gambroon Alexander Douglass, dated 6 June 1758, William Shaw recalled how the recent drought and famine which hit the region made it hard for English travellers and caravans to move between Aleppo and Basra. Unfortunately, he added, 'we have had a small caravan recently plundered' between Basra and Aleppo; 'also a Jew and a German doctor who were in another party arrived [in Basra] quite spoiled of every article' (104). In the same letter, Shaw explained how one Englishman, Captain Barton, last March, was robbed while travelling between Aleppo and Basra. For Shaw, Arab tribes plunder travellers in deserts, including Barton, because of the extreme 'dearth of grains and provisions' in the region which 'contributes to the Deserts being now so foul' (105). The 'Arabs rob everyone they meet', he explained, 'to obtain provisions and subsistence by taking the passengers' camels for food' (105).[49] Shaw was keen on communicating these observations to the East India Company post in Gambroon, which would in turn send them to the Company's presidency in Bombay. In so doing, Shaw aimed to help the Company determine whether it is a good idea or not to send goods, travellers or dispatches across the Persian Gulf into Basra, Aleppo and then to Europe.

Ives learned from Shaw about the experience of Barton in the Arabian deserts. This 'gentleman had it seems a few years before, acquired a handsome fortune in the East Indies, with which he returned to England settled at some distance from London in the character of a country gentleman, and served the office of high-sheriff for the country in which he lived' (Ives 1773: 232). William Shaw, who first mentioned the name of Barton in his letter, said nothing about Barton's social status. But Ives was right. Many Britons who returned to England from India used the newly acquired wealth to buy their way up the social ladder. Many in England called these men nabobs, referring to the dubious sources of wealth they had in the East.[50]

None of this bad talk about nabobs in England figured in Ives's account of Barton. In England, Ives noted, Barton acted like a gentleman, but among Arabs, he was far from being a gentleman. Barton 'held his cocked pistol towards the Arabs, and with a determined look, and high-toned voice', Ives noted, 'declared he would kill some of them, if they dared to approach any nearer' (Ives 1773: 232). Barton's previous experience in India could have taught him that the English were mostly respected and feared because of their sophisticated weapons with which they managed to win Plassey. But soon he realised that this might not be true in Arabia. 'By degrees', Ives noted, 'they [Arabs] surrounded him and with a blow on the head, he was brought to the ground and his pistol taken from him' (Ives 1773: 232). Barton's inability to show respect to the Arabs caused him a lot of trouble in the deserts. The Arabs 'stripped him quite naked, and leaving the servant a jacket and breeches, but not a drop of water, or morsel of provision for either' (Ives 1773: 233).

Barton's story among Arabs taught Ives and his fellow English travellers a great lesson about how Europeans should behave while encountering Arabs. For Ives, the first thing an Englishman needs to do here is heed an image the Arabs form of their English guests. 'After dinner Mr. Shaw [the EIC resident in Basra] carried us to see a long boat of his', Ives wrote [...]

> which he had fitted up as a little yacht and was so obliging as to offer us the use of it to carry us as far as Hilla, in our way to Baghdad. We gladly accepted it as being much more commodious than any of the country boats; and Mr. Alms undertook to sit her for the voyage. We likewise hired a Sandal or boat for carrying our baggage and the two horses we brought with us from Karec, to which Mr. Shaw also laid in a very large stock of fresh provisions before our passage up the river, and a letter of recommendation to the Roman nominal Bishop of Babylon. (Ives 1773: 234)

The mention of the yacht and horses in the preceding passage tells us a great deal about how the English wanted the Arabs to see them as gentlemen of higher status. James Silk Buckingham, who visited Mesopotamia in 1816, noted how the English Residency in Baghdad owned 'a large and commodious yacht' which 'always kept ready for excursions on the river [...]' (Buckingham 1827: 211). He further noted how the Residency also owned beautiful and expensive horses: 'the stud of horses was large and choice' (Buckingham 1827: 211). Buckingham realised these objects were mostly used by the English to impress the locals with English wealth. '[E]very thing belonging to the Residency', Buckingham wrote, 'was calculated to impress ideas of great respect on the minds of the inhabitants, who were witnesses of the manner in which it was supported and conducted' (Buckingham 1827: 211).

Ives, and later Buckingham, knew that a carefully choreographed image makes the Arabs friendly to the Britons travelling and residing in their land. As Ives explained, the 'yacht' the English resident in Basra prepared for his countrymen was designed to impress the Arabs and make them friendly towards the English. 'What seemed chiefly to attract the eyes of the Arabs, and surprise them most', Ives rejoiced, 'was the form of the yacht, the manner of rigging her, and above all, the carved work of a horse's head on the stem [...]' (Ives 1773: 242).

Ives and his fellow travellers carefully deliberated on what an ideal image of Englishness they needed to project on the locals. While his countryman Barton travelled with only one servant and two camels, Ives and his fellow English travellers hired a yacht with a lot of provisions and a few servants. While the Dutch in the region were known for being austere and thrifty, as the Dutch representative of the *Vereenigde Oostindische Compagnie* in the Persian Gulf told Ives, Ives and his fellow travellers cared to display expensive clothes and ride Arab horses. Ives and his fellow Britons living in the region knew that English pageantry insures the respect of the Arabs. Even many decades after Ives visited the region, the English knew that protecting their interests in the Arab region required more than just showing sophisticated weapons and ships:

'prestige' is the keyword that the English traveller and journalist Perceval Landen in 1915 asked his government to project on the natives in order to keep them under British protection in the face of rising Russian and German threats in the Middle East.[51]

For Ives, gentility does not require the show of force. Rather it requires the display of wealth and politeness. No more, no less. This tactic was confirmed when Ives and his friend reached the gates of Baghdad in May 1758; the English consul, Robert Garden, met Ives and his mates before they entered the city. Garden asked them to change their clothes, to wear English clothes and European hats. He also asked them to fix English stirrups on their horses. '[O]ur polite countryman Mr. Garden would not have us degrade the English name (which is here in high repute) by going into the streets on foot, and our horse furniture at present is much too mean to appear with [...]' (Ives 1773: 272). The English in the Levant and Mesopotamia, Ives rejoiced, gained the respect of the locals through the power of the image (clothes, horse furniture and polite manners) rather than the power of the pistol (as Barton mistakenly thought). '[V]ery many were the spectators here', Ives recalled, 'and much [to] their surprise, on seeing so many Frengees or Franks (the general name throughout Turkey for Europeans) and by the pleasure which appeared in the countenance of the boys, it seems they had never been so agreeably entertained before' (Ives 1773: 272). The English did not want to project an imperial image of their nation, as Ives showed; rather the English in the Middle East acted, in Guy Debord's phrasing, as 'a society of the spectacle' whose social relations with Arabs and Turks were all 'mediated by the image' (Debord 2014: 2). Such a spectacle made the English the talk of the city, which is what Garden, Shaw and Ives wanted in the first place. Thus, 'The hat, the hair differently dressed, wig, coat, and every part of our habits and accoutrements, even the horsewhip and European saddles', Ives added, 'were all matters of curiosity to men as well as boys; and yet not the least kind of incivility passed from any one of them' (Ives 1773: 272). These images, as Debord helps us to understand, are often successful in creating 'an objective reality': that is, they prove to be effective tools for suspending any sense of disbelief, whether by those who disseminate these images or those to whom they were directed (Debord 2014: 2). It creates a sense that what is being seen is real.

In an age in which English political interests in the Middle East were becoming increasingly vital for the protection of British imperial posts in India, Ives's definition of English politeness as a spectacle, a performance aided by objects (horses, yachts and clothes), was disseminated across the wider culture of British travels in the East. In the wake of Ives's journey, Britons, from both upper and middling orders, who reported about their travels in the Levant, recalled how a Briton in the East should impress the locals with his polite behaviour and genteel appearance. Lord Algernon Percy, who was in Cairo in 1776, knew that Christians were only allowed to ride donkeys within the city, but he bribed local officials so that he could enter the city on the back of his horse, an entry which suits what the traveller James Capper called an Englishman's 'proper character' (Capper 1783: 10). Another Englishman who lived in Aleppo in the eighteenth century, as Eyles Irwin recorded, brought into the city 'a capriole from London' which he 'drove on the road' (Irwin 1787: II, 295). This carriage was seen as an innovation in Aleppo, as Eyles Irwin wrote, so much so that many people gathered to view 'such a grand spectacle' brought into their city by an Englishman.

Such an anecdote, and the one told by Ives about the yacht, reveals how the English constantly cared about their image in the Levant. James Capper, who wrote about Lord Algernon Percy's horse-riding experience in Cairo, advised his countrymen who wish to travel in the region to project a genteel image on the locals. 'A person who from necessity is obliged, or from disposition inclined to be a rigid economist', he wrote, 'should not attempt to travel for curiosity or pleasure in the Levant; where the insolence and bigotry of the natives can only be got the better of by an appearance of wealth and liberality, should business oblige him to pass that way he must do the best he can' (Capper 1783: 10).

In the nineteenth century, the English in the Levant continued to use pageantry to impress the locals, but the spectacle they cultivated did not aim to gain the locals' respect; it was rather meant to install within them a sense of fear. In his *Narrative of the Euphrates Expedition* (1868), the English explorer Francis Rawdon Chesney recorded how in Bir, a town near the Euphrates, the steamer he built to explore the Euphrates and Tygris rivers fascinated the Arabs: when seeing it 'stemming a rapid current', he wrote, 'their astonishment knew no bounds'; 'ten Englishmen', he said, 'could take their town' (Chesney 1868: 223). Chesney, whose efforts to navigate the Euphrates and Tygris in the 1830s were supported by the British government and King William IV, recalled one benefit of English pageantry in the Levant. It evokes fears among the locals. In the following decades, Britons who visited and resided in the Arab-Ottoman world confirmed what Chesney previously observed – that is, British pageantry helps to make the Arabs submit to British power.[52] But this was not what Ives understood of the nature of his encounters in the Ottoman-Arab region. Ives found that those encounters unleashed huge possibilities of projecting his image of a gentleman and generous person, not just another British nabob whose only objective was to exploit the natives and siphon their wealth through illegitimate means, which could be further used to corrupt the body politic of a free nation.[53]

Meeting Polite Muslims

On 10 May 1758, Ives and his English friends anchored at 'small distance from Dewana commonly called (as is the province) Hasca' (Ives 1773: 259). Dewana (modern Al Diwaniyeah) is the capital city of Al-Qadisiyyah governorate in central Iraq. The city is now known as a railway corridor between Baghdad and Basra. William Shaw, the British resident in Basra, had previously advised Ives and his companions to show their utmost respect to Ali Agha, the ruler at the time, who controlled a large swathe of land between Basra and Baghdad. '[W]e are to salute [the Agha] with even number of guns, the more the better', Shaw said to them. Shaw has explained to his countrymen the etiquettes required in the presence of Muslim rulers: 'We must particularly remember to go in slippers, and be very careful not to thrust our legs and feet out, but to contrive (after the Turkish manner) to sit with them across' (Ives 1773: 235). The English in the Levant, as Ives and his countrymen living in the region recall, were not only respected in the region due to their well-orchestrated appearances; they were also respected because of their ability to show respect towards local culture, traditions and manners. Ives reported how entering the guest room, '[a]t our coming to the carpet we put off our shoes, which we had slipped down for that purpose before we left the vessel' (Ives 1773: 261). The governor greeted them and inquired about their health. 'He' also spoke about 'our company's affairs at Bengal', Ives wrote (Ives 1773: 261). He was curious about 'the revolutions which had lately happened there [...] our fleet in India [...] the several powers at war in Europe [and] the face of affairs there at present; and at last, the navigation of the river Euphrates of the latitude of Bassora, Dewana, &c'. (Ives 1773: 261).

Using the word 'revolution', Ives carefully chose to give the impression that this Ottoman governor was a neutral man; that is, he regarded the British expansion in India as simply one of change of government rather than a conquest. The word 'revolution' throughout the eighteenth century meant, as Raymond Williams explained, 'change', 'alteration' and 'movements of Fortune and Providence' and a 'necessary innovation of a new order, supported by the increasingly positive sense of progress'.[54] The use of the word 'revolution' here contradicts the official line of the Ottoman sultan, Mustafa III, and the sharif of Mecca at the time, who, as the English officer and traveller James Capper wrote in 1785, were concerned about British expansion in India to the extent that a ruling was issued in 1774 banning the English from trading in Egypt and the Arabian Gulf, calling the English violent and deceitful: the East India Company, as we read in the ruling, 'have obtained a footing in Hindostan' through 'deceit and violence'(Capper 1783: xvii). Ali Agha, Ives found, did not see the English in this light.

Ives's conversation with Ali Agha clearly aimed to show how the English were highly respected in the Arab-Ottoman world. The reality, however, was more complicated than this. In an age when the English vessels dominated the navigation of the Indian Ocean, Ottoman and Arab merchants feared British competition in the Red Sea trade. Such fear led to the issuance of an *Hatt-i Sharif* (edict) in 1779 barring the English from sailing and trading in the region.[55] The Hijaz rulers, including the sharif of Mecca, feared British expansions in India because they feared that British dominance in India could impoverish Muslim rulers who annually sent endowments to the holy cities of Mecca and Medina. But despite the fear of the Hijaz rulers, the East India Company presidency in Bombay did not stop Muslim rulers from sending gifts to the holy cities of Mecca and Medina because the East India Company, most notably Warren Hastings, cared about the idea of cultivating friendly relations with Ottoman and Arab governors of the region. Hastings often sought to open a line of communication between India and the Arab markets via the ports of Jeddah and Suez. To that end, aboard the ship *The Adventure* that sailed between Madras and Mocha in Yemen in April 1772, Eyles Irwin wrote, the English delivered 'a considerable sum of money [...] which was a present from the nabob of Carnatic to the temple of Mecca' (Irwin 1780: I, 18–19). Irwin further states that the English encouraged this tradition of delivering gifts from India to the Hijaz region, because doing so would make the Arabs friendly to the English: they will show them 'the utmost of favourable treatment in the neighbourhood of Medina' (Irwin 1780: 19).

Ives did not disclose whether he offered English presents to local rulers of cities and towns located between Basra and Aleppo, but he did talk about their hospitality towards the East India Company representatives in the region. Ives and his friends were entertained by Ali Agha:

> a small cup of coffee was brought, and after a short interval a small bason [basin] of warm sweet water scented with roses; lastly our handkerchiefs were wetted with rosewater, and our nostrils fumigated with the smoke of Ambergrease and Agala wood. (261)

The historian of Ottoman-British diplomatic relations Michael Talbot argues that offering coffee and other refreshments (such as sherbet and sweetmeats) constituted an essential part of 'Ottoman diplomatic hospitality' (Talbot 2017: 147).[56] Ives was clearly familiar with this tradition, showing how the English were highly respected in Ottoman-Arab land.

Such acts of gifting were seen by Ives as counterexamples to the idea prevailed in England about English officials in the East, the people who were often viewed by Britons as corrupt in their dealings with Eastern rulers. The presents the English travellers received from the governors of the Levant did not match in worth the expensive presents (jewels, money and land grants) English officials often received from Indian rulers. In fact, as most English travellers in Ottoman and Arab regions often complained, it was Muslim rulers, rather than English travellers and consuls, who often received English and European handouts in the form of presents.[57] Yet they admitted that Europeans benefitted from offering gifts to local rulers. Gifts bred peace and helped to ease trade between Europe and the Levant.[58]'[A]s soon as we got from our seats', Ives continued, 'Mr. Doidge, our elected chief, had a silk *Pelise* or vest put upon him, lined with Ermine, worth about ten pounds, for which he made one of his handsomest bows to Ally Aga' (261-2).[59] Such an expensive article of clothing was usually offered to men of higher office in the Ottoman Empire. The Greek merchant Elias Habesci in 1784 reported that 'When the Mufti', the supreme religious authority in the state, 'is elected he is ordered by the Grant Signor to repair to the palace, where he invests him in his dignity and office with his own hands, by clothing him with a pellicle of ermine [...]' (Habesci 1784: 111). Such a practice of honouring men of higher status in the empire was extended to include foreign ambassadors.[60]

By accepting such a symbolic gift, Ives showed his readers how he and his friends were seen by the Ottoman governor as men of public office. Henry Doidge, who received the gift, was Admiral Charles Watson's secretary in India. He and the rest of the English travellers (Ives, Captain James Alms, Captain Lindsey, Mr Pigot and Mr Pye) were Royal Navy personnel. The fact that these men were in the king's service explains why Ottoman governors gave them a formal reception. The idea that they were seen as, in Ives's phrasing, the 'men whose business was to serve King and country by sea' explains why the Ottoman governor gifted them 'a silk *Pelise*' (Ives 1773: 313).

It is revealing that the scene of hospitality in the preceding passage resembles the one we read in Ives's description of the encounter between the nabob of Arcot, Muhammad Ali Wallajah, and Admiral Watson in Madras in 1755. The nabob, Ives recalled, 'ordered a rich perfume of what is called Otta of roses to be brought to him, a few drops which, he put into his hand, and having himself opened the bosom of Mr. Watson's shirt, he rubbed the same over the admiral's breast' (Ives 1773: 72). The sexual illusion in the scene above was qualified when Ives insured that the Indian perfume touching the body of an English official represents 'the highest honour' an India ruler could show to an Englishman (Ives 1773: 72).[61] Ives's reference to the honourable exchange between Watson and the nabob above was meant to invite the reader to rethink the prevailing critique during the period of the corrupting influence of Indian wealth on English morals and body politic.

Ives noted how Indian rulers were not only interested in showering their English guests with expensive perfumes but with expensive gifts. Admiral Watson, however, Ives added, refused to accept gifts from Indian rulers. 'The Nabob appeared extremely surprised at this uncommon strain of generosity in the admiral', Ives wrote, 'though at the same time he could not be displeased with it' (Ives 1773: 72). In eighteenth-century India, the culture of the gifts between the English and local rulers, as many scholars indicate, was entangled in a web of corrupt relations that stirred a whirl of public outcry in Britain.[62] Local Indian rulers often offered diamonds, golden pieces and land grants which, as Natasha Eaton affirmed, put pressure on each party (the English and local rulers) to corner one another into a relation of indebtedness, a social and political relation which troubled British political and moral conception of virtue, one based on the inalienability of the self; indebtedness, as the ideologues of virtue argued, necessities loss of autonomy and opens the door for exchanging favours. It is expected to be shown by merchants and pedlars in the marketplace rather than by citizens living in a free polity.[63] To that end, many in Britain associated an Eastern gift culture with despotism and corruption, which put pressure on the British Parliament to investigate the case of British officials in India receiving hefty gifts from local rulers. 'The select committee of the House of Commons that sat in 1772-1773', the historian Nicholas Dirks wrote, 'estimated that "presents" worth of over two million pounds had been distributed in Bengal between 1757 and 1765' (Dirks 2006: 10). In response to this scandal at the centre of which was Lord Clive, whom Ives praised in his travel book, the government decided to outlaw receiving and distributing presents in India: this was mandated in the Regulation Act of 1773.[64]

If we juxtapose the two scenes of hospitality (Ottoman and Indian) in Ives's text, then we can see that describing a meeting between Englishmen and Eastern rulers was intended to placate moralists in England who accused English officials abroad of being corrupt. The politics of the gift here is important because in the early modern world, as scholars remind us, the idea of distributing gifts played an important role in the culture of obligation between the giver and the receiver.[65] In the early modern Middle Eastern state, the culture of the gift insured a road to peace, amity, trust and friendship, but it revealed the power of the giver over the receiver and the obligation of the later towards the former. For example, in 1743, when As'ad Pasha Al-Azem (1706–1758) was appointed governor of Damascus, the ruler of Acre at the time, Zaher Ul-Umar (1668–1775), sent him 50 loads of rice, sugar and cloth: these gifts were sent one year after Sulayman Pasha Al-Azem (d. 1743), the uncle of As'ad Pasha and ruler of Damascus before him, had attacked the castle of Tiberias where Zaher was hiding from the Ottoman sultan.[66] Sir James Porter, English ambassador to the Ottoman Porte between 1741 and 1761, recalled how in 1746 '[t]he Emperor of Morocco, with whom the Grand Seignior has scarce a connection, and who is almost unknown in Constantinople, sent very lately two ambassadors, with presents of great value, merely and solely to secure this pilgrimage [route] to his subjects' (Porter 1768: I, 33). Elias Habesci noted how many newly appointed Ottoman governors to rich provinces were 'obliged to pay the Vizir a considerable sum', and while serving in their posts they often sent to Istanbul 'annual presents' in order to lobby the central government to keep them in their posts (Habesci 178: 174).

That culture of the gift in the preceding examples suggests an imbalance of power between the distributer and receiver of gifts. Michael Talbot argues, however, that the exchange of the gift between British travellers and Ottoman governors included performative rituals and symbolic gestures that complicate a simplistic argument that one party felt superior to the other. For the English, as Talbot found in his work on the rituals of diplomatic receptions of European ambassadors in Istanbul, offering and receiving gifts 'was a public display of their status and wealth, a showcase of the dignity of the ambassador and of the British presence' (Talbot 2017: 148). For the Ottoman government, however, 'it was a demonstration to the populace of its capital of a foreign nation paying submission to the sultan, with a symbolic journey from "European" *Frengistan* to "Ottoman" land' (Talbot 2017: 148). Such a scene of diplomacy, one redolent with different assumptions, appeared in Ives's text. The Ottoman governor offered the English a silk gown worth £10, but in return the governor received an English bow. Ives and his friends, moreover, appeared during this reception as polite gentlemen who represented their country well, showing how the English and their king were highly respected in the East.

A Man of Improvement

Ives and his friends arrived in Baghdad on 20 May 1758. Before entering the city, they were welcomed 'in the most hospitable manner' by Robert Garden, 'an accomplished young gentleman' who worked as a writer in the 'company's service' in Bombay before he was 'later appointed second at Bassora and is at present engaged in business of consequence in Baghdad' (Ives 1773: 271–272). Ives recalled how Garden warmly received them in his house in Baghdad, but he also recalled how Garden instructed them about the correct way an Englishman is expected to carry himself among the locals. For example, he explained to them how the Arabs frown at foreigners who seek to chat with local women. Garden's sensitivity to the local culture was greatly appreciated in Baghdad so much so that, unlike the majority of Christians living in the city, he was allowed to wear clothes of green and white colours, which only Muslims were allowed to wear at the time. Such a privilege, Ives discovered, 'is permitted to strangers in a respectable station […]', hinting at the exaggeration of the reports of many European travellers on how Muslims often persecuted Christians who dared to wear colour green or even touch it in public (Ives 1773: 288).

Ives mentioned how his countryman, Garden, in Baghdad was granted a privilege rarely noted among the European community in the Levant. Garden gained such a higher status in Baghdad because of his commercial rather than political character. In an age in which the office of English resident in the region did not represent the British government but rather the East India Company, Garden's 'respectable station' in Baghdad was mainly earned through commercial relations.[67] In Baghdad, the British only succeeded in obtaining a 'Consulary Barat' from Constantinople in 1764, which means that English activities in the region during the time when Ives was there were mainly commercial and mostly dependent on friendly relations with local governors.[68] Garden's life and career in Mesopotamia could be seen as surprising for those versed in the writings of British residents and government agents who served in Mesopotamia in the nineteenth and twentieth centuries. James Claudius Rich (1787–1821) served as an East India Company resident between 1808 and 1814. Two years before he left the Residency, 'the designation of Resident was changed into that of Political Agent'.[69] What this meant was that the East India Company and the British government were not only interested in commerce but also in political conditions of the region. James Silk Buckingham who visited Baghdad in the early part of the nineteenth century recalled how Rich commanded, in additions to the servants, interpreters and administrators in the British residency, 'a company of [Indian] sepoys' who 'furnished a bodyguard'; he also commanded 'A troop of European Hussars [...]', showing the rising political and military power of the British in the Persian Gulf (Buckingham 1827: II, 211). 'Mr Rich was universally considered to be the most powerful man in Baghdad, next to the Pasha; and some even questioned whether the Pasha himself would not at any time shape his conduct according to Mr Rich's suggestions and advice, rather than as his own council might wish', Buckingham marvelled (Buckingham 1827: II, 211).

Unlike Garden, Rich showed no appreciation of the local culture. In his *Narrative of Residence in Koordistan* (1836), he compared locals with 'savage' tribes in the Pacific region and called them 'barbarous'; he even dehumanised them by comparing them with animals.[70] Rich did not show English politeness to those among whom he lived and worked. Nor did he exchange gifts and visits with Arab tribal leaders and Ottoman governors. As an unpublished account of the East India Company indicates, Rich did not seek to cultivate relations with local governors, which made the East India Company consider suspending him in 1815.[71]

While in office in Baghdad, Rich spent a great deal of his time studying the history and languages of the Levant and Persia. He collected coins, manuscripts, statues and inscriptions which, after he died, were purchased by the British Museum.[72] A careful reading of his first publication, *Memoire on the Ruins of Babylon*, first appeared in the Viennese journal *Mine de l'Orient*, will show the image of the scholarly traveller that Rich cared to present to his readers and interlocuters in the field of history, philology and archaeology. His investigations of Mesopotamia, which was associated in the European-Christian imagination with the site of Babylon, betrayed a scientific mentality rooted in the idea of conducting archaeological research in the field (observation), building on previous research and explorations (falsification) and clearing the muddled ground for future research and exploration (progress).[73] Rich was familiar with previous writings about Mesopotamia: the English translation of the Syrian geographer Abulfeda, the works of ancient writers such as Strabo and Pliney, James Rennell's *The Geographical System of Herodotus* (1800) and the travel book, initially published in French in 1748, of the Swedish scientist and antiquarian Jonas Otter who served as a French consul in Basra between 1742 and 1744. Dissatisfied with what these writers mentioned about Mesopotamia, Rich hired some Arab servants to find remains of the hidden architectural treasures hidden under the ground, showing how a traveller's role in the Middle East should not be focused on what is laid above the ground but rather on what is hidden underneath it.[74] With Rich, the age of European antiquarianism in the Middle East had come to an end. A new age of archaeology had just started.[75] In parallel to the idea of discovering the hidden truth of the past was that of distancing the self from the local culture.

Eighteenth-century Britons in the region – men like Garden, Ives and Carmichael (see Chapter one) – were not professional archaeologists whose search for antiquities coalesced with a rising imperial power in the Levant. Nor were they a breed of scholars who, in Bolingbroke's phrasing, uselessly spent their lives researching the 'dark mazes of antiquity' (Bolingbroke 1752: I, 14). Rather, they were humanist antiquarians for whom learning about the past of these lands offered a useful lesson for the moderns.[76] Most importantly, it is the social network with which they interacted that helped them to roam freely in the world of the ancients, that is, in barren spaces full of old stones and half-broken columns.

It is due to Robert Garden's relations with local governors and Arab tribes that Ives was able to reach *Tauk Kesra*, an ancient Sasanian-era monument now located in the modern town of Salman Pak, a few miles south of Baghdad.[77] Before visiting the site, Ives, unlike Rich, did not mention that he consulted previous writings about it.[78] Rather Ives, by measuring the monument, cared more about conveying the image of himself being a discoverer of something new in an age in which amateur antiquarianism secured many rich people from relatively humble backgrounds (one here recalls the story of rise and progress of the Scottish surgeon John Hunter who was also a collector of antiquities) a fast entry into the world of respectability and politeness, a world still dominated by men from the upper ranks. Ives was not a philologist, historian or astronomer: what he mostly cared about while dabbling in the world of ruins were two things – to raise his status as a man of taste and, like what we previously saw in Carmichael's account, to find a lesson about the past that could benefit modern readers.

Once in London, Ives met Charles Morton, the secretary of the Royal Society and chief librarian at the British Museum, who examined an old manuscript Ives bought in Gawerko near Mosul from 'one of the Deacons' who 'declared [it] to be a Gospel' (Ives 1773: 319). The act of buying 'the Gospel' here is revealing because it shows how one powerful force in modern culture (money) penetrated the souls of Christians living in a land known for its importance to the history of Christianity; these Christians, as Ives shows, exchanged a symbol of their faith with a few coins.[79] Ives experimented with this tension between money and faith after he read the French traveller, Jean Baptiste-Tavernier (1605–1689), who passed through the region in 1643. Tavernier offered two churchmen he met there '200 Piasters' to sell him an old Bible he saw in their church, but he was not successful (Tavernier 1678: 70). '[T]hey durst not sell it', he wrote, 'in regard it belonged to the Church and was not at their disposal' (Tavernier 1678: 70). Britain and France since Tavernier visited Mesopotamia changed: they became more and more distanced from an organised form of religion. Their print culture in both countries became increasingly sympathetic to Enlightenment ideas of universalism, scepticism and materialism. It was an Enlightenment culture which showed limited but visible toleration towards religious dissent, an attitude encouraged by governments actively seeking to dislodge residual power of the church.[80] Further, the Bible, in modern Britain and France, became, in a Voltairean sense, 'a product of human history and culture'; that is, as James M. Byrne argues, the dominant interpretation of the Bible moved beyond frameworks of Christian pietism into those of universal history (Byrne 1997: 12). Such cultural shift shaped Ives's admiration of the manuscript he bought in Mesopotamia, which he considered a valuable historical – not only religious – document. 'Dr. Morton', wrote Ives, 'decisively pronounced it [the Bible] to be the old or simple Syriac version of the Old Testament' (Ives 1773: 319).

Ives was successful in bringing to England a Christian manuscript from Mesopotamia which, like the fossils, medals and statues that many travellers and antiquarians collected throughout the eighteenth century, acquired various meanings throughout the course of their journey to European shores.[81] In Mesopotamia, the manuscript represented the triumph of the Market over Faith; in Britain the manuscript helped Ives to enter the social circles that would have been inaccessible had he returned empty-handed. Charles Morton never set foot in Mesopotamia, and yet he conversed with Ives about the authenticity of the manuscript. Like Ives, Morton was a medical professional. He read medicine in Leiden under the great medical celebrity of the Enlightenment, Herman Boerhaave (1668–1738), the man whose medical achievements were, as Samuel Johnson in an essay in *The Gentleman's Magazine* in 1739, wrote, 'so loudly celebrated' (329: 1787). Upon his return to England in 1745, Morton worked as a physician in a hospital in Kendal. In 1751, he was admitted to the Royal College of Physicians and on the establishment of the British Museum in 1765 he was appointed a librarian in the manuscript and medal department. In 1760, he succeeded Peter Duval as a secretary to the Royal Society. Morton's intellectual interests included medicine, astronomy and travel writing. Early in his career at the British Museum, Morton edited and published the travel narrative of Bulstrode Whitelocke who was sent on a mission by Oliver Cromwell to Queen Christine of Sweden in 1653 to negotiate an alliance with a fellow Protestant power.[82]

The act of buying the manuscript helped Ives to develop a contact with a celebrity antiquarian and physician of the period. Morton's fame as a scholar and gentleman reached many British and European scientists and antiquarians stationed in Britain and abroad.[83] He supported the British scientific expeditions which set out to observe the transit of Venus in the East Indies, St. Helena and North America.[84] He corresponded with John Swinton (1703–1707), an Oxford philologist, whose fame in England was shaped by his studies of ancient Roman and Greek coins and Palmyrine inscriptions.[85] Morton also corresponded with Benjamin Franklin (1706–1790) about how he could dispatch letters from the Royal Society to two British astronomers and surveyors, Charles Mason (1728–1786) and Jeremiah Dixon (1733–1779), who, in 1762, sailed to America to survey, map and mark the boundaries between Pennsylvania and Maryland.[86] Morton was an example of an Enlightenment scholar who believed that collective scientific collaboration between nations can sink sectarian and religious differences. To that end, he read to the Royal Society a scientific paper by a Jesuit missionary in China in the 1760s at a time when Britain was locked in a global war with France.[87]

Ives was not widely known in the scholarly world as Morton was, but Ives was aware of the period's scholarly interests and scientific networks. An example of how Ives was aware of these scholarly networks appears in the commentary he offered about one monument, a tower, he saw on the road between Baghdad and Aleppo. 'The present Turks, Jews, and Arabians are fond of believing this to be the identical ruin of the ancient tower of Babel', Ives wrote. But, he added, this cannot be true: 'to set about confuting them would be losing times in trifles' (Ives 1773: 298). Ives suggested that the tower was built by the ancients either to watch their enemy moves or to advance the state of knowledge in the field of astronomy. Babylonians, Ives wrote, were known for their efforts to advance knowledge about 'the various motions of the heavenly bodies' (298). Such an observation is not backed by evidence, but what it shows is that the debate in Europe about the importance of advancing scientific knowledge in the field of astronomy shaped his writing about Mesopotamian ruins.[88] Anthony Shirley, who visited the Babylonian tower in the last decade of the sixteenth century, consulted the Bible and concluded: 'a small part of the great Tower' is something 'which God hath suffered to stand [...] for an eternal testimony of his great worke in the confusion of man's pride' (Shirley: 21-22). Ives, unlike Shirley, did not consult the Bible while trying to understand the reason the ancients built this tower. Nor did he posit the tower as a testimony to the greatness of God and the limitedness of 'man's pride'. Rather the tower testifies to the great strides and improvements which man made in the past: the idea that the tower might have been 'used' as 'an observatory' for inspecting 'the various motions of heavenly bodies', wrote Ives, indicates that 'science was so much cultivated among the ancient inhabitants of this country, that even the Grecians [...] could never deny the Babylonians the honour of having laid the foundations of astronomy' (Ives 1773: 298). For Ives, the tower was a testimony to man's ability to innovate and improve, an idea that contrasts with what Carmichael's religious and moral sensibilities, as we saw in Chapter one, informed him: for Carmichael, ancients were honourable; for Ives, they were scientific and innovative people, just like the moderns in Europe.

Bourgeoise Values

Ives's conclusion about the limitless power of man appeared in an age in which the British were competing with the French not only for economic and military hegemony in Europe and the colonies but also in peaceful chambers of science: astronomy was a field of cooperation and competition.[89] For Ives, thus, the role of man is to build and improve his material conditions. Any talk of an unhappy life should direct the blame to people's unwillingness to improve rather than to the will of God. He made this claim while encountering ruins in the deserts. But he confirmed it after conversing with a few Muslims he met in the northern parts of Syria. 'While in the Kann [guesthouse]' in

Diyarbakir, Ives wrote, 'I ordered our interpreter Francisco to enter into a conversation with a poor Turk, relative to the late famine' which hit Syria and Mesopotamia in the 1750s (Ives 1773: 337). The man explained how 'dreadful' the situation was in these lands to the extent that people found nothing to eat except dead bodies. The Muslim man then was curious to know about 'the probability of such an event happening in our country', Ives added (Ives 1773: 337). Ives's reply surprised this 'poor Turk':

> a famine had not been known for more than a century, or hardly heard of us; and was in the utmost amazement to find, that by the laws of England a poor man could not starve, so long as there were any rich to provide him with food and raiment. This point about the poor laws, so struck the Turk, that with clinched hands, and eyes fixed towards heaven, he for a while seem employed in ejaculatory prayer: at last, he gravely, but with confidence replied, 'The happiness of this world is yours: Ours, in a future state'. (337)

This conversation between Ives and the poor Muslim man mostly focused on how the English were doing better than the 'Turks' in the field of helping the poor. But the conversation also reveals a tension between two different conceptions of the good life: one rooted in an immaterial conception of the meaning of life (which Ives associated with misery) and the other shaped by materialist thought focusing on replacing heavenly designs with human actions.

These two structures of feeling in Ives's text were not illustrative of a serious engagement with the plight of the poor both in the Levant and Britain. As the nineteenth-century English diplomat in the Ottoman Empire, David Urquhart, shows in his critique of European writings about the East, European travellers often neglect 'the moral and political interests which that land affords' and instead 'sketch external objects by the words which exist in the European language'; that is, they use a European frame of reference and pre-conceived notions to explain what they saw in their eyes (Urquhart 1838: I, xv–xvii). In the forgoing passage, thus, Ives had nothing to say against the political conditions of the region where rulers, as historians have argued, heavily taxed villagers, failed to improve the land, monopolised crops and accumulated large amounts of stolen capital in their coffers.[90] Nor was he interested in exploring the natural causes that led to famines during the period: extreme weather conditions and regular motions of locust swarms across the land.[91]

But the myopic vision in the said passage is rather understandable if we bring into the discussion the efforts of a man of middle-class background who wanted to convey the message to his reader that humans can make their own destiny rather than rely on an external and unseen entity to change their lives for the better. But while praising the efforts of the government and the elites in England who helped the poor, Ives said nothing about the difficult conditions of people in British workhouses.[92] Many scholars have demonstrated how in a period in which Britain's economy and empire were expanding, poverty remained a central concern for many social and political commentators of the period despite the efforts of the government to tackle poverty by creating an institutional framework rooted in the idea that the poor needed to be shepherded away from a life of idleness into that of economic productivity. In the first half of the eighteenth century, many people in Britain were below the bread line as food prices rose sharply. Parliament in 1722 legislated for the establishment of workhouses or poorhouses – 'sixty in the country and fifty in the metropolis', as Sir Fredrick Morton Eden wrote in 1779, where the poor were 'lodged, kept and maintained' (Eden 1779: I, 268–269).[93]

Alfred William Coats argued that the government was aware of this problem: in the second half of the century, the British government together with the rich in society encouraged philanthropy and actively sought reforms of the workhouse institution, a move which principally aimed to contain the social unrest caused by rising foodstuffs and bad harvests.[94] Ives, like many social reformers of the period, as Niall O'Flaherty showed, proposed that providing for the poor was the responsibility of the government and society. Those in government and the upper ranks were seen as duty-bound to provide for the poor.[95] Ives might have disagreed with one observer who in 1725 wrote that 'A Work-House is a name that carries along with it an Idea of Correction and Punishment; and many of our Poor have taken such an Aversion to living in it Upon that Account, as all the Reason and Argument in the World can never overcome' (Ives 1773: 35). Anna Moltchanova and Susannah Ottaway have shown how many voices throughout the period resisted the commonplace philosophy behind the institutionalisation of the poor in England: that is, they rejected the idea that in order to win the right of subsistence in workhouses, the poor had to forgo their natural and labour rights.[96]

Ives did not refer to the critiques the British government faced in its efforts to handle the problem of poverty.[97] Missing in his narrative, moreover, was the idea that the British government's pursuits of land enclosures impoverished many labourers and farmers in England and Scotland.[98] 'Proprietors of land', as Lord Kames wrote, used all measures 'to drive the poor out of the parish and prevent all persons from settling in it who are likely to become a burden: cottages are demolished and marriage obstructed' (Kames 1774: III, 45). Furthermore, Ives recalled nothing about the notorious mercantilism of the East India Company in Bengal in the early 1770s which impoverished and starved many people (Ives's book was published during the period in which many associated the horrors of the Bengal Famine with the monopolies and greed of the East India Company).[99]

It is also revealing that Ives recalled the philanthropic spirit of the British government and the English rich, but he did not mention anything about how the rich and government in the Ottoman land tackled poverty, a subject that fascinated many Europeans who visited the region. Early modern European travellers always praised the spirit of charity among Muslims, but they also found that the rich were not completely committed to it. Those who extended their charity to the sick, poor and animals often aimed to boost their image as men of power and prestige.[100] However, two eighteenth-century travellers mostly focused on the theological, instead of the social and political, context of charity. The French linguist and botanist Jean de Thevenot, who travelled extensively in the Levant in the second half of the seventeenth century recalled how 'The Turks Fourth Command is Charity, by that Command they are obliged to give yearly to the Poor, the fortieth part of their good if they have poor Kindred, they ought to prefer them before others; if they have none they should give their Charity to their poor Neighbours; and if they have no poor Neighbours, they give it to the first they meet' (Thevenot 1687: 50). 'This Command', he added, 'is not ill observed among the

Turks, for they are very charitable, and very willingly help the wretched, without minding their Religion, whether they be Turks, Christians or Jews' (Thevenot 1687: 50). Like Thevenot, the English churchman Richard Pococke admired the Islamic context of charity towards the sick and the poor when he visited Damascus in 1737. He noted how the 'Turks' built hospitals in the city to provide succour to the sick and the poor. Their 'charity consist in giving victuals to the poor once or twice a week; and sometimes in distributing medicines to the sick on certain days' (Pococke 1745: II, 122). Pococke, like Thevenot, noted how the idea of charity in Islam is rooted in a religious understanding of the sanctity of human life, which motivates Muslims to provide for the sick and the poor in their hospitals. On a wall in a hospital in the eastern part of Damascus Pococke, an inscription (translated) captured the theological context of charity: 'O God, for the sake of the leprous prophet, a friend of our prophet, and for the sake of all other prophets, give unto us health and peace' (Pococke 1745: 122).

Thevenot and Pococke were not the only European travellers who admired the charity of Muslims towards the sick and the poor. But they were, unlike most European travellers in the region, the only Europeans who focused on how Muslims associate charity with law and also consider it an act of devotion. Others, however, like the Scotsman Alexander Russell, used a secular frame in their explanation of Muslim charity. Russell, like Pococke and Thevenot, mentioned the idea that the rich and the government in Aleppo were concerned about tackling poverty: the rich give alms liberally, and the benevolent spirit of the government is reflected in the hospitals, fountains, bridges and *caravansaries* that it builds in the city. However, he explained how a culture of individualism sometimes affected people's understanding of the idea of poverty. The Ottomans do not have poor laws and workhouses, Russell wrote, and charity was mostly the responsibility of the individual, what Eyal Ginio called 'private altruism'(Ginio 2003: 166).[101] That the question of poverty need not be institutionalised in Aleppo, Russell added, was because 'the industrious poor' (here Russell may have referred to the poor in Britain) often 'support themselves by manual labour, and never have recourse to the public' (Russell 1794: II, 206). The poor in Aleppo, Russell concluded, were often in work except when there was 'dearth' which required the rich to step in to relieve them. None of the negative thoughts that many in Britain associated with the poor, such as their idleness and criminality, Russell noted, appeared in Muslim culture, thus hinting at the idea that criminalising the poor for not being in work in Britain is something Britons need to reconsider.

Like Russell, Ives agreed that people, including the poor, should oversee their own destiny. Yet, Ives had nothing to say about the Islamic conception of charity and how the Ottoman state tackled poverty.[102] Moreover, Ives did not mention how Islam or Christianity tackle poverty because if he stepped into that territory, then he would undermine his own secular understanding of well-being and happiness, as we previously noted. For Ives, man is responsible for his well-being, and if he failed to improve himself, then the state and the rich in society need to step in to help. Ives's understanding of poverty betrays the character of the rationalist for whom human faults, such as poverty, can be solved by exercising the laws, mobilising civil duty and energising social responsibility rather than using the religious framework of Christian or Muslim charity.

Thus, Ives did not appear to have been concerned about the role of faith in alleviating the suffering of people, a position which some Christian thinkers and writers during the period advocated, particularly those who were at the forefront of helping the poor in England, such as John Wesley (1703–1791).[103] It is in poor circles in Islamic land that Ives managed to confirm his bourgeoise ethics, one rooted in the awareness that he belonged to a class that was able to change their material condition and refine their manners, that is, become genteel.[104]

Conclusion

Back on the road, Ives and his fellow travellers joined the caravan of Abdullah Basha in Diyarbakir. The destination was now Aleppo where the English Levant Company held a trading post and consulate. Abdullah Basha had been appointed governor of Diyarbakir before the Ottoman court in Istanbul moved him to Aleppo. He was a friend of the English merchants and consuls in the region, mainly Alexander Drummond, the Levant Company representative in Aleppo, who warmly welcomed Ives and his friends upon their arrival in the city. After staying in Aleppo for a week, Ives and his countrymen joined a caravan heading to the port city of Latakia where they hired a boat to Cyprus and from there they sailed to Europe. The journey in the overland routes ended in Latakia, but the narrative of the journey offered a commentary on the human condition in modern times. Ives posited the land and the people whom he encountered on these routes as a blank screen upon which Enlightenment values of improvement, refinement and politeness were projected. For many Enlightenment literati, as we saw in the introduction, politeness is the trait of European commercial nations where arts and sciences were cultivated. In his travel account, Ives established the progressivist idea that material improvement produces social and moral improvements. However, he did not view Europeans as superior to Muslims, Arabs and Turks. Rather, improvement of manners as a trope in his *A Journey* was something of a global context in which all people can achieve, given that they overcome the hurdles of nature and step into the territory of culture. Improvement was real and happening, but people need to work hard to achieve it.

Despite the universal tone of his book, Ives was very much rooted in his English background. Ives's journey in the East showed how manners – not moral and religious convictions and social background – define a polite gentleman.[105] For Ives, politeness is a modern and democratising pursuit to which not only the aristocracy but also men of middle ranks subscribed. Such a democratising feature of modern life was called by Thomas Woodman 'social freedom' and noted in such spaces in England as the coffee houses, spaces 'set off [...] from the restrictions of courtly life' (Woodman 1989: 21). Yet the relaxed social mixing in this culture of politeness, as Woodman argues, should not be seen as an affirmation of the liberal and open nature of English society.[106] Rather it was 'a way of reconciling an aristocratic ethos with a limited acceptance of the aspirations of other classes in a laissez-faire economic system' (Woodman 1989: 22).[107]Ives, an English surgeon of humble background, found in the idea of travelling in the East 'an art', as Tobias Smollett put it in his *Travels Through France and Italy* (1778), 'that necessarily implies a sense of decorum, and a delicacy of sentiment', a performance which aimed to project a certain idea of Englishness centred around politeness; that is, politeness, he revealed, is a democratising move that creates new opportunities for people like him who aspired to move up the social ladder (Smollett 1778: I, 100). Polite manners – not privileges of birth – were all that Ives got. The journey abroad helped him to rethink the social hierarchy in England.

Notes

1 Dror Wharman, *The Making of the Modern Self: Identity and Culture in Eighteenth Century England* (New Haven and London: Yale University Press, 2004), 166; 179. Marshall Berman, *All That is Solid Melts into Air* (New York: Penguin Books, 1982).

2 A good explanation of this tension in modern time is Charles Taylor's *Sources of the Self: The Making of Modern Identify* (Massachusetts: Harvard University Press, 1989). See pages 25–28.

3 See the chapter titled 'The Patricians and the Plebs' in E.P Thompson's *Customs in Common: Studies in Traditional Popular Culture* (London: Penguin Books, 1991).

4 Kramnick, 113.

5 Daniel Defoe distinguished between those who were born with title and wealth, what he called 'the born' gentlemen and those who acquired gentility through elevating their material and social status in society, 'the bred' gentlemen. Defoe, *The Complete English Gentleman*, ed. Karl Daniel Bülbring (London, 1890), 3.

6 Oxford Dictionary of National Biography [http://www.oxforddnb.com/view/article/14499]. Date of Access: 23 August 2016.

7 *The Naval Chronicle* from *July to December 1799,* 38 Vols (London, 1799), Vol II, 549–550.

8 Louis H. Roddis, *James Lind: Founder of Nautical Medicine* (New York: Henry Schuman, 1950), 15–16.

9 A good account of this exchange can be found in H. W. Richmond 's *The Navy in the War 1739–1748* (Cambridge: Cambridge University Press, 1920), Vol I, 160–161.

10 See chapter four in Nick Robins, *The Corporation that Changed the World: How the East India Company Shaped the Modern Multinational* (London: Pluto Press, 2006).

11 On Lind's life and career, see Roddis. A good account on James Lind's discoveries in naval medicine is Stephen R. Bown's *Scurvy: How a Surgeon, a Mariner, and a Gentlemen Solved the Greatest Medical Mystery of the Age of Sail* (London: St Martin Publishing, 2005). On the life and career of Charles Morton, see *The Philosophical Transactions of the Royal Society of London, Vol X from 1750 to 1755* (London, 1809), 219.

12 Nikolai Detlef Falck, *The Seaman's Medical Instructor* (London, 1774), I. See the introduction to Pratik Chakrabarti, *Medicine and Empire 1600–1960* (London: Palgrave, 2014).

13 *Letter to Clive from Edward Ives* in the British Library, Ms G 37/57/4, November 1773.

14 Ives published his book in the same year in which the British Parliament issued the Regulation Act, which was meant to curb the despotic and monopolistic practices of the Company servants in India. But, as we shall see in the following chapters, the debate about how to combine rule with justice and virtue occupied British travel writings about the East for the rest of the century. For an excellent discussion of the tension in Britain between virtue and commerce in the context of British India, see Tillman Nechtman, 'A Jewel in the Crown: Indian Wealth in Domestic Britain in the Late Eighteenth Century', *Eighteenth Century Studies* 1 (2007): 71–86; see also his *Nabobs: Empire and Identity in Eighteenth-Century Britain* (Cambridge: Cambridge University Press, 2010).

15 George Edward Cokayne, *Complete Baronetage: Volume V* (Exeter, 1906), 119.

16 See Thomas Sheridan's *A Plan of Education for the Noble Youth Nobility and Gentry of Great Britain Most Humbly Addressed to the Father of His People* (London, 1969).

17 Adam Smith, *An Inquiry into the Nature and Causes of the Wealth of Nations*, 2 vols (London, 1776), Vol I, 415. My argument in this chapter about Ives's middle-class values resemble those advanced by Philip K. Wilson in his study of the life and work of the eighteenth-century English surgeon Daniel Turner. See Wilson's Surgery, *Skin and Syphilis: Daniel*

Turner (1667–1741) (Amsterdam: Rodopi, 1999), 6–7. A good discussion on how surgeons during the period used their professions to beat the boundaries of class was pursued by Wendy Moore in her book on the Scottish surgeon John Hunter (1728–1793). See Moore's *The Knife Man: Blood, Blood Snatching and the Birth of Modern Surgery* (New York: Broadway Books, 2005).

18 *Diary and Consultations of Mr Alexander Douglas, Agent of the East India Company at Gombroon [Bandar-e 'Abbās] in the Persian Gulf, commencing 1 August 1757 and ending 31 July 1758,* British Library: India Office Records and Private Papers, IOR/G/29/11, 22–23.

19 *Diary and Consultations of Mr Alexander Douglas,* 12.

20 Arnold T. Wilson, *The Persian Gulf: A Historical Sketch* (Oxford: The Clarendon Press, 1928), 177.

21 John Wainwright, 'Remarks on the navigation of the Persian Gulph, 1809–1810' in *Steam Navigation to Internal and External Communications of India,* Vol 8. British Library: India Office Records and Private Papers, IOR/L/MAR/C/570, 142. On the sickly environment of Bander Abbas, see the travel account of the early modern physician John Fryer, *A New Account of East India and Persia* (London: Printed for R.R, 1698), 227.

22 On how medicine turned into a tool and product of imperialism, see Jim Downs's *Maladies of Empire: How Colonialism, Slavery, and War Transformed Medicine* (Cambridge, MA: Belknap Press, 2021); Ishita Pande's *Medicine, Race and Liberalism in British Bengal: Symptoms of Empire* (New York: Routledge, 2010); Rohan Deb Roy's *Malarial Subjects: Empire, Medicine and Nonhumans in British India, 1820–1909* (Cambridge: Cambridge University Press, 2017).

23 Dror Whatman found a similar anxiety in the experience of encountering difference in Britain's North America colonies, *The Making of the Modern Self,* 213–215.

24 Mary Lindemann, *Medicine and Society in Early Modern Europe* (Cambridge: Cambridge University Press, 1999) 101.

25 See a pamphlet published by the Levant Company titled 'The case of the Levant Company, in relation to the bill now depending before this Honourable House, for performing quarentine' (London, 1721). See Patrick Russell's account of the plague in Syria in *A Treatise of the Plague.* Another account of the plague appeared in William Wittman's 'Historical Journal of the Plague' which appeared as an appendix to his *Travels in Turkey, Asia Minor and Syria* (London, 1803), 516–537. The French traveller and philosopher Constantine Volney considered the plague as an Ottoman disease; see his *Considerations on the War with the Turk* (London, 1788), 58.

26 The German traveller Carsten Niebuhr in Yemen recalled how local physicians use the Senna plant for treating different diseases such as diarrhoea and 'Cholera Morbus', *Travels Through Arabia,* 2 vols (Edinburgh, 1791), Vol I, 354–355. On the medical value of Senna in Britain, see James Miller's *Botanicum Officinale: Or a Compendious Herbal: Giving an Account of All Such Plants as Are Now Used in the Practice of Physics* (London, 1722), 409.

27 Anon, *Medical Observations and Inquiries,* 2nd edition (London, 1758), Vol I, VI.

28 Aaron Hill, who travelled in the Levant in 1700, recalled how the English import from the region 'fine Rhubarb, Opium, Aloes, Balm of Gilead, Cassia [Gum Arabic], Coffee, and a thousand other Drugs of noted efficacy in Medicinal Operations', *A Full and Just Account of the Present State of the Ottoman Empire* (London, 1709), 78. Clearly Hill in the early 1700s, like other medical professionals in England, saw coffee as a medicinal drug.

29 On the important of Ottoman and Arab herbs and cures in eighteenth-century European medical culture, see Mohammad Sakhnini, 'Eighteenth-Century European Medical Encounters with The Ottoman Levant', *Tarih Dergisi - Turkish Journal of History,* 73 (2021): 77–101.

30 It is revealing here that the British diplomat and historian John Gordon Lorimer who served in the Persian Gulf in the early part of the twentieth century recalled how 'gum arabic' in the city of Lingeh 'goes direct to the United Kingdom', *Gazetteer of the Persian Gulf,* Vol II, 1098.

31 Ogier Ghiselin de Busbecq, the sixteenth-century Austrian ambassador in Constantinople, spoke passionately about the wider admiration in Europe of the Balsam of Mecca; see his *Travels into Turkey Containing the Most Accurate Account of the Turks* (London, 1744), 269 and 289; François Baron de *Tott, Memoires of the Baron de Tott …* 3 vols (Dublin, 1785), 289. On Arabian plants in ancient writings, see Pedanius Discorides, *De Materia Medica* (Johannesburg:

Osbaldeston, 200), 84–85. Galen, *Method of Medicine, Book 5–9*, trans., Ian Johnston and G.H.R Horsley (Massachusetts: Harvard University Press, 2011), 105.

32 The nutritive properties of Gum Arabic which Hasselquist first noted in the Levant were later approved in England by another Richard Pearson, a physician and member of the Royal College of Physician; see his *Observations on the Nutritive Properties of Gum Arabic* (London, 1818).

33 Richard Hull, the chief merchant of the Royal African Company in James Fort, Gambia, in the 1730s, wrote about the importance for such a plant for European markets; he stated that 'Gum Gambia' was as good as those imported from Arabia and Senegal. See 'Appendix No IV' to Francis Moore*'s Travels into the Inland Parts of Africa* …. (London, 1738), 18–20.

34 Peter Forskal, *Flora Aegyptiaco-Arabica: sive descriptiones plantarum quas per Aegyptum inferiorem et Arabiam felicem*, (Hauniae, 1775). Joseph Pitton de Turnefort, *Materia Medica, or a description of simple medicines Generally Used in Physic* (London 1708).

35 Alexander Russel, *The Natural History of Aleppo and the Parts Adjacent* (London: Printed for A. Miller, 1756),99. Alexander Russell, *The Natural History of Aleppo*, 2 vols (London: Printed for G.G and J. Robinson, 1794), Vol II, 119–121; see also note XXX in the appendix. Leonhart Rauwolf, *A Collection of Curious Travels and Voyages*, 2 vols (London: Printed for S. Smith and W. Walford, 1693), Vol I, 2, 51, 54, 56, 67, 68, 84, 92, 97.

36 Tobias Smollett, *The Adventures of Roderick Random*, 2 vols (London, 1784), Vol I, 158.

37 See chapter two in Fiona Haslam's *From Hogarth to Rowlandson: Medicine in Art in Eighteenth-Century Britain* (Liverpool: Liverpool University Press, 1996). See also Zachary Dorner, *Merchants of Medicines: The Commerce and Coercion of Health in Britain's Long Eighteenth Century* (Chicago: Chicago University Press, 2020).

38 The chaplain and physician in the British embassy in Constantinople James Dallaway wrote in his travel diary of the Ottoman capital: 'Those who have attained to any high degree of lucrative practice in the seraglio, or as attached to suites of grandees, have not scrupled to administer nostrums, always iniquitous in their tendency, and very frequently fatal in their effect', *Constantinople Ancient and Modern with Excursions to the Shores and Islands of the Archipelago* (London: Printed for T. Binsley, 1709), 393.

39 Many voices during the period satirised, critiqued and criminalised the medical profession and its practitioners: doctors and surgeon (like Dr Slop, Dr John Misaubin and Gregory) were mocked by Laurence Sterne in *The Life and Opinions of Tristram Shandy* (1759), William Hogarth in *A Harlot's Progress* (1732), and Henry Fielding in *The Mock Doctor* (1732).

40 John Clark, *Observations on the Diseases in Long Voyages in Hot Countries* (London, 1775), 238. For the debate about this drug, see William White's *Observations on the use of Dr. James's Powder* (London, 1774).

41 Mary Montagu, *Letters from the Levant during the embassy to Constantinople, 1716–18* (New York: Arno Press, 1971), 149.

42 Russell, *The Natural History of Aleppo*, 2 vols (London: Printed for G.G and J. Robinson, 1794), Vol II, 125–129.

43 James Grehan, 'Smoking and 'Early Modern' Sociability: The Great Tobacco Debate in the Ottoman Middle East (Seventeenth to Eighteenth Centuries)', *The American Historical Review* 5 (2006), 1352–1377. See pages 1362–1363.

44 Ibid., 1355 and 1358.

45 The Scottish physician in Aleppo Alexander Russell recalled how smoking the waterpipe in the city was shown among people 'of easy circumstances who have lately adopted the Persian manner of smoking nargeery', *The Natural History of Aleppo* (1756), 82.

46 In England, the eminent physician Thomas Short spoke highly of the medical benefits of tobacco, but he reminded his reader that one needs to consume tobacco moderately if one wants to benefit from it. Among the benefits that Short listed: it invigorates the nervous system, keeps the body warm, helps to ease the circulation of blood, cleanses a muddled stomach, and treats toothache. See Short's chapter on tobacco in his *Discourses on Tea, Sugar, Milk, Made-Wine, Spirits, Punch, Tobacco* ... (London, 1750), 227–257. Before the nineteenth century, no British travellers in the Levant, including the Alexander Russell, commented on the negative impact of water-pipes on the smoker's health. This attitude changed by the time Edward William Lane visited Egypt in the nineteenth century. For Lane, thus 'The great prevalence of liver-complaints in Arabia is attributed to the general use of nargeeleh;

and many persons in Egypt suffer severely from the same cause', *An Account of the Customs and Manners of the Modern Egyptians* (London: John Murray, 1860), 137.

47 Longrigg, 168.

48 Justin Marozzi, *Baghdad: City of Peace, City of Blood* (London: Penguin, 2014), 218–219.

49 British Library: India Office Records and Private Papers, IOR/G/29/11.

50 A good account on how many in Britain viewed suspiciously those who worked for the East India Company is Tillman Nechtman's *Nabobs*.

51 Landen, Ibid., 514.

52 For example, Lord Curzon, the English viceroy of India, invited the Arab Sheikhs of the Trucial states to meet him aboard the HMS *Shoreham* in Dubai on 23 September 1933. In his speech to these Arab rulers, Curzon showcased English naval power in the region while aboard an English flotilla equipped with a Persian Durbar, an article of pageantry showing ostentatious ceremony. See Curzon's speech in 'Visit of 1st Destroyer Flotilla to 1933. Durbar of Trucial Sheikhs at Debai [Dubai]. Reaffirmation of Lord Curzon's Statement of Policy in 1903', British Library, India Office Records and Private Papers. IOR/L/PS/12/3773.

53 A good account on how British wealth obtained in the East was viewed by many British commentators as a dangerous intervention in the pure body politic of the nation, see Mark Knights's *Trust and Distrust: Corruption in Office in Britain and Its Empire, 1600–1850* (Oxford: Oxford University Press, 2021).

54 Raymond Williams, *Keywords: A Vocabulary of Culture and Society* (1976; Oxford: Oxford University Press, 2015), 210–212.

55 An extract of this edict can be found in James Capper's *Observations on the Passage to India ...* (London: 1783), vii-viii. A translated copy can also be read in full in Richard Scott, 102–113.

56 Suraiya Faroqhi, *Subjects of the Sultan: Culture and Daily Life in the Ottoman Empire* (London & New York, 1995), 220.

57 In 1797, the Anglo-Irish traveller Buck Whaley reported how the Ottoman governor of Acre, Ahmad Pasha Al-Jazzar, whom he met at the start of his excursion on the coast of Palestine, offered him a 'furred pelice', 'a handsome pipe and a few pounds of coffee'. Whaley, in return, offered the most powerful man in Palestine 'a pair of pistols, beautifully ornamented in gold and silver' which cost him '100 guineas', *Buck Whaley's Memoire Including His Journey to Jerusalem*, ed. Edward Sullivan Bart (London: Alexander Moring Ltd, 1906), 172.

58 Fatma Muge Gocek, *Rise of The Bourgeoisie, Demise of Empire: Ottoman Westernization and Social Change* (Oxford: Oxford University Press, 1996), 55. Seventeenth and eighteenth-century British travellers in the Levant often bribed Ottoman officials by sending them presents. Dudley North, the seventeenth-century English merchant in Istanbul, was able to make manage a successful business by cultivating friendships with 'a Cadi', as Roger North wrote, whom he kept 'in good humour by frequent though small presents [...] so the merchant [...] found great benefit and security thereby', *The Lives of the Right Hon. Francis North, Baron Guilford; the Hon. Sir Dudley North. and the Hon. and Rev. Dr. John North*, 3 Vols (London, 1890), 52.

59 It is important here to mention that it was an early-modern Ottoman diplomatic norm to gift long gowns to European ambassadors. See Careri, Giovanni Francesco Gemelli, *A Voyage Round the World: In Six Parts, viz. I. Of Turky, II. Of Persia, III. Of India, IV. Of China, V. of the Philippine-Islands, VI. Of New-Spain / by John Francis Gemelli Careri; written originally in Italian, translated into English*, [17–?], 150.

60 Aaron Hill, who visited Istanbul in the early part of the eighteenth century, referred to the account in the Bible about Joseph granting 'Raiment' to his 'Brethren'. He also noted how foreign ambassadors in Istanbul competed over obtaining these 'vests', since they were 'a Proof of the Respect they [the Ottomans] bore the Person they so honoured', *A Full Account,* 154.

61 British and European travellers in the East, mainly those who used their travel narratives to put themselves to their readers as men of high social status abroad, often showed how certain rituals of hospitality in Muslim *divans*-those including offering sherbets and incense-were meant to be offered to Europeans to show how their social status was highly respected. See how Lord Charlemont in 1749 enjoyed being seen as a man of rank among Ottoman officials while being given access to the *divans* of Ottoman officials in Istanbul who offered

him 'iced sherbet', 'rosewater' and 'burning perfumes', *The Travels of Lord Charlemont in Greece & Turkey, 1749.* Ed. W.B Stanford and E.J Finopolous (London: Trigraph, 1984), 166–167.

62 Historians call the period in which expensive gifts flowed from Indian rulers' palaces to British officials' residencies in India 'the age of plunder'; see Partha Chatterjee, T*he Black Hole of Empire: History of a Global Practice of Power* (Princeton: Princeton University Press, 2012), 39–44. William Dalrymple, *The Anarchy* (London: Bloomsbury, 2020), 99–136. Eddy Kent, *Corporate Character: Representing Imperial Power in British India, 1786–1901* (Toronto: The University of Toronto Press, 2014), 26–58.

63 Eaton, Ibid., 97.

64 The British government tried to regulate the despotic rule of British East India Company, and by 1773 the Regulation Act was passed in Parliament, but technically a bunch of British Nabobs, like their Muslim counterparts in the Levant and Persia, continued to act as the lords of the land until the government directly intervened in 1784 with the Pitt's Act.

65 Nicholas Thomas, *Entangled Objects* (Massachusetts: Harvard University Press, 1991), 14–21. See also the collection of essay in *Global Gifts and the Material Culture of Diplomacy in Early Modern Eurasia*, ed. Zoltan Biederman, Anne Gerristen and Giorgio Riello (Cambridge: Cambridge University Press, 2018).

66 Ahmad Bin Budairi Al-Halak, *Hawadith Dimashq Al Yawmiah* (The Daily incidents of Damascus) (Cairo: Al-Jam'iyya al-Misriyya 1959), 49.

67 Lorimer, Vol. I. 1225.

68 Terence Clark, 'Iraq' in *British Missions around the Gulf: 1575–2005: Iran, Iraq, Kuwait and Oman* (Folkstone: Global Oriental, 2008): 81–168; see page 84.

69 Charles Umpherston Aitchison, *A Collection of Treaties, Engagements and Sanads Relating to India and Neighbouring Countries* (Calcutta, 1892), Vol XI, 2.

70 Claudius James Rich, *Narrative of Residence in Koordistan*, 2 vols (London, 1836), Vol I, 170; 172.

71 The main dispute between Rich and the East India Company in the years between 1813 and 15 was because of his request to increase his personal allowance, his extended his stay in Istanbul on grounds of ill health in 1814 and the idea that he left for Vienna and Paris after a long stay in Istanbul without obtaining the permission of the Company. The details of this dispute can be found in 'Memorial from Mrs Rich' [f27r] (43/96), British Library: India Office Records and Private Papers, IOR/F/4/747/20396. See pages 9, 13, 41 and 49.

72 H. W. F. Saggs, *People of the Past: Babylonians* (Berkley: University of California Press, 2000), 10–11.

73 James Claudius Rich, *Memoir on the Ruins of Babylon*, 3rd edition (London: Longman, 1818), 1–4. The same argument was also made by Michael Seymour; see his 'Babylon' in *Cities of God: the Bible and Archaeology in Nineteenth-Century Britain*, ed. David Gange and Michael Ledger-Lomas (Cambridge: Cambridge University Press, 2013), 167.

74 Rich, *Memoire*, 25.

75 H. W. F. Saggs, 11.

76 Nadia Atia, 'A Relic of its own past: Mesopotamia in British Imagination: 1900–14', *Memory Studies* 2: 3 (2010), 232–241.

77 Historians agree that the Persian King Kohsrau I built the arch in 734 A.D as a sign of his imperial might. See Mehrdad Kia, *The Persian Empire: A Historical Encyclopedia* (Santa Barbara: ABC-CLIO, LLC, 2016), 112.

78 Ives was not the first European who visited and described the Arch of Kesra. The Italian traveller Pietro Della Valle, on his way back from India to Europe visited the monument on 9 June, 1625; he admired the material from which this monument was built, what he called 'an ancient great Fabrick', but he did not know whether the remains were those of a previous 'Palace, or Temple, or Castle', *The Travels of Pietro Della Valle into East India and Arabia Deserta* (London, 1665), 263. Like De Valle, the French traveller Jean de Thevenot visited the monument in the summer of 1657 and wrote a brief description of it: he recalled that all what he knew about the ruins was primarily derived from what the locals told him: the monument, he said, is called in the region 'the Persians tower', *Travels into the Levant: The Second Part* (London, 1687), 65. Ives, many decades after Thevenot visited the monument, spoke with the locals about the history

of the monument. They told him, via his interpreter, that it 'was not built by a Persian, Parthian, Turk, or any other Asiatic, but by a European prince, who came in this part of the world with a large army, and subdued it', *A Voyage,* 290.

79 My reading here of the powerful influence of money on the modern self is shaped by David Hume's essay 'Of Money' in which Hume associated modern cultural shifts such as individualism and self-interest with the accumulation and circulation of capital (money) in society. See *Essays and Treatises on Several Subjects* (London, 1755), 166.

80 Andrew D. Magnusson, 'A History of Violence? Islam, English Orientalism and the Bombay Riot of 1851' in *Britain in the Islamic World: Imperial and Post-Imperial Connections*, ed. Justin Quinn Olmstead (New York: Palgrave, 2019), 4.

81 See the collection of essays in *Eighteenth-Century Thing Theory in a Global Context*, ed. Eleana Baird and Christian Ionescu (London: Ashgate, 2013); Arthur MacGregor, *Curiosity and Enlightenment: Collectors and Collections from the Sixteenth to the Nineteenth Century* (London: Yale University Press, 2007); Joan Coutu, *Then and Now: Collecting and Classicism in Eighteenth-Century England* (Montreal: McGill-Queens University Press, 2015); Tom Stammers, *The Purchas of the Past: Collecting Culture in Post-Revolutionary Paris 1790–1890* (Cambridge: Cambridge University Press, 2020).

82 Bulstrode Whitelocke. *A Journal of the Swedish Ambassy: In the Years MDCLIII and MDCLIV,* 2 vols (London, 1772).

83 Claude-Nicolas Le Cat, 'An Account of Hydro-enterocele, appearing like Hydro-farcocele and ending in the death of the Patient. … In a Letter to Charles Morton …', *The Philosophical Transactions … for the Year 1767* (London, 1768), Vol LVII, 293–296.

84 A good account of the European race of the 1760s to advance the existing knowledge about astronomy is Andrea Wulf's *Chasing Venus: The Race to Measure the Heavens* (New York: Alfred A. Knopf, 2012). On Morton's role in the British expedition, see page 41.

85 Swinton John, 'Description of two Parthian coins, never hitherto published. By the Rev. John Swinton, B.D. F. R. S. Member of the Academy degli Apatisti at Florence, and of the Etruscan Academy of Cortona in Tuscany, in a letter to Charles Morton, M.D. Sec. R. SPhil', *Transactions of the Royal Society* (London, 1766) Vol 56, 296–301; 'Interpretation of the inscription on a Punic coin…In a letter to Charles Morton, M. D. Sec. R. S. from the Rev. John Swinton, B. D. F. R. S…', *Philosophical Transactions of the Royal Society* (London, 1768), Vol 58, 235–245; 'Description of a Meteor Seen at Oxford, October 12, 1766. In a Letter to Charles Morton, M. D. Sec. R. S. from the Rev. John Swinton, B. D. F. R. S. Member of the Academy Degli Apatisti at Florence, and of the Etruscan Academy of Cortona in Tuscany', *Philosophical Transactions,* 57 (1767), 108–110.

86 Thomas D. Cope, 'Some Contacts of Benjamin Franklin with Mason, Dixon and Their Work', *Proceedings of the American Philosophical Society,* 95 (1951), 232–238.

87 In 1768, he read to the Royal Society a paper written by a French Jesuit stationed in Pekin who argued that ancient Chinese and Egyptian systems of writing were identical; this paper is printed in *An Extract from the Journals of the Royal Society. Respecting a Letter Addressed to the Society by a Member of the House of Jesuits at Pekin in China* (London, 1770).

88 Curtis Wilson, 'Astronomy and Cosmology' in *The Cambridge History of Science*, ed. Roy Porter (Cambridge: Cambridge University Press, 2008), IV, 328–353. See pages 343–344.

89 Avraham Ariel and Nora Ariel Berger, *Plotting the Globe: Stories of Meridians, Parallels and the International Date Line* (Westport: Praeger, 2006), 19.

90 Yaron Ayalon, *Natural Disasters in the Ottoman Empire: Plague, Famine and Other Misfortunes* (Cambridge: Cambridge University Press, 2015), 17. On the heavy taxation and trade monopolies in Ottoman Syria, see Dick Douwes and Norman N. Lewis's essay 'Taxation and Agriculture in the District of Hama, 1800–1831' in *The Syrian Land in the 18th and 19th Century*, ed. Thomas Philips (Stuttgart: Steiner, 1992), 268–271. The eighteenth-century Damascus chronicler Ahmed Bin Budairi recalled that after the death of the ruler of Damascus Sulayman Al-Azem, the Ottoman state found large amounts of money hidden in his palace (850 sacks in total) in a period of extreme poverty in the region, *Hawadith Dimashq,* 54. See also Aysel Yeldiz's *Crisis and Rebellion in the Ottoman Empire: The Downfall of a Sultan in the Age of Revolution* (London: I.B Tauris, 2017) 49–50. William Eton, *A Survey of the Turkish Empire* (London, 1798), 255.

91 Semih Celik, 'Coping with Famine in Ottoman Anatolia, 1650–1850' in *An Economic History of Famine Resilience*, ed. Jessica Dijkman and Bas van Leeuwen (Abingdon: Routledge, 2020), 57. See also Yeldiz, Ibid., 48. Longrigg, 172.

92 Nicholas Rogers, 'Policing the Poor in Eighteenth-Century London: The Vagrancy Laws and their Administration', *Histoire sociale-Social History*, 24 (1991), 127–147. Jonna Innes, 'Managing the Metropolis: London's Social Problems and their Control, c. 1660–1830', in Peter Clark and Raymond Gillespie, eds, *Two Capitals: London and Dublin 1500–1840* (Proceedings of the British Academy, 107. Oxford, 2001), 35–79.

93 Poor laws in England go back to the Elizabethan period which required that to preserve the social order the rich needed to provide for the poor whether in the form of providing indoor relief for the sick among them, finding work for those who are able work in workhouses, and punish the vagrants in houses of correction. On the history of poor laws in England, see Lynn Hollen Lees, *The Solidarities of Strangers: The English Poor Laws and the People, 1700–1948* (Cambridge: Cambridge University Press, 1998), chs. 1 and 2. See also J. R. Poynter, *Society and Pauperism: English Ideas on Poor Relief, 1795–1834* (London, 1969), ch. 1.

94 A. W. Coats, 'The Relief of Poverty, Attitudes to Labour, and Economic change in England 1660–1782', *International Review of Social History* 21: 1 (1976), 98–115. See pages 108–109.

95 Niall O' Flaherty, *Utilitarianism in the Age of the Enlightenment* (Cambridge: Cambridge University Press, 2019), 267.

96 Anon, *An Account for Several Workhouses For Employing the Maintaining the Poor* (London: Printed and Sold for Joseph Downing, 1725), 45 and 76. On the daily routine in workhouses (the meagre diet and the monotonous routines of menial work, such as sewing old clothes or repairing sacks), see the pamphlet titled *An Account of the work-houses in Great Britain, in the Year M, DCC, XXXII* (London, 1786). Anna Moltchanova and Susannah Ottaway, 'Right and Reciprocity in the Political and Philosophical Discourse of Eighteenth-Century England' in *The Culture of the Gift in Eighteenth-Century England*, ed. Linda Zionkowski and Cynthia Klekar (New York: Palgrave, 2009). 25–36; see page 27.

97 Kames, Vol III, 47.

98 See chapter four in J. L. Hammond and Barbara Hammond's *The Village Labourer 1760–1832: A Study in the Government of England Before the Reform Bill* (London: Longmans, Green and Co, 1920).

99 Alexander Dow, *The History of Hindostan* (London: Printed for T. Becket and P. A. De Hondt in the Strand,1772), lxxxiv. Philip Lawson and Jim Philips, 'Our Execrable Banditti: Perceptions of Nabobs in Mid-Eighteenth Century Britain', *Albion: A Quarterly Journal Concerned with British Studies* 16:3 (1984), 225–241.

100 Paul Rycaut, *The Present State of the Ottoman Empire* (London, 1668), 161; Ogier Ghislain de Busbecq, *Travels into Turkey*, 223–224.

101 In Islam, well-off people are demanded to distribute one fortieth of their annual earnings on the poor. This obligation is called *zakat*. See Ingrid Mattson's 'Status-Based Definitions of Need in Early Islamic *Zakat* and Maintenance Laws' in 'in *Poverty and Charity in Middle Eastern Contexts*, ed. Michael Bonner Mine Ener and Amy Singer (New York: State University of New York Press, 2003), 31–52.

102 On poverty in the Ottoman Empire, see Hayri Gökşin Özkoray's essay 'Poverty, Law and Labour in the Ottoman Empire' in *The Routledge History of Poverty 1400–1800*, ed. David Hitchcock and Julia McClure (Abingdon and New York: Routledge, 2021), 309–321. See also Miri Shefer's 'Charity and Hospitality: Hospitals in the Ottoman Empire in the Early Modern Period' and Eyal Ginio's 'Living on the Margins of Charity: Coping with Poverty in an Ottoman Provincial City' in *Poverty and Charity in Middle Eastern Contexts*, ed. Michael Bonner Mine Ener Amy Singer (New York: State University of New York Press, 2003). Amy Singer, *Charity in Islamic Societies* (Cambridge: Cambridge University Press, 2008). Abdul-Karim Rafeq, 'The Poor in Ottoman Damascus. A Socioeconomic and Political Study', in *Pauvreté et Richesse Dans le Monde Musulman Méditerranéen* (Paris: Maisonneuve et Larose, 2003), 217–226.

103 Henry H. Knight, *John Wesley: Optimist of Grace* (Oregon: Cascade Books, 2018), 92–93. Niall O' Flaherty, 259.

104 On the relationship between bourgeoise morality and the question of poverty in England, see Marriot, 12–19.

105 Geoffrey L. Hudson argues that during the eighteenth-century English surgeon were often compared to 'butchers' who were 'sadistically indulging in excruciating bleedings, blisterings, and amputations'. He goes on to add that medical professionals in Georgian England were generally viewed as cruel people, quacks and money grabbers: 'This is the epithet which has been applied almost universally to medicine on the battlefield, in camps and on board ship', *British Military and Naval Medicine*, ed. Geoffrey L. Hudson (Amsterdam: Rodopi, 2007), 9.

106 Voices critiquing men of middling sorts who overrated their status in society were heard on the pulpit and the London stage. See Issac Kramnick, *Republicanism and Bourgeoise Capitalism* (Ithaca: Cornell University Press, 1990), 5. Edmund Burke, *Reflection on the Revolution of France* (London, 1790), 34. Brewer, 99.

107 The common consensus among eighteenth-century scholars is that politeness was an expression of a new bourgeoise sensibility which re-thought the old social, political and moral landscape dominated by the landed aristocracy and nobility. See Peter Earle's *The Making of the English Middle Class* (Berkley: The University of California Press, 1989), 13. In this changing scene, politeness was associated with middle-class values such as self-improvement and self-interest which redefined the classical notion of virtue. Such social changes were explained by Stephen Copley in the introduction to *Literature and Social Order in Eighteenth-Century England*, ed. Stephen Copley (London: Croom Helm, 1984). On how the press used the discourse of politeness to re-interpret social, political and moral landscape of Britain, see Copley's 'Commerce, Conversation and Politeness in the Early Eighteenth-Century Periodical', *The Journal of Eighteenth-Century Studies*, 18 (1995), 63–77. On the classical conception of virtue at the turn of the century, see Isaac Kramnick, *Bolingbroke and His Circle: The Politics of Nostalgia in the Age of Walpole* (Cambridge, MA: Harvard University Press, 1968); John Cannon's *Aristocratic Century* (Cambridge: Cambridge University Press, 1984); Quentin Skinner, *Visions and Politics: Renaissance Virtues* (Cambridge: Cambridge University Press, 2002), Vol II, 121–122. Laurence E. Klein, *Shaftesbury and the Culture of Politeness* (Cambridge: Cambridge University Press, 1994), 128.

Chapter Three

COMMERCE, VIRTUE AND IMPROVEMENT: ABRAHAM PARSONS'S *TRAVEL IN ASIA AND AFRICA* (1808)

There is scarce any country how rude or uncultivated soever, where the inhabitants are not possessed of some peculiar secrets, wither in nature or art, which might be transplanted with success.

—Oliver Goldsmith, *Citizen of the World* (1760–1761)

The Levant Company appointed Abraham Parsons as a consul in Iskenderun, Turkey, in 1767. Parsons served in the Levant for six years before deciding to retire in Leghorn in Italy where he died in 1785. Seven years earlier, Parsons had undertaken a journey of 'commercial speculations', as John Paine Berjew, the editor of Parsons's travel account, wrote in the preface to Parsons's *Travels in Asia and Africa* (Parsons 1808: iii). From his travel book, we learn that Parsons had joined an Arab caravan travelling between Aleppo and Basra where he lived for a few months before boarding a British ship sailing towards India.[1] In 1776, he arrived in Bombay, then moved to Surat and Madras before returning to Europe by way of Suez, Cairo and Alexandria. The details of this long journey were published posthumously in 1808 in a book many in Britain found somewhat repetitive and dull unlike most travel books of the period, which were known for the stories they told about their authors' adventures and suffering in exotic climes.[2] *The Monthly Review* suggested that Parsons's 'travels bespeak the man of business more than the man of letters and afford us the result of actual observation without much benefit from disquisition or research' (1810: 288). For the *London Review*, there is no doubt that Parsons's book lacks the literary and scholarly quality one finds in previous and contemporary accounts about the Levant. But what is even odd about the book is that it does little to explain differences between societies beyond just the Enlightenment discourse of progress. Parsons, *The London Review* in 1809 wrote, 'looks only on the artificial and obvious distinction between the modes of society in states: he knows nothing of the more recondite discriminations that separate, as it were, the souls of communities; and even, in the midst of the most liberal and enlightened intercourse, keep nation distinct from nation. Whilst passing with him through remote countries, we appear, as far as it relates to improvement, not yet to have quitted your own' (1809: 365). Parsons, *The London Rev*iew argued, was reluctant to view the people he encountered as nations with living traditions and practices different from other nations and cultures. He was rather a product of an Enlightenment age in which people were all seen as parts of the same human family with the only difference that some, judging from their material conditions, were able to improve while others remain static. The different communities and individuals that figured in Parsons's book did not seem to have been seen as living beings; rather they were seen as representations of larger economic and social forces, as fixed steps on the ladder of human progress.

Parsons, *The London Review* recalled, represents the kind of parochial English traveller for whom '[f]reedom [...] cannot emanate beyond the cliffs of Britain; civilisation is bounded by the Mediterranean and Red Seas; Asia was only created to supply England with teas; and Africa to furnish her with ship-loads of elephants' teeth' (1809: 365–366). Many, the journal continued, believe that commercial travellers have profound knowledge of the people they encounter because the nature of their adventure demands that they interact with and learn about different cultures. 'It is false, however' the article concluded, 'to estimate men merely by the situation in which they are casually thrown, and not by the capability they possess of benefiting from them' (Ibid., 364). It further states that the great value critics put on the accounts of merchants and tradesmen who travel in foreign nations is mistaken simply because these reports do not capture the 'soul', traditions and the living conditions of societies. Parsons was one such traveller, 'an ignorant man', who 'would scarce be the wiser, although he were transplanted into the moon [...]' (Ibid., 364). Such a view was confirmed by Joseph Emin, an East India Company soldier and a reputable figure in the Armenian liberation movement, who called Parsons after meeting him in Basra in 1774 'an Englishman, but not quite so sociable', hinting at the devious manners of Parsons from his countrymen whom Emin took to be sociable, polite and appreciative of other people (Emin 1792: II, 450).

Such an assessment of Parsons's book and character captures the values and purpose of travelling among and writing about Arabs and Muslims. Parsons's travel account, as this chapter shows, included many examples, insights and observations shaped by political, philosophical and economic debates during the period, like those in the writings of Smith and Hume who were ambivalent about the positive force of commerce and empire in society. Encounter with Muslims and Arabs gave Parsons the opportunity to reflect on Adam Smith's verdict on a commercialised society – that is, 'Commerce, which ought naturally to be, among nations as among individuals, a bond of union and friendship has become the most fertile source of discord and animosity' (Smith 1776: II, 82).[3] The idea that material advance generates happiness, security and liberty, one which was debated among Britain's most eminent literary and philosophical writers, troubled Parsons, a man of humble education, who travelled in and wrote about a region many votaries of commercial society in Britain associated with pastoralism and primitivism.

This chapter examines Parsons's encounters with cultural difference with the intention to find out how a commercial traveller responded to the challenge of improvement which was posed by Bernard Mandeville in 1717 but continued to trouble British writers throughout the eighteenth century. It is the challenge which underlines the tension between commerce and virtue. As Mandeville in the preface to *The Fable of the Bees* put it, it is impossible to enjoy 'all the most elegant Comforts of Life that are to be met with in an industrious, wealthy and powerful Nation', 'and at the same time be bless'd with all the Virtue and Innocence that can be wish'd for in a Golden Age'

(Mandeville 1723: A3). Most of the observations Parsons recorded in his travel book took place in 1775 and 1776, a period in which, in the wake of the Regulation Act of 1773, the East India Company's belligerent commercial and military policies in India, its corruption and cronyism troubled many to the extent that the government, to no avail, sought to directly intervene in regulating its affairs.[4] It is in this period that we find Parsons defending commercialism. But it is a sober and thoughtful defence based on a careful assessment of its costs and benefits: he disagreed with radical defenders of commercialism for whom people need to accept moral and political ills such as individualism and the pursuit of self-interest if they want to live in a prosperous society, a society in which wealth polishes manners and suppresses the residues of an intolerant, despotic and superstitious past. Parsons, however, was not a radical supporter of values of commercialism such as excessive self-interest, monopolies and competition: rather he, as this chapter shows, used his travel observations to reconcile, without being successful, between dominant values of commercial society and residual virtues of a pre-modern age.

Aleppo: Commerce and Toleration

In his travel book, Parsons mentioned how as a consul in Iskenderun he often visited the commercial 'capital of Syria'. He recorded his observations of the city in one last visit he made in 1773. 'This is the fourth tour which I have made from Scanderoon to Aleppo', Parsons declared, 'and having little else to do but to walk about and make observations, it has enabled me to see more than other persons who have resided here many years, as they had business of more consequence to take off their attention' (Parsons 1808: 56). Despite this claim, Parsons did not write about the natural history – animals and plants – of Aleppo which many travellers before him explored in detail. But he knew he did not have the knowledge, skills and sources to examine the flora and fauna of Syria. *The Natural History of Aleppo*, Parsons wrote, by 'Doctor Alexander Russell [...] who resided here many years', is the 'best' book which 'described' Aleppo (Parsons 1808: 56). Unlike Russell, Parsons was more interested in Aleppo's commercial culture, wealth and infrastructure than its natural history. 'This is by all (who have seen the capital of other great cities in Turkey) allowed to be the best built, handsomest, and cleanest of any city in the grand signior's dominions', Parsons stated, 'and next to Constantinople for size and number of inhabitants, being the capital of Syria' (Parsons 1808: 56).

Aleppo had always fascinated European travellers in the Ottoman Empire, not least because of its commercial and strategic importance; it was located on commercial routes widely seen as vital for transporting goods and travellers from India, Persia, Arabia and Europe. The French writer Volney, who visited Syria in the last part of the eighteenth century, observed that Aleppo 'is the emporium of Armenia and Diarbekar; sends caravan to Bagdad and into Persia; and communicate with the Persian Gulph and India, by Basra; and with Egypt and Mecca by Damascus; and with Europe by Scandaroon (Alexandretta) and Latakia' (Volney 1788: II, 150). As early as 1672, the French traveller in Syria, Abbé Carré, recorded his observations of the wealth of Aleppo which he called 'a splendid town' and 'the most flourishing in all Syria' (Carré 1947: 43). When the Dutchmen Johannes Aegidius van Egmond and Johannes Heyman visited the city in the early years of the eighteenth century, they noted how the commerce and wealth of Aleppo attracted many Europeans to the city. 'The English are much more numerous' than the French and 'while we were there' the English had 'twenty houses, besides temporary traders' (Aegidius van Egmond 1759: 346).

When Parsons visited Aleppo in 1773, British trade in the region was on its last legs in comparison to that of the French. Only 12 British merchants lived in the city, Parson found, while the French were 15 in total. Unlike the English, the French managed to revive their trade in the Levant because the cloth they sold in Syria was cheaper than that of the English.[5] Moreover, manufacturers in France's industrial heartlands found Syrian raw silk and cotton cheap.[6] Despite the fact that the French dominated the Levant trade throughout the eighteenth century, the English continued to send consuls to the city not least because they were hoping to beat French trade in the Levant. They also maintained commercial and diplomatic connections with the city because of Aleppo's strategic position on the overland routes to India.[7] Parsons was familiar with the importance of Aleppo for Europeans. While strolling in the city, he inspected the markets and discovered that 'immense quantities of the richest goods from India, Constantinople, Smyrna, Damascus, and other places, beside the various manufactures of Aleppo; all of which constitute an immense value' (Parsons 1808: 60).

Aleppo fascinated Parsons for another reason. He was keen on examining the extent to which a culture of commerce and enterprise, which he found in a metropolitan city like Aleppo, shaped people's manners. Parsons noted that the Alepines, regardless of their religion and culture, were an enterprising people. 'The weavers, whether Turks who live in the city, or Jews and Christians who live in the Jewdeda [suburb], have their looms in their houses. The masons, stone cutters, carpenters, joiners, and painters, either carry on their business at their own houses, or in some place near their homes, as there is no room to carry on this trade in the bazars' (Parsons 1808: 62). Aleppo's commercial environment, Parson found, was open to people from different religious backgrounds. In this commercial culture, Muslim, Christian and Jewish merchants made huge profits. '[S]ome of them are very rich, and have superb houses, with large gardens, hot and cold baths, and everything corresponding, either for convenience or luxury' (Parsons 1808: 56). It is true that Jews, Christians and Muslims lived in separate quarters, Parsons noted, yet the commercial life they led required that they mingle with each other in the marketplace. For example, 'The Jews or Christians', Parsons wrote, 'although not allowed to have dwelling houses in the city, yet such of them are merchants, or people in trade, have their accompting houses and shops in the city, as well as their magazines and warehouses, to which they resort in the morning, and return to the Jewdeda in the evening before the gate is shut' (Parsons 1808: 57). Parsons found in Aleppo a diverse commercial market which cut across boundaries of religion; the diversity of this culture was principally caused by the pursuit of self-interest.

But another Briton, whose book Parsons was familiar with, had a different story to tell about relations between communities in the city. In *The Natural History of Aleppo*, Alexander Russell recalled how church leaders in Aleppo often showed hostilities and sectarian prejudices towards members of the opposite sect (Russell 1794: II, 40).

Catholics, now supported by the French consul, often clashed with Greek Orthodox who suspected the intentions of Catholic missionaries to convert Orthodox Christians into Catholicism. Religious fears in Aleppo, Russell added, have 'contributed more to disseminate a narrow, contentious, and intolerant spirit, than to unite men, possessing the same faith, in the bonds of mutual good will: an opinion in the country where the effects are every day visible, not uncommon among the more sensible natives' (Russell 1794: II, 40–41). Such a 'contentious' religious culture dominated relations among Christian communities in the city. But it was also prevalent among Muslims who often showed, Russell wrote, an 'insolent petulancy' towards non-Muslims (Russell 1794: II, 42). For example, he added, although many held respectable positions in 'the Seraglio', Jews in Aleppo were often 'held in still greater contempt than Christians' (Russell 1794: II, 60).

The fact that Russell, as a physician, socialised and interacted with people from different walks of life suggests that his description of cross-religious relations in Aleppo may have been more credible than that of Parsons's. But as a medical man of secular learnings (he, during his student years at the University of Edinburgh, befriended social circles known for their rationalism, scepticism and empiricism), Russell's experience in Britain might have influenced the way he depicted Aleppo's complex religious landscape.[8]

The historian Bruce Masters doubted the credibility of Russell's characterisation of the relations between communities in Aleppo: 'Russell's characterization of "insolent petulancy" would hardly seem to qualify' (Masters 2001: 38). Masters, while rethinking Russel's limited knowledge of the relations between communities in Aleppo, examined 'law courts records' and many eighteenth-century '*fatwas*' in which he found that 'some Muslim intellectuals such as al-Nabulusi [the Syrian poet and jurist Abdu Ghani Al-Nabulsi] had genuine regards for their Christian contemporaries' (Masters 2001: 38). Masters also showed how people's social status determined the kind of attitudes they showed towards people from different faiths: Muslim people from lower classes often mixed 'with non- Muslims on a daily basis' and 'the *fatwas* show that their social acceptance of non-Muslims could vary almost as dramatically as could be found among the Muslim elites' (2001: 38). Yet Russell and others who complained of the religious intolerance in Aleppo, Masters concluded, were partially correct. 'There were [...] instances of violence. But indifference, perhaps tinged with contempt [...] rather than overt hostility seems to have been the emotional norm governing intercommunal relations in the period before the sectarian outbursts of the nineteenth century' (Masters 2001: 38). [9]

Masters's characterisation of the complex nature of cross-religious relations in Aleppo did figure in Parsons's text. Parsons saw in Aleppo an ideal place in which people from all walks of life care about labour, profit and material improvements rather than each other's religious convictions. Parsons did not speculate on the despotism of the 'Turk' and the religious prejudices of Muslims against non-Muslims, two famous tropes in eighteenth-century travel accounts about the Levant. Nor did he explain the legal context and laws governing the relations between Muslims and non-Muslims, what historians called 'the millet system' which 'institutionalised the idea of Muslim dominance' over non-Muslims, as Laura Robson argues (Robson 2020: 15). Rather

Parsons observed how Ottoman rulers often tolerated minorities and rarely interfered with their religious and civil affairs.

What intrigued Parsons was not only the absence of resentment by the subjects of the sultan against such an imposition by the government but also the idea that the government did not collect the poll tax directly, rather a community representative was tasked with collecting it on behalf of the government. 'Besides the Jews, here are four denominations of native Christians, who are called the four nations, viz. the Roman Catholics, Greeks, Armenians, and Syrians', Parsons noted, 'each of whom chuse a chief, who must be approved of by the cadi or Turkish judge, and who is accountable for the capitation tax, and any assessment made on them by the pasha (which is often the case) and must appear as their agent in any business pending between his nation and the Turks' (Parsons 1808: 57). Russell noted how the '*Wakeel*', an Arabic word for agent, occupied an honourable position in the eyes of the Ottoman ruler. This representative of a *millet*, however, Russell recalled, was often accused by Ottoman authority of 'partiality or peculation'. Similarly, this collector of the tax sometimes faced hostility from his own coreligionists who 'are never contended' (Parsons 1808: 41). Russell's characterisation of the local discontent caused by the poll tax did not find mention in Parsons's text.

Parsons's silence about the fraught political and religious landscape in the Levant in general and Aleppo in particular was odd. Eighteenth-century travellers in the Levant, particularly those who did not travel in the region in the capacity of merchants, often noted how Europeans in Aleppo were largely tolerated by locals, and they also noted the intolerance of rulers towards their Christians and Jewish subjects. When Bishop Richard Pococke visited Aleppo in the summer of 1737, he found that the people there 'often submit quietly when the governor squeezes their purses; and the tyranny this way often falls very heavily on their Christian subjects' (Pococke 1745: 151). The English naval officer Francis Vernon, who visited the city for a few days in the winter of 1785, mentioned how 'The Christians and Turks never associate, except to transact mercantile business, and then it is in the most laconic manner; for they consider us dogs [...]' (Vernon 1792: 161). Although Carsten Niebuhr did not rank Aleppo among those Levantine cities (Damascus, Cairo and Damietta) that harbour a culture of intolerance towards Christians, he observed that people and government in the Levant, especially what he called 'Turks', in contrast to those in the Hijaz and Yemen, often discriminate against Christians: 'so abject is the conditions of Christians, that they dare not complain of any injury suffered from a Mahometan' (Niebuhr 1792: II, 243). Niebuhr also complained of the large sums Christians were asked to pay because of their so-called inferior religious status: 'In the Turkish Empire, Christians are obliged to wear a badge, which marks their servile condition, and to pay a poll-tax' (Niebuhr 1792: II, 243). Indeed, this idea that Christians were asked to pay a special tax due to their different religious status was often seen by many European travellers in the Ottoman Empire as a sign of intolerance.[10] Girolamo Dandini, the Jesuit father who was sent by Pope Clement VIII in 1596 to investigate the conditions of the Christians of Mount Lebanon, noted how Syrian Christians often 'endured' an 'unsupportable' impositions of the 'Turks' (Dandini 1698: 51). Yet, he noted, many Christians, particularly those of Mount Lebanon, were too proud to submit to their oppressors: 'They choose rather to live in the poverty and affliction of a voluntary banishment, than to remain with their estates in their own country, under so unsupportable a tyranny' (Ibid.).

Despite most European travellers disliked the idea that Christians and Jews had to pay a special tax to Muslims, some British travellers, including Parsons, did not approach the subject from the perspective of a Christian reporting about the oppression his coreligionists suffer in Muslim land; rather they approached it from the point of view of the defender of government, stability and order as opposed to popular resentment and rebellions. Some eighteenth-century British travellers were dispassionate, nuanced and non-sectarian in their writings about the subject. Commenting on the Christians living in Cyprus in 1743, Alexander Drummond, the Levant Company representative in Aleppo, wrote: 'these taxes are exacted from all persons between the age of fifteen and seventy, that is, from all who are capable of labour' (Drummond 1754: 149).[11] Women and children, Drummond observed, were not required to pay this tax. Another example showing the complexity of travellers' views on the poll tax can be noted in Charles Thompson's observations of the Christian community in the Greek island of Chios. Thompson, who was in the Levant in the first half of the eighteenth century, noted how the Ottoman governor associated the Mastic tree with great medical benefits to the extent that the Christians who planted it were asked to 'pay but half of the Capitation Tax' and were 'allowed to wear white Turbans as well as the Turks, which is looked on as an extraordinary privilege' (Thompson 1767: I, 33).[12] The idea that Muslim rulers often raised funds from Christians and Jews because of their inferior religious status did not figure in Drummond and Thompson's accounts. While their countrymen in India and America at the time were immersed in raising taxes from non-Christian subjects, British travellers, including Parsons, had nothing to say against the religious nature of the 'Capitation tax'.

Parsons saw in the mechanism of collecting the poll tax in Aleppo a legal and political framework guaranteeing the institution of political order and protecting minorities; he did not see it an expression of Islamic intolerance against Christians and Jews. The view here about the Ottomans appointing Jewish and Christian representatives to collect the poll tax from their communities is seen in the context of British involvement in America and India. In the wake of Lord Clive's victory at the Battle of Plassey (1757), the Mogul emperor granted the East India Company a concession which allowed it to collect taxes in Bengal, Orissa and Behar: this privilege, which was called *Diwani*, granted many servants in the East India Company huge power over the locals and secured them huge wealth which many in Europe considered illegal, despotic and corrupt. As William Bolts observed, 'the DEWANNEE' was 'an office' the EIC 'invented for the private purposes of the Company and directors, and their servants and considerates [...] to screen on the seizing of the sovereignty of the country, by imposing upon and deceiving [...] not only the inhabitants of India and foreigners, but even the British nation' (Bolts 1772: 37). This critique of British involvement in raising revenues in their colonies was not restricted to India. Edmund Burke called the British system of raising tax in America 'an abominable project' which was 'obeyed solely from respect to the bayonet'; it denied Americans the right to tax themselves (1775: 27, 30). Burke reminded his audience in a speech he gave in the House of Commons in 1774 that George Grenville, prime minister between 1763 and 1765, toyed with the idea of granting the American some freedom to 'agree in some mode of taxation on the ground of an Act of Parliament', but 'he could never have proposed that they should tax themselves on requisition' (Burke 1775: 53). The consequences of Britain's policies in America, particularly those informed by the Navigation Act of 1765, were, Burke added, materialised in the 'universal insurrections' in the colonies and 'the discontent of the people from the taxes' (Burke 1775: 70). For Burke, the only way out of this crisis was 'to leave America, if she had a taxable matter in her, to tax herself' (Burke 1775: 89).

Taxing the self is what Parsons noted among the minorities in Aleppo in 1773, one year before Burke spoke to the House of Commons about the North American crisis. Unlike the American subjects of the British Empire, the Christian and Jewish subjects of the sultan, as Parsons showed, did not object to the idea of paying the poll tax, nor were there any clashes between the government and those who refused to pay the tax. Parsons made these observations at a time when Britain's North American subjects were resisting the Townsend Acts, a series of laws by the British government which introduced new taxes and strengthened British governors over the people. In Boston, this resistance culminated on 21 December with the Boston Tea Party, just 10 days before Parsons left Aleppo, an event which triggered the American Revolution.[13]

Seen in this context, Parsons's observations of the indirect interference of the Ottoman government in the affairs of minorities in Aleppo were informed by his understanding of British policies in the Empire. He praised the Ottoman system of taxing minorities in a period that saw huge debate in Britain about how monopolistic commercial ventures in both America and India threatened the freedom, liberty and trade of the British nation and those they governed in the name of improvement. Contemporaries of Parsons, such as Edmund Burke and Adam Smith, many scholars observe, were at the forefront of the broader opposition in Britain towards its mercantilist policies in India and America.[14] Burke in his speech to the House of Commons in April 1774 recalled how the British Empire was founded on 'a commercial system' which 'was wholly restrictive' and observed that 'this principle of commercial monopoly runs no less than twenty-nine Acts of Parliament, from the year 1660 to the unfortunate period of 1764' (Burke 1775: 38). Parsons did not critique British commercial ventures in America and India. Nor did he engage with the critique of oppression that many in Britain attributed to British political and commercial ventures in America. Yet the idea in his narrative that Jews and Christians had no objection to paying their taxes indicates how his views of Ottoman political and commercial systems were shaped by the debate in Britain regarding the problem of taxing Britain's colonial subjects.

Aleppo: Government and Peace

Parsons was one of those travellers and travel writers in the Levant who often found in the region some moral and political lessons he felt he should pass to his readers. One such lesson was about how polities dominated by commercial values and run by strong government enjoy prosperity and peace. Such an idea appeared in Parsons's observations of the commercial and political environment in Aleppo under the government of Muhsinzade Mehmed Pasha, who was previously a grand vizier in the Ottoman court. When Parsons was in Aleppo in 1773, this new governor arrived in the city with a mission to reinstitute order after a long period of civil wars between the *janizaries* and the local notables, commonly called *Ashraf*. This new ruler encouraged trade and established good relations with European merchants and consuls. He was a cosmopolitan Muslim; he often conversed with European guests about religion, culture and politics. 'I am told', as the Pasha said in a meeting he held in his palace with the English consul in the city, 'that among Christians there are many different sects',

> [...] and that each has a different way of worshipping God, and that the French and the English differ much: I do not pretend to know who is most right, but must observe, that if eighteenth French men must have upwards of thirty of the religious men of your church to superintend their conduct, and that twelve English men can be kept in order by one religious man's of their's, I must certainly give the preference to the English church; and 'if I will be Christian' [added he, smiling] 'I will be of their church'. (Parsons 1808: 59)

The reference in the passage above to the idea that the English abroad were men of religious and moral values in contrast to the loose French may have been recalled by Parsons as an attempt to diffuse critiques in England of the corrupt and un-Christian behaviour of the English in the East, mainly those commercially minded men serving in India.[15] But here Parsons did nothing new; he repeated what his countryman Henry Maundrell earlier in the century claimed. Writing from Aleppo to Mr Osborne, a fellow of Exeter College Oxford, in 1698, the chaplain in the Aleppo factory Henry Maundrell recalled how 'Our way of Life resembles, in some measure, the Academical. We live in separate Squares, shut up every night after the manner of Colleges. We begin the day constantly, as You do, with Prayers; and have our set times of Business, Meals and Recreations' (Maundrell 1703: 146). Despite the wild temptations prevalent in Aleppo, young and single Britons – as Maundrell and Parsons hinted to their readers at home – lived virtuously like the Christian Fathers.[16]

But Parsons's statement above passes another moral lesson in addition to the one about the discipline of the English in Aleppo – the idea that many French 'religious men' lived in the city refers to French missionary work in the region, which not only focused on the souls of European Catholics but also those from 'five of the historic Churches of the East: the Greek Orthodox, Armenian, Syrian, Nestorian, and Coptic' (Perry 2022: 207). Unlike the French, as Parsons implied, the Protestants had little religious presence in Aleppo. Simon Mills and Alastair Hamilton, in their different ways, show how the Protestant Church in the Levant mostly focused on preaching among British and some Dutch and German merchants in Aleppo rather than among local Muslims and other members of the Catholic and Greek churches.[17] Although some seventeenth-century Protestant churchmen in Aleppo, such as Edward Pococke (1604–1691) and Dr Issac Basire (1607–1776), toyed with the idea of shepherding the Levant to the fold of Protestantism, the British consulate in Aleppo was mostly concerned about trade rather than religion.[18] Unlike the French in the Levant, moreover, the British were relaxed in their relations with other Christian denominations in the region. In 1770, for example, members of the Aleppo factory, Robert Abbott, David Hays and Eleazar Edwards, attended the marriage of Charles Usgate, a British merchant in Aleppo, and Mariam, 'the daughter of Joseph Merdine', an Armenian. The marriage was 'performed according to the rite of the Armenian Church'.[19]

With the arrival of Robert Foster in Aleppo, the British factory in the city, in 1773, saw some missionary spirit. For example, Foster organised a public ceremony in which he announced the conversion of Maria Francesca Nicoletta, 'daughter of Peter Parker', an English merchant, 'and Apollonia his wife an Italian', to Protestantism.[20] In the spring of 1776, Foster led another ceremony in which another resident in Aleppo was 'received into the Church of England in the presence of the greatest part of the English Factory agreeable to his Request'. This ceremony was intended to 'publicly' baptize a man named Moise Va Islah who 'was born in Pisa in Italy of Jewish parents & educated in that Religion'.[21]

These two examples of the British missionary spirit in the Levant cannot be compared to the role which French missionaries played in Aleppo's religious landscape throughout the early-modern period. The English travellers who shared their experiences in Aleppo often recalled how their community did not care about the confessional divisions in the city. Rather they were concerned about showing the locals how the English were polite and commercial people, something which gained them a lot of friends from the Muslim community. Alexander Russell, whose travel account probably inspired Parsons to mention how the local governor hugely respected the English 'church', observed how the locals in Aleppo 'acquit us of being associates in several of the superstitious practices which they ascribe however impiously to the Christians of the country' (Russell 1794: I, 416). John Barker who presided over the English consulate in Aleppo between 1799 and 1825 recalled that '"*Parola Inglese*", or in Arabic "*Kilmet Inglee-zeeyay*", was a byword still in common use; by which was meant the truthfulness of England's sons, and respect and consideration Englishmen attached to the value of their pledged word' (Barker 1876: I, 24). John Jackson, the English merchant who travelled in the Levant in 1797, felt uneasy about the large presence of Catholic missionaries in the Levant. He called a Capuchin Friar, an Italian missionary, he met in Diyarbakir an 'extremely ignorant' and 'such a disgusting figure' (Jackson 1799: 164). From his interactions with Muslims Jackson learnt that the locals prefer the English over the French and the Italians because the English, like the Muslims, do not have 'crucifixes and images in their mosques' (Jackson 1799: 164). Muslims, Jackson added, 'entertained a more favourable opinion of the English' because they, like Muslims, do not worship any images or saints (Jackson 1799: 164).

Despite what Parsons thought about the moral superiority and integrity of his countrymen over the French, it was the French who enjoyed religious privileges the most among all Europeans in the Ottoman Empire. As Alexander Russell in *The Natural History of Aleppo* observed, Ottoman governors often gave French consuls a precedence over the English because of 'the prior establishment of the French factory in Aleppo' (Russell 1794: II, 2). France was the first European country to sign the capitulation with the Ottoman Empire in 1553. In addition to allowing the French to trade freely in Ottoman cities, the agreement gave Francis I the title of a protector of Christians in the Levant.[22] Buoyant with a sense of confidence after their countrymen signed the Capitulations agreement with the Ottoman Empire, Catholic missionaries started arriving in the region in the later part of the sixteenth century.[23] Successive Ottoman sultans allowed missionaries to operate in their land with the proviso that they do not preach among Muslims. As such, these men (Carmelites, Jesuits, Franciscans and Capuchins) established a close-knit network in the region. The English traveller Richard Pococke, while in Jerusalem, mentioned that the Latin convent housed many European missionaries. He counted 10 convents in Palestine and Syria, 'three in Egypt, under a vice-prefect, one at Cyprus, and another at Constantinople' (Pococke 1745: 11). Pococke and others knew that commercial agreements between the Ottomans and Europeans were accompanied by some religious and legal concessions. Ottoman governors and judges in different cities in the Levant did not interfere in the work of these missionaries despite the petitions of local Orthodox Christian leaders against European interventions in their communities. According to Bruce Masters, these petitions sometimes reached Istanbul which the Ottoman sultan would take seriously. As such, the sultan sometimes sent orders to Aleppo stating that European missionaries not be allowed to interfere in Orthodox Christian communities. But, as Bruce Masters observes, these rulings were largely ignored because Ottoman governors cared more about collecting presents and bribes than about enforcing the wishes of the sultan.[24]

The German explorer Carsten Niebuhr in 1761 wrote about how such network of power and corruption operates in Cairo. 'Here are Jesuits, Capuchins, Cordeliers and Fathers of the Society for the propagation of the Christian Faith', he observed [...]

> These monks are all eager to make proselytes, and sometimes succeed so far as to convert some schematic Christians of the East. The Government readily tolerates these modern apostles, on account of the profits which they derive from the quarrels which the conversion produced between the apostate, and the members of the Communion which he forsakes. The Pasha is often not content with fining the contending parties, but examines the affairs to the bottom, and exacts considerable sums from the monks besides. (Niebuhr 1792: I, 103)

The same point was confirmed by Alexander Russell in Aleppo: 'These religious contests have, as usual, been conducted with all the characteristic zeal and carried on at enormous expense [...] the Bashaw [governor of Aleppo], always perfectly indifferent to the merits of the cause, inclining steadily to the side which paid best' (Russell 1794: II, 29). Parsons did not report that Ottoman rulers of the period had an ulterior motive for allowing such large amount of 'religious men', missionaries, to live and work in Ottoman cities. In Parsons's account, Aleppo was projected as a city whose rulers encourage commerce, enforce the law and welcome foreign merchants and missionaries into their land.

But sometimes Parsons found that peace in a commercial city like Aleppo was fragile. He recalled how 'with the bravery of his janissaries' the governor 'quelled the rebellion' of the local notables known as *ashraf* 'and took and hung up above two hundred of the rebels, beside killing many in the conflict. This was a rebellion of the green heads, or descendants of Mahomet, of which there are said to be above thirty thousand at Aleppo, exclusive of women and children' (Parsons 1808: 64). The *ashraf*, the descendants of the Prophet Muhammad, were highly influential in eighteenth-century Aleppo. Dr William George Browne who was in Aleppo in 1797, estimated that around sixty thousand lived in the city.[25] The *ashraf* inhabited Aleppo at least since the Abbasids era, but upon the Ottoman conquest of Syria they enjoyed many privileges: they were exempted from paying tax, received salaries from the Ottoman treasury and dominated the religious and legal hierarchy in the empire. Many of them were engaged in trade and succeeded in accumulating huge wealth.[26] They derived political power from the law that prohibited the central government and its governors in the provinces to interfere in their affairs. As Carsten Niebuhr wrote, only the head of the *ashraf*, called 'Nakib', can prosecute a descendant of the Prophet Muhammad who commits a felony. But the Ottoman government, Niebuhr added, often found ways to limit their growing power and influence in Aleppo (Niebuhr 1792: II, 208).[27]

The Swiss explorer John Lewis Burkhardt wrote that in eighteenth-century Aleppo, the power of the *ashraf* grew to the extent that their representative in the city Muhammad Effendi Taha Zadah, a man of enormous wealth, 'obliged several pashas who would not yield to his counsels and designs to quit the town' (Burkhardt 1822: 649). Muhammad Effendi, Herbert L. Bodman in his *Political Factions in Aleppo: 1760-1826* (1963) observes, was then imprisoned and exiled because he was accused of hoarding grain which 'had been the cause for the scarcity of food in the city' (Bodman 1963: 101). Parsons was silent about all these developments, particularly about the hoarding of grain in Aleppo, perhaps because he was uneasy about the idea of critiquing a similar occurrence that troubled the waters of British-Indian relations in the 1770s. As many commentators during the period stated, the mismanagement of taxes and the economy by the East India Company in Bengal, in addition to the human miseries caused by droughts and crop failures, were responsible for the famine that hit Bengal in the 1770s.[28]

While some British travellers and those who examined their works considered rebellions in Aleppo and the Levant region as sign of Ottoman decline, Parsons, who supported the Ottoman governor against the rebels in Aleppo, saw it as sign of the victory of government over lawlessness.[29] Although Parsons lived for many years in Syria, he had nothing to say about the complex social and political landscape of government in Aleppo. Importantly, the fact that Parsons was on the side of government against disorder and rebellions indicates that British travel writers often portrayed the Levant in a way that reveals more about them and their nations than about the region they travelled: to that end, the inclination with peace and order that Parsons had in Aleppo was shaped by the agitation in Britain about the chaos and rebellion looming large in America. It is in the same year that Samuel Johnson, in *The Patriot* (1774), recalled how '[h]e is no lover of his country, that unnecessarily disturbs its peace' that we find Parsons cheering for the success of the Ottoman governor in crushing unruly factions (Johnson 1774: 7). Such an attitude was shown during a period when the British government was facing a growing rebellion in America centred around America's rejections of commercial monopolies and tax impositions. It is this political and economic context both in Britain and the empire that informed Parsons's observations of the political, economic and religious landscape of Aleppo.

Rebellious Arabs

On 14 March 1774, Parsons left Aleppo, heading towards Baghdad. Three Englishmen, the merchants William and Charles Smith and the chaplain Robert Foster accompanied him to the gates of the city. In a few hours, they reached 'the river Coie [Kwaik] where we found our servants had pitched my tent, and got everything ready for our reception', Parsons recalled (Parsons 1808: 75). Parsons joined a commercial caravan which 'consisted of near eight hundred camels richly laden, beside many mules, asses, and dromedaries, used by the sheik, his officers, and the passengers, for riding' (Parsons 1808: 76). The caravan was well-protected. 'We had one hundred and five Arab soldiers', he rejoiced, 'with their officers to guard the caravan; some of every tribe which is to be met with on the deserts, and twelve Turkish merchants, with their servants; all which, together with myself and two servants, made one hundred and thirty who carried fire arms, each of us having a musquets, a pair of pistols, and a sabre; besides all the cameliers (men who attend, feed, load, and unload the camels), about one hundred and fifty in number, had each a sabre and a pair of pistols' (Parsons 1808: 67). Normally across caravan routes, the cooperation of Arab tribes, mainly the Annazah (Arab) tribe confederation who migrated from central Arabia to southern Iraq and eastern Syria in the late seventeenth century, was considered essential for delivering goods and passengers between Aleppo and Mesopotamia.[30] To that end, Ottoman governors were keen on recruiting soldiers from these tribes to protect caravans. Parsons, nevertheless, noted a fierce enmity between the Ottomans (who were nominally responsible for the safety of the caravan) and the Arab tribes. 'It seems that they [Arabs] are fond of retaliating on the Turks', Parsons observed [...]

> for when they are in great cities or towns in Turkey, they are held in little account, and a sheik or emir (which is an Arabian prince), when summoned before a pasha, meets with no better reception than the poorest Turk; but in the desert he is a monarch indeed, and when he chuses to decamp, he stalks away, or mounts his dromedary (without designing to speak to anyone), and is immediately followed by his standard bearer, mounted on his dromedary, displaying Mahomet' standard on a pike, which is the signal for the cameliers to load and follow. If the gentlemen, or merchants chuse to stay behind, they may, as he takes no notice of any man. (Parsons 1808: 81–82)

Historians often attribute the political tension between Arab tribes and the Ottoman government during the period to the clash over the control of commercial routes that extended eastwards from Aleppo to the Persian front and pilgrimage routes that stretched westwards from Damascus to the holy cities of Mecca and Medina. According to author Karl K. Barbir, Ottoman governors often succeeded in securing a safe passage for travellers and goods cross Arab land via a system of patronage based on awarding large sums of money to tribal leaders.[31] This is not to say that the Ottoman government in Istanbul showed no interest in countering rebellious Arab tribes.[32] As Bruce Masters argues, 'When political manipulation failed, it was also useful on occasion for the central treasury to provide a large infusion of cash to buy the tribes' goodwill' (Masters 2013: 96). Parsons recalled how the Ottoman government often recruited members of

Arab tribes to protect caravan routes. But he noted that political relationships between Ottoman governors and Arab tribes were steeped in conflicts.

In an age in which Britain's American subjects were in an open rebellion against the British government, Parsons was impressed with the rebellious spirit of the Arabs, their ability to range across vast deserts uninterrupted from the imposition of the Ottoman government.[33] One Briton, who met Parsons in Aleppo several times, however, was nuanced in approaching the topic of political relations between the desert and the city. Patrick Russell, who served as a physician to the Levant Company factory in Aleppo between 1756 and 1771, recalled in a note attached to the 1794 edition of his brother's *The Natural History of Aleppo*, originally published in 1756, that one Ottoman governor of Damascus, Asa'd Pasha Al-Azem, was a seasoned Ottoman politician who knew how to win the approval and friendship of the tribes inhabiting the overland routes between Damascus and Mecca. 'Asa'd enjoyed the government of Damascus', Russell wrote, 'for many years, and in the character of Emeer Hadge (the commander of the pilgrimage), he had conducted the Mecca Caravans ten or twelve pilgrimages successively' (Russell 1794: II, 404). Russell further added that Asa'd was a popular governor among the Arab tribes, that when the Ottoman sultan decided to remove him from office the Arabs were outraged because 'they had not been duly prepared for the change [...] and the young' governor, who replaced Asa'd, 'neglected the proper means of conciliating their good will' (Russell 1794: II, 404). The result of such a renewed tension was the tragical event of 1757 in which the Arabs 'attacked and plundered' the Damascus pilgrimage caravan, an event which sent shockwaves across the Ottoman Empire because managing, funding and conducting the pilgrimage caravan in the Levant often lent the Ottoman sultan a layer of legitimacy in the eyes of his subjects.[34] This attack confirmed the weakness of the Ottoman sultan.

Such an event, Russell concluded, 'caused universal consternation in the Empire, particularly in the capital', an event which cost Asa'd, whom the Ottoman government in Istanbul suspected of being the perpetrator of this attack, his life (Russell 1994: II, 404). James Porter, the English ambassador to the Ottoman Empire at the time, to whom Russell owed his report about Asa'd's political influence among the Arab tribes, observed that in 1757 some Arabs attacked and plundered the Damascus pilgrims' caravan after Sultan Mustafa III suspended Asa'd, an ally of the Arab tribes, from office; As'ad was 'a man of sovereign credit' who 'married into one of their chief tribes'; he was hugely respected by the tribes inhabiting the Syrian routes to Mecca and Medina (Porter 1768: I, 28). During the 1790s, in a period in which the central government in London was actively recruiting men from Scotland, particularly from the clans in the Highlands, during the war with Revolutionary France, Russell spoke of a reconciliatory relation between government and tribes in Syria.[35] Russell (1727–1805) belongs to a generation that witnessed the brutal policies of the British government in its war against the Highlanders: perhaps a past strife between the British government and the clans in the Highlands of Scotland influenced his view of how one Ottoman governor was able to win the approval of the Arab tribes. Parsons, in 1773, however, associated tribalism with rebellion at a time when the American colonies were on the brink of a revolutionary war with the British government. Thus, his view of the political tensions between the Arab tribes and the Ottoman government was coloured by anxieties in Britain over the rebellion of the American colonies.

Publicly Spirited Arabs

Although both Parsons and Russell had different perspectives on the relationship between government and rebellious tribes, both agreed that Arabs inhabiting the deserts of Syria posed a problem to an Ottoman administration crippled by its inability to control the desert. In European thought, the trope about the independence of Arabs in their barren deserts and the inability of empires to subjugate them goes back to the time of the classical historian Diodorus of Sicily, who wrote about the failure of 'the kings of the Persians' and 'those of the Macedonians' to conquer the Arabs: 'this nation is one which loves freedom and under no circumstances submits to a foreign ruler' (Sicily 1946: I, 351). For Diodorus, Arabs were freedom-loving people; it was their barren and parched desert which protected them from foreign armies rather than their valour. In the eighteenth century, the trope of the freedom-loving Arabs continued to circulate in European writings, particularly the story about the failure of Alexander the Great to conquer Arabia.[36] Such a trope about the freedom of the Arabs in their deserts resonated with many eighteenth-century European philosophers and travel writers who interpreted the freedom of the Arabs in the context of what Christopher Berry called 'the dangers of commerce'; that is, the debate in Enlightenment Europe about the meaning of liberty in commercial polities in which relationships between people and their government are governed by contractual relationships in which individuals depend on and show obedience to a political entity which in turn lays the laws that protect individuals and their private possessions.[37]

For the French philosopher Montesquieu, the poor condition of living in barren deserts explains why the Arabs should be seen as free of 'servitude' in their societies; after all, they were unburdened with the contractual relationships of commercial society in which individuals are bound to submit not only to each other but also the law and government that protect their property.[38] Montesquieu's idea about the freedom of the Arabs was consistent with the French traveller and philosopher Constantine Volney who argued that hot climate prevents people from turning into settled agricultural communities and thus makes them unable to form a regular government: dearth necessitates wars and acts of pillage among tribes. But he also added that climate is not the only cause for the independence of Arabs in their deserts; the nature of their mode of subsistence demands that they move from one spot to another in search of pastures for their animals, which, Volney argued, explains why tribes do not seek to possess immovable property. The fact that their properties are not fixed but rather mobile means that their social units do not require complex laws guided by a regular form of government. For Volney, as well as for many Enlightenment philosophers, a milder form of government among Arabs can be attributed to their primitive modes of subsistence. The more materially advanced a society becomes, the more unequal it gets.[39] Volney agreed with Adam Smith who in *The Wealth of Nations* made it clear that 'Wherever there is property, there is great inequality' (Smith 1776: II, 314).

This materialist framework in eighteenth-century European thought which associated Arabs with a life of freedom and equality in comparison to those of commercial societies appeared in many British travel accounts about the overland routes to India. Bartholomew Plaisted, who travelled between Basra and Aleppo in the 1750s, noted how the Ottoman ruler of Baghdad was in an open war against the desert Arabs. Arabs, he wrote, cannot tolerate the idea of living under a regular government and 'will not bear to be rigorously dealt with, for they are a people, who are bold, cunning and revengeful' (Plaisted 1758: 22). Plaisted associated the lack of regular government, complex laws and hierarchical society among Arabs to their idleness and inability to understand the benefits of living in a modern society in which people are protected by their government. Like Plaisted, Niebuhr reported how the Arabs did not understand the concept of private property. Niebuhr stated that Arabs, unlike Europeans, do not submit to a ruler whose power is derived from owning land; their chiefs do not own the property that differentiates them from the common people. Among Arabs, what makes a man stand out in the crowd is his 'superiority of abilities' rather than his wealth, 'age or lineal succession' (Niebuhr 1792: II, 19). A 'right of election' requires that the ruler treat those beneath him as 'associates' rather than 'subjects, sharing with them his sovereign authority' (Ibid). It is because of their poverty (for the richest man among them cannot be richer than an ordinary citizen in Europe) and their primitive, non-commercial mode of subsistence that governance and law among Arabs appear mild. The lack of private property meant that the population there do not need a regular government. In 'The spirit of liberty, with which this warlike nation are animated', concluded Niebuhr, 'renders them incapable of servitude' (Ibid).

Like Niebuhr and Plaisted, Parsons explained the social and political nature of tribal life in the context of a developmental framework in Europe that associated commercial people with a life of interdependence rather than independence, with self-interest rather than civic virtues, with individualism rather than collectivism. While travelling in Arabian deserts and villages, Parsons was constantly looking for evidence that supports his preconceived notion about the lack of a culture of greed and individualism among the Arabs. For instance, he noted how 'their cotton, mulberry and olive grounds, and vineyards, as well as those fields where grain is sown, are all open, and in many places the public roads lead through them and their vineyards' (63). Land enclosures were not known in Syria and Mesopotamia. 'A large stone, set upright, marks each man's property in some places, in others, only a few sticks, as no man ever thinks of removing his neighbour's landmark' (36). Parsons here may have mounted a critique of the British government whose agricultural projects commonly associated with enclosing common land for improvement purposes alienated and dispossessed many in England and Scotland.

But what intrigued Parsons above anything else was the culture of collectivism among the Arabs. En route to Baghdad, Parsons, on 2 May, recorded how it was 'entertaining' for him to observe the camp of the Muntafiq Arab tribe 'decamp as nothing could be more regular'. Such an entertaining scene, however, encouraged him to reflect on the nature of political and social hierarchy in pre-commercial society: 'first went the sheep and goatherds', 'then followed the camels and assess', 'these were followed by older men and women mounted on asses surrounded by young men, women, boys, girls, on foot', and finally 'the procession is closed by the chief of tribe whom they call emir or father' mounting his horse and surrounded by chiefs 'all on horses, with many servants on foot' (110).[40] The idea that Arabs view their prince as father is quite revealing. Parsons's obsession with the nature of authority in primitive society was shaped by an Enlightenment discourse of improvement pioneered by Adam Smith who, in *The Wealth of Nations,* argued that rather than the 'superiority of fortune', it is 'the superiority either of age or personal qualities' that qualifies a man for leadership among tribes and clans in contrast to 'opulent and civilized society' where relationship are not necessarily paternal but rather based on what he called 'the authority of fortune' and that of 'birth' (Smith 1776: II, 317–319). Volney, who spent many years among the Arab tribes of Syria, explained Smith's assertion that there is a patriarchal relationship between leaders and their tribe members. Volney stated that as a man from a wealthy tribe, a commander of their army and their supreme judge, the chief commands the utmost reverence of the whole tribe to the extent that the members of his tribe 'are distinguished from' other tribes 'by the name of their respective chiefs or by that of the ruling family' (Volney 1788: I, 401). It is this patriarchal relationship that explains the sense of collectivism and lack of individualism in tribal culture: when Arabs 'speak of any of the individuals who compose them, they call them the children of such a chief, though they may not be all really of his blood and he himself may have been long dead since' (Ibid).

Parsons and Volney wrote about the social and political organisation of Arab tribes from an Enlightenment perspective. The idea of representing a political leader as 'a father' to his people reveals an Enlightenment developmental discourse, one in which pastoral societies do not show the same level of hierarchy that exists in civilised society. Whenever private property exists in society, such as that in Europe, then the line of hierarchy based on ownership of land sharpens the divide between peasant, aristocratic and ruling classes. In pastoral and agrarian societies, however, this hierarchy does not exist. Rather, as John Millar wrote, 'Superiority in strength, courage, and other personal accomplishments, is the first circumstance by which any single person is raised to be the leader of a clan, and by which he is enabled to maintain his authority' (Millar 1771: 121). Aware of this debate in Europe, Parsons found that an Arab leader did not act as a despot but rather as a father figure for the whole tribe; hence the symbolism in Parsons's statement above in which the leader of the tribe was 'a father' who protected his tribesmen. The observation in Parsons's passage above that the 'father' of the tribe stays far behind rather than at the front of a procession indicates how the emir was keen on protecting the tribe in case of enemy attack from behind and is also a reference to his humble character.

Ishmaelite Arabs

In European writings about Islam and the Arabs, the biblical characters of the Old Testament, Ishmael and Hagar, have often been recast to address European exigencies (religious, moral and social). In Medieval Europe, as Christine Petra Sellin in her book *Fractured Families and Rebel Maidservants* (2006) shows, European thinkers such as St

Augustine considered Hagar and Ishmael as the inversion of the pure, heavenly character of Sarah and Issac who represented a promise of salvation, a covenant with the Lord. For many who were inspired by St Paul and St Augustine, Ishmael and his mother represented exiled outcasts and enemies of the true faith [Figure 7]. Some Medieval Christians referred to them as Jewish.[41] For others, Ishmael 'stood for Muslims, who were considered Christendom's greatest enemies; Ishmaelites were thought to be the ancestors of the homeless Saracens' (Sellin 2006: 13). To that end, Pope Urban II, in his fiery sermon which opened the Crusaders campaigns of the eleventh century, invoked the image of the perfidious Ishmaelites to encourage Western Christians to 'cast out the slave women and her son' from the Holy Land.[42] In the seventeenth-century Netherlands, as Sellin observes, Ishmael and Hagar were shown some sympathy by a group of Dutch painters whose work was shaped by a broader cultural and religious currents prizing 'the primacy of the Christian family and order in domestic life' (Sellin 2006: 5). But the negative references to Ishmael and Hagar continued to be shown in early-modern European representations of Islam.

In European travel writings, the idea that the manners, traditions and politics of Bedouin Arabs resemble those of the followers of Ishmael can be traced back to the twelfth century. The medieval Jewish traveller Benjamin of Tudela, who travelled in Europe, Asia and Africa for eight years, between 1165 and 1173, recalled the biblical image of desert wars (Isiah X) when observing the manners of Jews and 'the Arabians their neighbours' who lead 'expeditions into distant provinces' to 'take the spoil and to take the prey' (Tudela 1840: I, 112–13). Tudela, whose native city Navarrese in Spain was mostly inhabited by rural communities, was fascinated with the manners and modes of subsistence of Arabs and Jews who lived in barren deserts. 'These Arabians are Bedouins, who live in tents in the deserts and have no fixed abode', he wrote, 'and

Figure 7 Expulsion of Hagar and Ishmael, Willem Thibaut, 1580. Source: Rijksmuseum, Amsterdam.

who are in the habit of undertaking marauding expeditions in the provinces of Yemen' (Ibid 1840: I, 113). Some of the Jewish people, he adds, 'cultivate land and rear cattle' but, like the Arabs, they are mostly 'a terror to their neighbours' (Ibid). This image of ungovernable desert dwellers – which owes its origin to the biblical Ishmael – continued to influence the observations of early-modern European travellers and commentators on the Arabs. 'Arabia signifieth Holy, as Solinsos [Solon] affirmth', wrote Samuel Purchas in *Purchas his Pilgrimage* (1629), '[b]ut in Scripture [...] Harabi signifieth both a robber by the way, and an Arabian' (Purchas 1626: 323). William Bidulph, the English chaplain in Aleppo in 1600, posited the Arabs as Ishmaelites: 'They call themselves Saracens, of Sarah', as Bidulph in his travel diary wrote, 'but they are Ishmaelites, of Ishmael, Abraham's son by Hagar and therefore also called Hagareens' (Bidulph 1609: 69). Ishmaelites 'are base, beggarly, and roguish people, wandering up and down, and living by spoil, which they account no sin, because they are Mahomet's countrymen, and he would allow them liberty to live by theft' (Ibid).[43] 'Mahomet' allowed them to pillage and rob people in the deserts.

Edward Gibbon, in his coolheaded analysis of the freedom and independence of Bedouin Arabs, critiqued the efforts of European writers to confirm 'the truth of Christianity' by referring to the manners, morals and mores of the inhabitants of barren deserts.[44] The fact that Gibbon critiqued the idea in Europe that the Arab manners confirm biblical reports about ancient Hebrews indicates how old tropes in Europe were not easily brushed away by dominant structures of feeling which explained differences between nations in culturalist and materialist rather than theological terms.[45] But despite Gibbon's critique of the residual religious tropes of modern Europe, the idea that the manners and traditions of Arabs corresponded with and confirmed what the Bible recorded about the Hebrews and the Gentiles did not have many advocates in Enlightenment thought. In a period in which Arabs and Muslims were no longer seen as a threat to Europe (the Muslim empires at the time, Ottoman, Mongol and Persian empires were commonly seen as inferior to those of the Europeans), descendants of Ishmael became synonymous with barbarism rather than infidelity. Barbarism here represented an inverted mirror image of modern Europeans widely seen as civilised, tolerant, peaceful and industrious in contrast to many non-European nations who do not encourage commerce and science.[46]

Seen in this context, the eighteenth-century Arabist, Simon Ockley, in his *The History of the Saracens* (1757), recalled how medieval Arabs produced great science, letters and conquests: 'their Progress in Learning once they had entered upon it, seeming no less wonderful than that of their Conquest' (Ockley 1757: I, xi).[47] But, Ockley added, the Arabs 'now' had nothing to do with the great medieval Arabs of the past; rather than continuing to evolve and improve, Arabs have regressed. Their modes of subsistence are mainly reliant upon robbing caravans and travellers in deserts. They 'excuse themselves by alleging the hard usage of their progenitor Ishmael, and think they have to indemnify themselves, not only upon the posterity of Isaac, but also upon everybody else who falls in their way' (Ockley 1757: I, 3).[48] In his *A Journal Kept on a Journey from Bassora to Baghdad over the Little Desert* (1779), the fervent Protestant Samuel Evers wrote an entire chapter on the 'the distinguishing particulars of ISHMAEL, and of his descendants to this very day' (Evers 1779: 88). Like Ockley, Evers saw no difference between the manners of the Arabs he encountered in the deserts and those of Ishmael he read about in the Bible. He noted that 'after the long space of above three thousand years, for it is to be remarked that according to the language of the scripture, what is spoken of the head or founder of any people, must be understood to be spoken of his descendants likewise and to be their general character, as well as his particular' (Ibid). For Evers, Arabs belong to a primitive and unpolished age rather than to one of civility: 'by this expression was meant that Ishmael and his posterity were to be wild, fierce, savage, ranging in the deserts, and not easily softened and tamed to society; And whoever hath read or known anything of this people, knoweth this to be their true and genuine character' (Evers 1779: 89–90). Arabs still bear 'bows and arrows', Evers adds, and 'to this day the greatest part of them are called the Wild Arabs' (Ibid).

Robert Hunter who travelled the Syrian deserts in 1780 recalled how Arabs did not care about settling in and cultivating barren land; rather they continued to practise the same primitive mode of subsistence that their ancestor Ismael pursued: 'Robbing is their trade by profession' (Hunter 1798: 192). While Arabs still bear arrows and bows, those who live in civilised societies use pens and shovels. While war and robberies are the skills Arabs are good at, commerce and agriculture remain the practices of those who live in modern and industrialised society. Eliot Eliot, who was in the Syrian deserts in 1750, confirmed this and suggested that 'As for the Arabs of the desert, I cannot see how they can be trusted; for they make a trade of robbery and are brought up to it from their infancy' (Eliot 1928: 98). Arabs, Eliot continued, 'are continually wandering from place to place and seeking whom they may devour and make no scruple of pillaging their own countrymen when they have a superior force'(Ibid). Nations who change their material conditions, Eliot added, normally find solutions to problems of poverty and religious prejudices. Arabs, however, he observed, resist change: 'Arabs of the desert [...] are ignorant, brutish, low-lived set of people, which is no wonder, considering their manner of life, and the meanness of their education, in a place where they can have little or no knowledge of the rest of the world' (Ibid). If modern, civilised nations are conscious of social hierarchies, Arabs pay no attention to this: 'they have no acquaintance with politeness or social virtue, and consequently have little regard for the distinction among mankind, or the difference which is due from inferiors to their superiors' (Ibid).

Many eighteenth-century writers used the image of Ishmaelite Arabs as a confirmation of how societies progress from primitivism to civilisation. Arabs no longer represented the people whose manners and traditions confirm the depictions in the Bible but rather they were seen as the unimproved pastoralists whose modes of subsistence, manners and mores remind modern Europeans of the material and political evolutions of their societies and also make them understand how other nations and cultures in different parts of the world have not yet been able to reach their level of civility. In most European accounts of non-Europeans, barbarism as a secular category referred to the primitive manners and traditions of nations whose economic modes of subsistence were perceived to be backward.[49] Rather than being measured with the yardstick of their closeness or distance from Christianity, Arabs were considered by the rationalist and progressivist as purposeless nomads with the mode of subsistence and manners nowhere close to those of commercial and civilised society. This materialistic discourse in Europe in which politics, manners and morals of a society were measured by the yardstick of progress shaped Parsons's characterisation of the political and social character of the Arabs: 'the Arabs are Ishmaelites', Parsons noted, 'which they are fond of telling into Europeans, thinking, and indeed believing, that their origin is not known to the inhabitants of Europe' (Parsons 1808: 110). However, Parsons did not recall that Europeans are superior to the Arabs.

Parsons was familiar with the developmental discourse in Europe, but his travel account revealed none of the above prejudices expressed by his countrymen (Hunter, Elliot, Eversfield and even the Arabist Ockley) who wrote about the Arabs. Instead, he admired their collectivist and cooperative culture which he contrasted with that of modern Europe. A publicly spirited culture among Arabs, he wrote, guarantees social equality: 'this, however, can be truly said to their praise that there are not any lazy people among them, nor any beggars. The poor are industrious, and the aged, sick, blind, and lame, are maintained by the public, when they cease to be able to work' (Parsons 1808: 147). Like Ives, as we saw in Chapter two, Arabs, for Parsons, constituted a screen upon which his fears of the loss of public virtue in modern society were projected.

After many years of living in Syria, Parsons learned that Arabs do not show vanity, corruption and individualism which many European moralists associated with modern, commercial societies. While Ives (in Chapter two), commenting on the poverty of the Arabs, praised British efforts to help the poor and establish workhouses, Parsons found the collectivist spirit in Arab culture far superior to anything else he had seen.

Parsons, while travelling among the Arabs, proposed an alternative world to his British readers, one in which happiness is predicated upon collectivism, moderation, temperance and sympathy rather than avarice, competitiveness and vanity which many during the period associated with commercial society. Near Coote, a city on the banks of the Euphrates which his caravan passed through on the route to Basra, Parsons observed a big camp. 'Here I saw above twenty tame ostriches, with red woollen cloth collars about their necks, and small brass bells' (Parsons 1808: 148). As a merchant, Parsons 'asked the price of a pair' but 'was told that they belonged to the prince and were not to be sold [...]' (Ibid). Parsons learned from his interactions with Arabs that although their tribe was 'famous for breeding horses of the best race [...]' (Parsons 1808: 149), their love of horses is not only for making profits. They bred animals such as 'greyhounds and falcons, both for sale and use' (Ibid). Parsons praised this and suggested that 'no people are more fond of hunting and hawking than the Arabs, as there are plenty of antelopes and hares in most parts where they reside' (Ibid). Parsons might have known that Arab tribes in Syria, Iraq and the Gulf were actively engaged in a lucrative horse trade with India and Europe, one in which Arab horses were exported as items of luxury and for purposes of horse-breeding.[50] For Parsons, however, Arabs were little concerned about accumulating wealth and more interested in sports, just like the Spartans of ancient times whose virtue was predicated on their military rather than commercial character. The idea in Parsons's account that the virtuous character of Arabs is inextricably linked to their military and non-commercial pursuit caught the imagination of Edward Gibbon in his *The History of the Decline and Fall of the Roman*

Empire (Vol 5, 1788), who associated the Arabs with a pastoral stage in which people are imaginative, sporty, austere and free from social and political hierarchies known in commercial society.[51]

Siege of Basra: Commerce, Virtue and Corruption

Parsons left Aleppo on 14 March and reached Baghdad on 7 May. He stayed in Baghdad for the whole summer of 1773. He left the city on 22 October accompanied by Major Knudson of the East India Company, Marcad Awed, an Armenian merchant, and Joseph Emin, an Armenian officer who was described by Parsons as an 'imposture who had passed himself off in London' a few 'years back as Prince Heraclius of Georgia' (Parsons 1808: 139). Clearly, Parsons did not hold a lot of respect for Emin who was in the service of the East India Company at the time.[52] Parsons and his fellow travellers reached Basra on 11 November 1774. In Basra, he found the East India Company's representative in the city, Henry Moore, embroiled in local political and commercial conflicts. Basra, like Aleppo, was important for British commercial and political interests in the Levant and the Persian Gulf. English commercial relations with Basra date back to the late sixteenth century when the East India Company joined the rulers of Persia, Oman and Baghdad in their aim to expel the Portuguese ships and settlers from the Persian Gulf.[53] Before the arrival of the English in the Persian Gulf, the Portuguese had held the upper hand in the region for more than a century.[54] After the Portuguese left in the seventeenth century, the English became the dominant naval power in the Persian Gulf: they established a factory in Basra in 1640 and 'obtained a license from the Turkish Basha to land' their 'goods under favourable circumstance' that none of 'any other European nations enjoyed'.[55] Other European nations such as the Dutch and the French traded and settled in the Persian Gulf in the seventeenth and eighteenth centuries.[56] However, Britons benefited most from their dominance of the region, politically and commercially on account of a host of reasons. First, the British ships were sophisticated which helped in navigating and expanding their commercial interests. Their military posts in India provided a strong background. Second, their friendly relations with Ottoman, Arab and Persian rulers and the commercial networks they established with diverse groups such as the Armenian, Jewish, Ottoman and Arab merchants consolidated their position. And finally, their resolve in combating piracy in the Persian Gulf made them a force to reckon with.[57]

The English first appeared in the Persian Gulf in the city of Bandar Abbas (known by European travellers at the time as Gambroon) where they, throughout the seventeenth century, traded (without paying any taxes) in British woollen cloth, steel and Persian silk.[58] Throughout the eighteenth century, however, Persia was in a state of political turmoil which impacted the supply of silk to the Bandar Abbas port. The English then decided to move their factory to the port of Basra. Moreover, the East India Company quit Bandar Abbas in the wake of a French attack on the Company's establishment in 1759.[59] They never thought of returning.[60] Consequently, in 1763, Basra replaced Bandar Abbas as the Company's post in the Persian Gulf, and a year later the English agent in the city was given diplomatic status as a consul. Basra was an important trading station for the British in the Persian Gulf: Surat cloth and wool which arrived via English ships were sold in Basra at exorbitant prices to the extent that the Ottomans, Persians and local Arab rulers constantly 'vied for authority over it'.[61] Politically, Basra was part of the Ottoman *Pashalik* of Baghdad, but economically it mainly depended on the flourishing trade of the Indian Ocean which connected India, Syria, Anatolia and mainland Europe.

Throughout the eighteenth century, Basra and Baghdad were constantly ravaged by the plague (the worst was in 1773) which disrupted trade and reduced the number of inhabitants, as Parsons reported, from 300,000 to 50,000. And, as a result of the plague, the East India Company suspended its production in April 1773. Henry Moore and his fellow Britons from East India Company left Basra for Bombay on the 26th of April. Yet, as soon the plague subsided, Basra bounced back. Henry Moore and William Digges La Touche returned in October 1773.[62] Basra quickly recovered, and Britons resumed business in the city.[63] John Griffith, who visited Basra in 1786, recalled how the city was 'the emporium of this quarter of the world' (Griffiths 1805: 389). It is through Basra that Indian goods reached as far as Aleppo and Istanbul, thus supplying the East India Company with much-needed revenue necessary for its battles in India. 'It is here that richly laden ships', continued Griffiths, 'from every part of India, pour in their valuable cargoes' which include 'pearls, elegant gold and silver cloths, shawls and other splendid articles of dress' (Ibid). These ships carry back to India 'specie or jewels' and 'a certain number of highly bred Arab horses' mainly bought by the English, those 'gentlemen who promoted the pleasures of the turf and chace' (Griffiths 1805: 389–390). 'It is a place of very great trade, owing to it's convenient situation', Parsons wrote, 'as merchants can here purchase the produce of most parts of India, Persia, and Arabia, at the first hand, the ships from these countries bringing their rich cargoes immediately from the place of their growth, or manufacture, to this port' (Parsons 1808: 154).

Europeans, Parsons added, never lost the chance of collecting 'specie' in the city. '[Merchants] bring, for the most part', Parsons wrote,

> [...] specie in gold or silver of Turkey and Persia, or Venetian zechins; but the merchants who come from Aleppo bring European goods for sale, (chiefly from Venice), which they sell and return with piece goods from India, coffee from Mocha, and many kinds of drugs from different parts of Arabia and Persia; all which are conveyed from Bussora to Aleppo, either directly by caravans of camels, or first to Bagdad by water, and from thence by camels to Aleppo. From Bagdad great quantities of piece goods are sent to Smyrna and Constantinople; but most of the drugs are sent to Scanderoon, from whence they are shipped for London, Venice, Amsterdam, Marseilles, and Leghorn; excepting the goods which are carried directly from Bussora to Aleppo by caravans, and the small quantity which is consumed at Bussora the remainder, which is immense, goes first to Bagdad, and from thence to Damascus, to Constantinople (by the way of Ezerum), and to Trebisond, in the Black Sea ; excepting what is consumed at Bagdad and its dependent territories. (Parsons 1808: 155)

Merchants in the region found in Basra a global magnet. 'Christians, Jews, Arabians and Indians', John Griffiths who visited the region observed, 'are more or less engaged in commercial transactions' (Griffiths 1805: 390). 'Jews and Indians seem to have engrossed that branch which is more immediately connected with jewels, the precious metals and exchange of money', he added, whereas the Armenians 'attend to the general concerns of an import and export trade' (Ibid). 'In consequence of these advantages', Parsons stated, 'here are many rich Armenian and Jew merchants, as well as Turks and Christians, both natives and foreigners, who purchase either on commission, or on their own account on speculation, and resell to such foreign merchants as come here at stated times to purchase' (Parsons 1808: 154). Basra was the commercial hub of the Persian Gulf.

Parsons was also ware of the political importance of Basra. It was an important strategic position on the routes to India. The British factory in Basra was vital for forwarding letters and dispatches to Aleppo, Constantinople and India, especially during periods of wars between the East India Company and its rivals in India. British agents stationed in Basra often reported to the East India Presidency in Bombay about political activities in the region.[64] They were also tasked to spy on French activities in the Levant and the Persian Gulf.[65] In Basra, Parsons stayed with two men who played an important role in the history of British relations with the Persian Gulf: Henry Moore, the East India Company consul in Basra, and his assistant William Digges La Touche, who succeeded Moore as an agent in late 1775. Moore, who had a 'peculiar and flighty character', was hostile to Persian rulers.[66] His anti-Persian policy – which is a line he took in total disregard to the official policy of the East India Company – risked British commercial and political interests in the Persian Gulf and triggered the Persian military campaign which occupied Basra in 1775.

Unlike Moore, La Touche had friendly relations with the Persians, Ottomans and Arabs. His amiable character won him the affections of the inhabitants of Basra, the friendship of Solyman Agha of Basra and the trust of Karim Khan Zand of Persia.[67] One reason why Britons, including Moore, preferred the Arab-Ottoman part of the Persian Gulf was their ability to exert their political will over the government of Baghdad because of the huge loans they often provided to local rulers.[68] La Touche, with the assistance of the British ambassador in Istanbul Robert Liston, lobbied the Ottoman Porte in favour of appointing Solyman Agha, a friend of the English in the Persian Gulf, as a governor of both Baghdad and Basra in the hope that, as La Touche and George Abraham of the East India factory of Baghdad wrote in a letter in 1779, 'the Basha continuing to show our factory in particular, every indulgence and favours in his power' (4).[69] English merchants preferred the cities of Basra and Baghdad over Bander Abbas, Bushehr and Shiraz because of the liberal tax policy of Ottoman governors with whom the East India Company was often on good terms. 'The pasha of Bagdad', Parsons noted, 'is always sure of receiving two customs on all goods which are sent from Bussora, viz. three per cent, from Europeans (Franks), and eight per cent, from all Turks, or Turkish subjects, Persians, and other Asiatics' (Parsons 1808: 155). Due to this liberal tax policy, as the English saw it, the East India Company made huge sums of money from the Basra-India trade. 'All goods brought in English ships', Parsons noted, 'pay a duty and consulage to the East India Company, which amounts to six per cent; this duty is over and above what is paid to the pasha of Bagdad; and as all the goods from India are brought in English ships, it amounts in the year to a considerable sum' (Parsons 1808: 158). While the English traveller John Griffiths superficially noted how the rich market in Basra was open for all trading communities, Parsons, a merchant himself, noted that this market was though open for all but was not necessarily a level playing field. He knew that his countrymen in Basra were the winners in such a commercial context because of their monopoly of trade in the region, one rooted in what David Hume called 'the jealousy of trade' which the East India Company adopted in India, China and America throughout the eighteenth century.[70]

Parsons observed how the expansion of trade in Basra, of which the English were the main players, occurred at the expense of other trading ports in the region. 'It is about five years', Parsons wrote, 'since the company ceased to have a factory at Bushear; for the two last years that the factory subsisted little business was done, as ships from India bound to Bussora did not so frequently call at Bushear in their way as heretofore they were accustomed to do' (Parsons 1808: 185). From the Persian point of view, the man to blame for this loss of trade in the ports of Persia was Henry Moore, the East India Company representative in Basra who often rejected Karim Khan's offers for reviving British trade in Persia. 'This alteration the khan attributed to the agent of Bussora', Parsons recalled, 'who, he was informed, had given orders to the masters of all ships from India to Bussora, not to put any goods on shore at Bushear' (Ibid). The tension between the Company and the Persians seemed to have been aggravated by the 'unaccountable antipathy which the agent [Moore] at Bussora seemed to have conceived against the Khan'.[71] Karim Khan, Parsons further recalled, took revenge against the Company by capturing one English ship, *The Tyger*, which was on its way from Basra to Bombay in 1773. Two Englishmen on board – Beaumont and Green – were captured and taken to Shiraz. They were released in 1775 after the East India Company agreed to resume their commercial activities on the Persian coast of the Gulf. Before this development took place, Karim Khan [Figure 8] had long angered the English with his piratical activities. With his own permission, a group of Arabs from the coast of Persia chased and captured the *Britannia*, an East India Company ship loaded with cargoes heading for Basra. Moore wrote to the company asking for military enforcements against Karim Khan Zand, but the Company rejected his demand.[72]

For Parsons, the pursuit of commerce not only brings many benefits to those involved in it but also, as Adam Smith suggested, leads to clashes and conflicts once it transgresses collaboration and breeds jealousy and resentment.[73] Parsons noted how Karim Khan Zand's revenge against the English was illustrated by the military campaign he led against Basra. 'On this account, the khan was much irritated against the English', Parsons observed, that 'he declared that since Bussora had all the trade from India with the English (to the exclusion of his country), he would be revenged by destroying Bussora' (Parsons 1808: 150–156). Parsons opined that Karim Khan invaded Basra because he thought he was unfairly excluded from the prosperity and wealth of the region, but here Parsons was clearly not concerned with the causes of the conflict in the region beyond just the problems of monopolies and trade rivalry.

In the preface to *The Dynasty of the Kajars* (1833), translated to English from a Persian manuscript owned by the Persian ruler Fath-Ali Shah Qajar, the English diplomat and

Figure 8 Karim Khan Zand with an Ottoman ambassador, Iran; c. 1775. Source: Parkmuseerne.

author Sir Harford Jones Brydges, recalled that the main reason why Karim Khan invaded Basra is because Omar Pasha, 'a weak and needy ruler' of Baghdad, often mistreated Persian 'pilgrims' and 'merchants' who passed through Baghdad and Basra on their way to the pilgrim sites in Karbala, Mecca and Medina (Brydges 1833: cix). Kareem sent an envoy to the Ottoman court asking for an explanation but he failed to get satisfying answers; what he mostly received were empty promises. As such, 'the spirit of the Vakeel' was 'roused' and 'very early in 1775, he sent against Bussora a large force, under the command of his brother Sadik Khan; with a view as he declared in a sort of manifesto published on the occasion to, "to open the eyes of the sleepy-headed Turks"' (Brydges 1833: cx). John Gordon Lorimer, a diplomat in the British residency in Bushehr in 1913–1914, recalled that one important reason why Karim Khan invaded Basra was because of the British and Ottoman refusal to assist him in his war against the Imam of Oman. 'Mr Moore', Lorimer observed, 'apprised the Pasha of Baghdad that, so far as far as British vessels were concerned, the Vakil's demand was inadmissible' (Lorimer

1915: I, 1245). For Parsons, however, the Persian invasion in 1775 was principally a trade war in which both Karim Khan and the East India Company engaged in all kinds of treachery and deceit in their efforts to control the navigation of the Persian Gulf.

The biggest losers in this war, Parsons found, were the people of Basra and their ruler, Solyman Agha, 'who is not only very brave, but active and vigilant' during the siege (Parsons 1808: 163). Solyman, a man of Georgian origin, was appointed as an Ottoman governor of Basra in 1771.[74] He was not necessarily on good terms with Henry Moore because the latter refused to directly intervene in the war against the Persians: 'we were only merchants in Bussora', Moore told him, and so 'we had nothing to do with the disputes between the Country powers'.[75] Moore, despite his personal animosity towards the Persian ruler, was not often on good terms with Solyman: he often complained to the governor of Baghdad, Omar Pasha, about the despotic and extortionate policies of Solyman. In a letter he sent to Baghdad in January 1774, Moore complained that merchants informed 'me' that 'they have met with' the most 'oppressive and injurious treatments' from 'the government here during eight months in which I have been absent, money extorted from them by imprisoning their persons, and other proceedings shocking to freedom, and human nature'.[76]

For Parsons, however, Solyman Agha, who was appointed in 1797 as the governor of Baghdad, was a virtuous leader unlike the East India Company servants, Moore and La Touche, whose trade policies in the Gulf encouraged Karim Khan to invade Basra.[77] Karim Khan, who figured in eighteenth- and nineteenth-century British commentaries on Persia as a champion of trade, prosperity and peace in the region, nevertheless, appeared in Parsons's account as a brutal man who resorted to violence for commercial gains.[78] Parsons recalled how Karim, via his brother Sadik Khan who led the military campaign of 1775, sent an envoy to the Ottoman ruler of Basra and to Henry Moore demanding 'twenty-five lack of rupees for the ransom of the city [Basra]; if this is refused, the Persian general threatens to take it by storm in five days' (Parsons 1808: 167).

Despite this threat, Karim was keen on reviving trade in his country through peaceful means. Karim rose to power in 1751 after Persia had long suffered from a period of devastating civil wars after the assassination of Nadir Shah.[79] His reign was known for political stability. He was determined to restore the old reputation of Persia as a trading hub in the region. Sir Percy Sykes, in his *The History of Persia* (1915), recalls that Karim Zand in 1763 'gave exhausted Iran two decades of sorely needed rest' (Sykes 1915: II, 375). He granted the English merchants many privileges in the hope of reviving trade in Persia. Sykes quotes the *firman* which Karim issued in full in 1763: 'The English Company may have as much ground, and in any part of Bushire, as they choose to build a factory on, or at any other port in the Gulf [...]they may build factory-houses in any part of the kingdom they choose' (Sykes 1915: II, 357).

Parsons had nothing positive to say about Karim's polices in the region. For Parsons, the siege and the occupation of Basra mostly occurred because Karim's commercial mindset resembled that of the English: one of monopoly and violence. For Parsons, commerce generates wealth, prosperity and happiness, but when it lacks the spirit of collaboration, sociability, progress and diplomacy, it can be a cause of conflict. An example of this figured in Parsons's account when he recorded his observations of 9 April 1775. Parsons was happy that people in the city across all religions were in 'high spirit', vigilant and active, intending to defend their city: it is a 'noble defence' indeed (Parsons 1808: 176).[80] But he was disgusted when he discovered that 'The heads of the twenty-one Persians, who were pulled down from the ladders over the walls, lay exposed all this day; I saw twelve at the Baghdad, and nine at the Zobeir gate' (Parsons 1808: 177). 'It was a shocking site', Parsons added, 'to behold with what cruelty and barbarity the lifeless heads were treated, as scarce a man that passed would dart his lance in the faces, using every insolent expression with which low minds are too apt to treat a vanquished enemy' (Parsons 1808: 176).

Parsons's use of the word 'barbarity' here is not directed at a particular culture, religion or a social group: for he mentioned how people from different religions in Basra defended the city against the Persians. Rather the word 'barbarity' here was used as a rhetoric to illustrate the point that sometimes the excesses of mercantilist policies breed violence. Like what we saw in Carmichael's account in Chapter one, travellers in the Levant and Arabia often voiced their concerns over an Enlightenment discourse of improvement in which commercial polities were meant to replace the Hobbesian state of nature. For Parsons, commerce can lead to civility, but it can also plunge those who pursue it into violence. The association of commerce with violence goes back at least two hundred years before Parsons visited the Persian Gulf. Throughout the period from the sixteenth till the eighteenth century, the pursuit of monopolies was part of an early-modern commercial reality in the Indian Ocean and Persian Gulf. It was the sixteenth-century Portuguese, as the historian K. N. Chaudhuri observes, who established their commercial supremacy in the Indian Ocean and the Persian Gulf by virtue of their naval power; they were followed by the Dutch and the English in the seventeenth and eighteenth centuries despite 'naval warfare' for the English was 'a deterrent than a tactical weapon' (Chaudhuri 1985: 126).[81] One of the most powerful responses to English mercantilism in Asia came from Adam Smith who accused the EIC officials of being 'nuisances in every respect; always more or less inconvenient to the countries in which they are established, and destructive to those which have the misfortune to fall under their government' (Smith 1776: II, 256).

In the Persian Gulf, the English projected an image of neutrality during periods of fierce wars between the Ottomans and Persians. But, as Parsons realised, this image of English neutrality was not something that locals, whether Turks, Persians or Arabs, trusted and believed. 'I walked alone and heard myself and countrymen cursed by most of the Arabs and Turks whom I met; saying that the English agent was the sole cause of all their present troubles' (Parsons 1808: 176). Parsons was not prepared to defend the East India Company who let down the people of Basra in their wars against the Persians. Nor was he prepared to support the East India Company's decision regarding English neutrality in the region. He disliked the idea that all what Moore could do is to pack his bags, collect his goods, secure his cash and then depart the city. Before the fall of Basra to the Persians, Parsons noted, 'the agent went on board the Eagle: the treasure and valuables had been sent on board this ship before, at a place of much greater security then the factory seemed to be at this critical period' (Parsons 1808: 166).

In Parsons's travel account, Moore's selfishness stands in stark contrast to the heroism of the Ottoman governor. Parsons criticised the British agent in the city, but he was aware of the *realpolitik* of the world of trade: it is a world of self-interest rather than virtue. At the beginning of the Persian siege of Basra, Parsons decided to offer his service to defend the city. He, as a man of great experience in maritime affairs while serving as a consul in Iskenderun, came up with a plan to block the Persian vessels crossing the Tygris to reach Basra. But such a plan did not see the light of day as the Bombay government in mid-March 1775 sent a dispatch to Henry Moore asking him to remain neutral and never interfere in the conflict. Parsons was not in favour of this decision. But the volunteering work that he did in the city reveals how, contrary to the calls of the moralists of the period, a merchant can also be virtuous, publicly spirited and benevolent or at least he wanted his readers to believe. The Muslim rulers in Basra, moreover, were open to the idea of Britons helping them to push back against the Persians. But Parsons knew that the Company representatives in Basra only acted from the position of self-interest rather than duty. In all dispatches of the period between the East India Company residents in the Ottoman-Arab region and the Company's presidency in Bombay, the word 'honourable' was often addressed to the East India Company and its residents in the region. However, Parsons's experience in Basra taught him that there is nothing honourable about the Company. '[T]he poor Bussorians are deserted', he wrote, 'by those whose duty and interest it was to assist them to the utmost of their power: had they been so assisted, not the whole power of Persia, would be able to take the city' (Parsons 1808: 186).

Conclusion

Parsons has shown how travelling and travel writings allow the person to reflect on what has gone wrong in modern commercial society. Admiring the independent spirit of the Arabs in the deserts while deploring the competitions over trade and resources in Ottoman cities, Parsons addressed some British concerns of the period relating to the British Empire in India and America, mainly those associated with corruption, despotism and monopolies. Though a merchant himself, Parsons was a moralist who lamented the loss of virtue, public spirit and collectivism in modern commercial nations. Parsons's complex reflection on the benefits and disadvantages of commercialism allows us to rethink dominant views in some nineteenth- and twentieth-century commentaries on British political and commercial relations with the Middle East. For these commentators, Parsons's account of British political and commercial relations with the Levant and the Persian Gulf was informed by the rising British power in the Middle East. Such a view reveals the extent to which historians' readings of Enlightenment-era travel books about the Arab-Ottoman land were coloured by the Orientalist model proposed by Edward Said, a leading cultural critic of modern times.[82] As this chapter argued, Parsons's worldview is not illustrative of a Briton who envisaged himself as a deliverer of civilisation to barbaric societies. Nor did Parsons see the British as the model of progress the world needs to emulate. Parsons did not dismiss Arab and Muslim societies as being naturally despotic and inferior to Europeans. He was far from holding the notion that one particular religion, race, culture or nation is superior to another. Rather he saw the world as being a global unit inhabited by different nations that not only trade with each other but also compete among themselves over resources and wealth. Parsons was sceptical of the idea that the pursuit of progress constitutes a stable safeguard against political, religious, social and economic conflicts.

Notes

1 Aleppo, the city from which Parsons bought his merchandise, is not on the Mediterranean. And the trade caravan that travelled overland to India used to operate between Aleppo and Basra, a city on the Persian Gulf. The commodities in this caravan moved back and forth between India, Mesopotamia, Syria and Europe. During the eighteenth century, there were also trade caravans that operated between Syrian coastal ports, such as Latakia, Antioch and Tripoli. From these coastal cities, many India and Syrian commodities set out for Europe. The caravan journeys which J. Griffiths undertook in 1785 from Antioch to Basra reveal how the caravan trade routes during the period plugged Europe, the Levantine Mediterranean, Aleppo, Basra and the Indian Ocean into a global circuit of trade. See Griffiths' *Travels in Europe, Asia Minor and Arabia* (London, 1805).

2 One such famous and popular example during the period was John Harriot's *Struggles Through Life, Exemplified in the Various Travels and Adventures in Europe, Asia, Africa and America*, 2 vols (London: Printed for the Author by C. and W. Galabia, 1807). The trope of adventurism in the context of British encounters with non-Europeans abroad also appeared in the fictional scene of the period as evidenced by William Rufus Chetwood's novel *The Voyages, Dangerous Adventures, and Imminent Escapes of Captain R. Falconer* (London: Printed for S. Fisher, 1801).

3 On the debate on how commerce and material wealth was seen as a source of civility in seventeenth- and eighteenth-century England, see Keith Thomas' *In Pursuit of Civility: Manners and Civilisations in Early Modern England* (Massachusetts: Brandeis University Press, 2018), 140.

4 Peter James Marshall, *Problems of Empire: Britain and India 1757–1813* (London: Allen and Unwin, 1968), 33–36.

5 Andrew Archibald Paton, *The Modern Syrians; Or, the Native Society in Damascus, Aleppo, and The Mountains of the Druses From Notes Made in those Parts During the Years 1841-2-3. By an Oriental Student* (London, 1844), 265. A good account of the period about why the English trade declined in the Ottoman Empire is James Porters' advertisement to his *Observations on the Religion, Laws, Government and Manners of the Turks, The Second Edition, Corrected and Enlarged by the Author to Which is Added the State of The Turkey Trade from its Origin to the Present Time* (London: Printed for J. Nourse, 1771). On the condition of French trade in Aleppo, see section V in Porter's, 396–406.

6 French trade with the Ottoman Levant during the eighteenth century was estimated at around 60% of the total European trade in the region; see Edhem Eldem's 'French Trade and Commercial Policy in the Levant in the Eighteenth-Century', *Oriente Moderno*, 1 (1999), 27–47. See also Pococke, 151.

7 For example, the English writer Arthur Young, known in England for his support of improvement projects in the English countryside, wrote about the decline of English trade in the Levant, proposing that the English could beat the French and Dutch in the Levant trade by offering 'a bounty [...] upon the exportations of those druggets [fabric]' so that the English could 'beat our rivals at their own weapons [...]'. Young, like many during the period, critiqued the inability of the Levant Company to compete with the French who produced the woollen cloth that suited the weather and patterns of taste in the Levant and cost less than that of the English, *Political Essays Concerning the Present State of the British Empire* (London, 1772), 223. The historian Fredric Hervey in 1779 made the same point Edward Young and others made earlier in the century that the Levant Company has lost its competitive edge in a market dominated by the French, but he also recalled how the Parliament in the 1740s debated the option of reforming the Levant trade and considered the calls to abolish its monopolies and 'entirely open [it] to all

British subjects', *The Naval History of Great Britain: From the Earliest Times to the Rising of Parliament in 1779,* 5 vols (London, 1779), IV, 381.

8 On 2 October 1969, the Yorkshire physician John Fothergill read a paper titled *An Essay on the Character of the Late Alexander Russell* in which he states that while Russell was reading medicine at the University of Edinburgh, he and other notable medical personalities such as William Cuming of Dorchester and the Scots George Cleghorn 'formed a Society for their mutual instruction and advancement in their studies. Every student of a certain standing, who distinguishes himself by his diligence, capacity and conduct was initiated into this little assembly. Here the opinions of the Ancients, of their Contemporaries [...] were frequently discussed; and two of the members were always charged with the task of providing instruction and entertainment for the next meeting of the Society. Questions, no doubt, were here disputed and decided, which long experience would have declined. But it exercised their faculties, gave them both sides of arguments, taught them to doubt, and habituated them to observation', (London: Printed in the 1770), 7–8.

9 There are excellent studies on the millet system in the Ottoman state. Some powerful studies are selected here. Bruce Masters, 'The Millet Wars in Aleppo, 1726–1821: An Ottoman perspective' in *Aleppo and Its Hinterland in the Ottoman Period*, ed. Stefan Winter and Mafalda Ade (Amsterdam: Brill, 2019), 130–151; *Christians and Jews in the Ottoman Empire: The Roots of Sectarianism* (Cambridge: Cambridge University Press, 2001). Halil Inalcik, Suraya Faroqhi, and Donald Quataert, ed., *An Economic and Social History of the Ottoman Empire 1300–1914,* 2 vols (Cambridge: Cambridge University Press, 2004). Benjamin Braude and Bernard Russell, ed., *Christians and Jews in the Ottoman Empire: The Functioning of a Plural Society*, 2 vols (New York: Holmes and Meier, 1982).

10 Humphrey Prideaux, in *The True Nature of Imposture Fully Displayed in the Life of Life of Mahomet* (1679), once wrote: 'even unto this day, all who live under any Mahometan Government, and are not of their religion, pay an annual tax for a constant Mulct of their Infidelity (which in Turkey is called Caradge) and are sure to be punished with death, if not in the least they contradict or oppose any Doctrine that is received among them to have been taught by Mahomet' (London: Printed for E. Curll, 1716), 77–78. Prideaux never travelled in the Levant. The idea in the above statement about the stringency of Islamic laws towards minorities was borrowed from Jean De Thevenot's *Relation d'un voyage fait au Levant* (1665). Thevenot's commentary on the Islamic view towards non-Muslims and the poll-tax that Jews and Christians had to pay to Ottoman authority can be found on pages 38 and 83 in the English translation, *The Travels of Monsieur de Thevenot into the Levant* (London: Printed by H. Clark, 1687).

11 Drummond's comment about Cyprus was also confirmed by the Italian traveller Giovanni Mariti who visited the Levant in 1769. 'They [Ottoman governors] fall upon the people', Mariti wrote, 'with furry; and their subtle tyranny invents a thousand means to get possession of their wealth, and to extort from them the fruits of their labour and toil', *Travels through Cyprus, Syria and, Palestine,* 2 vols (Dublin, 1792), Vol I, 10

12 Edward Barker, who served in the British consulate in Cairo between September 1830 and 1834, remarked that during the eighteenth-century Christians in the Levant 'were not allowed then to wear white turbans, nor bright colours, nor yellow shoes, nor red shoes, nor to ride on horseback in towns', *Syria and Egypt Under the Last Five Sultans of Turkey.* [...] Vol II (London: Samuel Tinsley, 1876), 322. This quote is taken from Vol II.

13 On British mercantilist attitudes in America and India, see P. J. Marshall's *The Making and Unmaking of Empires: Britain, India and America 1750–1783* (Oxford: Oxford University Press, 2005); see also Jonathan Eacott's *Selling Empire: India and the Making of Britain and America 1630–1830* (Virginia: The University of North Carolina Press, 2016).

14 In his Speech to the House of Commons in April 1774 about excessive British taxes in America, particularly those related to Chinese tea imported by the East India Company, Burke observed, '[i]t is indeed a tax of sophistry, a tax of pedantry, a tax of disputation, a tax of war and rebellion, a tax of anything but benefit to the imposers, or satisfaction to the subject', *Speech of Edmund Burke on American Taxation, April 19, 1774* (London: Printed for J. Dodsley, 1775), 19–20. On Burke's opposition to British mercantilist policies in America and India, see chapters six and nine in Gregory M. Collins' *Commerce and Manners in Edmund Burke's Political Economy* (Cambridge: Cambridge University Press, 2020).

15 On these critiques, see Mahesh Gopalan's 'Maritime Society in an Early-Modern Port City: Negotiating Family, Religion and the English Company in Madras' in *The East India Company, 1600–1857: Essays on Anglo-Indian connection* (Abingdon: Routledge, 2017), 114–125.

16 Alexander Russell observed that prostitutes 'are licensed in Aleppo' by the governor, 'whom they pay for protection'. Their clients were mostly soldiers. But men from the upper classes in the city could also be found in their quarters. *The Natural History of Aleppo*, Vol I, 263. Contrary to the expectation of many in Britain who associated travels abroad with sexual adventures, Parsons and other travellers like Dr John Griffiths often spoke of the morality of the English abroad. Others, however, mainly the travellers who were in the armed forces like Francis Vernon and Samuel Evers, did not hesitate to show their interests in, what Evers called, 'sexual favours' in regions they passed through. See Evers's *A Journal Kept on a Journey from Bassora to Baghdad.* (Horsham, 1784), 29.

17 Alistair Hamilton, 'The English Interests in the Arabic-Speaking Christians' in *The 'Arabick' Interest of the Natural Philosophers in Seventeenth-Century England*, ed. G. A. Russell (Leiden: Brill, 1994), 30–53. Simon Mills, *A Commerce of Knowledge: Trade, Religion, and Scholarship between England and the Ottoman Empire, 1600–1760* (Oxford: Oxford University Press, 2020). See also Mill's 'The English Chaplains at Aleppo: Exploration and Scholarship between England and the Ottoman Empire, 1620–1760', *Bulletin for the Council for British Research in the Levant*, 6:1 (2011), 13–20.

18 Basire was a naturalised Briton. He was born in France to a French Protestant family. On his missionary work in the Levant, see *The Correspondence of Isaac Basire: With a Memoir of His Life* (London, 1831), 202; *Dictionary of National Biography*, ed. Leslie Stephen (New York: Macmillan, 1885), Vol III, 356–357.

19 *The Pedigree Register*, ed. George Sherwood (London: Published by the Editor, 1913–1916), Vol III, 226, 125.

20 Ibid., 227.

21 Ibid., 293.

22 James Finn, *Stirring Times or Records from Jerusalem Consular Chronicles of 1853-156*, Vol I (London: C. Kegan Paul and CO., 1878), 56. Andrew Lake, *The First Protestants in the Arab World: The Contribution to Christian Mission of the English Aleppo Chaplains 1597–1782. 2015.* Melbourne School of Theology, PhD thesis, 117.

23 Alastair Hamilton, 'The English Interests in the Arabic-Speaking Christians', 31.

24 The French traveller Laurent d' Arvieux, who visited the Levant in the second half of the seventeenth century, noted how the Ottoman governor of Sidon (*Saida*) who controlled most parts of north Palestine 'gives a Particular Protection to all the Christian Profession in the East, and that the Missionaries Prosecute their Labours under that Protection', *The Travels of the Chevalier Laurent d' Arvieux in Arabia the Desert* (London: Printed for B. Barker, 1732), 2. In a letter sent by Father Verzeau, a Jesuit in Syria, in 1694 to Father Fleuriau, of the Society of Jesus in France, we read how the Greek Orthodox bishops in Aleppo bribed the judges of the city so that they could secure the position of the Patriarchal See for themselves although the position was occupied by a Roman Catholic. 'They sacrificed with pleasure their Jewels and whatever they had most precious to corrupt the judges and render them favourable to their false Patriarch [...]', *Edifying and Curious Letters of Some Missions of the Society of Jesus from Foreign Missions* (Printed in the Year 1709), 6.

25 William George Browne, *Travels in Africa, Egypt, and Syria* (London: Printed for T. Cadell), 385.

26 George Fowler, *Turkey or a History of the Origin, Progress and Decline* (London: T.H Rees, 1854), 477. Elias Habesci recalled that 'almost all the dealers in slaves, or slave merchants, are of the emir [*ashraf*] race', *The Present State of the Ottoman Empire* (London, 1784), 116. See also Aaron Hill's *A Full and Just Account of the Present State of the Ottoman Empire* (London, 1709), 56.

27 Francis Vernon, *Voyages and Travels of a Sea Officer* (London, 1792), 168–169. Johan Ægidius van Egmond and the Orientalist Johannes Heyman, *Travels through Part of Europe, Asia Minor, the Islands of the Archipelago* (London, 1759), 344.

28 Adam Smith's *An Inquiry into the Nature and Causes of the Wealth of Nations* was published in 1776 while Parsons was touring India. In the book, Smith commented on the monopolising efforts of the East India Company in Bengal and in so doing he presented the Company

officials as men of power and authority over the natives which confirms what Parsons found while visiting the Company factory in Surat. According to Smith, 'It has not been uncommon, I am well assured, for the chief, that is, the first clerk of a factory [in Bengal], to order a peasant to plough up a rich field of poppies and sow it with rice or some other grain. The pretence was, to prevent a scarcity of provisions; but the real reason, to give the chief an opportunity of selling at better price a large quantity of opium, which he happened then to have upon hand. Upon other occasions the order has been reversed; and a rich field of rice or other grain has been ploughed up, in order to make room for a plantation of poppies; when the chief foresaw that extraordinary profit was likely to be made by opium. The servants of the company have upon several occasions attempted to establish in their own favour the monopoly of some of the most important branches, not only of the foreign, but of the inland trade of the country', *An Inquiry into the Nature and Causes of the Wealth of Nations,* ed. Edward Cannan, 250. For an eighteenth-century critique of the East India Company's monopolising activities in India, see Alexander Dow's *The History of Hindostan.* (London: Printed for T. Beckett, 1777), lxxxvi–ix. For a scholarly account of the East India Company's monopolies in India, see Emily Erikson's *Between Monopoly and Free Trade: The East India Company 1600–1757* (Princeton: Princeton University Press, 2014) and chapter two in Robert *Travers's Ideology and Empire in Eighteenth-Century India* (Cambridge: Cambridge University Press, 2007).

29 Many European historians and travel writers considered the eighteenth-century political unrest in the Ottoman Empire as a sign of political decline; the late eighteenth-century traveller William George Browne commented on the state of Ottoman decline in his *Travels in Africa, Egypt and Syria*, 386. Edward Barker, the English consul in Aleppo between 1803 and 1829, recalled how the constant rebellions in the empire were harbingers of 'rapid decay'; Barker was certain that the 'decay' was happening, but he was convinced the Ottoman Empire will not 'die a natural death'; rather it will disappear once the European powers, England and France, decide to 'swallow up' its territories, *Syria and Egypt Under the Last Five Sultans of Turkey*, 2 vols (London: Samuel Tinsley), I, 70. The same trope in European writings about the relationship between decline and rebellion continued in the early decades of the twentieth century with the writings of the the British historian and army officer Stephen Hemsley Longrigg; see his *Four Centuries of Modern Iraq* (Oxford: The Clarendon Press, 1925), 198.

30 Jane Hathaway, *The Arab Lands Under Ottoman Rule, 1516–1800* (London: Routledge, 2013), 183.

31 Karl Barbir, *Ottoman Rule in Damascus 1708–1757* (Princeton: Princeton University Press, 1980), 105–106.

32 For example, the Ottoman Sultan asked his governor in Baghdad in 1787 to 'send the head of Twiny to Constantinople': Twiny was the leader of Al-Montafiq tribe who attacked Basra in April 1787 and expelled its Ottoman governor; see William Francklin, *Observations Made on A Tour from Bengal to Persia* (Kolkata, 1788), 119.

33 James Capper who travelled in the Syrian deserts in 1774 recalled how the Arabs were the people who greatly value their independence from the Ottoman governors: 'They acknowledge no superior but their own Sheicks, nor do they like most of other tribes pay a tribute to any of the Bashaws belonging to the Ottoman government', *Observations on the Passage to India,* 65.

34 Bruce Masters, 'Aleppo: The Ottoman Empire's Caravan City' in *The Ottoman City between East and West: Izmir, Aleppo and Istanbul* (Cambridge: Cambridge University Press, 1999), 145.

35 See chapter three in Atle L. Wold's *Scotland and the French Revolutionary War, 1792–1802* (Edinburgh: Edinburgh University Press, 2015).

36 See George Sale, *The Koran, Commonly Called the Alcoran of Mohammed* (London, 1734), 13. William Guthrie, *A General History of the World*, 12 vols (London: J. Newbury, 1764), Vol VI, 22. Volney's *Travels Through Syria and Egypt*, 2vols (London, 1788), Vol I, 90. See also the chapter about the history of the Arabs in *An Universal History from the Earliest Accounts to the Present Time* (London: Printed for C. Bathurst, 1780), Vol XVI, 319–321.

37 Paul Sagar, *The Opinion of Mankind: Sociability and the Theory of the State from Hobbes to Smith* (Princeton: Princeton University Press, 2018), 169. See also chapter six titled 'The Dangers of

Commerce' in Christopher J. Berry's *The Idea of Commercial Society in the Scottish Enlightenment* (Edinburgh: Edinburgh University Press, 2013).

38 See the chapter titled 'On the Liberty of the Arabs and servitude of the Tartars' in Montesquieu's *The Spirit of the Laws*, 2 vols (London: Printed for J. Nourse, 1750), Vol I, 389–399. On a good discussion on this trade-off between liberty and material progress, see Dennis C Rasmussen, 'Does 'Bettering Our Condition' Really Make Us Better Off? Adam Smith on Progress and Happiness', *The American Political Science Review* 100:3 (2006), 309–18.

39 This idea of the inequality of commercial society in contrast to the natural conditions of primitive, no-commercial clans and tribes was first analysed and popularised in Europe by Jean-Jacques Rousseau in his *A Discourse Upon the Origin and Foundation of Inequality Among Mankind*, first published in 1755. Rosseau was avidly read by Scottish Enlightenment theorists of commercial society, by men like Hume and Smith; see, for example, Michael Ignatieff, 'Smith, Rousseau and the Republic of Needs,' in *Scotland and Europe 1200–1850*, ed. T. C. Smouth (Edinburgh: Edinburgh University Press, 1986), 187–206.

40 Despite that eighteenth-century travellers in the Levant and Arabia offered a sociological analysis of why Arabs pursue such a warlike life, what Lord Kames in *The Sketches of the History of Man* called 'the clan spirit', this image goes back to the time of Lodvico di Varthema for whom what Parsons considered as entertaining was actually 'a sad appearance', *The Travels of Lodvico di Varthema* (London: the Hakluyt Society, 1863), 18.

41 See chapter sixteen in Michael F. Kuhn's *Finding Hagar: God's Pursuit of a Runaway* (Carlisle: Langham Global Library, 2019).

42 Elaine James, 'Sarah, Hagar, and their Interpreters' in *Women's Bible Commentary*, ed. Carol A Newsom, Sharon H. Ringe, and Jacqueline E. Lapsley (1992; Louisville: Westminster John Knox Press, 2012), 51.

43 It is striking that Carmichael, as we saw in Chapter one, used the same phrase 'Mahomet countrymen' to describe how Arabs boast of their independence in the deserts. See Carmichael's 'A Journal', 52.

44 Edward Gibbon, *The History of the Decline and Fall of the Roman Empire*, 5 vols (London, 1788), Vol V, 179.

45 In his travel book, for example, the British traveller in the Levant Richard Tyron observed how the primitive manners of the descendants of Ishmael confirm the 'ancient predictions of Scripture, we will find them literally fulfilled concerning them', *Travels from Aleppo to the City of Jerusalem in 1776* (Glasgow, 1785), 20.

46 A good discussion of this inverted mirror image in Enlightenment thought is Fredrick J. Whelan's *Enlightenment Political Thought and Non-Western Societies: Sultans and Savages* (Abingdon: Routledge, 2009).

47 This view about the great medieval Arab contribution to arts and sciences appeared in many accounts during the period. William Eton wrote: 'Under the splendid reign of Abdurrahman, the founder of the Arabian monarchy in Spain, it assumed a more civilised form. That political sovereign promoted intermarriages between Mahomedan and Christian subjects and favoured the natural propensity of the Arabs to literature and science, at a time when the rest of mankind were sunk in ignorance and barbarism', *A Survey of the Turkish Empire*, 195–196. This view on the impact of Arab sciences and arts on medieval Europe also appeared in the example put forth earlier in the century by the writer of the chapter on Arabia in *The Modern Part of The Universal History Compiled from Original Writers' By the Authors of the Antients which will Perfect the Work, and Render it A Complete Body of History From the Earliest Account of Time, to the Present.* In a footnote, the author cites a letter sent by one Mr Ames, the secretary to the Society of Antiquarians in London, to the famous English astronomer and physician Dr John Bevis. In the letter Ames wrote: '…our numerical characters were first brought into England at the return of Richard I from the holy wars, and that probable our people learned them among the Saracens [Medieval Arabs]' (London: Printed for T. Osborne, 1765), Vol XLIII, 68.

48 The English translator of Jean de La Roque's *A Voyage to Arabia the Happy: By the Way of the Eastern Ocean, and the Straights of the Red Sea Performed by the French for the First Time A.D. 1798, 1709, 1710*, recalled how 'Ockley invites all traders, and other persons who have any such letters by them to communicate them to him; because he is persuaded that these sorts of letters, which discover to us the genius of the language and the Eastern way of expression, will

be very useful for the clearing up several passages of the holy scriptures', ix. The English translator of *The Travels of the Chevalier d'Arvieux in Arabia the Desert ; Written by Himself and Publish'd by Mr. De la Roque* wrote a fascinating footnote about the Biblical origin of the Arabs: 'The Arabs in general have two Originals, they derive the first one from Joktan, Shem's Great grandson, whose children peopled the Peninsula, since called Arabia, from the name Jarab one of his sons, or from Arabat, the name of a Country in the same Peninsula. The second Original of the Arabs is what they derive from Ishmael, Abraham's and Hagar's Son, who came and settled himself in the same Place those first and ancient Arabs and was the Father of the Arabian Ishmaelites, some tribes of whom applied themselves to trade and husbandry; and the others, the greater number, possessed the deserts and led a sort of life which they thought the most agreeable to their condition and Original...whom the Scriptures likewise calls Kedarens, Hagarens, and sometimes the Children of the East', 96. Robert Heron, the Scottish translator of Carsten Niebuhr's *Travels Through Arabia and Other Countries in the East*, wrote: travel writings about Arabs 'throw much new light on the historical events, the laws, the worship, and the customs recorded in the Old Testament', Vol I, xii. Billie Melman has demonstrated how many nineteenth-century European writings often associated Arabia and its inhabitants with the textual universe of the Bible. These accounts, Melman maintained, were written by middle class and fervent Christian travellers whose journeys mainly aimed 'to corroborate God's revealed text' (2002:109). The author of the chapter on Arabia in *The Modern Part of The Universal History* argued that ' Some derive' the name of Arabia 'from the Hebrew [...] *Harabi*, which signifies a robber or freebooter , as that nation is known to have always bee; others from another signification of that Hebrew word implying mixture, or a mixt multitude...and are accordingly styled by the prophet Jeremiah, 'the mixed people that dwell in the wilderness''(London: Printed for C. Bathhurst, 1783), Vol XXXVI, 430. The same trope about Arabs as the inhabitants of Biblical deserts, a changeless people in a changeless land, as Rosalynn Haynes has argued, appeared in many nineteenth-century travel accounts such as those of Richard Francis Burton, Charles Doughty and Edward Robinson; see her 'Travel Writing and the Desert' in *The Cambridge History of Travel Writing* (Cambridge: Cambridge University Press, 2020), 315–329; see particularity pages 318–319.

49 Nathaniel Wolloch, *History and Nature in the Enlightenment.* (London: Routledge, 2016), 211.

50 Hala Mundhir Fattah, *The Politics of Regional Trade in Iraq, Arabia, and the Gulf, 1745–1900* (New York: New York State University Press, 1997), 160. See also James Haynes, *Travels in Several Parts of Turkey, Egypt and the Holy Land* (London, 1774), 11.

51 Gibbon, Ibid., Vol V, p. 180. On Gibbon and primitivism, see Jeremy Black's 'Gibbon and International Relations' in *Edward Gibbon and Empire*, ed. Rosamond Mcktitterick and Ronald Quinault (Cambridge: Cambridge University Press, 1997), 220–221. On Gibbon and Islam, see Bernard Lewis's 'Gibbon on Muhammad', *Daedalus*, 105:3 (1976), 89–101.

52 Emin later became a prominent figure in the Armenian national movement which aimed to liberate Armenia from Persia and the Ottoman Empire. On his rise into prominence, see Louise Nalbandian, *The Armenian Revolutionary Movement* (Berkley: University of California Press, 1963), 23.

53 Captain Cope, *A New History of the East Indies...* (London, 1754), 210–211.

54 J. G Lorimer, Vol I, 20–23.

55 *The East India Company's connection with Turkish Arabia*, 1646–1846, Vol 24, British Library: India Office Records and Private Papers, IOR/L/PS/5/345, 43.

56 On the Dutch expansion in the Persian Gulf in the early modern period, *The Dutch and English East India Companies: Diplomacy, Trade and Violence in Early Modern Asia*, ed. Adam Clulow and Tristan Mostert (Amsterdam: The University of Amsterdam Press, 2019). Also see Willem Floor's 'Dutch Relations with the Persian Gulf' in *The Persian Gulf in History*, ed. Lawrence G. Potter (New York: Palgrave, 2009).

57 Joseph Emin, a prominent eighteenth-century Armenian nationalist and friend of Edmund Burke, passed through Basra on the way back from India in 1775. He was in the same ship, *Revenge*, with Abraham Parsons, Henry Moore, the East India Company factor in Basra, and Colonel Christian Knudsen of the Bengal Army. Amin, in 1775, noted how Henry Moore employed an Armenian, Markar, as an agent of the Company. Markar worked 'partly for the gentlemen of Bosra and mostly for the Jews', *The Life and Adventures of Joseph Emin an Armenian*,

2 vols (London, 1792), Vol II, 449. This example shows how Britons cooperated with different communities in Basra including Armenians.

58 John Struys, *The Voyages and Travels of John Struys Through Italy, Greece, Muscovy, Media, Persia.* (London: Printed for Abel Swalle, 1684), 351.

59 Throughout the eighteenth century, Britain's policy in the Persian Gulf was mostly focused on countering French influence in the region but the French managed to attack the British factory in Bander Abbas in 1759, Sir Arnold Wilson in 1928 recalled, and destroy it: they 'landed troops and heavy guns, battered the building' of the English factory before burning it, 'and the defenders were forced to surrender', *The Persian Gulf: An Historical Sketch from the Earliest Times to the Beginning of the Twentieth Century* (177). Not only fear of the French encouraged Britons to desert Bander Abbas. After the assassination of Nader Shah in 1747, Persia plunged into a civil war that was only stopped by Karim Khan Zand who succeeded in gaining the support of tribal leaders. Still, the East India Company did not find it profitable and safe to operate in a politically instable Persia, which made the Bombay government keen on strengthening their position in Basra. On the way back from India to Europe, in 1750, Bartholomew Plaisted, who served in the East India Company, stopped at Bander Abbas. He logged in his diary: 'It is easy to conceive what dreadful Confusion reigned throughout the whole Kingdom during these changes and revolutions, and therefore it would be deemed downright madness to travel throughout the Country at this Time', *A Journal from Calcutta in Bengal, by Sea, to Busserah from thence Across the Desart to Aleppo.* (London: Printed for T. Kinnersly, 1758), 14.

60 In 1746, the British established a factory at Bushehr but in 1769 the British trade in the Persian Gulf shifted totally to the port of Basra due to the rising tension with Kerim Kan, the Persian ruler. The Bushehr factory, however, did not close but Basra was their main port in the Persian Gulf.

61 Rose Greaves, 'Iranian Relations with the European Trading Companies, to 1798', in *The Cambridge History of Iran: From Nadir Shah to the Islamic Republic*, ed. Peter Avery, Gavin Hambly, and Charles Melville (Cambridge: Cambridge University Press, 1991), 361.

62 The plague however was not new to the region in the eighteenth century. Plaisted, who was in Basra in 1750, recalled in his travel book that 'In 1691, this City was depopulated by a Plague, of which 80000 of the Inhabitants died, and the rest ran away', Ibid., 23. Henry Moore explained the direful effects of the plague on the trade of the region: see IOR/L/PS/20/C227, pp. 275–276.

63 Sir Arnold Wilson, 183.

64 In the record of the East India Company, we find many letters sent by La Touche and Moore to the East India Company directors and governors in India in which they reported about the political situation of the region. See for the example 'Letter from Henry Moore, East India Company Agent at Bussora [Basra], and his assistant, John Beaumont, to James Morley, East India Company Resident at Bushire, and his assistant, George Green', British Library: India Office Records and Private Papers, IOR/R/15/1/1, f 35v 1. See also 'Letters from William Digges Latouche, Resident at Bussora [Basra], to Edward Galley, Resident at Bushire', British Library: India Office Records and Private Papers, IOR/R/15/1/4, ff 26v-27.

65 *En route* from India to Britain, John Jackson visited Basra in June 1797. He met Samuel Manesty, the East India resident in the city, who mostly focused assisting the British government in its war against the French. The French at the time were preparing to occupy Egypt, an idea which scared the British. Mr Manesty's 'conduct', Jackson wrote, 'is most truly that of an English gentleman; and he has rendered Government very essential services during the present war, by seizing the French dispatches, and preventing that nation from carrying on any correspondence with India by land', *Journey from India Towards England in the Year 1797* (London: Printed for T. Cadell, 1797), 29.

66 John Gordon Lorimer, Vol I, 1227. See also 'Selections from State Papers, Bombay, regarding the East India Company's Connection with the Persian Gulf, with a Summary of Events, 1600–1800', British Library: India Office Records and Private Papers, IOR/L/PS/20/C227, p. 289. See also *Life and Adventures of Joseph Emin,* 2 vols (London: Printed in the year 1792) Vol II, 454.

67 Letter No. 29: William Digges Latouche and George Abraham, Officials at Bussora [Basra], to [John Beaumont, Resident at Bushire] [f2v] (2/2), British Library: India Office Records and Private Papers, IOR/R/15/1/4, f 2 2.

68 Henry Moore, the British resident in Basra, mentioned the governor of Baghdad owes the East India Company over 6, 000,000 Persian Toman. In British currency, this amount was over £187, 500. IOR/L/PS/20/C227, 272. Upon his release from captivity in Persia, Solyman Agha, the governor of Basra, secured a huge loan from La Touche in order to be able to secure the Pashalik of Baghdad from central government in Istanbul. See Harford Jones Brydges's *An Account of the Transactions of His Majesty's Mission to the Court of Persia.* 2 vols (London, 1834), Vol I, 191.

69 British Library: India Office Records and Private Papers, IOR/R/15/1/4, f 21. Vol 4, pp.4.

70 Hume, a proponent of commercial civility, lamented the moral failings of modern commercial nations: 'Nothing is more usual among states which have made some advances in commerce, than to look upon the progress of their neighbours with a suspicious eye, to consider all trading states as their rivals, and to suppose that it is impossible for any of them to flourish but at their expense', *Essays and Treatises On Several Subjects,* 2 vols (Edinburgh: Printed for T. Cadell, 1793), Vol I, 325. A good discussion on how 'the jealousy of trade' debate in eighteenth-century Britain and France was meant to correct the moral failings of some mercantilist policies and, additionally, wrap the mantle of civility, improvement and cosmopolitanism around sociable commercialism, see Istvan Hont's introduction to *Jealousy of Trade: International Competition and the Nation State in Historical Perspective* (Massachusetts: Belknap Press, 2005).

71 This quote is taken from a note written by Amy Apcar, the editor of *Life and Adventures of Joseph Emin,* the second volume, page 454. Apcar draw this conclusion from Emin's book and also from the proceedings of the Bombay governments for the year 1775.

72 IOR/L/PS/20/C227, pp. 274–277.

73 Smith's argument about conflict and clashes generated by what Istvan Hont called the 'jealousy of trade' appeared in his critique of the monopolistic activities of the East India Company throughout the eighteenth century; see Smith's chapter titled 'causes of the prosperity of New Colonies' in *An Inquiry into the Nature and Causes of the Wealth of Nations,* 2 vols (London: Printed for W. Strahan, 1776), Vol 1, 157–190. In his sixth edition of *The Theory of Moral Sentiment,* originally published in 1759, Smith also examined the moral failings associated with 'the jealousy of trade'; he distinguished between two kinds of commercial competitions between nations: emulation (positive) and envy/resentment (negative); see *The Theory of Moral Sentiment,* 2 vols (London: Printed for A. Strahan, 1790), Vol II, 79–80. Smith's argument about the jealousy among trading nations was taken from David Hume's essay titled 'Of the Jealousy of Trade', first published 1742.

74 Longrigg, 187.

75 IOR/L/PS/20/C227, p. 284.

76 Ibid., 281.

77 On Solyman's life and career, see Longrigg, 187–211.

78 Francklin, 122.

79 Greaves, 351.

80 Even Catholic missionaries in the city joined the Ottomans and Arabs in their efforts to defend the city against the Persian invasion. See Longrigg, p. 191.

81 On the Portuguese trade and naval expeditions in the Persian Gulf, see chapter eight in Sir Arnold T. Wilson's *The Persian Gulf: An Historical Sketch from the Earliest Times to the Beginning of the Twentieth Century* (Oxford: The Clarendon Press, 1928).

82 J. G Lorimer read Parsons's chapter about the East India Company's response to the Persian siege of Basra in 1775 as a confirmation of Britain's rising military and naval power in the region. Parsons in Lorimer's book appeared as an eyewitness of Britain's superior ships and trade in the region; see *Gazetteer of the Persian Gulf, Oman and Central Arabia,* 2vols (Calcutta: Superintendent Government Printing, India, 1915) Vol I, 159. Similarly, George Nathaniel Curzon referred to Parsons's account to drive home a point that it was because of British presence in Bushehr, 'a town without a history' or at least with some history that began after the British landed on its shores as merchants, 'such a history as an existence of 150 years can supply' that trade started to prosper in the region. Upon the opening of the British factory in Bushehr, Curzon added, 'the mercantile marine of the gulf was developed' and 'Bushire grew in size and importance', *Persia and the Persian Question.* 2 vols (London: Longman, Green

and Co., 1892), Vol I, 231. A recent scholarly account found in Parsons's book a confirmation of the notion that the eighteenth-century discourse about Arabs in British travel writings should be read in the context of the rising British power in the region: 'we find in Parsons' account', Hiāl Ḥajarī wrote, 'an early indication, within British travel writing on Oman, of a hegemonic discourse', *British Travel Writing on Oman: Orientalism Reappraised* (Bern: Peter Lang, 2006), 87.

Chapter Four

HENRY ABBOTT: A COSMOPOLITAN IN CITIES AND DESERTS

We have obligation to others, obligations that stretch beyond those to whom we are related by the ties of kith and kin, or even more formal ties of a shared citizenship.

—Kwame Anthony Appiah, *Cosmopolitanism: Ethics in the World of Strangers* (2015)

Henry Abbott was born in 1764 in Pera, a suburb of Constantinople, to a well-to-do family of expatriated merchants and consuls, among whom he was brought up in Ankara and Aleppo before moving to India. Abbott lived and worked in India between 1785 and 1802.[1] He died in Blackheath, Kent, on 12 February 1820, age 55.[2] In Calcutta, he married Margaret Welsh, the daughter of William Welsh of Edinburgh, with whom he had several children, all of whom were influential in the British military and diplomatic service in the East. His son James Abbott (1807–1896) served as the deputy governor of the district of Hazara in North-West India.[3] Fredrik Abbott (1805–1892) joined a British military regiment, the Bengal Engineers, in 1823 and fought in the first Burmese War (1824–1826). Saunders (1811–1894) and Augustus (1804–1867) served in the British army in Bengal. Keith Edward Abbott (1814–1873) served as the consul-general of Great Britain in Tehran and Tabriz (1842–1856).[4] Henry's family in the Levant were mostly based in Ankara, Istanbul, Thessaloniki, Aleppo and Beirut. His father Joseph Abbott, as Henry wrote in his diary, established 'a mercantile house of business' in Ankara (Abbott n.d: 3). His uncle George was 'a very affluent man' in Istanbul (Ibid). Another uncle Bartholomew Edward Abbott, a Levant Company proconsul and merchant, was one of the richest men in Ottoman Salonica.[5] His uncles John, who held the position of a consul to the Levant Company factory in Aleppo from 1770 until his death in 1783, and Robert, a merchant, were responsible for Henry's education after he moved to Aleppo in 1774.[6]

In Aleppo, Henry was brought up in an enterprising family of merchants who lived and worked in the Levant for many years.[7] The Levant Company chaplain at the time, the Reverend Robert Foster, 'a man of education & talents & an excellent scholar', as Abbott wrote in his memoire, had tutored the young Henry (Abbott n.d, 9). Foster, Henry wrote, 'was steady & indefatigable in discharging trust reposed to him to the best of his abilities both on my literary studies & on my moral principles' (Ibid). The way Henry was brought up in Ankara and Istanbul was unlike what he later experienced in Aleppo. Unlike his brothers John and Robert in Aleppo, Henry's father, Joseph Abbott, was 'upright, conscious & religious man, a good Classical scholar, of much rewarding

& and sound judgement', a man mostly committed to his family and God (Ibid., n.d: 7). He often read to his children passages from 'the Old and New Testaments, explaining, commenting as he read, upon the moral to be derived from those holy records; the purpose of which Man was created so much more perfect than other animals, his duty to his God, to his parents, and to the rest of Mankind' (Ibid). Henry's father was wholly committed to the religious education of his children: 'incubating into our young minds those principles of religion and probity which are of the utmost consequence of our happiness in after life' (Ibid). In Aleppo, Henry was a pupil of a Protestant chaplain who often reminded him of how Christians need to abjure earthly pleasures and instead focus on heavenly rewards. Yet in Aleppo, in contrast to the austere life he had in Ankara, Abbott was immersed in earthly strivings and rewards. At the age of 15, his uncle Robert and the servants in the Aleppo factory, he recalled, taught him the skills to manage 'merchants accounts & the general routine of commerce' which prepared him for a prosperous career in India (Ibid., n. d, 20). In addition to learning business skills in Aleppo, Abbott cultivated the habits widely pursued in bourgeois England: he learned Italian and developed a passion for reading novels, romances and plays. He also enjoyed riding and hunting in the countryside of Aleppo. He was a polite gentleman who often socialised with members of the European community and tribal leaders in the region.

In the middle of 1783, Abbott's career in Aleppo took a different turn. His uncle John died which caused the steady decline of the Levant Company trade in the region.[8] His uncle Robert, as Henry recalled, did little to revive British trade in Aleppo. During this period, it was the French, rather than the English, who dominated trade in the Levant.[9] Because of that, Henry envisaged leaving the Levant altogether. This was a period in which many Britons of his generation flocked to Bengal and Madras, a quick route to wealth in a region ridden with diseases and wars but also full of opportunities.[10] Henry left Aleppo in July 1784 with the hope of finding a better opportunity in Calcutta. His uncle Robert helped him to secure letters of recommendation from the British ambassador in Istanbul Robert Ainslie. These letters directly addressed the governor general of the East India Company, Warren Hastings, who was in Calcutta at the time and whom Henry met briefly. Henry knew that the East India Company under the leadership of Warren Hastings had created many opportunities for young Britons, mostly from the lower and middle classes, who made huge fortunes in India.[11] But he also recalled how it was tough to find employment in the East India Company amid the rivalries of its members over trade, wealth and power. Through the connection of his family with the East India Company representative in Basra, Samuel Manesty, however, Abbott was successful in obtaining a position in the office of Edward Hays, the secretary of the East India Company.

While working in Hays's office, Abbott realised how British travels on the overland routes to India were immensely vital for the Company's dispatches and for the diplomatic relations between Europe and Asia. With the aim of offering himself as an expert on the Desert Mail routes, Abbott wrote a travel account in which he showed how travelling among Arabs in the Syrian and Mesopotamian deserts is not redolent with risks as many Britons, including Edward Hays, believed. In his *Journal with Occasional Remarks*

Made on a Trip from Aleppo to Bussora across the Grand Desert of Arabia (1789), Abbott showed how the experience of travelling in the 'Grand Desert of Arabia' was not only worth the risk; it carried many opportunities of entertainment and education. En route to India, as Abbott wrote, his experience was rooted in the immediacy of personal contact. Abbott learned from his encounters that societies are shaped by different historical and economic contexts, and the best way for a European to understand human differences is to tap into what Herder called 'a reservoir of human experiments', that is, to develop the traits of an Enlightenment sceptic and inquirer for whom human diversities and differences represent a strength of the human family rather than a weakness.[12] While so doing, Abbott showed a hospitable attitude towards Arabs rarely seen among travellers of his generation: for Abbott, each society and cultures, that is, each member of the human family, contributes to the advance of humanity in their own way.

Abbott published his travel book in the same year in which the French Revolution took place which explains how he figured in his narrative as a man of cosmopolitan leanings. Contemporaries of Abbott, those who discussed the idea of universal sympathy such as the philosopher Adam Smith, the cleric Richard Price, the sceptic David Hume and philosopher Jean-Jacques Rosseau, adopted the Ciceronian argument that one often finds stronger attachments towards those living closer to home than those living abroad.[13] As Rosseau in *The Discourse on Political Economy* explains, 'It seems that the sentiment of humanity evaporates and weakens as it extends itself across the globe' (219). The idea of distance here, as the Scottish philosopher James Dunbar in his *Essays on the History of Mankind* (1780) argued, can be seen as a metaphor of religious, cultural and moral differences that 'have grown immense in the revolutions of time' (Dunbar 1781: 154). Others who lived in the same period, however, mainly in Germany, such as Christopher Martin Wieland and Emmanuel Kant, spoke of the possibility of establishing – in Kant's words – 'a federation of nations where every state even the smallest, could expect its security and right not from its might, or its own juridical judgement, but only from this great federation of nations' (Kant 2009: 16). 'This gives hope', Kant wrote, 'finally that after many reformative revolutions, a universal cosmopolitan condition which Nature has as her ultimate purpose, will come into being as the womb wherein all the original capacities of the human race can develop' (Kant 2009: 20–21).[14]

Kant and the aforesaid scholars all argued for the possible development of 'the human race', but they had no doubt that only the bourgeois, literate classes in Europe were at the peak of civility in modern times. Abbott did not tell us that he read these scholars. Yet his narrative clearly shows he was aware of the debate in Britain and France about the universal cosmopolitan condition. Sometimes Abbott showed in his account of his encounters with the Ottomans an exclusionary understanding of Englishness, one premised on a political rather than racial marker of identity which we find in Onni Gust's recent study of how eighteenth-century diasporic Britons in different imperial posts understood 'home' in the context of an imperialist 'self-fashioning' and self-identifying as 'white' (Gust 2021: 11). But, as this chapter shows, Abbott's experience in the Levant produced a cosmopolitan Self rooted in the idea that encountering other cultures strengthens rather than threatens and dilutes one's attachment to her national and cultural roots – a kind of cosmopolitanism in which an attachment to one's nation and culture is not necessarily a marker of racial superiority as Gust saw it. It was one that many Enlightenment universalists (e.g. Herder and the Scottish historian William Robertson) showed in their writings; that is, the idea that encounters between different cultures, religions and nations foster improvements of the human family.[15] Buoyed up by moments of hopes in Europe in the wake of the American Revolution and on the eve of the French Revolution, Abbott, while reporting about what he saw across the 'Grand Desert' route, challenged established habits of thought in Britain in which the idea of improvement of any nation is measured by their material advance: that is, by their achievements in the world of arts, sciences and commerce. All nations and cultures, Abbott emphasised, had something to add to the march of humanity forward towards a universal cosmopolitan culture.

A Cosmopolitan in Aleppo

Abbott lived in a late eighteenth-century era in which the language of political rights, balance of power and peace between nations, as Lynn Hunt has convincingly argued, came to the fore.[16] In Europe, many saw the idea of culture – mainly the dabblers in Orientalism who replaced, in historian Thomas Carlyle's words, 'the old insular home-feeling' with 'attenuated cosmopolitanism' – as a conduit of constant exchange between East and West (Carlyle 1869: II, 36). During the early-modern period, as the latest scholarship has demonstrated, many cosmopolitan minds in Europe were fascinated with Arabic culture and literature. Many in Europe collected and translated Arabic books, offering a model of scholarship shaped by a cosmopolitan understanding of the meaning of human improvement.[17] Abbott lived in this age – in both the Ottoman Empire and Europe – in which many called for learning about and from cultural traditions and experiences of foreign nations. Although in the Ottoman Empire, the cosmopolitan spirit of the European Enlightenment – one which pervaded the writings of William Jones in Britain, Voltaire in France and Emmanuel Kant and Johann Gottfried Herder in Germany – did not necessarily take place, Ottoman elites were aware of the need to learn about and from Europeans, especially in regard to battlefield.[18] In Ottoman cities known as magnets for European merchants and diplomats, such as Aleppo and Constantinople, members of the Christian community were in close contact with European missionaries, ambassadors and merchants for whom they worked as interpreters, assistants and guides. In these cities, many Ottoman subjects, albeit Christians, developed the linguistic skills which helped them to read and translate European books and introduce the printing press.[19] This contact between Europeans and local Christians in the Levant encouraged changes of attitudes towards old mores, traditions and values governing the relationship between East and West.[20] Christians in the Ottoman Empire experienced this change but so did the Muslims. Author Ethan L. Minchinger argues that Ottoman elites saw their empire and society sliding into chaos, decline and, therefore, 'tried vainly to hold on to their sense of mission' (Minchinger 2017: 7). To that end, they issued, Minchinger adds, 'a bold and wide-ranging reform program in the empire's military, administrative, fiscal, and social spheres' in which the idea of borrowing from Europe played an important part in the efforts to modernise the state (Minchinger 2017: 10).

While Abbott was growing up in Istanbul and while he was training as a merchant in Aleppo, political elites in the Ottoman state were fiercely debating reforms. The Ottoman grand vizier, Halil Hamid Pasha (1736–1785), relied on French officers to reform the army, opened a naval engineering school and encouraged the efforts to publish French military and topographical books.[21] Reformers such as Ahmed Vasif, Dürrî Mehmed Efendi and Canikli Ali Pasa turned to the past in search of inspiring personalities and victories – like that of Sultan Süleyman I, Mehmed II and the early followers of Islam – in the hope to explain how the heavy defeats of their empire at the hands of Europeans, primarily the Russians, did not mean that it would not stand again on its feet in the future.[22] In their search for changing what they considered the decayed condition of their empire, however, the superior technology of Europeans fired their imagination. Ibrahim Mutefferika and Ahmed Resmi Efendi, to mention two ardent reformers during the period, spoke of the need to improve the military institutions of the empire in order to address the rising threat of European powers, mainly the Russians and the Austrians. To that end, they urged their rulers to learn from Europe.[23] Mutefferika, a Protestant from Transylvania by birth, converted to Islam after he was captured as a young boy by Ottoman soldiers near the Habsburg frontier in 1692. Heather Sharkey studied the contributions of Mutefferika to the Ottoman age of Reforms. He introduced, she wrote, 'the first Islamic-state approved press, dedicated to publishing works for Muslim audience in Ottoman Turkish' (Sharkey 2017: 99). Mutefferika printed books on the politics of different nations, the history of America and the achievements of European scientists and philosophers such Galileo and Descartes. One scholar considered him as a leading voice in 'Ottoman Enlightenment'.[24]

Abbott lived in Istanbul and Aleppo in an era in which the Ottoman elites looked to the modern world which Europeans indulged in. Notwithstanding the concerns of the conservative reformers of the age who looked for restoring rather than replacing the old order and despite the popular rage of the period against the Russian annexation of the Crimea in 1783, Sultan Abdulhamid (r. 1774–1789) and Selim III (r. 1789–1807) were admirers of European cultures, arts and sciences. According to Thomas Milner, 'while a somewhat strict observer in general of the Mohamedan law', Abdulhamid 'allowed himself a beverage which the Koran [Quran] interdicted, and is said to have observed jocosely to some of his European guests, that if he were to become an infidel, he should embrace the Roman Catholic communion, since all the best wines grew in their countries' (Milner 1799: 176). The successor of Abdulhamid, Sultan Selim III, was also an admirer of European modernisation projects. He sent an ambassador to France, corresponded with Louis XVI and examined 'the history of his country, and the general history of Europe; cultivated correspondence with intelligent natives and distinguished foreigners and conceived the bold design of becoming the regenerator of the empire' (Milner 1799: 177).[25] Both Abdulhamid and Selim III suffered heavy defeats from the Russians, but both were concerned about the future of their empire.[26] However, in a period in which the Ottoman Empire was in a state of war with both Russia and Austria, many conservatives in the empire rejected the idea of borrowing from Europe.

Foreign consuls faced the anger of local mobs.[27] Even Sultan Selim III was deposed, as George Larpent in his *Turkey: Its History and Progress* (1854) put it, because of his 'partiality for foreigners' (Larpent 1854: I, 199).

Such was the political and cultural milieu in which Abbott lived in Pera, Ankara and Aleppo, one in which European elites were widely respected in elite Ottoman circles. In Aleppo, Abbott's community was composed of rich Europeans who felt free to socialise among themselves and with the local elites.[28] In his excursions to Iskenderun, Abbott in his memoire recalled that he visited the Ottoman governor of Baylan with whom he conversed in Turkish. But in Aleppo he also spoke Italian, the lingua franca in Aleppo, with Dr Salina, 'a very respectable man who had two daughters & three sons grown up all of whom were fond of me, & as I generally met good company there, I passed my evenings very agreeably with them when I was not otherwise engaged' (Abbot n.d: 11). Abbott spent many evenings among the European community in Aleppo reading and rehearsing Italian plays. 'The language we spoke was always Italian', Henry added,

> the young ladies with great good will corrected my errors. We often read together & frequently got up plays from Mitastasio & Goldoni in which I always had a part, & whenever we were sufficiently perfect, my uncle the Consul generally invited a party of select friends to form the audience which we exhibited upon a neat little theatre he had built for the purpose at his own house. The characters in general well supported, & the whole together formed at once, a pleasing, innocent & instructive amusement, much to be desired amongst a circle of friends in any part of the world. (Ibid., n.d: 12)

Abbott's account of the cosmopolitan world of Aleppo was confirmed by James Capper who visited the city in the late 1770s: 'The Europeans by a general subscription have built a small theatre, which they have fitted up with great taste' (Capper 1783: 178). 'During the winter season they perform French and Italian comedies, and even sometimes attempt operas with very great success', he added (Ibid). Henry Maundrell, late in the seventeenth century, once described his countrymen in Aleppo as 'academical' and pious Protestants who often socialised among themselves (Maundrell 1703: 146). Abbott and Capper, late in the eighteenth century, however, saw their countrymen as men of cosmopolitan leanings: they spoke Turkish, Arabic, Italian and French; they often joined European parties and celebrated the famous Christmas carnival in Aleppo in the company of other Europeans.[29]

In an age redolent with tensions among European states over the safety and prosperity of their trade and settlements in different parts of the world, many European residents and merchants in Aleppo found such a cosmopolitan space in which they were encouraged to set aside their political and religious differences. It is true that at a time of war between England and France, as Alexander Russell in his *The Natural History of Aleppo* put it, 'public ceremonies between the Consuls were suspended' (Russell 1794: II, 13). 'The Franks, in general', however, 'live together in harmony', Russell added, and 'the private relation of men brought together by accident in a distant country, whom choice had led to form friendly connections, still remained sacred' (Ibid). In Aleppo,

Europeans cultivated peaceful relations, and in so doing they created in the eyes of their Muslim neighbours an ideal image of European unity. Even Catholic missionaries in the Levant were keen on developing harmonious relations with fellow Protestants. As Russell reported, 'A Missionary, describing the ceremonial visit made by Europeans at the annual [Muslim] feasts', [...].

> justly remarks to his correspondent, that he need not be surprised at those mutual civilities among people of different countries, for the French, English, Italian, and Dutch, in respect to the people among whom he dwelt, considered themselves as persons of the same country, and in that light, were viewed by the natives, who, without distinction reckoned them all Franks. (Russell 1794: 14)

Russell published his *The Natural History of Aleppo* in 1756 in the same year in which Europe was going through the atrocities of The Seven Years War. It is in this context of war that we find Russell and other Europeans living in Aleppo quite keen on rethinking their nations' hostilities towards each other. They did this while living in one of the most tolerant and cosmopolitan cities in the Levant.

Abbott enjoyed living in this cosmopolitan culture which Richard Pococke who visited Aleppo in the 1730s called 'sociable' (Pococke 1745: 137). Britons in Aleppo 'live very sociably with one another', Pococke wrote, 'and pass two or three days in the week either in the gardens, or under a tent in the country, or else amuse themselves in the season with country diversion' (Ibid). Russell also reported about these 'country diversions'. The English often pitched their tents in land known as Ain al Embarakey which belongs to the Ottoman governor Ragib Pasha, who was friendly with the European community in the city. 'The hawks and greyhounds are placed near the tent', Russell wrote, 'and various kinds of game are hung up in trophy at the entrance' (Russell 1794: II, 16). The English sometimes hosted local grandees. Russell recalled how one Arab emir often visited the tent while on 'his way to or from the city' (17). 'He is always received with great civility', Russell added, 'and together with his retinue (which seldom exceeds five or six persons), is treated with wine, or spirits, either being more agreeable to the Emeer than coffee' (Russell 1794: II, 17).

Europeans in Aleppo often showed friendly attitudes to the local elites, and these attitudes were reciprocated by their Muslim neighbours.[30] Under John Abbott's consulship in Aleppo, the East India Company and Levant Company cultivated amicable relations with the locals.[31] There were constant exchanges of presents and favours between the English and the tribes inhabiting the routes between Aleppo and the port city of Iskenderun where the Levant Company received and exported its goods.[32] Henry Abbott recalled how he used his friendly connections with the Ottoman governor of Baylan (Belen) to release one Turkman, a notorious robber in the region, from prison. This robber's father, a leader of his tribe, had previously entertained Abbott in his tent; he offered him a shelter while travelling between Aleppo and Iskenderun. These encounters show how Britons in the Levant were often prepared to cross into the other culture, whether by necessity or choice, but it was a crossing nevertheless which influenced residual cultural and religious prejudices.[33] *The Pedigree Register* (1913) recalled that

Roxana Vernon, the widow of Thomas Vernon, a British merchant in the Levant, was married in the Aleppo factory to one Abdullah Zaida, a Syrian Muslim from the city of Edlib, who signed a document in the consulate stating that he allow his wife to pass her property (worth 6,000 dollars) to her three daughters by her late husband whenever she sees fit and also agrees to pay Roxana's daughters 10,000 dollars.[34] The idea that this contract was signed in the presence of the English residents in the city indicates that John Abbott, the consul, and other members of the British community did not object to the marriage and shows how local elites were welcomed by the British in their factory. The English mostly socialised among themselves and other Europeans who lived in the city but also mixed with the locals.

Britons in Aleppo and its environs were sometimes exposed to local prejudices but, as Russell recalled, this was found in 'certain remote parts of the town' where the locals scarcely met Europeans (Russell 1794: II, 24). In Aleppo, Britons sometimes expressed narrow nationalist and religious sentiments. However, they knew that a hospitable attitude to others was a good way to survive and prosper in the East. When, in 1760, the Armenian nationalist Joseph Emin, a friend of Lord Bolingbroke and Edmund Burke in England, tried to recruit men from Armenian and Turcoman tribes to take over Aleppo from the Ottomans, two Britons – Patrick Russell, a Scottish physician in the Levant Company, and David Hays, a merchant – dissuaded him from such a dangerous undertaking. In a letter published in Emin's memoir, Russell explained to the earl of Northumberland, Emin's patron in England, why he and Hays prevented Emin from doing anything that would disturb the religious and cultural harmony in Aleppo: 'If he had not hearkened to us, the consequences of his enterprise would unavoidably have been fatal to all the Christian subjects of the Othman empire; nor could Europeans have been prevented from sharing their fate' (Emin 1792: I, 185). Russell was, as Emin noted, widely regarded in Aleppo so much so that he was allowed, unlike other Christians and Europeans in the city, to wear a white turban, a privilege only the elite enjoyed (Emin 1918: II, 503). Like Russell, Hays was a cosmopolitan Briton in Aleppo. His cosmopolitanism was reflected in the way he raised his daughter Marianne, who went on to marry John Barker (1771–1894), the British consul in Aleppo between 1809 and 1825. John Griffiths, who visited Aleppo in 1785, noted that Marianne spoke five languages: 'at the tender age of seven she spoke fluently Arabic, Greek, French, Italian and English languages' (Griffiths 1805: 335). Griffiths admired the cultural mixings in the Hays family home in Aleppo. 'On the right hand of the square of the first apartment was a dinning-parlour, generally furnished in the English style' (Ibid). But this English gentleman, David Hays, Griffiths added, was not strictly 'Englished' in the way he chose the design of his house. Like the houses of the upper classes in Aleppo, Griffiths added, Hays's home boasts of a 'fountain constantly playing' in the yard and in the divan 'a marble fountain in the middle, and cushions upon a raised platform along three of the sides' (Ibid). Griffiths was impressed with what he called this 'luxurious retreat' that was 'fitted up with much taste', a taste fusing East with West (Ibid). Like Griffiths, Francis Vernon, who visited Aleppo towards the end of the century, was surprised when seeing how most of English and European houses in the city 'were elegantly furnished, with carpets, sophas, cushions, &c, the manufacture of Persia' (Vernon 1792: 161).

Britons, including Abbott, enjoyed living in a city known for its luxuries and rich cultural fusions between the East and West. They also enjoyed a culture of toleration in a city whose main raison d'etre was to attract goods and merchants from all over the globe. As Richard Pococke, an eighteenth-century English traveller in the Levant, wrote, 'The English pass their time here very agreeably; and in the excursions which they make for pleasure they are commonly respected by the Arabs, Curdeens and Turcomen, there being very few instances of their having been plundered by them [...]' (Pococke 1745: 152). Russell further added that Europeans in the city did not feel pressured to learn Arabic. 'Of the Europeans, even those who live long in the country, very few acquire more knowledge of Arabic, than is barely sufficient for familiar conversation, and it is very rarely than any of them take the trouble of either learning to read or write it' (2). Nor did the 'Franks' feel pressured to conform to the local dress code: 'The Consuls and several of the private gentlemen, retain the European dress' (Russell 1794: II, 2). 'It was formerly the custom of all, or most of the Franks', Russell recalled, 'to wear the Turkish dress, retaining the hat by way of distinction; but of late, the far greater part of the English dressed in the European fashion' (Ibid). Even the Catholic missionaries in Aleppo, Russell marvelled, wore 'the proper habit of their order' (Russell 1794: 7). In a period when few Muslims turned up on European shores, Aleppo, as Russell noted, tolerated foreign habits. Europeans felt free to 'entertain reciprocally; they have card parties, weekly concerts, and sometimes, in the Carnival, masquerades', Russell added (Russell 1794: II, 12). 'Neither competition in trade nor the intervention of national ruptures in Europe, broke off the social intercourse in Syria' (Russell 1794: 13). Even the dishes and drinks served up in these parties indicate the cosmopolitan culture which European cultivated in the city. 'The tables of Europeans', Russell added,

> are well supplied with provisions of all kind, except sea fish, which can only be procured fresh in the winter. The cooks, as well as most of the other menial servants, are Armenians, but have been taught French or English cookery, and only now and then, by way of variety, serve up some of the country dishes. [...] The wines in common use are the dry white wine of the country, and a light red Provencal wine. The French present Liqueurs at the Desert. The English drink a draught of very weak punch, before dinner and supper; a custom found so deliciously refreshing, that most of the other Europeans, many of the native Christians, and some even of the Turks have adopted it. (Russell 1794: II, 10)

Russell noted how sometimes locals ('native Christians and some Turks') adopted European habits. But European and British merchants in Aleppo, he added, also adopted local habits, mainly those of the elites. As Griffiths noted of the lifestyle of his countrymen in Aleppo: 'An early breakfast of coffee, served without ceremony, precedes the pipe; in attention to business [...] or a short walk, or in absolute inactivity, [they] pass the hours until the hour of dinner, which is in general more frugal than supper' (Griffiths 1805: 539). 'After dinner, the siesta, or afternoon's nap', Griffiths added,

> is resorted to, and shorten the time until the ladies and gentlemen assemble for the evening, by invitation or otherwise; when a well sup- plied table, and social conviviality, detain the guests till nearly midnight, when each returns home. (Ibid)

For Griffiths, English residents in Aleppo were not only concerned about conducting business and making profits; they also found many opportunities of 'conviviality' and conversations.

In *The Modern Syrians: Or, Native Society in Damascus, Aleppo, and Other Mountains of the Druses* (1844), Andrew Archibald Paton, who lived in Damascus and Aleppo between 1841 and 1844, recalled how his countrymen who visited and lived in the city during the eighteenth century were sociable and cosmopolitan. Paton examined the archives of the British factory in Aleppo and found an account – he did not mention who wrote it – about how Europeans conducted their affairs in the city. He related how once 'in carnival time', the French were having 'a picnic party' where they were all dressed up for this occasion. While this event was taking place, he added, one Englishman Francis Vernon, who was passing through Aleppo on his way to Europe, borrowed the Ottoman governor's uniform and headed to the 'picnic party' without informing the French consul who was then enjoying himself in the company of other Europeans. On the spot, a messenger was dispatched to inform the French consul about a sudden visit of the Ottoman governor of Aleppo. The Frenchman felt embarrassed because he was not wearing his official clothes. 'Harlequin', as Paton described the French consul,

> wishing the Pasha at the bottom of the koik [river in Aleppo], stumbled out an expression of the delight which his visit would give him. The nation, his subjects, aggravated his torments by their suppressed laughter; so he cast away mask and sword, and borrowing a wig from one, a cocked hat from another, and covering harlequin's jacket with a cloak, begged them to suspend their merriment until the redoubtable visit was terminated. But in vain did he arrange his wig, and frown them into decorum; the cloak, however skillfully spread out, still left exposed a pair of legs resplendent with all the colours of the rainbow, and an uncontrollable burst of laughter rung round the tent; just at this moment the dragoman re-entered: His Excellency is come. The Consul is at his last gasp, when Mr. Vernon and suite make their appearance, and join their laughter to that of the French. (Paton 1844: 256)

As the passage above shows, Vernon aimed to poke fun at the French consul. But what Patton's anecdote here reveals is that Britons and other European residents in Aleppo felt free to hold carnivals and masquerades in the city; Britons participated in these acts in the context of friendship and amity with local Muslim governors and fellow Europeans. In his travel book *Voyages and Travels of a Sea Officer*, Vernon wrote about the Christmas carnival Europeans held in the city and mentioned how Europeans passed the time there with 'one continued circulation of entertainment, at the French, Venetian, Dutch, or English consuls; where the society of many respectable European families was heightened by the splendour of Eastern magnificence' (1792: 161). Europeans in Aleppo were free to have their own parties where men and women mix, a tradition that did not exist among the locals, including Jews and Christians. 'We frequently formed balls and masquerades, thereby giving an opportunity for the ladies to convince us', Vernon wrote, 'they were by no means deficient in polite accomplishments' (1792: 161). This convivial culture was enjoyed by Donald Campbell, a Scot of aristocratic and military background, who visited Aleppo in 1786. 'Parties of pleasure had no intermission', Campbell added, 'while I was there; and as the ladies of Europe or of European extraction in that country are highly accomplished, speak many languages, are indefatigable in their efforts to please, and receive strangers from Europe with a joy and satisfaction not to be described' (1795: 55). Such was the cosmopolitan culture in which Abbott grew up in Aleppo.

Cosmopolitan in Deserts

In *The Present State of the Ottoman Empire* (1784), a book translated to English from the French, Elias Habesci, a Greek merchant who previously served in the office of Ottoman vizier Halil Hamid Pasha, the reformer who was executed in 1785 for his alleged involvement in a scheme to depose Sultan Abdul Hamid I and replace him with his nephew Selim III, narrated a story of a Persian princess, the daughter of Karim Khan Zand who governed Persia between 1751 and 1779.[35] He recalled how the princess, 'a powerful' woman 'accompanied by a train of ladies, who were all very rich', in 1776 joined the Basra pilgrimage caravan heading to the holy cities of Mecca and Medina. An Arab 'chief of the tribe' in Basra negotiated with the Persians the expenses of conveying them across the deserts to Damascus. Initially, he was dazzled by 'the great splendour and riches of this [Persian] caravan', which encouraged him to ask for 'a more considerable sum than usual to conduct them' (Habesci 1784: 99). The Persian pilgrims 'refused to pay and addressed themselves to the chief of another tribe' (Ibid). The Arab chief with whom they first negotiated, however, did not put the matter to rest. Thus 'when they [the Persian caravan] were in the heart of the desert', he 'with his followers' attacked the caravan,

> of whom they made a great slaughter. They then stripped all of the pilgrims, not sparing even the daughter of Kerim-khan, and plundered the caravan, leaving the travellers afterwards to pursue their journey to Damascus, where they arrived in a miserable condition. (Ibid)

In Damascus, the Persian princess received little help from the Sunni 'Turks', Habesci added, but one European, a Frenchman, 'generously offered her his purse, which she accepted'. After her return to Persia, Karim Khan 'remitted' to the Frenchman 'the original sum' with 'double interest' and gave him many 'magnificent presents' that made him one of the richest people of Damascus (Habesci 1784: 100). Immediately upon hearing the news of the attack, Karim Khan dispatched his ambassador to the Ottoman sultan to ask for an explanation: all he could get for an answer, Habesci added, was 'the Arabs are rebels, and the tribe who committed the outrage inhabited the territory of Bassora which was subject to the government of Bagdat, it, therefore, belonged to the Bashwa of that city to indemnify him' (Ibid). As a direct reaction to such a cold answer, Karim marched to Basra and occupied the city.[36]

Abbott doubted the veracity of Habesci's account of the Ottoman Empire, but one idea that Abbott responded to in Habesci's book was that Arabs attack travellers in their deserts because of their avarice and violent culture. For Abbott, Arabs did not attack caravans because they were naturally cruel and covetous of other people's wealth; nor was it because, as many in Europe at the time, including Habesci, wrote, Ottoman rulers failed to bring them into the fold of government. Rather it was because travellers in their land often flout Arab rules of hospitality. One can win the friendship and protection of Arabs, Abbott learned, by showing them genuine respect. Abbott recalled how one Englishman, Mr Hare, who made 'his fortune in the law line in Bengal', was attacked and killed while he was on the overland routes to India in 1783 (Abbott 1789: 7). In the wake of this incident, many Britons accused the Arabs of being barbaric murderers. Few of them bothered to examine why Hare was attacked. Hare's 'behaviour to the Arabs was very rude, and disagreeable', Abbott lamented, since he

> would often gather such of them as he thought deserving of attention, and amuse them with the sight of diamond rings, gold snuff-boxes, chains and such like gewgaws as proofs of the wonderful ingenuity of European artists; and the more he saw their admiration kindled, the more fuel he would add to it, by producing something new. (Abbott 1789: 9)

Hare may have afforded to buy these 'gewgaws' by using the money he and many Britons during the period acquired while serving in India. Yet the main point in the passage above was that Hare insisted on reminding his Arab companions of their poverty, lack of innovation and industriousness. 'By the time they had been together eight or ten days', Abbott wrote, it became impossible for Arabs to tolerate Hare's behaviour: 'he [Hare] had carried his behaviour to such extremities, that neither the dictates of their religion, not their natural pride, could allow them to let it pass over with impunity' (Abbott 1789: 7). Abbott was clearly of the view that neither Arab traditions nor their religion encourage cruelty and aggression towards others, a view that Habesci clearly disagreed with when he wrote: 'Mohametanism having been established by violence [...]' (Habesci 1784: 139). For Abbott, 'Arabs are not treacherous, they are not wantonly cruel, not unworthy of trust, nor hypocrites, nor are they mercenary' (Abbott 1789: 12). Rather, they are 'hospitable, even to excess; if a party of Arabs are setting, and a stranger passes by, be he a Christian, Turk, a Jew, or an Infidel, they never fail to invite him to partake of their fare, and will hold it as a mark of disrespect, if the passenger does not honour their invitation, by dipping his fingers in the dish, and taking, though it were only a mouthful' (Abbott 1789: 13–14).

Abbott chose to correct British views about Arabs at a time when many in Europe wrote about the danger of travelling in the deserts of Syria and Egypt. The story of the suffering of Captain Barrington and his fellow Europeans in the deserts of Egypt in 1779 sent shock waves across Britain so much so that the British press continued to publish the story years after the incident. Captain Barrington, a Dutchman named Vendelwelden and other French passengers aboard the *Nathalia* (12 in total) reached Suez in June. They had originally loaded the ship with Indian commodities worth £40,000. In Suez, they formed a caravan with the aim to cross the deserts towards Cairo. En route, the caravan was attacked by a party of Arabs.[37] Eliza Fay, who passed through the deserts of Egypt on her way to India in August 1779, recalled how the Arabs brutally treated Barrington and his European companions; they confiscated their merchandise and left them alone naked in 'the blistering heat' and 'utterly destitute of sustenance of every kind; no house, tree, or even shrub to afford them shelter' (Fay 1908: 53). *The Annual Register* in 1781 described the scene in a harrowing language and recalled how the deserts for Captain Barrington were a 'murdering space' where one could expect 'death, hunger, thirst, suffocating heat by day, mortal cold by night, excessive fatigue, and destructive sting of the insects, the fire and sword of Arabs, the grief of seeing his companions perish, and his inability to succour his brother [...]' (1781: 55–57). Indeed, the attack on Barrington's caravan was orchestrated by the Beys of Egypt who had been honouring the ruling issued by the Ottoman sultan, Mustafa III, in 1778. The new law banned the East India Company travellers and merchants from approaching the port of Suez, which was then considered of immense importance to the East India Company posts in India. For Fay and *The Annual Register*, the dispute over trade in the region was not the main cause for such an attack. Rather it was because Arabs were naturally cruel to foreigners. The French writer Gullaume Thomas Francois Raynal, who never visited the deserts of Arabia, confirmed in his *Histoire des Deux Indes* (1770) this point: Arabs are 'so human, faithful, and disinterested towards each other' but 'savage and rapacious in their transactions with foreigners' (Raynal 1779: I, 289).

Abbott did not agree with this view and further argued that one needs to live among the Arabs to be able to judge their manners. One traveller who offered an 'erroneous' view of Arabs and Muslims, Abbot postulated, without living among them, was John Carmichael, who travelled the overland routes in 1751. Carmichael's geographical skills, which focused on calculating distances between cities and towns across the deserts, were praised, as we saw in Chapter one, by grand authorities of Eastern travels and travel writings in late eighteenth-century Britain. Eminent men such as the physician of the Levant Company Patrick Russell and the East India Company geographer and surveyor James Rennell spoke highly of Carmichael's scientific rigour; they also admired the great service Carmichael offered his countrymen by reporting about important landmarks in the desert routes to India. Abbott said nothing about the contribution of Carmichael to his country's effort to unearth the geographical mysteries of the Syrian deserts. He rather saw Carmichael as a prejudiced and ignorant Briton. 'Mr Carmichael, in particular', Abbott wrote of Carmichael's travel account, 'represents the inhabitants of Mahshed Aly as the most barbarous and inveterate enemies to the name of a Christian, though he owns at the same time that he never was at the town' (Abbott 1789: 71). Abbott's view of Carmichael bears a resemblance to what a contemporary of Abbott, the philosopher James Dunbar, wrote about the naivety of many in Europe who expressed a 'simple criterion of civilisation and barbarity' in their reports about non-European nations and cultures (Dunbar 1780: 142). For Dunbar, as his *Essays on the History of Mankind* showed, one 'essential' feature to 'the character of civilised people' is to show 'equity and humanity in their conduct towards strangers' (Dunbar 1780: 134). But this trait, Dunbar argued, was hard to find in contemporary Europe where many reports about non-European cultures showed prejudices towards others. Importantly, he added, these reports encouraged Europeans to send their settlers and armies to foreign climes in the name of civilising their inhabitants.

The reference in Abbott's text, thus, to the idea that Carmichael accused Arabs of being barbarous without interacting with them is indicative of the fact that Abbott was aware of the debate throughout the period about how one can expand sympathies to people who belong to different cultures and traditions without socialising with them, living among them and learning about their culture.[38] What Abbot shows here is the complexity of expressing one's openness to others: for Abbott, this is a dilemma fraught with problems of difference and distance. Striking a balance is not easy but what is certainly dangerous, as he showed in correcting Hare and Carmichael's views of Arabs, is seeing one's nation and culture as superior to those with whom many Britons were bound to meet, the people who live in an important region that offers a bridge between Britain and British settlements in India.

'I am an Englishman'

We read in Abbott's memoire that while on a trip outside Aleppo, he stayed in a guest house in a village near the Salt Lake area 'on the skirts of the desert' (Abbott n.d: 15). In that village, he encountered two Ottoman soldiers who showed no sign of respect to him and the people in the village. They confiscated the 'fine grass' which Abbott had already brought for his horse. Abbott objected to such oppressive behaviour and made it clear to them: 'I am an Englishman & not afraid of Pashaus & Dellybashes nor will I be treated as you treat these poor people' (Ibid). As a member of the English trading community in the Levant, Abbott may have known that his property was protected by the Capitulation agreement between the British monarch and the Ottoman sultan which on several occasions prevented British merchants from being subjected to impositions by local Ottoman officials.[39] Captain Richard Scott of the East India Company who visited the Levant in 1780 excavated the register of the Aleppo Consulate and found one important exchange between the British ambassador in Istanbul, Robert Ainslie, and one representative of the British government who was in Cairo on a mission to investigate the late Ottoman edict which banned the English from trading in Egypt. Scott reported that the British government representative reminded Ainslie of how the Ottoman sultan did not have the right to confiscate the property of English merchants because the Capitulations signed between the British and the Ottomans secured the property of British merchants and residents in the Levant. Scott also recalled how the government representative emphasised that the Ottoman government did not have the right to enslave 'English subjects' who, as their 'constitution' mandates, were free.[40] Abbott might have learnt from his uncle John Abbott, who was entrusted with this government correspondence, about the exchanges between Robert Ainslie and the British government. But Abbott's notion of English freedom was imagined at a moment of encounter with what he considered oppressed villagers and oppressive soldiers. Indeed, Abbott enjoyed his freedom in an Ottoman world in which it was well known among European travellers and residents in the region that Ottoman officials would not spare a moment to imposes extra taxes and fees upon European residents and travellers who happened to trade in or pass in their land.[41] But the association between Englishness and freedom in Abbott's statement above shows how Abbott's understanding of Englishness was imagined during a moment of encounter with difference. In her *The Genius of the English Nation: Travel Writing and National Identity in Early Modern England* (2008), Anna Suranyi has argued that the 'discourse of differences' in early-modern English travel writings and ethnographic literature 'proved to be eminently suitable for expressing English proto-nationalism and justifying future colonial encounters in the early modern world' (Suranyi 2008: 19).[42] Abbott's memoire and travel narrative sometimes expressed an idealised image of Englishness rooted in a 'discourses of difference' studied by Suranyi, but his conception of Englishness as a marker of difference in his account was not wrapped up with a rhetoric of colonisation and certainly did not show a sense of superiority to those among whom he lived, travelled and worked.[43] It was rather a rhetorical gesture conjured up in a moment of fear from the other: Abbott was fearful of losing his life and property while encountering Ottoman soldiers outside cosmopolitan Aleppo, his place of residence, where the English were much respected and protected.

The association between Englishness and freedom in Abbott's memoire was also shaped by the debate in Europe between revolutionaries and conservatives in the 1780s and 1790s, the debate in which fears were alleviated by using tropes of Islamic despotism.[44] Elias Habesci's book, which was published a few months after the fall of the 13 British colonies in America, might have been a valuable source of information for the young Abbott who might have heard about the American Revolution while living in Aleppo. In *The Present State of the Ottoman Empire* (1784), Habesci capitalised on an Orientalist discourse by offering his reader a harrowing image of Ottoman despotism. The Ottoman monarchy, he wrote, 'is one of the most despotic on earth' and 'the Turkish government, properly speaking, is a system of slavery' (Habesci 1784: 285). The despotic nature of the Turkish government, Habesci added, was derived from an Islamic theological context that legitimised violence: 'Mahometanism having been established by violence [...]' (Habesci 1784: 139). To that end, he added, we should not be surprised to find 'heads [...] taken off in Turkey with as little ceremony as an English gardener would cut off a parcel of cabbages from the stalks, and that without any apparent reason' (Habesci 1784: 257).[45] In an age in Europe and North America in which discourses of rights were becoming popular among radical circles, Habesci's image about Islamic despotism might have struck a chord in Abbott. Abbott, however, did not use any of the rhetorical flourishes which Habesci and his English translator used to turn their book into a bestseller in a British print culture which, for fear of censorship, was fertile ground for foreign writers who, in their books, critiqued despotic governments. Despite being aware of Habesci's work, Abbott said nothing about the despotic nature of Islam. Nor did he speculate on the idea that, as George Baldwin, the Levant merchant and diplomat on Egypt, who travelled between Istanbul and Aleppo in May 1780, conjectured in his travel account, Ottoman '[o]ppression will beget rebellion' (Baldwin 1785: 133). Rather, as a friend of the elites in Aleppo and its surroundings, all what Abbott cared to show while reporting about oppression in the Ottoman Empire is the notion that he was a free Englishman. To be an Englishman, as

Abbott realised, involves rejecting oppression. But this is where it stops. Abbott might have known that a radical espousal of freedom and liberty in the wake of the American Revolution and on the eve of the French Revolution was problematic for many in his native England. Thus, all what Abbott cared to show the locals was his sympathy with their plight rather than encouraging them to rebel against their oppressors: 'pity for the sufferers under such government was all the consolation in my power to offer them' (Abbott n.d: 15). Abbott here uses a sentimentalist discourse widely known in the print culture of the period which illustrated how a bourgeois subject avoided showing a serious engagement with the notion of universal freedom; the unwillingness to call for changing the status quo or advocate a radical notion of freedom was cloaked in a rhetoric of sympathy.[46]

In his memoire, Abbott offered a version of Englishness rooted in what might be called a qualified notion of liberty while in his travel account he offered another version of Englishness rooted in a discourse of hostility to France. Abbott's hostile attitude to the French appeared while he was en route to India, specifically when he conversed with the Ottoman governor of the city of Najaf about England's wars in India. 'I thought', Abbott wrote, 'a slight fib on this occasion, not only excusable, but necessary; and therefore, told him, that we were messengers from the King of England, going to India with instruction for the prosecution of the war against the French [...]' (Abbott 1789: 69). Although he was not carrying letters or dispatches from Europe to India, Abbott played the role of a patriot whose duty was to defend his country's settlements in India against the enemy. We know, as he told us in his account, however, that the main reason Abbot went to India was to seek employment in the EIC. Still, at the time when English trade in the Levant was in rapid decline and in a period in which the French commercial and political relations with the Ottoman court dwarfed those of the English, Abbott, with all the cosmopolitanism he showed towards Muslims and Europeans in Aleppo, could not hide his hostility to the enemies of his country, the French.[47] To that end, Abbott disagreed with Habesci who argued that the French, not the English, were highly respected in a late eighteenth-century Ottoman court. 'The decline of British commerce with Turkey, and the ascendancy which France, the perpetual rival of England', Habesci wrote, 'has evidently gained in the political state of Europe, have contributed to lessen the consequence of the English nation at Constantinople' (Habesci 1784: 310). For Habesci, the English were feared by the Turks who detested the idea that British commerce and maritime power were superior to theirs. Thus 'whenever they drew comparisons', he wrote, 'the Ottoman pride broke forth in excretion against this formidable nation' (Ibid: 309). For Abbott, 'notwithstanding what Mr Habesci said in the *History of Turkey* [...] the levity of the French has rendered them very obnoxious to the inhabitants of these countries, and that neither the Turks nor the Persians, are well wishers to that nation [...]' (Abbott 1789: 70). Whenever they go in the Levant, Englishmen, unlike the French, were often welcomed by locals who show them 'great civility' because the English respected local traditions, mores and manners (Ibid., 69). Abbott told the story that the East India Company representative in Basra, William Digges La Touche, was highly regarded by the locals because he was friendly to them; he even helped to release many of their relatives from Persian imprisonment in the wake of the Persian occupation of Basra in 1775.[48] 'The English nation is much respected at Bussora, and the liberality, prudence and humanity of Mr Latouche, during a period of seventeen years among these people', Abbott recalled, 'have so far attached them to him, that his word is the law' (Ibid., 98).

In the context of encountering Ottoman soldiers and heavily taxed Ottoman subjects, Englishness, Abbott showed, meant freedom. While encountering Muslim rulers, governors and caravan leaders, Englishness meant civility, politeness and hostility to the French. Among his countrymen in India, however, Englishness acquired different meanings. Immediately after he arrived in Calcutta, Abbott discovered how the British community had been riven with competitions. Among the self-interested East India Company servants, Abbott felt a complete 'stranger'. Despite those men of power and influence in the British state and East India Company, figures such as Sir Robert Ainslie (1730–1812), the British ambassador in Istanbul, and Samuel Manesty, the East India Company resident in Basra, wrote recommendation letters on his behalf to Warren Hastings and other powerful men in India, Abbott struggled to find employment in the East India Company. Abbott's views of the English community in India was captured by his friend Jeremiah Church of the Calcutta Supreme Court: Englishmen in India are 'complete Courtiers, from whom hardly anything need be expected beyond the sweet words and some good dinners' (Ibid., 25). Seen in this context, Abbott's Englishness in his memoir and travel narrative was not a fixed essence: that is, Abbott's views of Englishness in these accounts express what Stuart Hall called 'the process of identification', one concerned with 'taking up positions, rather than identity as a fixed essence because identification in this sense is never complete, is always in process' (Hall 2017: 127). Abbott's Englishness was a process of identification shaped by different social circumstances, what author Kathleen Wilson called 'a relation' which emerges 'through dialogic engagement with the social' (Wilson 2003: 2).

The Value of Cultural Crossings

Abbott showed cosmopolitan attitude towards Arabs which effectively emerged in the context of a social encounter in which conversing with others, as the philosopher Sonia Sikka found in the writings of Herder, constitutes an important prerequisite for 'self-knowledge' and 'salutary change' (Sikka 2011: 22). It was this idea of sociability that encouraged Abbott to critique a dominant view in Europe which measured the improvement of nations with the yardstick of material advance mainly in the fields of arts and science. This method of measuring the advance of what eighteenth-century philosophers of progress called 'nations' disregarded the lived traditions, habits, manners and feelings of different cultures and peoples whom European travellers did not find it easy to understand beyond their own cultural framework, as Tala Asad brilliantly argued, but nevertheless found in them 'the possibility of learning something important for' their 'own form of life that might help to transform how that life is understood' (Assad 2018: 9). James Dallaway, the late eighteenth-century physician and chaplain to the British embassy in Istanbul, illustrated how the Enlightenment method of measuring difference worked: 'when we reflect that a people whose government is systematically corrupt and proportionably feeble, whose recourse are neither understood nor applied, without commerce and without manufactures for foreign consumption' we should immediately conclude that '[s]o distant is the remark in Shakespeare from present application: "We must not think the Turk is so unskilful/To leave the latest, which concerns him first"' (Dallaway 1797: 49–50). Dallaway, who was a contemporary of Abbott, saw Muslims in eastern and western provinces of the Ottoman Empire as essentially the same, that is, materially unimproved and, thus, politically and culturally primitive. Unlike Dallaway, Abbott did not judge the civility of societies by using utilitarian framework. The complexity of encounter in Abbott's travel account meant that he was willing to reflect on the extent to which all societies, whether those that Europeans consider as civilised or not, contribute in their own ways to the development of human life.[49] A position like this was known in the writings of the Orientalists of the period. Take, for example, William Jones's view on Asian cultures:

> although we must be conscious of our superior advancement in all kinds of useful knowledge, yet we ought not therefore to contemn [condemn] the people of Asia, from whose researches into nature, works of art, and inventions of fancy, many valuable hints may be derived for our own improvement and advantage. (Jones 1799: I, 11)

It is true that Jones's frame of reference, in the passage above, was mainly European, which explained why he viewed the different cultural traditions in Arabia, Persia and India as essentially Asian. Yet Jones was aware of the need to rethink the utilitarian framework in Europe which does not appreciate different human contributions beyond the realms of commerce and science. Jones, who wrote these words while working for the East India Company in Bengal, was convinced that modern Europe is far more advanced than Asia, mainly in fields that do not require the work of 'fancy': that is, in the fields of sciences, manufacturing and trade. But this does not mean that people in the East do not produce ideas which benefit Europeans, most notably in the field of poetry and oratory.[50]

Abbott, like Jones, used a similar non-utilitarian view to critique dominant rationalist, empirical and utilitarian ideologies in Europe. For example, he reported in his travel narrative about how he in the Syrian deserts learned a useful lesson about how humans should view non-human animals beyond the framework of utilitarianism. He recorded in his travel book how he once saw in the deserts a monument an Arab built to the memory of a mare which had saved his life before she died. After catching 'a bullet in her leg', as Abbott was told by an Arab in his caravan, the mare did not give up on her owner who relied on her 'mettle' to escape a hostile attack: 'such was her goodness and mettle', Abbott wrote, 'that without halting in the least, she outran the enemy's horse, nor would she stop till she reached this hill where she fell dead, after saving the life of her owner, who to her memory created this dome over her grave' (Abbott 1789: 42). Abbott did not doubt the veracity of this story, nor did he comment on the *ghazi* or raiding culture of the Arabs, a tradition which, as we previously saw, European travellers in the region often interpreted in the context of the biblical reference to the violent Ishmael of the deserts. Rather, for Abbott, the affection the Arab man showed towards his horse represents an admirable relationship between human and non-human animals, one rooted in the exchange of affections and benevolence. This sentimental varnish on the story may have been recalled in Abbott's text to critique the utilitarian discourse in Europe in which relations between humans and non-human animals were primarily shaped by an anthropocentric ideology.[51]

Abbott's admiration of Eastern people's love for their horses was deeply rooted in a historical moment of exchange between Britain and the Levant. Abbott, like most British travellers in the Levant, greatly admired Arab and Turkish horses many of whom were imported from the Levant to England throughout the seventeenth and eighteenth centuries for purposes of leisure and also to improve the 'English breed'.[52] Donna Landry observes that 'Between 1660 and 1750, more than 200 horses designated as Oriental were imported into England' and men of aristocratic backgrounds such as Sir Edward Harley (1689–1741), the Earl of Oxford, 'enacted' their Englishness 'on the back of horses whose equine superiority owed its very existence' to British encounters with the Ottoman Empire (Landry 2009: 115). Abbott recounts how on a visit to a Turkman tribe near Aleppo he was impressed with how 'mares& horses' were 'fed, groomed and kept in the highest order' (Abbott n.d: 20). It was, Abbott wrote in his memoire, 'a gratifying sight' to see 'the finest and most esteemed horses [...] bred by Turkmens' (Ibid). Abbott accepted a gift, a horse, from a Turkman chief who held a great deal of respect for Abbot because he helped him to release his son from an Ottoman prison: this young man was imprisoned by the governor of Baylan because of his notorious attacks on caravans.

For Abbott, if Europeans in modern time show improvements in the arts and sciences, this does not mean that non-European cultures are inferior to those of Europe. Arabs and Ottomans had many traits, habits and manners in their daily lives that no rational European would have seen as primitive and uncivilised. In his travel account, Abbott admired the Arab method of roasting camel meat: 'we had ours [camel meat] roasted, which I found pretty tender, and not inferior to coarse beef; but my companion, from his prejudice against the animal when alive, could not bear the thoughts of fasting on its flesh' (Abbott 1789: 52). Abbott did not reveal why Captain Rochfort, his companion, was 'prejudiced against the animal': perhaps Rochfort was familiar with the prohibition against the consumption of camel meat in the Old Testament.[53] Perhaps he was surprised to find that Bedouin Arabs, who were often seen by Europeans as the descendants of the ancient Hebrews, consumed the same meat which Moses had previously been told to abstain from, a prohibition which encouraged English scholars of Islam and Arab history like George Sale to compare Jewish with Muslim dietary laws.[54] Maybe Rochfort, to recall what the seventeenth-century Italian traveller Giovanni Francesco Gemelli Careri observed in Persia, was like those 'Christians [who] eat not of these creatures [camels], because of the superstitious Words they [Muslims] utter when they kill them' (Careri 1700: 143). Abbott, however, had no theological argument to make against the Islamic method of slaughtering the camel: the only objection Abbott made in this regard was concerned with some unhygienic habits that he thought would endanger lives if they continued to be followed in the deserts. 'Knife was an instrument which they were not much accustomed to use at meals', he regretted, and Arabs kept raw meat 'on the back of a camel all the next day exposed to the sun' (Abbott 1789: 33). Despite these objections, Abbott did not pass a sweeping moral judgement on Arabs. His only concern was rather focused on the idea of falling ill in places in which it was difficult to find a physician or effective remedy.

Yet Abbott, like most travellers in Arab caravans en route to India, enjoyed his meals with the Arabs. From what we learn from the accounts of these travellers, Europeans knew that sharing food with Arabs was a good strategy the traveller should follow to gain their trust and ensure a safe passage across the deserts.[55] Abbott understood this well, but he also used the opportunity of sharing meals with Arabs to critique the epicurean culture of the rich in Europe. 'After hunting a few hares', as Abbott wrote of the Arab method of cooking in the deserts, an Arab 'first dug a hole in the sand wherein he kindled a large fire, and as soon as the flames and smoke were out, he buried the hare whole, skin and all as it was, in the hot ashes: having remained there for somewhat better than an hour, it was taken out, skinned and served up' (Abbott 1789: 48). Abbott admired this method of cooking which many people in Europe, he objected, might find it uncivilised. 'ODD as this cookery may appear to modern epicure', he concluded, 'I think it far preferable to roasting hare; for by this mode the skin prevents the gravy from running out, and the meat is rendered more tender and richer' (Abbott 1789: 49).

John Jackson drew on Abbott's appreciation of the simple methods of cooking in the desert when he commented on the Arab way of baking bread: I was 'amused', he wrote, 'by observing the dexterity of Arab women in baking bread' (Jackson 1799: 50). 'If they were not exceedingly quick at their work, the heat of the oven would burn the skin from off their hands and arms; but with such amazing dexterity do they perform it, that one woman will continue keeping three or four cakes at a time in the oven till she has done baking' (Ibid., 51). But why did Jackson admire the Arab way of baking bread? 'This mode' he explained, 'does not require half the fuel that is made use of in Europe' (Ibid). Jackson's description of the Arab method of baking bread was published in *The Edinburgh Magazine* in 1799 and in *The Universal Magazine in Knowledge and Pleasure* in 1800, which shows how before the high age of industrialisation – the nineteenth-century 'great transformation' in Karl Polanyi's phrasing – Eastern traditional artisanship was appreciated in Europe. [56]

In the eighteenth century, Britons who travelled and resided in the Arab-Ottoman land admired many traditions and habits which they considered useful for their readers at home to learn about. John Griffiths, while travelling in the Levant, wrote about the Arab traditions of using brass mortars to grind their coffee. 'To do away the reproach which foreigners never fail to urge against the coffee presented to them in England', Griffiths suggested,

> [...] I could wish to recommend the above method of making it [Arab method]; premising, however, that not only the quantity of powder generally allowed in England is insufficient to make coffee as strong as foreigners drink it, but also the powder itself is never sufficiently ground by the mills in use; a second, therefore, should be employed, so as to reduce it to an impalpable powder; and, if that cannot be effected by a mill, a pestle and mortar should be substituted. (Griffiths 1805: 358)

Griffiths did not object to the idea that coffee should be served as thick and suggested that the English, by adopting the Arab ways of making coffee, could improve their hospitality, particularly when hosting 'foreigners'. Griffiths was not the first European who suggested that the tradition of making coffee in Arabia was superior to that of Europe: twenty years earlier Carsten Niebuhr observed in Yemen that he 'found the taste of the pounded coffee much superior to that of the ground' to the extent that he and his European companions decided to leave 'off using our mills' and instead use the Arab mortar to make their coffee. 'The pounding seems better to express the oily part of the bean', he observed, 'which give the coffee its peculiar relish' (Niebuhr 1792: II, 229).

Before the advent of European steamboats into the Middle East, that is, before 'the age of steam which is the age of gold', many British and European travellers admired the craftsmanship of the region (baking bread, cooking, making coffee, operating public baths, catching pearls, weaving cotton and silk and building boats).[57] It is true that Britons were busy building an empire of commerce and arms in the East, but this did not stop some from appreciating the traditions and cultures of those among whom they lived and worked. Abbott was a member of this multilingual, multicultural community in the Levant, for whom travelling among and living with people of diverse cultural and religious backgrounds was an opportunity for improvement, an enabling exercise which is 'apt to dissolve' rather than consolidate European cultural certainties.[58] A peripatetic experience in the Middle East, thus, opened for European travellers many possibilities for improvement.[59]

Conclusion

Abbott's cosmopolitan experience took place in a world of constant blending and merging between cultures. The constant vacillation between the local and the global in Abbott's texts may be described as 'attenuated cosmopolitanism', as Carlyle put it. But it did not display any form of cultural superiority while interacting with Arabs. To that end, cosmopolitanism in Abbott's text is intrinsically a social act, one which recognised the equality of all cultures while being rooted to local traditions. Abbott's life and journey in the East were centred around this idea of personal advancement and financial gains, but he was aware that one's progress cannot be distanced from those among whom one lives; that is, the love of one's family, community and country, as he showed, should not be seen as a hindrance to respecting and appreciating foreign cultures, habits and mores. Abbott found in the idea of writing about his experience among Arabs a good opportunity to explain to his countrymen that cultural, religious and national prejudices hinder the person from being enlightened. The majority of travellers report false information about Arabs, he noted, 'without having had the sufficient leisure of inquiry on the spot or the necessary knowledge of the country language, to render their accounts and observations as correct as they might have wished' (ii). In setting out to correct British views about Arabs, Abbott rethought his relationship with his own community and nation (a relationship framed by national and class rather than ethnic or religious imaginary) while living and travelling in the Ottoman-Arab region. Bourgeois travellers such as Abbott not only highlighted the importance of encounter for an Enlightenment notion of cosmopolitanism but also raised larger questions about the ways in which that encounter created cosmopolitan identities. These identities, as author Stephanie Barczewski found in the cosmopolitan contexts of the eighteenth-century English country house, 'were historically and geographically contextualised by the specific global influences that were filtering into contemporary England' (Barczewski 2013: 42).

Notes

1 Ralph Davis notes that 'the Levant merchants in this period were rich because it was hard for anyone not born into well-to-do family to enter the Levant trade at all', *Aleppo and the Devonshire Square: English Traders in the Levant in the Eighteenth Century* (MacMillan: London, 1967), 224.

2 Henry was buried in the Church of St Mary's in Lewisham, London. *The Monumental Inscriptions in the Church and Churchyard of S. Mary, Lewisham*, ed. Herbert Charles Kirby and Leland Lewis Duncan (Lee: Printed by Charles Forth, 1889), 1.

3 The city of Abbottabad was founded and named after James Abbott. James, like his father, was keen on socialising and interacting with the people among whom he lived and served. He spoke Urdu and was keen on learning about local cultural and literary traditions of the Hindus and Muslims in colonial India. According to the British official Charles Raikes, 'everyman, woman and child in the country knew him personally, and hastened from their occupation to welcome and salute him as he came their way. The children especially were his favourite. They used to go to Kaka Abbott (Uncle Abbott) whenever their mouths watered for fruit or sugar plums. He never moved out without sweetmeats in his pocket for the chance children who might meet him, and as plentiful a supply of money for the poor. He literally spent all his substance on the people, and left Huzara, it is believed, with only his month's pay', *Notes on the Revolt in the North-Western Provinces of India* (London, 1858), 28. James Abbott was also a prolific writer. Like his father he was steeped in both worlds, East and West. He wrote two long tales *Prometheus Daughter* (1861) and *The T'Hakoorine: Tale of Mandoo* (1841): the former was a re-reading of the Greek myth of Prometheus whereas the story of the later was derived from a local tradition he learned in the city of Malwa, in West India, which he visited in 1832. His travel account about a journey he undertook between India and Russia in 1840 was published under the title of *Narrative of A Journey from Heraut to Khiva, Moscow, and St. Petersburg (*1843).

4 In1842, Keith Edward Abbott published 'Notes of a Tour in Armenia in 1837' in *The Journal of the Royal Geographical Society of London.*

5 A good account of Bartholomew Edward Abbot's family business, wealth and social connections in the Levant, see chapter eleven in Despina Vlami's *Trading with the Ottomans: the Levant Company in the Middle East* (London: I.B Tauris, 2015).

6 Robert Page Abbott served as Levant Company consul in Aleppo between 1797–1799. John Barker, *Syria and Egypt Under the Last Five Sultans of Turkey*, I, 17.

7 Laidlaw, *The British in the Levant*, 213–214. Ralph Davies, *Aleppo and Devonshire Squire*. 225.

8 A sign of the decline of the Levant Company during the eighteenth century was that John Abbott, 'although the Levant Company's Consul, he lived, as a private person, as economically as possible, unable to bear the great expenses attendant on a public character, and that he found himself also in much the same predicament, because the Levant Company would no longer pay a salary (as the decline of trade has diminished their fees) to the Consul, but only a sort of gratuity for the Consul's trouble in forwarding their packets' from Aleppo to Basra and from there to India, *Syria and Egypt Under the Last Five Sultans of Turkey*, I, 76–77. Despite this decline of trade, many Britons kept their commercial connections with the city, as the Syrian raw silk was still of greater demand in England. Jonas Hanway, a well-known merchant and traveller in Persia and Russia wrote about the decline of trade in Ottoman cities. He, in 1753, confirmed that 'Yet is not the trade entirely sunk; on the contrary it is said, that from Aleppo we annually import six hundred bales of raw silk. This alone is a very great

national object.', *An Historical Account of the British Trade Over the Caspian Sea with A Journal of Travel From London through Russia into Persia; and back through Russia, Germany and Holland* (Dublin: Printed for William Smith, 1754), 32.

9 John Jackson, *Reflections on the Commerce of the Mediterra*nean (London: Printed for W. Clarke and Sons, 1804), 7.

10 Nicholas B. Dirks, *The Scandal of Empire: India and the creation of imperial Britain* (Massachusetts: The Belknap Press, 2006), 38. H.V Bowen, *The Business of Empire: The East India Company and Imperial Britain, 1756–1833* (Cambridge: Cambridge University Press, 2006), 3.

11 As many historians of the period show, the East India Company service was open to many Britons from humble backgrounds. These men went to India to improve themselves, but the reputation of corruption in India accompanied them when they went back to England. In this period, these men were called Nabobs, a term which referred to the culture of bribery and exploitation in these men's service in the East Indies. And the term itself marked the controversy in Britain surrounding the British rule in India. For an excellent discussion of this problem in England, see Nechtman, 'A Jewel in the Crown', 71–86.

12 I take the quote here about the value of cultural differences in Herder's work from Charles W. J. Withers's *Placing the Enlightenment: Thinking Geographically about the Age of Reason* (Chicago: The University of Chicago Press, 2007), 138.

13 On Rosseau's rejection of cosmopolitanism throughout the period, see Helena Rosenblatt's 'Rousseau: The Anti-Cosmopolitan', *Daedalus*, 137:3 (2008), 59–67; see particularly page 64.

14 Genevieve Lloyd reminds us that 'Kant's emphasis is on cosmopolitanism as a political idea—as an ideal for the organization of collective life, rather than as an individual character trait'. This is true, but Kant in his essay *Idea for a Universal History of a Cosmopolitan Aim* (1784) also spoke of a universal human history in which emphasis was not only given to politics but also to, as Amelie Oksenberg and James Schmidt put it, 'human strivings' which 'bring about a realization of chiliastic hopes within human history'. In other words, Kant focused on cosmopolitanism from the perspective of a political scientist, but he was also philosopher and historian. See Lloyd 's *Enlightenment Shadows* (Oxford: Oxford University Press, 2013), 141. See also Oksenberg and Schmid's 'Introduction: history as philosophy' in *Kant's Idea for a Universal History with a Cosmopolitan Aim: A Critical Guide*, ed. Amelie Oksenberg and James Schmidt (Cambridge: Cambridge University Press, 2009), 2.

15 The Scottish historian and philosopher William Robertson decried what he considered the violence and religious superstitions of medieval crusading missions in the Holy Land. However, Robertson continued, 'It was not possible for the crusaders to travel through so many countries, and to behold their various customs and institutions without acquiring information and improvement', *Works of William Robertson with An Account of His Life and Writings*, Vols 9 (London: Printed for Whitmore and Fenn, 1824), Vol III, 32.

16 While Abbott was living in Aleppo, in Britain, Gotthold Ephraim Lessing's play *Nathan the Wise*, (originally published in German appeared) in print, 'a philosophic Drama' , the English translator wrote, 'which was not written for the stage, but was intended as an antidote against the rancour of religious bigotry with which the Jews are still treated in many parts of Germany', *Nathan the Wise: A Philosophical Drama from the German*...(London: Printed for J. Fielding, 1781), 2. Emmanuel Kant's essay *Idea for a Universal History of a Cosmopolitan Aim* was published in 11 November, 1784, ten days after Abbott arrived in Bengal. In this essay, Kant advocated for a cosmopolitan federation of states united to defend peace. Like Abbott, Kant's criteria of inclusion in this cosmopolitan public sphere is the acceptance of people to live and 'do business' with others who are radically different from them; such cosmopolitan order is formed out of what Kant called 'unsociable sociability'. For an English translation of Kant's essay and also for novel critique of his philosophy of cosmopolitanism, see *Kant's Idea for a Universal History with a Cosmopolitan Aim: A Critical Guide*, ed. Amelie Oksenberg and James Schmidt (Cambridge: Cambridge University Press, 2009). On the wider European debate regarding dissent, see Lynn Hunt, *Inventing Human Rights* (New York: W.W Norton, 2007). See chapter four on the debate in late eighteenth-century Europe and the United States about religious and political rights for religious minorities, slaves and women. On the cosmopolitanism of the public sphere in late eighteenth-century Europe, see chapter two in Michael Scrivener's *The Cosmopolitan Ideal* (London: Pickering and Chatto, 2007).

17 See the collection of essays in *The Teaching and Learning of Arabic in Early-Modern Europe.*, ed. Jan Loop, Alastair Hamilton and Charles Burnett (Leiden: Brill, 2007). See also Alexander Bevilacqua, *The Republic of Arabic Letters.*

18 Heather J. Sharkey, *The History of Muslims, Christians and Jews in the Middle East* (Cambridge: Cambridge University Press, 2017), 95.

19 Natalie Rothman, *The Dragoman Renaissance and the Routes of Orientalism* (Ithaca and London: Cornell University Press, 2021), 5. Peter Hill, *Utopia and Civilization in the Arab Nahda* (Cambridge: Cambridge University Press, 2021), 61. Maurits H van den Boogert, 'Ottoman Intermediaries in the 18th Century: Analysis of a 'Dirty Trade'', *Oriente Moderno,* 93:2 (2013), 515–530.

20 Sharkey, 98.

21 Stanford Shaw, *History of the Ottoman Empire and Modern Turkey*, (Cambridge: Cambridge University Press, 1967), Vol. 1, 251. A Turkish press at the residence of the French ambassador produced translations of military texts for use in the schools established by the mission. They printed many books such as *Elémens de castramétation et de fortifications passagère,* by La Fitte-Clavé, and *Traité de la manœuvre pratique* by Laurent Jean Francoise Truguet. The French ambassador Choiseul-Gouffier produced a Turkish grammar book in French and topographical maps of Istanbul and the Bosphorus. See Virginia H. Aksan's *Ottomans and Europeans: Contacts and Conflicts* (Istanbul: The Isis Press, 2004), 65.

22 Historians have often associated the onset of modernity in the Ottoman Empire with the adoption of European military and technological innovations. These borrowings shaped the worldview and lifestyle of many in the Empire. Hence the debate during the period, as Ethan L. Minchinger shows, about the disruption that borrowings brought into society, morality and religious world views. As Minchinger argues, 'The very act of borrowing required deliberation on the part of the statesmen and thinkers. It forced them to grapple with new and at times profoundly unsettling ideas', *The First of the Modern Ottomans: The Intellectual History of Ahmed Vasif* (Cambridge: Cambridge University Press, 2017), 8; 85–86.

23 Sharkey, 100.

24 Ibid. See also Shaw's *History of the Ottoman Empire*, Vol. 1, 237–38.

25 *Turkey: Its History and Progress,* 195. Shaw, *History of the Ottoman Empire*, Vol. 1, 260–261.

26 Abdul Hamid I accepted the treaty of Küçük Kaynarca in 21 July 1774 in which he allowed Russia to intervene on behalf of the Greek Orthodox subjects in the Ottoman Empire. For details about this treaty, see George Larpent's *Turkey: Its History and Progress from the Journal and Correspondence of Sir James Porter…*, Vol 1 (Hurst and Blacket Publishers, 1854), 193–194. See also Stanford Shaw, *Between Old and New: The Ottoman Empire Under Selim HI, 1789–1808* (Cambridge, MA: Harvard University Press, 1971), 73.

27 According to Aksan, 'After the outbreak of the Russo-Turkish war of 1787, chaos reigned in Istanbul and Choiseul- Gouffier', the French ambassador, 'was attacked at his residence', *Ottomans and Europeans*, (Istanbul: Isis Press, 2004), 64.

28 In late February 1786, the English officer Francis Vernon recalled how the English in Aleppo often blended in like locals. In his travel journal, he, the Levant Company consul Charles Smith, and other members of the English community visited a pleasant garden on the banks of the river Queik. They had 'an excellent entertainment, partly in the European, and partly in the eastern style'. A local dish which Vernon and his countrymen enjoyed was 'an Omelet made of an ostrich's egg, lately brought from the Desert, and sufficiently large for three people to dine off'. Such a hearty meal was followed by 'coffee and excellent wine', he added, 'and some neighbouring Arabs, forming a dance, at the entrance of the tent, enlivened the scene', *Voyages and Travels of a Sea Officer* (Dublin, 1792), 175.

29 Vernon, *Voyages and Travels*, 179. Eyles Irwin, *A Series of Adven*tures, 2 vols (London: Printed for J. Dodsley, 1782), Vol II, 282.

30 In *Directions for Passing Over the Little Deserts,* Captain Elliot Eliot, who passed the deserts in 1750, showed how the English were greatly respected in the region. 'But with regard to grown persons your being well known will rather command the greater respect, especially as you will have passes from Bashaws, which are easily obtained by Europeans'. Eliot's journal was published as an appendix to Bartholomew Plaisted Journal from Calcutta in Bengal, by Sea, to Busserah, 2nd ed. (London: Printed for T.K Kinnersly, 1785), 202.

31 Richard Scott, 133.

32 Captain William Beawes who served in the East India Company was in the Syrian deserts in 1745. In his journal, he advises his countrymen to 'To visit the principal Shaik with a small present, as a vest of cloth or the like', *Remarks And Occurrences In A Journey From Aleppo to Bassora*....in *The Desert Route to India Being Journals of Four Travellers By the Great Desert Caravan Route Between Aleppo and Basra, 1745–1751*, ed. Douglas Carruthers (London: Printed for the Hakluyt Society, 1929), 7.

33 Dr John Fothergill (1712–1780), an English physician and plant collector, recalled how his friend the Aleppo physician Alexander Russell found a name for himself as a friend of the locals, regardless of their religion. Such an amicable relation he found in the city helped him to examine the regular bouts of the plague and also collect plants such as Scammony which not only reached notable collectors of plants in Britain, such as James Gordon and Peter Collinson, but also crossed into Britain's North American colonies. See *An Essay On The Character of The Late Alexander Russel MD, F.R.S* (London, 1770), 10; 15.

34 *The Pedigree Register*, ed. George Sherwood.... Vol III (London 1913–1916).

35 According to Virgina H. Aksan, Halil Hamid was 'one of the most reform-minded of the eighteenth-century grand viziers', *Ottomans and Europeans,* 64. Shaw's *History of the Ottoman Empire*, Vol. 1, 256–257.

36 Habesci's narrative about the Ottoman Empire is dubious. The Persian siege of Basra took place in 1775, not 1776, as Habesci wrote, and the reason for launching the Persian military campaign against Basra was not the idea that the caravan of Karim's daughter were attacked by Arabs but rather that Omar Pasha, the governor of Baghdad, was constantly imposing restrictions and taxes on the Shi'a pilgrims heading to the Holy Shrines in Najaf and also because Omar Pasha was constantly interfering in the affairs of the Persian backed authority in the Kurdish principality of Baban. Habesci was no friends of the Ottomans. Abbott had nothing to say about what Habesci mentioned about the siege of Basra: 'many able pens have already given circumstances of' (95–96). Nor did he mention anything about the biased views Habesci expressed regarding the Ottoman Empire and Islam.

37 The historian Maya Jasanoff has argued that the horrific reception which some Europeans faced in the deserts of Egypt in the summer of 1779 indicates the difficult business of Empire in the eighteenth and nineteenth centuries; Barrington and his European companions' fate in the deserts of Egypt 'encapsulated both the troubles and temptations facing would-be European imperialists in Egypt', *Edge of Empire: Lives, Culture, and Conquest in the East, 1750–1850* (New York: Vintage Books, 2016), 240.

38 A good account on the cultural and nationalist debates throughout the period about cosmopolitanism between is Helena Rosenblatt's 'Rousseau: The Anti-Cosmopolitan', *Daedalus* 137:3 (2008): 59–67. On the history of British traditions of cosmopolitanism, see Richard J. Evans's *Cosmopolitan Islanders: British Historians and the European Continent* (Cambridge: Cambridge University Press, 2009). On the philosophical traditions in Europe associated with the concept of cosmopolitanism, see Martha C. Nussbaum's *The Cosmopolitan Tradition: A Noble but Flawed Ideal* (Massachusetts: Belknap Press, 2019).

39 John Gordon Lorimer, *Gazetteer of the Persian Gulf, Oman and Central Arabia,* Vol 1, 1192. Roger North, *The Lives of The Right Hon. Francis North, Baron Guilford; The Hon. Sir Dudley North. And The Hon. And Rev. Dr John North*, 3 Vols (London, 1890), 101.

40 Richard Scott, 118–119.

41 Ives, 208–212; Eversfield, 55–56. Howel, 43.

42 Many studies showed how the literature of travel widely read in seventeenth and eighteenth-century England forged an image of Englishness firmly rooted in jingoistic rhetoric associating empire with trade and liberty. See Katherine Turner's *British Travel Writers in Europe, 1750–1800: Authorship, Gender and National Identity* (London: Ashgate, 2001), 10. Matthew Day, ''Honour to Our Nation': Nationalism, *The Principal Navigation* and Travel Collections in the Long Eighteenth Century' in *Richard Hakluyt and Travel Writing in Early Modern Europe*, ed. Daniel Carey and Clare Jowitt (2012; Abingdon: Routledge, 2016), 77–86.

43 On how many people in eighteenth-century England showed awareness of their imperial nation's sense of mission, see chapter two in Krishan Kumar's *The Idea of Englishness: English Culture, National Identity and Social Thought* (London: Ashgate, 2005). See mainly pages 37–38. Several scholars, notable among them is Linda Colley, wrote profusely about how British identity was constructed during an age redolent with wars and conflicts between Britain

and France. This is certainly true as some British travellers in the Levant during the period openly expressed their antagonism to the French. But little in the scholarship about British identity of the period has been shown regarding the idea that Britons in the Ottoman-Arab region sometimes developed a sense of Englishness and Britishness which in the context of showing anti-French sentiments. On the anti-French rhetoric in Britain, see Colley's *Britons: Forging the Nation 1707–1837* (Yale: Yale University Press, 1993).

44 A good account of this discourse is Alain's Grosrichard's *The Sultan Court: European Fantasies of the East* (London: Verso, 1998).

45 Baldwin, 'A Journey from Constantinople to Aleppo' in James Capper's *Observations on the Passage to India Through Egypt* (London: Printed for W. Faden, 1785), 97–158; This quote is from page 133.

46 Habesci wrote his account of the Ottoman Empire while he was on a business trip in London. In *The Partition of the Dominion of the Pope Preceded by that of the Ottoman Empire* (1790), he recalled how while on a short visit in London he was 'advantageously known to the Ministry and Other Noblemen, one of whom he wished me to write on the then present state of Turkey' (1). His circle of friends in London included John Elphinstone, lately a British commander in the Russian fleet, who contributed to the defeat of the Ottomans in the Battle of Chesma (1770). By the time Habesci's book was published, the Russians, succeeded in defeating the Ottomans by annexing the Crimea-an Ottoman territory- to their empire. An arch enemy of the Ottomans, Empress Catherine II 's 'ultimate aim', Habesci reported, 'has long been to remove the seat of her empire from the North to the South, from the icy religion of Petersburg to the serene climate of Constantinople' (289). European powers at the time, mainly France and Britain, were keen on keeping the balance of power between the Ottoman Empire and Russia. Habesci prayed that the Ottoman Empire will fall sooner than later. He regretted that European powers, mainly the French, were helping the Ottomans in 'the discipline of their land-forces and of their marine' (306). To that end, the French, not the English, have gained the trust and respect of the Turks.

47 On the decline of British trade in the Levant in the last quarter of the eighteenth century, see chapter four in Despina Vlami's *Trading with the Ottomans: the Levant Company in the Middle East* (London: I.B Tauris, 2015). Baldwin was attacked and his property and papers were robbed on the road between Istanbul and Aleppo in 1780. Once in Aleppo, he told John Abbott, the English Consul, that if the East India Company is serious about protection its interest in the region, they should conquer it by force. The Company considered this dangerous; it did not agree with Baldwin. This anecdote and the reaction to it by the Company were reported by Richard Scott; see page 89.

48 William George Digges Latouche (1747–1803). He arrived in Basra with Henry Moore, whom he succeeded as resident. He often helped British travellers in the region and showed kindness to the local inhabitants. During the Persian wars with the Ottomans in Iraq in 1757, he ransomed the inhabitants at his own expense to save them from slavery. At the siege of Basra in 1775, he sheltered many people in the British factory. He retired in 1784. He married Grace Puget, the daughter of John Puget, a London banker. He was the grandson of David Digges La Touche, who belonged to the Huguenot regiment, and who came to England with William of Orange. *The Life and Adventures of Joseph Emin, An Armenian* (London, 1792), 451. See also *Dictionary of National Biography*, ed. Sidney Lee (New York: Macmillan and Co, 1892), Vol XXXII, 182.

49 This cultural relativism was common in the work of John Gottfried Herder in Enlightenment Germany. Herder was a contemporary of all the travel writers I examine in this book. On Herder's culturalist theory, see Sonia Sikka's *Herder on Humanity and Cultural Difference: Enlightened Relativism* (Cambridge: Cambridge University Press, 2011).

50 See chapter five in Michael J. Franklin's *'Orientalist Jones': Sir William Jones, Poet, Lawyer, and Linguist, 1746–1794* (Oxford: Oxford University Press, 2011). See the introduction in Michael. D. Dodson's *Orientalism, Empire, and National Culture: India, 1770–1880* (New York: Palgrave, 2007).

51 Erika Cudworth and Stephen Hobden, 'Civilisation and the Domination of the Animal', *Millennium*, 3 (2014), 746–766.

52 William Guthrie, *A New System of Modern Geography*, 3 vols (Philadelphia, 1795), Vol II, 139.

53 See the entry on 'Camel' in Samuel Johnson's *A Dictionary of the English Language*, 2 vols (London, 1755), Vol I.

54 *A Complete History of the Arabs from the Birth of Mohammed to the Reduction of Baghdad*, 3 vols (London, 1761), Vol I, 362. George Sale, *The Koran*, 128.

55 Howel, 46.

56 *The Edinburgh Magazine, Or, Literary Miscellany*, (Edinburgh, 1799), Vol 14, 168; *The Universal Magazine of Knowledge and Pleasure* (London, 1800), Vol 106, 130.

57 On manufacturing in Aleppo, see Richard Pococke's *Description of the East and Some Other Countries*, 2 vols (London: Printed by W. Boyer, 1745), Vol I, 151. See also Parsons' *Travels in Asia and Africa*, 47, 52 and 55. This quote about the age of steam is from Paton's *The Modern Syrians*, 190. On the Arab tradition of building boats used in the rivers Euphrates and Tygris, see John Jackson's *Journey from India*, 39–40. The English traveller James Capper admired the public bath in Egypt in the 1770s; see his *Observations on the Passage to India*, 15. *The London Magazine* published Capper's observations of the Turkish bath without mentioning his name, an indication of how Capper's experience in the bath was appropriated by the magazine to entertain its bourgeois readers, *The London Magazine Enlarged and Improved*, II (1784), 364–365. Sir Arnold Wilson, the British diplomat in the Persian Gulf in the early decades of the twentieth century, summarised this change in the region in the following words: 'Nowhere were better or faster ships built than on the Oman and Arab coast of the Gulf, no nation had more skilful sailors or more enterprising merchants. But steam ruined the industry and dealt a blow at the maritime Arabs from which they have never recovered, for they have neither the capital, the knowledge, nor the resources to stand up against European steam vessels'; 'A Periplus of the Arabia Gulf', 237.

58 Vanessa Smith, *Intimate Strangers: Friendship, Exchange and Pacific Encounters* (Cambridge: Cambridge University Press, 2010), 14. The idea that an encounter in liminal spaces (such oceans) creates multiple possibilities and opportunities that de-centre and re-centre the traveller (in her relationship to his/her nation, gender and class) is brilliantly examined by Emily Burns' essay 'The Old World A New: The Atlantic as a Liminal Site of Expectation' in *Framing the Ocean, 1700 to the Present ': Envisaging the Sea as Social Space*, ed. Tricia Cusack (2014; Abingdon: Routledge, 2016), 37–54.

59 I take the cue here from George Santayana's essay 'The Philosophy of Travel', *The Virginia Quarterly Review*, 1 (1964), 1–10. For Santayana, travel is an exercise that encourages discoveries and is fraught with promises and expectations, a constant search for the novel, the new and different. Expectations and promises may give way to disappointments, but travellers should not give up looking for change. See page 6.

Chapter Five

EYLES IRWIN'S TRAVELS: THE POLITICS OF ADVENTURE IN THE LEVANT

The flow of ideas and civilization was for long ages from the East to the West, and not as is now the case, from the West to the East.

—Charles MacFarlane, *The Romance of Travel: The East* (1846)

Eyles Irwin was born in Calcutta, India, in 1751. His father, James Irwin, was a merchant in St Helena and Java in the 1730s. In the 1740s, he 'received direct employment by the [East India] Company', the historian Barry Crosbie wrote, which allowed him to make fortunes that enabled him to buy the Hazeleigh estate in Essex (Crosbie 2011: 40). At an early age, Eyles Irwin's father sent him to England to study at a private academy in Chiswick. In 1771, via his family's connections with the director of the East India Company at the time Laurence Sullivan, Irwin was offered a position in the Madras civil service and a few years later he rose in the EIC ranks to be a 'superintendent of the company's grounds within the bounds of Madras'.[1] While in Madras, Irwin succeeded to gain the trust of the governor of Madras, Lord Pigot (George Pigot [1719–1777]), who was appointed to restore the province of Tanjore to the Rajah.[2] Irwin's ambitions were shaken when Pigot died in his prison in St Thomas Mount in 1777shortly after the Madras Council ousted him. Immediately after Pigot passed away, Irwin was suspended because he didn't follow the new leadership headed by George Stratton, Henry Brooke and Charles Floyer.[3] Soon after, Irwin returned to Britain by the Red Sea route via Suez, but two years later he was reinstated to the service. In 1783, he returned to India by the Syrian-Mesopotamian routes. In the same year, Lord McCartney (George McCartney), the governor of Madras, endorsed Irwin's talents to the East India Company. He appointed him to administer the provinces of Tinnivelly and Madurah. In 1793, Irwin was further promoted: he sat on the 'Secret and Superintending Committee of Supra Cargos for the Company's Affairs in China'.[4]

Irwin's colleagues and friends in Madras and Bengal consisted of Britons who had powerful connections and possessed huge wealth both in India and Britain. One such Briton was the rich money speculator Paul Benfield who was stationed in Bengal but was involved with commercial affairs in Madras. Benfield, who was known for offering loans to the Nawab of Arcot, had clashed with Irwin's erstwhile boss, Lord Pigot, over the restoration of Tanjore to Thuljaji Bhonsle, the head of the Bhonsle dynasty which ruled Tanjore for decades before the Company, now in an alliance with the Nawab of Arcot, Muhammad Ali Wallaja Khan, seized its government.[5] Benfield was singled out by Edmund Burke, the arch-critic of the East India Company during the period, who considered Benfield one of the most corrupt British servants in Bengal.[6] Benfield was known for his notorious business deals with local Indian rulers for whom he was a spokesman in the British Parliament to which he was elected after he returned to Britain in 1780. Benfield's involvement with loans and speculations in India secured him a fortune of £500,000, which allowed him to bankroll his parliamentary seat and purchase Woodhall Park in Hertfordshire.[7] He was called 'Count Roupee' by the artist James Gillray in 1797: Gillray's satirical portrait showed how the wealth Benfield collected in India enabled him to show the trappings of a gentleman, but the polished façade was not successful in undoing his enslavement to the grand 'Roupee' [Figure 9].

Irwin's other colleagues were also accused of corruption. Warren Hastings, the tragic hero of Edmund Burke's impeachment saga in the British Parliament between 1787 and 1795, was the second in charge of the Madras Council between 1769 and 1771. In 1771, Hastings was appointed governor of Calcutta. Upon returning to Britain with huge sums in 1784, Edmund Burke accused Hastings [Figure 10] of corruption and claimed that Hastings granted a contract to Stephen Sullivan, son of Laurence Sullivan, 'for the provision of opium, without advertising for proposals'. Hastings, Burke continued, aimed to help the young Stephen secure 'instant fortune' because of 'the support and attachment of his father' (Burke 1885: IV, 402). Irwin was close to the circles of Hastings and the Sullivans whom Burke accused of corruption.[8]

But Irwin was not only friends with men whom many in England accused of being corrupt. As a poet and writer, Irwin nurtured a friendship with men known in Britain

Figure 9 A small ugly man rides a galloping horse in profile to the left, his leg thrust forward. He wears spectacles, and his complexion is dark. There is a background of grass and trees, and in the distance a building with a pediment, evidently the new Knightsbridge Barracks (see 'Gent. Mag.', July 1797, p. 545, pl.). 5 June 1797. Hand-coloured etching. Source: The British Museum.

Figure 10 Warren Hastings on his Arabian Horse, 1796. Source: Yale British Centre.

and India as erudite scholars and respectable gentlemen. Irwin was also friends with William Jones, a man whom Warren Hastings patronised and supported in his efforts to create a layer of respectability and scholarship around the East India Company which many in Britain associated with corruption. Jones was appointed as a judge in Bengal in 1784. His reputation as a scholar of Oriental literature and history drew the attention of Hastings who wanted to curb the corrupt practices of the Company and understand Indian customs, laws, cultures, manners and traditions in order to govern the country more efficiently.[9] Besides his professional duties, Jones presided over the Asiatic Society of Bengal, a gentlemanly club modelled after the Royal Society in London in which men from military and commercial backgrounds dabbled with Oriental archaeology, natural history, law, religions and poetry.[10]

We do not know whether Irwin was a member of The Asiatic Society or not, but in his *Occasional Epistles* (1783), he celebrated the poetry of Jones and called him the 'the British Hafiz' (Irwin 1783: 27).[11] Irwin shared with Jones a penchant for an eighteenth-century poetic tradition to which famous literary minds in Britain, such as William Collins and Samuel Johnson, contributed. In the Anglo-Oriental poetry written in Britain and Calcutta in the second half of the century, as the author James Mulholland points out, Arab, Indian and Persian characters were given opportunities to speak about contemporary British anxieties over imperial and commercial expansions, loss of virtue in modern commercial times and dangers of revolutions in America and France.[12]

Irwin was no stranger to this literary phenomenon in British culture. *The European Magazine*, in an essay titled 'Memoires of Eyles Irwin' published in March 1789, made it clear that Irwin's 'literary pursuits' in England were abandoned for a more prosperous career path in the civil service in Madras, but the magazine also argued that India offered him an opportunity to grow as a writer while keeping an eye on 'improving his fortune' (1789: 179). Irwin was, *The Annual Biography* recalled, 'a native of the East [whose] life, talents and character, all tend to prove that virtue and abilities are not to be exactly measured by degrees of longitudes and latitudes as some philosophers have pretended' (1818: II, 221). Irwin's travel writings and poetry (which appeared in the 1770s and 1780s) were powerful testaments to the fact that young Britons found in the East an opportunity to cultivate their literary talents as well as get an imaginative space to reflect on Britain's troubled political climate.[13]

Three years after the death of Pigot in Madras, Irwin wrote *An Epistle to the Right Honourable George Lord Pigot* (1780) in which he eulogised Pigot's military achievements while lamenting his demise: 'Behold the Man who toils and dangers brav'd/Check'd Gallia' progress, and the Decan sav'd/Now own'd the leader of unconquered bands/And now a captive in ignoble hands!' (9). In *St. Thomas' Mount, a Poem* (1771) and *Bedukah, an Indian Pastoral* (1776), Irwin glorified Indian fables, religious rituals and landscape, but in so doing, he allegorised the political challenges which the Company and the British government faced in the 1770s, namely anxieties surrounding the American revolution and the threat of Hyder Ally, an arch-enemy to the Company whose death Irwin captured in a poem titled *Ode to Robert Brooke, Occasioned by the Death of Hyder Ally* (1784).

Irwin served and wrote in Madras in a political climate in the 1770s and 1780s, known as, in Edmund Burk's phrasing, the 'greater disorder' (Burke 1852: III, 486). The Indian historian Ishwari Prasad explained how this disorder was illustrated in the '[t]he conditions of Madras' which 'had grown from bad to worse. Corruption was rife everywhere, and the harmonious working of the administration of the Government had become difficult' (Prasad 1973: 124–125). This 'disorder' was often attributed to the political uncertainties facing the British Empire in the wake of the fall of the American colonies and the rising French threat in India. Twenty years after the signing of the Treaty of Allahabad (1765), which entrenched the Company's rule in Bengal, local Indian forces headed by Hyder Ally and his son Taipo Sahib, now supported by the French, posed existential threat to the Company settlements in the South.[14] Irwin's life, career and writings during the period were shaped by this troubled political context.

This chapter asks why the East in Irwin's travel writings turns into an imaginative space that enables the traveller to reflect on and alleviate his political anxieties, mainly those related to commercialism and empire, prevailing in Britain during the 1770s and 1780s. In steering Irwin's travelling experience in the Levant in the direction of some political and ethical issues that dominated late eighteenth-century discourse in Britain, I follow the lead of Benjamin Colbert, Robin Jarvis and Nigel Leask who, in their different ways, showed how eighteenth-century romantic travellers and travel writers were conditioned by specific political and cultural contexts in which they laboured.[15]

Nigel Leask's idea of 'antique land' is helpful in this regard because it helps us to understand how Irwin's aesthetic images of Arabia were shaped by and contributed to a political and philosophical culture in Britain which yearned for a sanitised and virtuous past different from a contemporary time redolent with corruption. While doing so, Leask asserts, 'European travellers constantly "temporalized" the antique lands (and especially their modern inhabitants) by comparing them with more familiar classical, biblical, or medieval worlds, at the same time as they incorporated them into a "universal" grid of geographical orientation based in Europe' (Leask 2002: 2). Encounter, a form of 'intellectual, cultural, or sometimes critical stimulation', helped Irwin to sanitise and rethink dominant ideologies during his lifetime.[16] In so doing, as Benjamin Colbert argues, Irwin was conditioned by 'culturally located act of observation' in which 'the eye represents some form of motivated perception, in which aesthetic, moral or political judgements are brought to bear on the observations of buildings, scenery, people, or complex tableaux containing many referents' (Colbert 2005: 5–6). As this chapter shows, aesthetic representations of Arabia allowed Irwin to celebrate and rethink, in Terry Eagleton's phrasing, modern values of 'political order' and 'social harmony', which many during the period feared being subverted (Eagleton 2014: 37).[17] For Irwin, pictorial representation of the Euphrates valley and sentimental descriptions of powerful rulers in the Levant speak to contemporary fears of the loss of British colonies in India and America . While structures of powers are at their best when they succeed in infiltrating 'structures of feelings', in Raymond William's phrasing, that is, if poetics tends to submit to politics, then an effective (travelling) subject is not totally dissociated from popular ideologies of reason, order, progress and empire: affective responses, as this and the next chapter show, provide compliments as well as critiques of these ideologies.[18]

A Travel Writer

On 2 April 1771, Eyles Irwin, Major Anthony Hammond and Major Alexander of the East India Company arrived in Mocha in Yemen. They carried with them a substantial amount of money, expensive diamonds, gold, silver rings and jewels that they acquired during many years of service in India.[19] From Mocha, they headed to Jedda and then to the port of Suez before joining an Arab caravan to Cairo. In Cairo, they were received by the English resident and diplomat George Baldwin who facilitated their move to Alexandria where they boarded a French ship, *The Cleopatra*, aiming to reach Europe after a long and arduous journey across the deserts of Arabia. Throughout the journey in Egyptian deserts, they were extremely worried about losing their possessions. The people among whom they travelled, their companions and the people they encountered en route knew that Englishmen who served in India often returned home with huge sums and expensive jewels.[20] Irwin's narrative of his journey is filled with anecdotes about how he and his English companions were constantly stopped and searched on the coast of Arabia and Egypt. In a letter to the Court of Directors of the East India Company, dated July 1778, Irwin asked for compensation for 'his expenses for travelling overland' and complained that 'I was unfortunate enough to be engaged of more valuables than Mr Hammond, the Booty which the Arabs obtained from me was consequently greater' (Irwin 1778: 21–22).[21] Because of the slow response of Company officials to his demand for compensation, Irwin found in the idea of writing a travel book an opportunity to recover his financial losses in the deserts. Perhaps the sum of money (£6,000) that the author John Hawksworth, well known in Britain for collaborating with Samuel Johnson in founding a periodical called *The Adventurer*, received upon compiling and editing Captain James Cook's official account of his travel in the South Pacific inspired Irwin to explore the prospects of travel writing.[22]

In fact, Irwin wrote his travel account with the purpose of selling books. Irwin's narrative about his journey along Egyptian routes figured in his *A Series of Adventures in the Course of a Voyage Up the Red Sea* (1780). Immediately upon its publication, the book became a sensation. A second edition appeared in the same year of its publication. One reason why the book drew a massive readership was the way it was written. Irwin's style of writing resembles that of Hawksworth. In both books, detached descriptions were replaced by personal and sentimental reactions to people and nature. What the editors of *A New and General Biographical Dictionary* in 1784 wrote about Hawksworth could have applied to Irwin: 'Works of taste and elegance, where imagination and the passions were to be affected, were his province; not works of dry, cold, accurate narrative' (1784: 477). Many readers enjoyed reading books that drew on sentimental experiences of travellers, but among commentators on travel writing in the British press, however, this new trend in travel books could jeopardise the 'real' value of the genre: that is, readers should be introduced to detached observations rather than aesthetic and sentimental reactions to and impressions of exotic landscapes and people. *The Critical Review* in 1780 believed that *A Series of Adventures* 'has perhaps as fair title to success as most of its predecessors' because although it is true that readers cannot resist books that include marvellous, romantic and exotic descriptions, '[t]hese Adventures' are 'not very interesting or important' despite that they are 'entertaining' (1780: 405, 411). Irwin resisted an early eighteenth-century tradition in travel writing which mostly focused on the idea of recording detached observations, and in so doing he had to face the critics in the English press who were suspicious of the turn inward which pervaded the genre of travel writing in the second half of the eighteenth century. '[H]is good understanding must soon convince him', *The Monthly Review* in 1780 concluded, 'that this affected mixture of simple narrative and inflated description is a blemish in his work and ought most carefully to be avoided by every writer who aims at the approbation of the sensible and judicious class of readers' (1780: 409). The critics of Irwin's style of writing mostly focused on the turn inward in his book, but as the *Monthly Review* above suggested Irwin joined the chorus of travel writers who understood well the growing fascination of the period with inward and everyday experiences of writers, what historian Mark Salber Philips called 'the social and sentimental interests' of eighteenth-century British 'culture' (Philips 2000: 8).

While being subject to ridicule in Britain, Irwin's travel book was popular in other parts of Europe. In Leipzig, a German edition appeared in 1781 with the title

Begebenheiten einer Reise auf dem rothen Meer, auf der arabis. In Paris, the book kept circulating in the press long after it was first published in England: two editions in French appeared between 1792 and 1793.[23] One reason why *A Series of Adventures* was widely read in the continent, mainly in France, was because Irwin's style was appealing to a readership familiar with the Orientalist traditions rooted in exoticism, embellished language and inflated imagery. 'French travellers', *The Critical Review* in 1799 noted, 'always invent and embellish', whereas those who published in Britain, such as Richard Pococke and Fredric Norden, 'are grave and voracious writers' whose books 'are confined to the shelves of men of science' (1799: 286).

Seven years after *The Series of Adventures* was published, Irwin brought out a new edition, but this time he aimed to balance a sentimental style with one that showed disenchanted, rationalist and empiricist descriptions of places and people he encountered: the new book included a narrative about Irwin's journey in the Syrian-Mesopotamian overland routes, which Irwin undertook in 1783. The book was well-received by the British press in comparison to that of his first account of the Egyptian journey. However, the third edition was not regarded in any way as beneficial to readers because it was deficient of new descriptions of lands, people and routes seen as immensely important for an expanding British Empire in India. Irwin's description of the manners of Arabs and the villages located 'on the banks of this great river [the Euphrates]', *the Monthly Review* noted, 'will be acceptable to the reader who is curious and inquisitive in regard to subjects of this entertaining kind' (1788: 520). But the *Monthly Review* added, 'The journey through the Deserts is similar to that described by other writers' and 'the particulars of this voyage are not very interesting' (1788: 520). Even the geographer James Rennell, who admired the efforts of Irwin to measure the distance between Aleppo and Basra by calculating the steps of his camel, concluded that Irwin's calculations were less accurate than those who travelled before him: John Carmichael and James Capper. 'Mr Irwin', Rennell wrote in his article 'On the Rate of Travelling' published in *The Philosophical Transactions* in 1791, 'took the bearing of his course by a compass, though not so much in detail as Mr. Carmichael' (Rennell 1791: 138).

Irwin thus faced the dilemma of being a travel writer in a late eighteenth-century Britain in which travel and travel writing were no longer seen as merely an individual enterprise. It was rather shaped by national concerns about protecting trade routes, finding new markets and expanding the empire.[24] One the one hand, Irwin was accused of being a romancer; on the other hand, he was viewed as an observer of a region that many travellers before him had already described.

Irwin's travel observations found mention in four letters (two about his travels in Egypt in 1779 and two about his passage from Europe to India across Syria). The 1787 edition was revised and published in two volumes that included four new engravings, one map and two illustrations. He also added many footnotes confirming what Pococke and Norden previously discovered in Egypt, which indicates that Irwin paid heed to critiques of 1780 and finally turned to an empirical style widely popular among travel writers and readers. Yet, his narrative, as this chapter shows, cannot in any way be considered as scholarly, curious or even scientific.

Indeed, the idea that Irwin added the account of his Syrian journey to the third edition was in line with the work by previous travellers such as Richard Pococke and James Capper who first published their accounts of Egypt before that of their Syrian journeys. To entertain his readers, Irwin did not write as a journalist or a scientific traveller but rather as a man of letters. Like many travel writers of the period, such as Alexander Drummond (*Travels Through Different Cities* [...] 1754), Alexander Jardine (*Letters from Barbary* 1788) and Henry Rooke (*Travels to the Coast of Arabia Felix* 1783), Irwin chose an epistolary form, showing an effort to tap into the success of such phenomenon among a readership for whom, as Jean Viviès reminds us, 'the fictional travel narrative and the travel narrative are not clearly demarcated categories but poles which reveal a continuum' (Viviès 2002: 27).[25] Such a form could be found in travel books on the Levant as mentioned before. But the popularity of the epistolary form in travel writings speaks to a larger cultural concern. Epistolary travel books were meant to address a bourgeois reader living in a modern age in which attempts to preserve old vestiges of classical virtues against 'the encroachments of the new economy' were effectively negotiated in the realm of feelings and sentiments; the realm of feeling and sentiments, to which the epistolary form organically belonged, was meant to help writers alleviate concerns about the modern commercial and imperial experience.[26]

Finally, one cannot finish explaining the kind of travel writer Irwin was without recalling how cross-cultural encounter shaped his identity as a servant of the British empire and as a member of the Enlightenment republic of letters. Not only the wealth he collected in India but also the huge volumes of travel experiences he wrote helped to earn him respectability in Britain and Ireland.[27] '[I]f he [the traveller] has rather consulted the public amusement, than the gratification of his vanity', he wrote, 'this early publication, with all its imperfections, will not want an advocate among the literati' (I, viii).[28] In writing huge volumes, Irwin craved literary immortality. The *Monthly Review* in 1779 was critical of the idea of publishing huge travel books and considered such a phenomenon an imitation of what was in vogue in Europe at the time: 'we are sorry to see that even some of their [German] best writers have not yet divested themselves of their national prejudice in favour of huge volumes; as to write a great deal, and to make large books, was the way to literary immortality' (1779: 303). The medium of travel writing offered Irwin an opportunity to pursue 'literary immortality' despite criticisms ridiculing his efforts.

Travel and Pleasure

In the wake of Mary Montagu's travel letters about the Ottoman Empire, travellers in the Levant, including those who went through the overland routes to India, revived the old style of travelling in the region which included surveying and classifying the land and its people. The 'patterning instinct' integral to the Western tradition of understanding the relationship between man and nature, to use Jeremy Lent's phrase, no longer satisfied middle- and upper-class travellers looking for variety, irregularity and difference (Lent 2017). The trope of novelty, of seeing the land and its inhabitants in 'a new dress' (the idea of seeing the land and its inhabitants in pictorial and sensuous terms), replaced an early-modern one in which the Levant (Syrian-Palestine and Egypt) was often seen as an intellectual experiment in which travellers looked for such precious things as relics, medals, manuscript and plants that encouraged them to authenticate ancient classical and biblical knowledge about the land. The patterning instinct of the early-modern period did not die out in the second half of the eighteenth century. It rather evolved into a discourse of aestheticism, particularly in the writings of middle- and upper-class Britons who had no university education and little knowledge of the classical and biblical history of the region (Donald Campbell, whose travel account is the subject of the next chapter, belongs to this category of travellers). The literary critic Elizabeth A. Bohls has brilliantly argued that the late eighteenth-century privileged classes in Britain often affirmed their taste and accumulated 'cultural capital' by searching for aesthetic experiences in foreign landscapes and among 'exotic' and 'primitive' people; while doing so, they showed how 'picturesque aesthetics' is rooted in 'intercultural' and imperial encounter (Bohls 2016: 248–249). For Romita Ray, who studied the hybrid nature of British aesthetic traditions that appeared in British paintings and writings about India, the empire offered a vast field for aestheticism.[29] Seen in this context, the sensuous language which dominated late eighteenth-century British writings about the Ottoman Empire and Arabia was a manifestation of this new cultural tradition shaped by Britain's expanding empire, trade and travels in the East.

The *Monthly Review* in 1792 captured this shift in British travel writings about the Levant. Geovanni Mariti's *Viaggi per l'isola di Cipro e per la Storia e Palestina fatti dall'anno 1760 al 1768* (*Travels Through Cyprus, Syria and Palestine*, translated into English in 1792), as *The Monthly Review* stated, belonged to an earlier tradition of travel writing which put a premium on empirical observations of flora and fauna rather than on the affective responses of the traveller to whatever he encounters. 'This long detail, though fraught with much useful information', *The Monthly Review* observed, 'had drawn on the author the censure of some critics, who have charged him with having, in this instance, practised the art of authorship, in order to swell out and make the most of whatever materials he could procure, that bore any relation to the main subject of his narrative' (1792: 527). For a constituency of readers now bombarded with an unlimited supply of travel books, reading books of dry history became as boring and tedious as reading narratives of pious travellers in the Holy Land. Marti is one such traveller. His account, *The Monthly Review* concluded, is littered with 'tedious accounts of departed monks, and saints and ruined monasteries [...]' (1792: 528).

As *The Monthly Review* suggested, contemporary readers are instead looking for pleasure and entertainment, not piety, religiosity or dry reporting of latitudes and longitudes. They are looking for examples in which the self appears in charge of its agency in a culture dominated by impersonal and abstract forces such as order, reason and productivity. The pushback against the hegemony of reason was captured by travel writers in the second half of the eighteenth century. In *Letters from Barbary* (1788), the British army officer Alexander Jardine addressed the general public – he did not refer to men of authority and powers, politicians, historians, ecclesiastics and antiquarian, those who for long had dominated the constituency of readers of travel books in Britain – telling them that his account was not written with the intention of confirming what previous writers had already reported about Morocco, France and Spain. '[R]egularity and system', Jardine continued, does not lead to the advance of knowledge. An entertaining travel book should be one in which [...]

> the author has digressed to a variety of subjects [...] and has indulged in reflections which seemed then of importance. Some of them may still appear new, others perhaps interesting, and even the most singular may appear acceptable to some readers; for, it is imagined that by following only his ideas and opinions, he is more likely to be original, and different from other letter writers of the same kind. (Jardine 1788: I, vii)

Despite the claim of authenticity and personal experience, Jardine, and many travel writers during the period, did not produce a narrative free from discursive influences and dominant tropes prevailing at the time. Jardine's observations of the manners and modes of subsistence of the unruly tribes of North Africa confirmed what the Scottish school of conjectural history had advanced regarding the causes of primitivism in pastoral societies: that is, the absence of vigorous capitalist culture and lack of efficient state bureaucracy. Furthermore, he was sympathetic to what his countryman Daniel Defoe advocated earlier in the century in his *A Plan of the English Commerce* (1728): that is, North African countries make excellent European colonies (Jardine 1788: I, 106–108), and every European power 'should possess the least in Proportion to the Forces employed in the conquest of it' (Defoe 1728: 322). But what emerged in Jardine's, and to some extent in Irwin's, work was the idea that travel abroad produces the sensate and aesthetic rather than scientific self. Bart Ooghe was correct when he concluded that late eighteenth-century British and European travel accounts about the Near East, including Irwin's account about Syria and Mesopotamia, revealed 'a purely tourist attitude, far removed from any desire to be scientifically informative [...]' (Ooghe 2007: 249). Like Jardine, Irwin was not keen on this idea of regularity and order which dominated earlier travel accounts. 'The reader who looks for connected accounts, Ciceronian epithets, and polished expressions, in these rambling pages', Irwin confirmed in *A Series of Adventures* (1780), 'will be greatly mistaken in the intention of the author; whose highest aim is amuse the curious and touch the humane' (Irwin 1780: I, 121). With Irwin, travel writing in the Levant and the overland routes to India was meant to touch hearts and raise laughs, mainly to entertain rather than to educate.

Imaginative Escape

Robert Heron, the British translator of Niebuhr's *Travels in Arabia*, which was first published in English in 1792, captured this 'amusement' trope to which travel writing responded fairly strongly in Britain in the last three decades of the eighteenth century:

> To wander from city to city, from hill to vale, from vale to hill; to see one new extent of horizon open upon the eye after another, and landscape after landscape, display sublimity and beauty in all their varying forms, affords perhaps the most delightful, at least the most improving amusement of which the human mind susceptible. (Niebuhr 1792: I, vii)

For Heron, travelling experience that includes 'wandering' and 'seeing' a variety of 'landscapes' enriches one's soul. It is an aesthetic experience which prioritises the act of 'seeing' over that of cataloguing, classifying and measuring nature, what Mary Louise Pratt called Europe's 'planetary conspicuousness' shaped by a strong connection during the Enlightenment between travel writing and the scientific field of natural history (Pratt 1992: 9).

For Heron, travelling is a delightful pursuit rather than a laborious act wrapped up with a layer of duty and mission.[30] Despite being a supporter of the new tradition in travel writing, Heron is averse to replacing an earlier tradition in which nature appeared as a mystery that required the scientific traveller to discover its laws with a new one in which nature appears as a landscape that invites the tourist to devour its beauty. Rather he is showing that a new tradition can do an equally effective job by merging values of utility with those of beauty, values that suit the lifestyle of the bourgeois traveller and reader whose civility and improvement are dependent on consuming diverse articles of luxury, building picturesque gardens and indulging in landscape paintings. Both styles, however (one dominated by aesthetic responses to nature and the other dominated by empiricist terms emphasising regularity and uniformity rather than variety), share a common trope: the annexation of new land into the empire of the eye. As the previous passage by Heron reveals, the movement of the eye between different landscapes resembles the activity of what Pratt calls 'the seeing man' whose 'imperial eyes passively look out and possess', an activity that replicates the British Empire's effort to expand territories and markets: imperialism and commercialism here are aided by new discourses of beauty, sentimentalism and picturesque aesthetics (Pratt 1992: 7).

Niebuhr and his fellow travellers, who mounted an expedition in Arabia funded by the Danish Crown, were men of scientific zeal and passion for natural history, but it was the passages in their accounts about the picturesque mountains of Arabia, particularly the coffee plantations on the mountains of the Yemen, which fascinated Heron (the English translator and editor of Niebuhr's account) in a period in which the East India Company was heavily investing in coffee trade in India and the Caribbean and also in a period in which coffee in Britain was often seen as an article of luxury the consumption of which was a sign of gentility and status.[31] To that end, Heron added in his English translation of Niebuhr's book an engraving [Figure 11] prepared by Daniel Lizars, one titled 'Prospect among the Coffee Mountains of Yemen', which shows how a representation of the mountains of Yemen was shaped by the late eighteenth-century discourse of the picturesque popularised in Britain by William Gilpin whose book *Observations Relative Chiefly to Picturesque Beauty* (1785) enjoyed a huge popularity.[32] None of the German and French editions of Niebuhr's book included picturesque mountains in Arabia.[33]

The representation of landscape in the example above is essentially a political act that has little to do with the mountains of Yemen that Niebuhr visited and more to do with pressing political and commercial concerns of late eighteenth-century Britain. Irwin's representation of different Oriental landscapes resembles that of Heron's. In his first published poem *Mount St Thomas* (1774), the engraving of Mount St Thomas in Madras showed a space of harmony, order and stability, a reference to Irwin's desire for peace in a period known for uncertainty for the East India Company in its wars on the

Figure 11 Daniel Lizars, a coffee plantation in Yemen in Carsten Niebuhr's *Travels Through Arabia and other Countries in the East*. Credit: The British Library.

coast of the Coromandel. In his *Series of Adventures*, the engraving about the mountains of Egypt showed rugged and broken surfaces which, according to Edmund Burke's theory of the sublime popularised in his *A Philosophical Inquiry* (1757), create 'stronger "effects" on the viewer than any "smooth and polished" spaces' (Burke 1757: 52).

Heron's and Irwin's rendering of Arabia as the land of the picturesque and the sublime revealed how British travel writers, painters and translators of travel books during the period accommodated popular aesthetic ideologies for purposes of alleviating the political concerns of their nation: aesthetic responses to landscape appeared in Britain in a period in which the East India Company was immensely concerned about securing safe routes of travel between Britain and India across the Levant and the Arabian Gulf. For those in the Company Presidency in Bombay and the Court of Directors in London, the safety of communication across shortcuts between Britain and India, mainly in the wake of the loss of the American colonies, during the Anglo-French War (1778–1783; 1793–1802) and the Second and Third Anglo-Mysore Wars (1780–1784; 1790–1792) was hugely important.[34]

In many places in his narrative, Irwin used popular aesthetic discourses in Britain for political ends, one of which was the notion that the traditions of the marvellous, exotic, utopian and fabular arrived in Europe from the East.[35] One such fabular export was the story of the Garden of Eden in the Bible which, as Francis Wilford in his essay in the *Asiatic Researches* mockingly wrote, 'there is hardly a country on earth, or a region in heaven, but has been ransacked in search of it' (Wilford 1801: VI, 488). Even the Hindus, Wilford stated, have their own traditions about it: 'they place it on the elevated plains of Bukhara the lesser, where there is a river which goes round Brahmapuri or the town of Brahma' (Wilford 1801: VI, 488). Many European travellers in the Levant, as we saw in Chapter two, attempted to locate the biblical Garden of Eden while passing through fertile lands in Syria, Mesopotamia and Asia Minor (Joseph Pitton de Tournefort supported the idea that it was in Armenia, Richard Pococke found it in Damascus and Charles Thompson located it on the banks of the Tygris). These travellers mostly aimed to settle modern uncertainties about biblical geography. For an aesthetic traveller like Irwin, however, a desire for negotiating political anxieties in Europe and India meant that the biblical Garden of Eden – now stripped of its religious significance – was a metaphor for human stability, peace and contentment. 'For my own part', wrote Irwin of the banks of the Euphrates:

> I am content to see that there are no traces of this delightful spot -if that happy situation be excepted-to justify the assertion of: or, if I could adopt the opinion, I should draw the conclusion from it of uncertainty of the human possessions. (Irwin 1787: 360)

In her essay on European encounters with Polynesia, Sarah Johnson has shown how European explorers in the South Seas, such as William Dampier and Captain Cooke, located the Garden of Eden in Tahiti. For these explorers, Johnson has suggested, Tahiti was seen as a land of primaeval innocence and freedom. None of the corruptions of modern Europe exist in Tahiti. For European explorers, Tahiti was a metaphor of equality, justice and prosperity. But these explorers, Johnson showed, feared that Tahiti was bound to fall because of its contact with commercial and corrupt Europe. Travellers, Johnson wrote, often 'humanely and sadly expressed the belief that Europeans would corrupt South Sea islanders' and '[i]nevitably the islanders would want to trade, and inevitably their new wants would make them unhappy' (Johnson 2006: 186). As Sarah Johnson was correct to argue, the writing about paradise in European travel culture was not as much an act of displaying piety as it was an enabling practice that helped Europeans to negotiate and alleviate fears of false promises of modernity by conjuring up idealised images of the Garden of Eden.[36] Here the trope of paradise does not appear as a mobiliser of Christian piety but a psychological escape that opens new possibilities for the traveller concerned about the plight of modernity. Seen in this context, Irwin used the Garden of Eden analogy to critique what he considered the uncertainty of material progress in modern times. The reference here to the uncertainty of 'human possessions' in the present age appeared in a period known for anxieties in Britain over the loss of America and the possible loss of Madras to the Kingdom of Mysore. In the 1780s, British settlements on the Coromandel coast faced existential threats posed by the Kingdom of Mysore and their European allies (the French and the Dutch still held a few settlements in the region).[37]

The rejuvenating experiences in the Garden of Eden thus belied a deep anxiety in Irwin's book over the loss of the empire. But the reference to the Garden of Eden had another function in the narrative. For Irwin, Arabia, as his reading of Sir William Jones's *On the Poetry of the Eastern Nations* (1772) convinced him, was the land of 'balm-dropping woods' and 'delightful vales' where 'the fruits of every climate court his taste and the breezes of cassia refresh his senses' (Irwin 1780: 15). Irwin and Jones's image of Arabia as the land of 'balm' is derived from the biblical references to the Balm of Gilead, a medicinal plant located in Palestine, Egypt and Arabia, which in British literature, at least since the Renaissance, was 'stripped of its overly biblical context' and rather 'conveyed something soothing to the mind by focusing largely on earthly remedies rather than spiritual cures' (Jeffrey 1992: 72). But the mention of the variety of fruits in Irwin's statement above refers to the Islamic paradise as mentioned in the Qur'an: 'And fruits numberless, Unending and unforbidden [...]' (the Qur'an, 56). In Britain, Mahomet's paradise, as it was called, was seen as a repository of rivers, food and drinks, plenty of sensual pleasures and a ceaseless fountain of gratifications.[38] Christian Lange has perceptively argued that informed by St. Augustine's doctrine of the original sin, Christian monastic repudiations of bodily pleasure and sexuality and the Enlightenment age disenchantment with scriptural literalism, many European polemicists critiqued what they considered an excessive Islamic paradise. Some contrasted it with the spiritual heaven of Christianity.[39] Eighteenth-century scholars of Arabic and Islam who accessed Arabic sources (for example, Adriaan Relend in the Netherlands and George Sale in England), Lange wrote, rethought Europe's 'long held polemical assumptions' about the Islamic paradise of the Qur'an, but with these writers' 'enlightened critique of religion resulted in an entrenchment of common perceptions of the Islamic otherworld as exceedingly sensual, permissive, and misogynist' (Lange 2016: 23–24).[40]

Langue's critique of the Enlightenment conception of the Islamic paradise is sufficient but incomplete. In the field of travel writings, the way writers engaged with the Islamic idea of paradise was more complicated than what Langue found in the writings of the Arabists in Europe. Irwin did not necessarily recall the anti-Islam polemic in Europe in which the Islamic conception of the 'otherworld', in Lange's phrasing, constituted 'the favoured battlefield' between the Orthodox Christians and deistic, rationalist, sceptical writers (Lange 2016: 18). Rather what mattered for Irwin was the idea that a paradise is a land of plenty (fruits from every clime) and health (balm-dropping woods): these images figured in the first edition of his narrative which he published after a journey he made across the overland routes in 1771, just one year after the Bengal famine which many during the period associated with destructive East India Company policies which bled Bengal, 'the granary of nations', dry (Fullarton 1787: 40). Irwin's description of Arabia above marks a subtle admiration of the Muslim paradise, one which addresses the senses rather than the mind, one in which people do not compete over resources and wealth (unlike what he saw in India in the war over trade and profits between the Dutch, French and English powers and local Indian rulers).[41]

Irwin, however, was not the only eighteenth-century Briton who used the trope of the Islamic paradise to create an alternative reality to the anxieties in Britain about contemporary politics. Muslims, the English traveller in the Ottoman Empire Mary Montagu wrote, 'have a right notion of life. They consume it in music, garden, wine, and delicate eating, while we are tormenting our brains with some scheme of politics, or studying some science to which we can never attain, or, if we do, cannot persuade other people to set that value upon it we do ourselves' (Montagu 1771: III, 80). Women, in such a situation from Arcadia, Montagu noted, in contrast to what many in Europe believed, can share the joy: Prophet Mohammed 'promises a very fine paradise to the Turkish women' (Montagu 1771: IV, 55). For Montagu, paradise in Islam is a space of domestic Utopia which excludes virgins and widows (the reference here is to Catholic nuns and the widows whom society derides for choosing to remarry) but accommodates married women. Montagu clearly knew little about the description of paradise in the Qur'an, but what appeared here as relevant to our argument is that she used the metaphor of Islamic paradise to negotiate her society's dominant attitudes towards marriage and domesticity. Other writers, however, rejected Montagu's notion that the Islamic paradise accommodates women. But they agreed that the depiction of paradise in the Qur'an teaches Christians what went wrong in their own society; 'Paradise, or the state of bliss', the traveller John Griffiths wrote,

> which will be the ultimate attainment of all Mussulmauns, is supposed to be the residence of our first parents Adam and Eve; it is represented in the fervour of the Mussulmaun's imagination, and conformably to the assurance of his prophet, as a place where every excitement, and perpetual renovation of, happiness and pleasure eternally await him. Splendid palaces, cooling grottos, trees of all the previous metals, and mountains of all the precious jewels; murmuring fountains, shady bowers, flowery meads; and every object that the most enraptured fancy can suggest [...] [...] subject to no influence of time, but ever varying, ever new. (Griffiths 1805: 130)

It is no surprise that senses starved of stimulation during dreary months in Arabian deserts and physically fatigued by shortage of food and water made Griffiths and Irwin titillate with an Islamic conception of paradise. But the idea in Griffith and Irwin's books that an Islamic paradise does not seem to have been subjected to a linear conception of progress recalls how both were concerned about the voices in Britain which associated an excessive pursuit of wealth with corruption and moral degeneration.[42] Like Montagu, Griffiths, in the above passage, does not seem to have read George Sale's dispassionate and scholarly analysis of how paradise in Islam meant different things for different people. What he mostly confirmed is the trope in Europe that Islam is a religion of the senses rather than the soul, but it was this notion of endless pleasure which offered Griffiths the material with which he worked out how dabbling in earthly pleasures is futile. Modern Europeans could possibly be materially and scientifically advanced, as Montagu, Griffith and Irwin implied, but such progress is not something that guarantees permanent pleasures. Progress carries seeds of the big fall: corruption. In an Islamic paradise, people do not follow a linear path which includes progress and fall, a popular Enlightenment trope as we saw in the introduction and Chapter one. In an Islamic paradise, there is a constant renewal of pleasures, an idea which fascinated both Griffiths and Irwin in the 1780s, a period in which Britons lost their American colonies and were constantly fearful of a French invasion.

Novelty, Travelling and Politics

In 1784, Henry Abbott, whose book we examined in Chapter four, mentioned how his travelling experience in Arabian deserts was 'a party of pleasure', referring to the joyous experience he had among his countrymen and among fellow Arab travellers in the caravan. On Saturday, 17 July 1784, Abbott's caravan arrived at the bank of the Euphrates after a 12-hour 'march' in 'the scorching heat of the sun' (Abbott 1789: 54). The beauty of the 'meandering stream' reminded him of Eyles Irwin's sentimental poems composed on the banks of that great river of Mesopotamia: 'Had our friend Irwin been here, he would have found subject enough for his lyric muse to have favoured the world with half a dozen eclogues; but you know I am no poet [...]' (Abbott 1789: 54). Abbott was clearly familiar with Irwin's musings over the beauty of the villages situated on the banks of the Euphrates which appeared in his *Eastern Eclogues, Written during a Tour through Arabia, Egypt, and Other Parts of Asia and Africa* (1780) and also in the third edition of the *Series of Adventures* (1787). But Abbott was clear to his reader about the difference between his writing style and that of Irwin. Irwin was less concerned about adhering to truth; rather he was more concerned about singularity and novelty: 'drawings of particular scenes, in which' he was 'engaged, and representations of the singular customs of the country, would have brought them forward to the reader's eye' (Irwin 1787: I, ix). Irwin cared more about the eye than the mind, which again recalls the late eighteenth-century picturesque theory of travel. As William Gilpin wrote in his essay 'On Picturesque Travel', 'it is not from [...] scientifical employment that we derive our chief pleasure'; rather '[w]e are most delighted, when some grand scene [...] strikes beyond the power of thought'.

Irwin referred to eminent figures in the field of Middle Eastern travels throughout the period, Fredrick Norden and Richard Pococke, whose drawings of Egyptian pyramids and antiquities reflected a popular passion during the period for classical style of architecture, which reflected a careful balance between lines, proportions and structures. Despite their informative style, Pococke and Norden, Irwin comments, failed to offer novel and sensuous representations of the countries in which they travelled. To that end, Irwin saw in Richard Dalton's engravings of Egyptian and Turkish rulers, manners and customs, what he called 'a remedy at hand for those who delight in novel pictures' (Irwin 1787: ix). In 1749, Dalton accompanied James Caulfield, the fourth Viscount Charlemont, in his Grand Tour to Constantinople, Greece, Malta and Egypt.[43] After Dalton had returned to London, he published a collection of prints advertised as *Musaeum Geracum et Egyptacum or Antiquities of Greece and Egypt, illustrated by Prints, engraved from Drawings taken on the Spot by Mr Richard Dalton, in a late Voyage to the Levant, in the Company of the Right Honourable Lord Viscount Charlemont and Francis Pierpoint Burton, Esq* (1751). This was followed by a series of prints in 1752, 1781 and 1790, culminating in the full edition of 79 plates and etchings entitled *Antiquities and Views in Greece and Egypt with Manners and Customs of the Inhabitants from Drawings Made on the Spot, AD, 1749* (1791). Irwin was aware of Dalton's work, particularly the account which Dalton in the 1780s was preparing for the press, *Remarks on Prints*, published just one year after *A Series of Adventures*.

What Irwin, drawing on the work of Gilpin and Dalton, aimed to achieve in his aesthetic approach to travel is to arrest rules and unleash imaginations. In *Remarks on Prints*, Dalton emphasised the notion that it is the present rather than the past of Arabs and Turks that he cared to represent in his work, unlike Pococke and Norden who were mostly concerned about confirming biblical and classical references to Egyptian antiquities and manners. For Dalton, both Pococke and Norden's descriptions of Egypt are authentic; yet Pococke lacked 'a proper skill in drawing' and did not express 'the objects as they appeared' which 'has greatly diminished the Value of his Labours' (Dalton 1781: 2). Norden, Dalton continued, produced 'good engravings with regards to the Antiquities in Upper Egypt as also the towns and villages in the lower' but several of his drawings, particularly those of the pyramids, were lost which made his editor rely on other drawings, 'very erroneous ones', published in Benoît de Maillet's *Description de l'Egypte* (1735). Especially authentic in Norden's account, Dalton added, were the plates drawn by the German engraver Carl Marcus Tuscher, which were added to the French edition of Norden's *Voyage d'Egypte et de Nubie* (1755) in which not only rocks and statues were drawn but also people in their daily life performing acts like farming and playing music. These plates were all approved by Dalton: they 'are etched with great Taste' (Dalton 1781: 3). But Tuscher and Norden failed in their efforts to draw accurate images of Egyptian people because they failed to appreciate the fact that the Ottoman Levant is a region of diverse populations with different cultures. Tuscher's 'Figures are taken' [...]

> from the Turks, the Inhabitants of Constantinople, and from other parts of Turkey, and not from the Natives of Egypt, who are a mixed Race, the lower Class of whom in the Towns and Villages, are nearly the same. But the Arabs and Moors, from the different Parts of Africa, are clearly distinguished from the Turks, or slaves in Turkish Habits, who being afterwards made free, and holding the chief Rank, reside principally at Cairo. (Dalton 1781: 3)

In his *Antiquities and Views in Greece and Egypt with Manners and Customs of the Inhabitants from Drawings Made on the Spot, AD, 1749* (London 1791), Dalton strived to show the diversity of Egypt, and the Levant in general, which included, as many observers during the period noted, settled Arabs (town and village dwellers, men and women), Bedouins, African slaves (men and women), Georgian slaves turned governors and men of rank, among others. All these people figure in Dalton's plates, but other groups in the country such as local Christians, Jews and European residents in the region did not capture his attention, which indicates the difficult task that Dalton sets for himself while aiming to capture the diversity of Egyptian society in his drawings.

Indeed, during a period of revolutionary politics which rocked Britain for the publication of his *Remarks on Prints* and *Antiquities*, it appeared that Egypt was an ideal world from which Dalton found a means to rethink contemporary British anxieties about political radicalism and the abolition of slavery. Thus, one Egyptian ruler, known as Ali Bey Al-Kabir, one who rebelled against the Ottoman authority and declared Egypt an independent state, figured in Dalton's plates as a gentleman 'of amazing Feats as a Marksman, in shooting at Burdacks, or Water-Pots, and firing when the horse is on full Speed' (Dalton 1791: 28). Not only was a political rebel seen by Dalton as gentleman. Also, slaves in Egypt, as Dalton recalled in his remarks, were better treated than their brethren in regions where Europeans were heavily involved in slave trade: 'These slaves meet with far better treatment than most of those from other parts of Africa, with which the West-India Islands, and Part of the Continent of America, are stocked' (Dalton 1781: 33–34). In short, the Levantine world which appeared in Dalton's drawings was one of

Figure 12 An Arab sheikh hosting Lord Charlemont in his house. Richard Dalton's *Antiquities and Views in Greece and Egypt*. Source: SPL Rare Book Collection.

harmony and concord rather than struggle, poverty and revolutions, which indicates the extent to which Orientalism was not necessarily a means to control the Orient but rather to alleviate anxieties of European travellers about pressing political concerns their nations faced.

In his account of Egypt, Dalton inspired Irwin to compose in his travel narrative an Orient constituting an imaginative escape from political anxieties in Britain. In one plate in Dalton's account, an Arab Sheikh [Figure 12], a man of fair complexion (the lower classes in Egypt appeared as dark skinned), appeared as a hospitable man who invited Europeans (Dalton, Lord Charlemont and their companions) to share a meal with him in his house: this Arab 'does honour to human nature' (Dalton 1791: 30). Similarly, for Irwin, in his account of his overland travel to India via Egypt, the Arab Sheikh, whom he named Isman Abu Ally, appeared as a hospitable man of 'grey eyes' and 'very fair complexion', a man of polite and gentle manners different from the lower-class Arabs, 'the dross of the nation', he encountered in the desert. 'It was reserved for this moment', Irwin added,

> for us to meet with the polite gentleman and the honest man, comprised in the person where they ought to be found, in the representative of his people. Happy the subject of a virtuous land, who at once possess and imitates so rare an example! But how sunk in the abyss of infamy are the race, who wholly deviate from the standard of rectitude; and through daily reproached by the life of their monarch, are not to be reclaimed by the tone of authority, or the elocution of active virtue. (Irwin 1780: 264)

The description of the Arab Sheikh in the passage above might have been written by Irwin with the aim to praise the character of the English monarch, King George III, whose American subjects were not then content with the English "tone of authority."

In May 1801, the name of the Arab Sheikh, Isman Abu Ally, whom Irwin met in Egypt in the 1780s, appeared on a Dublin stage as a character in a musical written by Irwin under the title *The Bedouins or the Arabs of the Desert*. While Isman Abu Ally figured as a firm ruler in *A Series of Adventures*, he appeared as a loving father and tolerant Arab in the *Bedouin*: he welcomed Europeans into his territory and agreed to marry off his adopted daughter (originally a Greek) to an Englishman: the reference here is to the idea that Greece belongs to Europe despite that Muslims had long controlled it. *The Bedouin* was written and performed in a period when Britain, upon the failure of the French campaign in Egypt in 1801, was actively seeking to exert its influence on a region which was then considered by many, including Irwin, as an important station on the Indo-European overland routes.[44] In Irwin's foray into the stage, politics and aesthetics were inextricably related. The *Bedouins* received lukewarm reviews in the British press. *The British Critic* disliked the extravagance of 'the dramatic effects' of *The Bedouin* which seems to have 'scenic attractions [...] of the strongest kind' (*The British Critic* 1802: 433). When it was first staged in May 1801, in Dublin, very few people attended the show. Irwin, in a letter he sent to the great collector of ancient poetry and lover of literary primitivism Bishop Thomas Percy in April 1801 explained why the opera was not widely popular in Dublin: 'I tell you the Opera was played three nights with great applause to very fashionable and select, though not crowded audiences' (Irwin 1858: 360). It is to the fashionable and the select audience that Irwin wrote his play, showing how in a work aiming to promote his literary credentials among the Irish middle classes he could smuggle laudatory references to the humanity of the British Empire towards the Arabs and the Greeks. The Protestant elites of Dublin might have agreed with Irwin, but not the Catholics who might have held a different view on the British Empire, especially in the wake of the annexation of Ireland to the United Kingdom under the Act of Union which came into force in January 1801.

Nature, Art and Culture

In the wake of Adam Smith's book *The Theory of Moral Sentiments*, which blended values of beauty with those of utility, and in a period in which Britain's middle classes developed an unprecedented passion for fine arts, the idea of representing nature as a picture dominated the British travel writing scene. As early as 1642, James Howell's *Instructions for forreine Travell* made it clear to British travel writers that 'I say the eye taketh in farre deeper Ideas, and so makes firmer and more lasting impressions' (Howell 1642: 12). Howell realised that an image creates a lasting impact on the viewer not least because the act of seeing helps to construct an air of authenticity around reports of travel; it eventually helps both travel writers and readers to dispel inaccuracies inherited from the scholastic traditions which valued the word over the experience.[45] Brian W. Ogilvie has suggested that early-modern writings about nature sometimes used 'pictorial' language, but, in the main, 'a technical descriptive language [...] eventually took precedence [...] over pictures' (Ogilvie 2006: 6). This is certainly something noticeable in late seventeenth- and early eighteenth-century travel books such as those written by Henry Maundrell, Richard Pococke and Fredric Norden. Late eighteenth-century British travel books about the Levant and Arabia ceased to use 'technical descriptive language' and further utilised the language of feelings widely disseminated in fictional writings of the period (Festa 2006). Eighteenth-century writings which represented nature in pictorial terms benefitted from available optical and aesthetic theories in which nature triggered mental associations: grandeur, wonder, dignity, novelty and grace. According to John Barrel, many writers such as James Thomson and Arthur Young associated improved and cultivated land with peace, harmony, productivity and order while others such as those who abhorred cultivation, such as William Gilpin, found beauty in wild nature in which travellers and artists encounter 'a force powerful enough to resist the advance of an increasingly rationalist and scientific civilisation [...]' (Barrell 1972: 79). Despite the seemingly radically different attitudes towards nature in the writings of these two groups, they have one thing in common. Their writings, as Barrel states, 'can be seen as part of a wider movement in the eighteenth century, to explain the countryside, open it out, and make each particular place more available to those outside it' (Barrell 1972: 84). One central problem of this aesthetic discourse, as Eva Gottlieb and Juliet Shields argue, was the threat it creates to local features and living conditions of the people who inhabit sublime and picturesque spaces: the traditions and habits of poor communities who live in the countryside and anxieties about the scale of changes in their villages were often sublimated by pictorial representations.[46]

Irwin was no stranger to this debate. En route to India in 1781, he visited a few churches in Venice and found that the Catholic Church relies on the power of arts for elevating the piety of worshippers. Irwin was intrigued with the power of images in Catholic Churches: for example, he admired Jacopo Bassano's *The Building of the Ark* and *Animals Entering the Ark* (1578) which, he wrote, 'evinced the facility of raising devotion, by this appeal to the senses' (Irwin 1787: 168). In his artwork, Bassano turned the story of the flood in Genesis into a series of images in which the Patriarch appeared busy conversing with God while his wife, children and their spouses were engaged in manual labour: building a ship and saving animals from the flood. Such labour imbalance was mystified in a beautiful and harmonious scene, one of order, stability and industriousness. Irwin was no admirer of Catholicism. But he wished that Protestant churches in Britain would show similar approaches: that is, using 'ceremony' and 'instructive morals of the pencil' to 'impress proper sentiments of religion on the lower classes' (Irwin 1787: 168). Art can uplift morals and transform piety into obedience, which prevents superstition, idleness and rebellion. Art plays an important role in policing the lower classes, an idea which occurred to Irwin in the wake of the Gordon Riots (1780).

For Irwin, art can please and relieve the eye of the bourgeois traveller, but it can also be an effective tool to control the masses, particularly those who show disenchantment with one symbol of the state: the church. Irwin's aesthetic response to landscape paintings revealed an enlightened attitude to art in which the artist is now burdened with a social and political responsibility that previous centuries accorded to ecclesiastics, an idea which also emerged in the writings of reputable commentators on British art during the period such as the poet William Hayley (Irwin's friend), Sir Joshua Reynold (who drew a portrait for Irwin, now in the British Museum) and the reverend William Gilpin.[47]

The political context of the early 1780s influenced Irwin's aesthetic representations of spaces he visited. It also influenced Irwin's friend, the artist Richard Dalton. In his *Remarks on Prints* (1781), which he prepared for the press while working as a librarian to King George III, Dalton described an engraving (which was published in *Antiquities and Views in Greece and Egypt*) of 'the holy Camel', that is, the lead camel in the pilgrimage caravan to Mecca which he saw in Cairo in 1750. The description and the engraving emphasised the importance of creating pleasing images to the eye: the tent attached to the camel is embroidered with gold, and colourful trappings on the head were made of ostrich feathers. Despite its intended pleasing effects to the eye, the drawing revealed a serious political point beyond just pleasing the spectator. The cover of the gilded tent included a verse from the Qur'an (chapter three): God 'had revealed to you 'O Prophet the Book of truth, confirming what came before it, as He revealed the Torah and the Gospel' (my translation). The message of this verse is that Islam, Christianity and Judaism belong to the same monotheist root, a verse which appealed to Dalton in an age in which the debate around Catholic emancipation was on the ascent in Britain's public sphere. Indeed, the verse above figured [Figure 13] in Dalton's *Antiquities* which was published in the same year in which the Parliament passed the Roman Catholic Relief Act, which removed certain educational, political and religious restrictions on Catholics.

The political tension which Dalton's Oriental engravings were meant to alleviate might have been inspired by one Arabic line written on a wall inside the Alhambra mosque built for King George III at Kew Gardens in 1761 by the architect Sir William Chambers [Figure 14]. Chambers, with the help of Charles Morton, the principal librarian of the British Museum, added a few sentences taken from the Qur'an which, as he told us in *Plans, Elevations, Sections and Perspective Views of the Gardens and Buildings at Kew in Surrey* (1763), emphasised the oneness of God and discouraged the imposition

Figure 13 Seven plates from Antiquities and views in Greece and Egypt, with the manners and customs of the inhabitants, from drawings made on the spot, *AD 1749* by Richard Dalton (1791). Source: Holding Museum: Khalili Family Trust – Hajj and the Arts of Pilgrimage Collection.

Figure 14 A view of the wilderness, with the Alhambra, the Pagoda & the Mosque in the Royal Gardens at Kew c. 1763. Courtesy: Royal Collection Trust.

of one's religious view on others. William Chambers translated the Qur'anic sentences into Latin: 'no sit coactio in religione/ non est deus ullus praeter deum/no ponatis deo similitudinem' (Chambers 1763: 6). These Qur'anic verses were translated from Arabic into English in the following words: 'There is no compulsion in religion (from Al-Baqara 256)/ There is no god but God (Muhammad 47)/ There is nothing like unto Him (Al-Shūrā 42)'.

Like Dalton, Irwin used a pictorial language to describe the camel on which he rode across the deserts of Egypt in 1780 and Syria in 1783, but what Irwin mostly shared with Dalton, as we previously saw in his appreciation of the Bassano paintings, was the idea that politics is mostly effective when it infiltrates the domain of aesthetics. Such infiltration appeared in many places in Irwin's travel narrative. An attitude showing how an aesthetic discourse is politically motivated figured in Irwin's description of the gardens of the richest person in Bagdad at the time, the wife of Omar Pasha who governed the Iraq pashalik between 1746 until his assassination in 1776. Irwin did not recall that he spoke with the Pasha's wife or any of the people who worked in her gardens, which could make the reader doubt the whole report of his excursion in these gardens. But what emerged from this report is that the gardens of the rich in Baghdad resembled those owned by the elites in eighteenth-century Britain:

> We ranged about this wilderness with infinite pleasure and could not stir a step, without brushing off the surrounding blossoms, which fell before us, and returned an odour from the pressure of the foot. The borders were lined with rose-trees, which were beginning to bud, and to invite the hand. Nor statues, nor fountains, nor vistos, were here, to astonish by their grandeur or taste. Nature, simple and unadorned, was the disposer of these shades, where the naiads, visible to imagination along, conducted the Chrystal rills, to improve the treasures of the Eastern Pomona. (344)

The pleasurable walk in the garden has a deep implication on how Irwin understood the idea of landscape. In a politically charged period, Irwin's walk in the gardens helped him to escape a troubled political context in India. In Baghdad, Irwin spent a few days 'amusing ourselves, as well as we could, after hearing of the signal success of Hyder Ally in the Carnatic, and the perilous situation of the Company's affairs in India; an event, that in a manner precluded the advantages, which must otherwise have attended a war with the Dutch in the quarter!' (Irwin 1787: 376). Enjoying being in nature, however, did not only alleviate anxieties about the political situation of empire in India. It also helped Irwin to merge values of utility with that of beauty. In the above passage, the liberty of the traveller to furnish the land with imaginary 'rills' is one such effort. Irwin's response to landscape (wild, undressed and adorned) which he, as a poet and traveller, dressed and adorned by invoking the image of 'naiads' improving 'the treasure of Eastern Pomona' recalls a dominant standard of taste in late eighteenth-century Britain which, as Paul Smethurst argues, weaved 'an ethos of development and progress' within an aesthetic discourse (Smethurst 2012: 143).[48]

To that end, Irwin enjoyed the idea of seeing nature as a picture. But an unadorned nature includes faults that only the pencil of the poets and the shovel of the farmer – that is, the correct strokes of culture over nature – can improve, dress up and adorn: that is, for nature to turn into picture it must undergo some cultural work. Such an ethos which combined aestheticism with progress also appeared in Irwin's reflection on the improvement projects of the late Solayman Pasha who governed Baghdad between 1780 and 1802.[49] Solyman was 'attached' to British interests in the region, Irwin wrote, and displayed 'an enterprising spirit' in his efforts to drain the marshes of Basra where Arab tribes, who openly defied government, often found a refuge from military attacks. Travelling in the Levant in a period in which the East India Company was in an open war against the Polygars (tribes) of the south of India, Irwin admired the warlike achievement of Solyman Pasha in the Ottoman-Persian war in the city of Basra in 1787, but he mostly praised this ruler's efforts to discipline 'the Ghuzzals' or Al-Ghazalat, a branch of Al-Muntafiq tribe who, as Irwin wrote, inhabited the banks of the Euphrates and regularly attacked caravans in the region. 'For this purpose', Irwin added, Solyman

> collected a force, consisting of 4,000 janizaries, and 6,000 Arabs, and marched against them. The Ghuzzals retired into their swamps; and depending on their inaccessible situation, set his arms at defiance. When Solyman perceived, that much time and many lives would be lost, in driving them from their fastness, he adopted a measure, that decided the contest without drawing a sword; and in its magnitude and splendour perhaps rivals the most celebrated achievements of past ages. He put some thousands of hands at work, in cutting a channel for the river, opposite the swamps; and by turning the stream into a new course, he proposed to drain the places, to which the Ghuzzals retreated. The novelty of the enterprise struck these people with surprise; as the idea of being forsaken by the waters, on which they rested their security, impressed them with such terror, that they quickly proffered terms, to which the pacha acceded. (Irwin 1787: 342)

Viewing such an act of war from the vantage point of enforcing the law and restoring order in places marred by chaos and rebellion, Irwin confirmed a commonplace trope in Britain which kept circulating in print at least since the defeat of the Jacobins in the Battle of Culloden. It is the idea that uncultivated, swampy and unimproved land often turns into a refuge for the kind of people (rebels, vagrants, robbers and nomads) who pose a real threat to the dominant political, social and economic order. As Susan Oliver has argued in her interpretation of the impact of the ideology of improvement on late eighteenth and early nineteenth-century Scottish literature, mostly notably on Walter Scott's *Waverly*, the diffusion in print of the positives of improvement not only revealed the disruptive effects of utilitarian projects on complex ecosystems around 'moorland' and 'wetland' areas in Scotland but also, on a political level, aimed to show how land improvement projects were intended by the government to 'prevent future emergence of weed species or any uncanny seeds of rebellion' (Oliver 2021: 79). Seen in this context, the improvement projects which Irwin found in the work of Solyman Pasha in Basra were seen as helpful in that they stop the 'depredations' of 'contending hordes of Arabs' who lived in barren and swampy lands with no 'useful ornamental projects' (Irwin 1787: 342–343). Irwin attributed the lack of development in Basra to the idle inhabitants and to the weak administration of government, but he believed that a strong ruler, like Solyman Pasha, can change the conditions of the population: 'in truth, nothing, but the expectations which are formed of Solyman Pacha, could have brought back the inhabitants to their wretched dwellings' particularly after the war with Persia in 1779 nearly destroyed the city. If Solyman Pasha embarks on a project of improving the city by building a quay alongside Basra's creek, where the English factory is based, Irwin suggested, then 'I know not a city which could show a more handsome and useful canal' (Irwin 1787: 380). Local people will benefit from such a project: 'it is possible that a change might be affected in points in such moment to the welfare of inhabitants'. The projects which included clearing up trees and enclosing land in the Highlands of Scotland and in India will also work in Basra. Such 'a favourable alteration' will eliminate regular visitations of the plague, increase the population and establish law and order.

Irwin's encounter with and responses to what he saw in Arabia is shaped by eighteenth-century aesthetic discourse in which the beautiful and the pleasing for the eye could not be dissociated from a political context charged with tropes of productivity and progress.[50] The mixing of values of beauty with those of utility in Irwin's travel text reveals how British travel writings on the overland routes to India in the late eighteenth century sanitised British ideologies of improvement but also revealed concerns about the effectiveness of pursuing them. In 1781, Irwin was appointed as a civil commissioner of the districts of Madura and Tinivelly. He succeeded in raising revenues of the Company by crushing rebellions of the Polygars (mountaineers) and forcing their leaders to pay fixed tributes. He also developed plans aiming to improve the land.[51] In 1783, Irwin supported Captain William Fullarton who led a regiment against the tribes of Madura who threatened the Company's rule in south India. Particularly he was commissioned to fight the tribes 'who have hitherto defied the powers of the crescent and the cross', Captain Fullarton wrote, 'and, under cover of woods, mountains, and inaccessible retreats have asserted independence' (Fullarton 1787: 51). 'Mr Irwin, superintendent of Madura and Tinivelly', Fullarton added, was determined to subdue these mountaineers: he 'had repeatedly urged me to proceed against the Polygars, in order to restore tranquillity and recover the revenues' (Fullarton 1787: 121). For Irwin, however, as he wrote to the Madras presidency in 1783, tribal 'licentiousness not having been curbed or checked for these five years past, they are now become so hardened in their contumacy as to render it impracticable to reduce them to a proper sense of their interest and duty but by force of arms'.[52] These tribes posed a real threat to the security of the Company's rule in Madras. As historian G. J. Bryant observes, the Polygars were seen by Company officials as 'feudatory chiefs of backward areas in dense jungles, not worth much but symbols of resistance that would have to be neutralised' (Bryant 2013: 197). Thus, it is this political context which involved Irwin in the Company's war against the Polygars in the 1780s, and the fact that the Polygar tribes were allies to Hyder Ally in his war against the East India Company in the 1780s shaped Irwin's aesthetic descriptions of places he visited on the Syrian and Mesopotamian routes to India.[53]

Conclusion

Irwin was the first eighteenth-century British traveller along Syria and Egypt who offered his readers some amusing and entertaining sketches of his encounter with antique and ancient land, sketches in which the landscape, the people and animals were seen from the eyes of the romantic traveller. This was the start of a new development in British representations of Arabia in which the romance of travel began to replace scientific travels. With Irwin, the deserts as a curious object, a relic from some biblical, Greek and Roman past turned into a landscape; the Arabs, who were previously seen as the descendants of the biblical Ishmael, turned into rebels who discredited the government under whose nominal jurisdiction they lived. While constantly reminding his reader of the pleasurable effects of travelling along Syria, Irwin reflected on the political and social landscape of his nation. Politically, Britain, in the 1780s, experienced uncertainties in its imperial ambitions in America and India. Within Britain, the middle classes and gentry, to which Irwin belonged to, appreciated the development projects in the British countryside by using terms such as 'picturesque' as dreary land could be transformed into beautiful land. Travel writing about Arabia may have been written with the spirit to entertain, but in essence the sentimental reflection on landscape, communities, tribes, ruins and mountains fused the aesthetic with the political. Samuel Johnson travelled all the way from commercial London to what he considered the barbarous and barren Highlands, that is, the spaces in need of British improvements, to make sense of the value of the utilitarian ideology of modern times. Similarly, Irwin, an Anglo-Irish man, found in the Arabian space – one of dreary wastes and nomadic people – an opportunity to reflect on his nation's political conditions and in so doing he fused aesthetic discourse with political ideology, a combination comprising beauty, order, stability and prosperity. The next chapter, as we shall see, shows how the eighteenth-century discourse of sentimentalism enabled one British traveller to intervene in contemporary debates on political radicalism; the chapter will demonstrate that sentimentalism not only accommodates utilitarian values but also actively departs from them.

Notes

1 Sidney Lee, *Dictionary of National Biography* (New York: Macmillan and Co, 1892), Vol XXIX, 57.

Laurence Sullivan was an Irishman of great fortune, powerful connections and business enterprises in Britain and India. Sullivan served as a director of the East India Company for many years between 1755 and 1786; he also served as an MP for Taunton and Ashburton. He was 'a person of great authority and influence in the direction of the Company affairs' even after his retirement, as Edmund Burke wrote (402).

James Irwin, Elyes's father, was Laurence Sullivan's uncle. See Barry Crosbie's *Irish Imperial Networks: Migration, Social Communication and Exchange in Nineteenth Century India* (Cambridge: Cambridge University Press, 2012), 45.

2 *Copies of Papers Relative to the Restoration of the King of Tanjore*, 2 vols (London, 1777), Vol I, 2.

3 See Sudip Bhattacharya's *The Strange Case of Lord Pigot* (Cambridge: Cambridge Scholars, 2013).

4 Earl H. Pritchard, 'The Instructions of the East India Company to Lord Macartney on His Embassy to China and His Reports to the Company, 1792–4. Part I: Instructions from the Company', *Journal of the Royal Asiatic Society of Great Britain and Ireland* 2 (1938), 201–230; On Irwin's duty in China, page 207. On Irwin's life and career, see *Annual Biography and Obituary For the Year 1818,* Vol II (London: Printed for Longman, Hurst, Press, Orme, and Brown, Paternstoer-Row, 1818), 321–337.

5 On the clash between Benfield and Pigot over the restoration of Tanjore, see *Copies of Papers Relative to the Restoration of the King of Tanjore* [...], Vol I, 159.

6 As Burke, in 1785, recalled in a speech on the East India Company's corrupt activities in India, 'a few innocent, inexperienced young Englishmen, such as Mr. Paul Benfield, for instance, without property upon which any one would lend to themselves a single shilling, are enabled at once to take provinces in mortgages, to make princes their debtors, and to become creditors for millions', *Speeches of the Right. Hon, Edmund Burke with Memoir and Historical Introductions* (Dublin: Published by James Duffy, 1854), 316. See also Jerry Z. Muller, *The Mind and the Market: Capitalism in Western Thought* (New York: Anchor Books, 2002), 123.

7 Margot Finn and Kate Smith, 'Introduction' in *The East India Company at Home, 1757–1857*, ed. Margot Finn and Kate Smith (London: UCL Press, 2018), 8.

8 Hastings and Eyles Irwin were close friends. In a letter written to his wife Marian in 1783, Hastings recalled that in Calcutta 'Mr Irwin breakfasted with me and appeared in such Spirits that I ventured to make Inquiries about his wife', *The Letters of Warren Hastings to His Wife*, ed. Sydney C. Grier (Edinburgh: Blackwood and Sons, 1905), 95.

9 Bernard S. Cohn, *Colonialism and Its Forms of Knowledge: The British in India* (Princeton: Princeton University Press, 1996), 68.

10 On the history and scholarship of the Asiatic Society in Bengal, see chapter VIII in Garland Cannon's *Oriental Jones: A Biography of Sir William Jones* (1746–1794) (Mumbai: Asia Publishing House, 1960).

11 The medieval Persian poet, Hafiz, was first introduced to the English-speaking world by Sir William Jones. In his *Grammar of the Persian Language* (1771), Jones translated one of Hafiz's poems called 'A Persian Song', 137–140. The song was reprinted in Jones' *Poems* (1772), 71–76.

12 See chapter four in James Mulholland's *Sounding Imperial: Poetic Voice and the Politics of Empire, 1730–1820* (Baltimore: The John Hopkins University Press, 2013). Many scholars examined this phenomenon in Anglo-Oriental poetry. See Michael J. Franklin's *Orientalist Jones: Sir William Jones, Poet, Lawyer and Linguist* (Oxford: Oxford University Press, 2011); 'Accessing India: Orientalism, anti-Indianism and the Rhetoric of Jones and Burke' in *Romanticism and Colonialism: Writing and Empire, 1780–1830*. Ed. Tim Fulford and Peter J. Kitson. Cambridge: Cambridge University Press, 1998), 84–676; James Watt, *British Orientalisms 1759–1835* (Cambridge: Cambridge University Press, 2019); Javed Majeed's *Ungoverned Imaginings: James Mill's The History of British India and Orientalism* (London: Clarendon Press, 1992); V. de Sola Pinto, 'Sir William Jones and English Literature', *Bulletin of the School of Oriental and African Studies, University of London* 11:4 (1946), 686–694.

13 In *The Failure of the French Crusade or the Advantages to Be Derived by Great Britain from the Restoration of Egypt to the Turks* (1799), a book which defended British efforts to block Napoleon's imperial

ambitions in the Arab world, Irwin shared with William Jones the idea that Britons needed to collect and translate Oriental manuscripts because such an effort will help to improve knowledge. To that end, he, in the 1790s, praised the scholarly effort of one Englishman, Sir William Ousley, an Orientalist and a scholar of Persia, whose *Oriental Collections* (1797–8) and *The Oriental Geography of Ebn Haukal, an Arabian Traveller of the Tenth Century* were widely celebrated in Britain. See page 25 of *The Failure of the French Crusade.*

14 Collins, *Commerce and Manners*, 351.

15 Robin Jarvis, *Romantic Poets as Travel Readers in Romantic Poetry and Transatlantic Travel: Expeditions and Tours in North America, 1760–1840* (Farnham: Ashgate, 2012). Benjamin Colbert, *Shelley's Eye: Travel Writing and Aesthetic Vision* (London: Ashgate, 2005). Leask, Nigel. *Curiosity and Aesthetics of Travel Writing.*

16 Christopher M. Keirstead, 'Travel and Poetry' in *The Cambridge History of Travel Writing*, ed. Tim Youngs and Nandini Das (Cambridge, Cambridge University Press, 2020), 448.

17 On these modern values were sanitised by bourgeoise artists of the period, see John Barrell's *The Dark Side of the Landscape: The English Poor in English Painting 1730–1840* (Cambridge: Cambridge University Press, 1980).

18 Recent studies of eighteenth-century British Orientalism have confirmed one important argument in Edward Said's *Orientalism*: that is, the expansion of colonies in the East cannot be dissociated from the expansion of knowledge in Europe about the Orient; the appropriation of Oriental voices in British poetry is one phenomenon of this expansion; see James Mulholland's *Sounding Imperial* and Ashok Malhotra's *Making British Indian Fictions: 1772–1823* (New York: Palgrave, 2012).

19 Irwin did not declare all the wealth he had amassed while serving in India, but he told us he managed to carry with him across the deserts 'about lool.... Venetians and guineas, which, with a gold watch, and a ruby ring of some value concealed in a handkerchief about my waist'. His companion Anthony Hammond transported around '1000 l. in specie' and '500 venetians', *A Series of Adventures in the Course of a Voyage Up the Red-Sea* (London: Printed for J. Dodsley, 1780), 194.

20 Eliot Eliot who travelled there in 1741 wrote, 'that in these Parts of the World they [Arabs] look upon all Europeans to be as rich as Craesus [Crassus], and everyone will be ready to impose upon you if you will let them', *The Desert Route to India: Being the Journals of Four Travellers by the Great Desert Caravan Route Between Aleppo and Basra 1745–1751*, ed. Douglass Carruthers (London: Hakluyt Society, 1929), 213.

21 IOR/1/63 ff. 21–22v. British Library, India Office Records and Private Papers.

22 Hawksworth's work was published in *An Account of the Voyages Undertaken by the Order of His Present Majesty for Making Discoveries in the Southern Hemisphere* (1773). On Hawksworth's involvement in the marketplace of travel writing, see Isabella Alexander, 'Copyright and the Circulation of Geographical Knowledge in Eighteenth-Century Britain' in *Forms, Formats and the Circulation of Knowledge: British Printscape's Innovations, 1688–1832*, ed. Louisiane Ferlier and Bénédicte Miyamoto (Leiden and Boston: Brill, 2020), 87–111; see particularly p. 108.

23 *Voyage de l'Inde en Europe par l'Égypte, par M. Irwin* (Paris: Chez Fuchs, 1793). *Voyage a la Mer Rouge, sur les cotes de l'Arabie, en Egypte, et dans les déserts de la Thébaide: suivi d'un autre de Venice à Bassorali* (Paris: Chez Briand, 1792).

24 A good account on the relationship between travel writing and imperial concerns, see Innes M Keighren, Charles Withers, Bill Bell's *Travels into Print.*

25 Jean Viviès, *English Travel Narratives in the Eighteenth Century: Exploring Genres* (Aldershot: Ashgate, 2002), 27.

26 John Barrell, 'The Dark Side of the Landscape' in *Value: Art: Politics: Criticism, Meaning and Interpretation after Postmodernism*, ed. Jonathan Harris (Liverpool: Liverpool University Press, 2007), 23–62; this quote is from 28.

27 In the 1790s, Eyles Irwin was a member of the Royal Irish Academy. In 1792, his letter to another reputable figure in Britain and Ireland in the field of travels, Lord Charlemont, the President of the Royal Irish Academy, appeared in *The Transactions of the Royal Irish Academy* (Vol 5) under the title 'An Account of the Game of Chess as Played by the Chinese [...]' (Dublin: Printed by George Bonham, 1792), 53–59.

28 The English poet William Hayley in 1789 recalled how Irwin often craved a life of fame. Hayley mentioned how Irwin once told to him about his close friendship with the Russian

Emperor Paul I, who was then a political and military ally of Britain against France. 'I have received [...]' Hayley wrote, [...]

> [a] most singular intimation in a very kind letter from my old friend, Eyles Irwin-that I have been honoured in a most unexpected manner by the Emperor of Russia, who, according to this friendly correspondent, has sent me his portrait in return for the pleasure he has received from my publications. I am inclined to suppose, (as I have heard nothing before of this Imperial favour,) that it must be a mere vision of my gentle enthusiastic Irish friend, who is too much a man of serious integrity and benevolence to invent such a story, as a source of laughable illusion.

However valid the argument that Irwin was constantly looking for opportunities to gain access to a literary scene dominated by the likes of Hayley and Jones, he was not sure his talent would be recognized. The quote is taken from *Memoirs of the life and writings of William Hayley, the friend and biographer of Cowper,* 2 vols (London: 1823), Vol II, 446.

29 Romita Ray, *Under the Banyan Tree: Relocating the Picturesque in British India* (New Haven: Yale University Press, 2013).

30 On how nature was constructed in early modern scientific thought, see the Introduction to Sarah Irving's *Natural Science and the Origins of the British Empire* (2008; Abingdon: Routledge, 2016).

31 Brian Cowan, *The Social Life of Coffee: The Emergence of the British Coffeehouse* (Yale: Yale University Press, 2005), 30.

32 Fabricant, 61–62.

33 *Reisebeschreibung nach Arabien* (Kopenhagen : Gedrluckt bey N. Moeller, 1774); *Voyage en Arabie et en d'autres pays circonvoisins.* 2 vols (Amsterdam: S,J. Baalde, 1776).

34 George Baldwin, the East India Company representative in Egypt in the last three decades of the eighteenth century, recalled how 'I had the satisfaction also to convey the first advice of the war in 1778 to the East Indies; by means of which we were enabled to the astonishment of all England, when the news arrived, to expel the French from India, before the succour could reach them, and to add their possessions to our own', *Political Reflections Relating to Egypt* (London: Printed for H. Baldwin and Son; New Bridge Street, 1801), 6–7. Although the French after 1787 were less threating for the British from within India, they were Britain's powerful competitor in the East, mainly in Egypt and Syria, since France, throughout the century, was stable ally of the Ottoman Empire in its war with the Russians. On George Baldwin's activity in Egypt and on the rising British interests in the Levant in general and Egypt in particular, see Rosemarie J. Said's 'George Baldwin and British interests in Egypt *1775 to 1798*. PhD thesis. SOAS University of London (1968).

35 In 1779, an article published in *the Westminster Magazine* which recalled how European troubadours' songs were filled with Oriental imagery, with 'the extravagancies of Asiatic fiction, dwarfs, giants, dragons, and necromancers' which inflamed the imaginations of those minstrels who accompanied princes and nobles during the Crusaders campaigns to the Holy Land, *The Westminster Magazine or the Pantheon of Taste* (London, 1779), 450–451. A similar trope appeared in William Franklin's commentary on an Oriental tale he translated from the Persian into English in 1793. For Franklin, an East India Company officer in Bengal, many vivid images in the book reminded him of Lodvico Ariosto's *Orlando Furioso* (1516). Franklin goes on to mention the influence of the literary culture of the East on that of the West, stating that 'Many of his [Aristo's] wild stories are unquestionably of Oriental fabric, from which a very inference may be drawn that those highly romantic tales so prevalent in Italy during the first centuries, are of Asiatic origin, and were introduced into Europe about the time of the first crusades, or perhaps at the still earlier period of the Saracenic invasion of Spain and the Western provinces of France [...]', *The Loves of Cámarúpa and Cámalatà: An Ancient Indian Tale : Elucidating the Customs and Manners of Orientals* (London, 1793), 280–281.

36 Johnson's argument about the connection between the Garden of Eden trope and anxieties in Britain about the promise of material progress resembles what Raymond Williams showed in his *The Country and the City* (New York: Oxford University Press, 1973), 10–12.

37 'Memoirs of Eyles Irwin', *The European Magazine and London Review* (London: Printed for J. Sewell, 1789), Vol XV, 180.

38 James Porter, *Observations on the Religion, Law, Government and Manners of the Turks* [...] 2 vols (London, 1768), Vol I, 74.

39 Christian Lange, *Paradise and Hell in Islamic Traditions* (Cambridge: Cambridge University Press, 2016), 17–24.

40 Lange showed how Relend in his *De religione Mohammedica* (1705) relied on Arabic writers in his intellectual project set upon complicating dominant images of Islam in Europe: that is, he showed that some Muslim writers thought about paradise metaphorically; some conceived it to be a spiritual place in which one unites with the Creator. The same idea in which Islamic thought showed some descent regarding the dominant interpretations of paradise appeared in George Sale's *The Koran* (43), but Sale went even further than Reland in showing how some Islamic philosophical groups, like the Mutazilites, doubted the whole idea of the paradise of the senses in the hereafter; he also cited the Muslim philosopher, Al Ghazali, arguing that the Islamic paradise is also a spiritual, not only a sensual, place unlike what many in Europe think. Sale, a republican in an early eighteenth-century England riven with political disputes between orthodox Christians and dissenters, mentioned twice in his section on Islamic paradise that the Muslim heaven is not only open for the rich but also for the poor. Lange, *Paradise and Hell*, 17–24; Sale, *The Koran, Commonly Called the Alcoran of Mohammed* (London, 1734), 95–103.

41 G. J Bryant, *The Emergence of British Power in India, 1600–1784* (Suffolk: Boydell Press, 2016), 191–192.

42 *The European Magazine and London Review* suggested that unlike many Britons who returned home loaded with plundered wealth from India, Irwin retired in Britain with 'perfect contentment in his lot', 181.

43 Caulfield's account of the Ottoman Empire is edited by William Bedell Stanford and E. J Finopolus, *The Travels of Charlemont in Greece and Turkey, 1749* (London: A. G. Levntis Foundation, 1984).

44 In a later stage in his life, mainly in the 1790s when France set out to block British access to India by occupying Egypt, Irwin turned to Egypt as a source of literary inspiration. He wrote: *Inquiry into the Feasibility of Buonaparte Expedition to the East* (1796), *Buonaparte in Egypt* (1798), *Nilus, an elegy on the Victory of Admiral Nelson* (1798) and *The Failure of the French Crusade* (1799).

45 See chapter one in Sam Smiles's *Eyewitness Artists and Visual Documentation in Britain 1770–1830* (Abingdon: Routledge, 2018).

46 Gotllieb and Shields, 'Introduction' in *Representing Place in British Literature and Culture, 1660–1830* (Abingdon: Routledge, 2013), 5. See also Peter Womak, *Improvement and Romance: Constructing the Myth of the Highlands* (Basingstoke: Macmillan, 1989), 85.

47 The image in Irwin's travel narrative about the power of the 'pencil' is borrowed from William Hayley's *An Essay on Paintings in Two Epistles* (1781): 'Blest be the pencil which from death can save/The Semblance of the virtuous, wise and brave/That youth and emulation still may gaze/On those inspiring forms of ancient days/And from the force of bright example bold/Rival their worth, 'and be what they behold' (London, 1781), 8. In his speech to students in the Royal Academy (11 December, 1769), Reynold recalled the same idea about the power of the artist's pencil. He stated that 'a promising young painter' needs to be 'vigilant, whether at home or abroad, in the streets or the fields. Every object that presents itself, is to him a lesson. He regards all nature with a view to his profession; and combines her beauties or corrects her faults', *The Works of Joshua Reynolds,* 2 vols (London: Printed for T. Cadell, 1801), Vol 1, 32.

48 On the unity between aesthetic and economic criteria in the Enlightenment discourse of improvement, see Womak, 61–65.

49 In April 1820, Claudius James Rich, a scholar of Eastern antiquities, was in Baghdad. He reported about the family and reign of the last governor of Baghdad Solyman Pasha 'who was a Georgian slave of his predecessor but was a man of considerable ability; and by his energy and promptitude and wisdom, subjected the various tribes within, and kept in awe those without, his dominions. Agriculture and commerce were thus promoted; and Baghdad became very flourishing under his paternal and judicious government', *A Narrative of Residence in Koordistan*, 2 vols (London, 1836), Vol 1, 4.

50 On how encountering nature contributed to the inventing of the character of an improved and heroic European traveller, see Cian Duffy's *The Landscape of the Sublime, 1700–1830: Classic Ground* (New York; London: Palgrave, 2013), 25.

51 Robert Caldwell, *A Political and General History of the District of Tinnevelly in the Presidency of Madras* (Chennai, 1881), 147.

52 Quoted in Caldwell, 148.

53 It is fascinating that Irwin associated mountaineers in India and the Levant with anarchy and barbarism. Another Briton who served in India in the last few decades of the eighteenth century, Major John Taylor, admired the hospitality and courage of the inhabitants of the chain of mountains on the Malabar coast, the people whom the East India Company was successful in subjugating. See *Taylor's Travels from England to India,* Vol II, 160–165.

Chapter Six

POLITICAL AND MORAL IMPROVEMENT: DONALD CAMPBELL, *A JOURNEY OVERLAND TO INDIA PARTLY BY A ROUTE NEVER GONE BEFORE BY ANY EUROPEAN* (1795)

Man lives in this in-between, and what he calls the present is a life-long fight against the dead weight of the past, driving him forward with hope, and the fear of a future (whose only certainty is death), driving him backward toward the quiet of the past with nostalgia and remembrance of the only reality he can be sure of.

—Hanna Arendt, *The Life of the Mind* (1977)

With the publication of Donald Campbell's *A Journey Overland to India Partly by a Route Never Gone Before by Any European* (1795), British travels along and travel writings about Middle Eastern routes to India had come a long way. Campbell's travel book was the first of its kind which described an overland journey to India that included a passage through the Low Countries (Holland, Germany and Austria). Almost all travellers who travelled to India overland avoided this route; they preferred the sea route which included a stop en route to the Italian port of Venice; this route was popular because it was quicker, less expensive and offered travellers opportunities to see the architecture, museums and churches of Italy.[1] But there is another reason which makes Campbell's book different from all previous accounts about the overland routes to India. Campbell, like Irwin, was little concerned about confirming or falsifying what previous travellers and historians mentioned about the region. Rather he was mostly interested in describing his own personal experiences abroad. And while doing so, he, unlike what we saw in Chapter five, received positive reviews in the British press. *The Analytical Review* recalled the names of some travellers who previously described a large portion of the land in which Campbell travelled, but '[c]circumstances may, however, occur', the paper added, which 'render personal adventures of a traveller going this route very interesting, and afford much entertainment' (1796: 355). With the publication of Campbell's account, travel books had already become less burdened with the question of truth: Campbell wrote his book with the sole purpose of entertaining and enlightening his children.[2] But the book was immensely political: it expressed personal – sometimes contrarian – opinions about some pressing political and social issues of the day.

Once it was published, the book enjoyed a huge popularity; two editions appeared between 1795 and 1796. Many abridgements of the book came out under the title *A Narrative of Extraordinary Adventures and Sufferings by Shipwreck & Imprisonment of Donald*

Campbell, EsQ. Of BARBRECK with The Singular Humours of His Tartar Guide, Hassan Artaz Comprising the Occurrence of Four Years and Five Days, Overland Journey to India; this title appeared at least in four editions between 1769 and 1801. Donald Campbell was a Scottish Highlander of rank. He was born in 1751 to family with a long history of service in the army in Britain and India. His father Charles Campbell and uncle Donald Campbell were military officers in the East India Company: both commanded East India forces in the war with Hyder Ally in the 1760s.[3] Clan Campbell, during the Jacobite Rebellion, joined the Hanoverian Crown in its battle against rebellious Scottish clans. After the battle of Culloden, clan Campbell helped the central government in London in its efforts to annex the Highlands of Scotland into market capitalism.[4] Many members of clan Campbell served in different posts in the British Empire throughout the eighteenth and nineteenth centuries.[5] Campbell himself served in the British army in the Carnatic region. He was a captain of a cavalry regiment serving under the Nawab of Arcot, Muhammad Ali Khan Wallaja, who was an ally of the East India Company in its war against the Kingdom of Mysore in Southern India.

Campbell, as he described himself in his *Journey*, was not a man of letters; nor, as we previously saw with the Irishman Irwin, did he hope to be one. Rather he was 'born, bred and habituated to the life of the Soldier', a lucrative profession which during the period attracted many young Britons of aristocratic background (Campbell 1795: 44).[6] Campbell joined the East India Company in 1781, as he wrote in his diary, after the 'War in India had interrupted the regular remittance of my property from thence' (Campbell 1795: 11). Campbell, although from an aristocratic background in Scotland, was clearly in deep financial troubles in the 1780s and 1790s. His father owned expensive estates in India and Argyllshire, but, as Fredrick, his son, in his *A Letter to Mrs. Campbell of Barbreck, Containing an Account of the Campbells of Barbreck from the First Ancestor to the Present Time* (1830) wrote, Charles Campbell was 'a person of expensive habits, and of a very generous disposition [...]. [before] his death in 1792; and this led to the alienation of the greater portion of his property, soon after his decease' (Campbell 1830: 28). Following the footsteps of his father, Donald Campbell collected huge amounts in India which allowed him to buy an expensive property in Britain, as Fredrick in *A Letter* recalled, 'Situate[d] in that part of Argyllshire called Kentyre, four miles from Campbell Town: consisting of about 8000 English acres, 1200 of which are hilly, the remainder cultivated and as level as the country round London' (Campbell 1830: 33).

The reward which Campbell reaped after many years of service in India is an indication of how the empire was a good source of financial improvement for young Britons. Yet, in his travel account and also in a letter he wrote to the Duke of Argyll, *A Letter to the Marquis of Lorn on the Present Times* (1798), Campbell did not appear as a man of commerce and private interests but rather one of virtue and public duty.[7] In *A Letter to the Marquis of Lorn on the Present Times* (1798), Campbell recalled how living in commercial London weakens the sense of duty and dulls one's public spirit. The duke of Argyll, Campbell recalled, should do better than choosing to stay in corrupt London. 'You are called upon, then, by every public principle', Campbell wrote, 'as well as every private motive, to reside a great deal in that country of which you are one day in the course of nature (if the active energy of Jacobinism, and the unjustifiable indolence and supineness of the propriety of the land, do not overturn all property), to be chief' (Campbell 1798: 56). For Campbell, sympathies to Jacobinism in Scotland were increasingly spreading among the lower classes: the result was the emergence of a 'spirit of revolt' (Campbell 1798: 57). 'Those things could not well happen', he concluded, 'if every great man remained upon his estate, by his presence and counsel to give a proper direction to the sentiments and opinions of his people' (Campbell 1798: 57).

As this chapter shows, it is this concern with re-channelling the 'sentiments' of the 'people' that invited Campbell, a man of upper-class background, to write a travel book in which he aimed to show the danger of revolt. The social and political hierarchies of the Ottoman Empire influenced the mind of the young Campbell who was concerned about the efforts of many in Britain who wanted to see the established religious and political order radically changed, who wanted the common people to follow the path of the French. Seeking to diffuse this danger, Campbell projected himself as a man of feelings in his writings: one sensitive towards those he passed through and socialised with. Critics have long argued that the flow of emotions and feelings in eighteenth-century writings appeared at a time when Europeans were actively expanding their colonies and trade abroad. 'Sentimental sympathy', Peter Hulme has argued, 'began to flow out along the arteries of European commerce in search for its victims' (Hulme 1986: 299).[8] This chapter complicates this designation of sentimentalism as a tool reifying colonialism. Sentimentalism in Campbell's text allowed the British self to sympathise with Muslims, thereby showing the extent to which travelling and learning about the world of others was a transforming experience.[9] But it also allowed him to critique late eighteenth-century political views which called for dismantling established political traditions in the name of liberty and reason.[10] If, as Elizabeth A. Bohl and Ian Duncan argued, '[s]entiments' in the late eighteenth century 'became a medium for heterodox views, including political radicalism', Campbell's sentimentalism was a tool of conservatism. It acknowledged the need for improvements but also rethought radical calls for change that gripped many dissenting and revolutionary minds during the period (Bohl and Duncan 2005: 3).[11]

Islam, Tradition and Dissent

In *Early Romanticism and Religious Dissent* (2006), Daniel E. White has perceptively argued that 'Many Orientalist texts throughout the seventeenth and eighteenth centuries drew analogies between East and West in order to critique and indeed subordinate dissident groups within the West itself' (White 2006: 126). 'The consequence of this perspective', he added, 'is a far less unified discursive field, involving Orientalisms that either represent a coherent Europe as superior to its Other or suggest a fragmented and unstable Europe in which alien cultures could be homologous to dissident religious and political groups vying for supremacy within the state and civil society' (White 2006: 126). Seen in this context, in a late eighteenth-century Britain known for rising political tensions between radicals and loyalists, conservative defenders of the established order and their critics used Islam, the Qur'an and 'Mahomet' as props to critique the opposite ideological and religious camp.[12] This ideological war was largely shaped by anxieties over the growing sympathies in Britain towards radical political changes in France and over an expanding British imperial sphere in India and Canada where British officials found themselves governing many Muslims and Catholics.[13] In *Considerations on the Present Internal and External Condition of France* (1794), Maurice Morgann, a colonial administrator in Canada and a secretary to Lord Shelbourne for many years, expressed his frustration of the radical revolutionary politics in France whose proponents he associated with violence and atheism. 'I would not swear that we should not behold another Mahomet in Robespierre', he wrote, 'and find Atheism and Fanaticism very lovingly shake hands together' (Morgann 1794: 21). The barrister James Bowles, in his *The Real Grounds of the Present War with France* (1795), ridiculed the French Jacobins and compared their pursuit of liberty to Islamic conquests of past ages: 'Under the mask of Religion, the arms of Mahomet established the empire of the Saracens – and under the mask of Liberty, the French seek to establish the infinitely more formidable empire' (Bowles 1794: 25). Such fear of radical politics was also expressed by the arch-conservative politician, writer and philosopher Edmund Burke who considered Jean-Baptiste Cloots, a Prussian philosopher who supported the French Revolution and wanted to see its principle of universal fraternity embraced across the globe, an absurd atheist.[14] 'If he was asked what the French confraternity bore any kind of comparison? he would readily answer, To the confraternity of Mahomet. This imposter did not profess any schemes or views of conquest: but with his Koran in one hand and his sword in the other, he spread over a considerable part of the world, the yoke and faith of the Mussulman' (*Parlimentary Register* 1793: 85).[15] From the point of view of English radicals, however, as James Gillray's satirical print of 1799 showed, it was the conservatives in Europe who were the ardent supporters of 'The Pale of the Church of Mahomet' [Figure 15].

Campbell wrote his travel account in this political climate in which Mahomet and Islam appeared as foils for conservative critiques of radical movements and radicals' critiques of conservatives, loyalists and the government.[16] Campbell found in the Qur'an an excellent constitution which protected people from despotic rulers. '[B]y [...] provision of the Constitution', he wrote, 'the power of the Monarch is limited' (Campbell 1795: 13). Campbell's reading of the Qur'an displayed a liberal frame of mind in which the Qur'an did not appear as a belief system. Rather it was a body of legislations and laws that protected both the people and monarch.[17] Campbell did not care to compare the Bible with the Qur'an, preferring one over the other. Nor was he interested in the popular tropes in Europe which posited the Qur'an as a forged book written by a false prophet, an imposture and 'heresiarch' as the Prophet Muhammad was known in Europe.[18] He rather posited the Qur'an as an excellent system of laws, a political document and constitution which organised the power relations between the ruler and the ruled. As Robert Forster, the editor of *The Most Celebrated Voyages and Travels* (1818), put it, 'Mr Campbell thinks the Turkish constitution not nearly so bad as it is conceived to be' (Forster 1818: IV, 98).

Campbell was a deist and critic of the corruption of the ruling classes, but he was not politically revolutionary and ideologically committed to radical principles aiming to dismantle the old alliance between the established church and the monarchy.

Figure 15 James Gillray, 1799. Théologie a la Turque. The Pale of the Church of Mahomet. Source: The British Museum.

After all, he was a member of the ruling elite in Scotland and an officer in the British army in India; that is to say, he was a member of the ruling British establishment. Yet Campbell was a man of reforms. He found in travelling and writing a travel book about the Ottoman-Arab land an opportunity to pass some moral and political lessons about the necessity of reforming the British political system in which the relationship between the ruler and ruled is imbalanced. To that end, he found in Islam one important political lesson that his fellow Britons could learn from. He found in the Qur'an a moral and political system in which three groups (the monarch, clergy and people) divided powers equally between them. He recalled how Muslims are loyal to their ancient political traditions, unlike many eighteenth-century Europeans who actively sought to overturn their monarchies with all the political and religious traditions they represented.[19] Campbell maintained that despite the Qur'an does not encourage the people to topple their rulers, it guarantees them dignity and liberty. Unlike what many Europeans claim, Campbell wrote, the Qur'an does not grant a ruler an unlimited power over the people. 'Were our opinions to be directed by the general belief of Europeans', he wrote,

> we should suppose that the life and property of every being in that vast Empire were irremediably at the mercy of the Grand Signiore – and that without the laws to protect, or any intermediate power whatever to shield them, they were entirely subject to the capricious will of an inexorable tyrant, who, stimulated by cruelty, sharpened by avarice, and unrestrained by any law human or divine, did everything to oppress his subjects, and carry destruction among Mankind. (Campbell 1795: 11)

Campbell's fascination with the Qur'an as the constitution of 'Turkey' enabled him to respond to the calls for constitutional reforms in late eighteenth-century Britain.[20]

In many European writings about Islam and the Ottoman Empire, such as those by Alexander Dow, Montesquieu and Voltaire, we find the same idea that a ruler in an Islamic polity enjoys an unlimited power over his subjects. But one book disseminated this trope widely in Europe: it was Sir Paul Rycaut's *The Present State of the Ottoman Empire*, first published in 1665 and went into six editions between 1665 and 1688. Rycaut served as a private secretary to the British ambassador to the Ottoman Empire (1660-1667). The book appeared in England in a period in which many feared the return of the revolt because of King James II's rivalry with the anti-Catholic Parliament. This historical context explains the views Rycaut held towards the Ottoman Empire. He reported on the cruelty of the Ottoman ruler, what he called the 'absolute' and 'unlimited power' of the Muslim 'Prince' (Rycaut 1682: 5). He mentioned how the Ottoman Empire was governed according to laws originally 'founded in three Books, which may not properly be called the Codes and Pandects of the Mahometan Constitutions' (Rycaut 1682: 185). The 'Alchoran' is the first; the second is 'the Consent or Testimony of Wisemen, called the Assonah, or the traditions of the Prophets; and the third, the Inferences or Deductions of one thing from another' (Rycaut 1682: 185). 'Mahomet wrote the Alchoran, and prescribed some laws for civil government' but the laws were later modified by the successors of 'Mahomet' until 'by the force of the sword transferred' from the Qur'an to the 'Mufti', the chief religious authority in a Muslim state. While the power of the state lays in the hand of the *Mufti*, the supreme religious authority, it is the case that the sultan's rule cannot be disputed even by the *Mufti*. '[I]ndeed', Rycaut wrote, 'I have considered seriously the contexture of the Turkish Government, the absoluteness of an Emperor without reason, without virtue, whose speeches may be irrational, and yet must be laws; whose actions irregular, and yet examples; whose sentence and judgement, if in matters of the Imperial concernment, are most commonly corrupt, and yet decrees irresistible [...]' (Rycaut 1682: 2).

Rycaut's book continued to be read and cited by most eighteenth-century commentators on Islam and the Ottoman Empire, including Edward Gibbon and William Robertson.[21] Campbell was aware of Rycaut's book but did not agree with his verdict on the undisputed authority of the ruler in Islam. 'I firmly believe, that, from the combination of ideas arising from those prejudices', Campbell interjected, 'there are few Christians who think or hear of the Grand Turk, that do not, by an involuntary act of the mind, instantly think of blood and murder, strangling with bowstring, and slicing off heads with cimeters' (Campbell 1795: 12).[22] For Campbell the Ottoman ruler is not an Oriental despot with limitless power, one unchecked by the law. 'It is obvious his power is limited and under control', Campbell observed (Campbell 1795: 12). 'Rather than autocracy or theocracy', '[it]is equally certain that the Turkish Government is partly Republic' (Campbell 1795: 18). Such a division of power in the Ottoman political system is derived from the Qur'an.

Rather than positing the Qur'an as a tool legitimising despotic government, Campbell found it a well-crafted constitution which balances power between the ruler and the ruled: the sultan is the head of the state and the Ulama, the religious class who act on behalf of the people, perform their duties as judges with complete independence. The Ulama, a body of scholars 'composed of all the members of the Church and the

Law, superior to any Nobility, jealous of their rights and privileges, and partly taken from the People, not by election but by profession and talents' (Campbell 1795: 13). This religious class form 'an intermediate power which, when roused to exertion, is stronger than the Emperor's, and stands as a bulwark between the extremes of Despotism and them' (Campbell 1795: 13). The Ulama guard the laws of the Qur'an which equally divides power between the ruler and the ruled. In so doing, they check despotism and the possibility of bloody revolutions. The Ulama 'derive their authority as much as the Emperor from the Koran, and when necessary, act with all the firmness resulting from a conviction of that authority [...]' (Campbell 1795: 13). They can easily 'rouse the people to arms, and proceed to dispose', but 'the Emperor cannot be disposed without their concurrence' (13).

Campbell borrowed the idea that the Qur'an was a balanced system from James Porter's *Observations on the Religion, Law, Government, and Manners, of the Turk*, first published in 1768. Campbell did not name the writer of his source, but he described Porter as 'the best and most liberal of our Historians on that subject, and which is of too great notoriety to be doubted' (Campbell 1795: 15). Porter served as an ambassador to the Ottoman Empire between 1747 and 1761. He was a scholarly man, but he was also a fervent Christian; he could not escape the hostile view in Europe towards the false divinity of the Qur'an: he saw the Qur'an as a forged document written by 'Mahomet', whom he considered 'so absolute and so able an imposture' (Porter 1768: I, 65). However, Porter found many things to admire in the world of Islam. He praised the Qur'anic laws which balance power relations between government and the people. 'I must [...] observe, that some of its [the Quran] laws, if not rigidly just, are yet an effectual security against despotism, and the oppression of the people, especially such as relate to private property, widows, orphans, inheritances, legacies, and crimes, &c.' (Porter 1768: I, 76).[23] Such a statement appeared in print in the same year in which John Wilkes was imprisoned for writing an article in the *North Briton* about King George III being a puppet in the hand of the Earl of Bute's ministry.

Porter's book appeared in a period in which the question of the rebellion of the colonies occupied the hearts and minds of the people in England. The trope about the despotism of the British King (George III) and the Grenville ministry, who were seen by many as responsible for imposing taxes on the American colonies without the consent of the American people, appeared in the radical print media of the period in Britain and America.[24] Porter was aware of the radicalism of the period; therefore, he tried to intervene in the political debate of his age by using the Qur'an to warn people of the danger of changing the established political structure but equally to warn government of the danger of disregarding people's rights. For Porter, Qur'anic laws protect the ruler against the ruled, but the people, not the ruler, often disturb the balance of power. 'Notwithstanding the transcendent expressions the Turks use when speaking of their Sovereign', Porter stated,

> they will frequently murmur, talk freely, abuse him and his ministers, throw anonymous scurrilous papers into the moschees (mosques), and seem ever ripe for rebellion, if outraged by frequent and unusual oppression and tyranny. They are taught that he is established by

> God, that he is a descendent of their prophet, thro' whose mediation they expect salvation; and yet in a moment they will deprive him of his throne, of his liberty, and even of his life. (Porter 1768: I, 107)

Porter here was referring to the insurrection which took place in Istanbul in 1730 and which led to the deposition of Sultan Ahmed III (1673–1736). But the political tension in the passage above was meant to remind his fellow Britons of the danger of rebellion. In a period in which there was a heated debate in Britain about the future of the American colonies, Porter posited the Qur'an as an excellent system balancing power between the ruler and the ruled.

Like Porter, Campbell found in the Qur'an some excellent laws which protect people from the tyranny of government; he suggested that such a system also lays to rest the fear of the tyranny of the masses. Campbell was aware of the political tension between the radicals and loyalists which kept circulating in print in Britain and North America throughout the revolutionary era of the second half of the eighteenth century. In 1795, a feeling of discontent against King George III and the Pitt ministry reached an unprecedented level. While King George III was on his way to open the Parliament in October of that year, angry protestors stoned his carriage, an incident which encouraged the government and the Parliament to issue the Treason Act suspending political meetings and banning publications which critique the king and government.[25] Radicals, however, found different ways to critique the government: in their commentaries on contemporary politics, they substituted the ancients for the moderns, Islam for Christianity and the Ottoman sultan for the English king. Issac D'Israeli's Citizen's Rant in *Vaurien: or Sketches of the Times* (1797) commented on this role-reversal in the radical political scene of the period: they 'talk of Constantinople while everyone know' they 'mean London, of Mahomet while' they 'strike at Jesus'.[26]

In this context, while referring to Constantinople and the Ottoman Sultan, Campbell critiqued the British government and the king. He reported a story in which he recalled that when the Ottoman Sultan, Mustafa III, in 1755, formed a plan to rebuild his 'burnt down' palace, 'it was determined that the only certain means' to prevent future accidents like this was 'to leave a space of clear ground all around it, for which purpose the contiguous houses should be purchased from the proprietors, and demolished' (Campbell 1795: 15). One owner, Campbell continued, refused to sell, advancing the claim that 'she was born and had lived here all her life, in that spot, would not quit it for any one' (Campbell 1795: 15). The sultan could not force her to leave the house.[27] The *Ulama* and magistrates in Constantinople, Campbell argued, consulted the Qur'an and ruled in favour of the people: 'No [...] it is impossible! It cannot be done! It is her property', they declared (Campbell 1795: 15). The laws of the Qur'an, Campbell, echoing Porter, added, 'the actual written laws of the realm are, if duly administered, are sufficiently adequate to the security of property, the regulation of commerce, the repression of vice, and the punishment and prevention of crimes' (Campbell 1795: 16). Contrary to the laws in Britain which permitted the enclosure of common land in the name of improvement, the laws of the Qur'an guarantee the protection of the property of the 'common people'. 'Now in England', Campbell protested, 'for the convenience of a private canal, the Parliament would force her [the woman] to sell' (Campbell 1795: 15). In the Ottoman Empire, however, 'the common people are more free, and that property and life are better secured in Turkey, than in some European countries' (Campbell 1795: 16–17). 'Their internal policy is, in many respects', he added, 'excellent, and may be compared with advantage to that of any Nation in Europe' (Campbell 1795: 17). Qur'anic laws, if properly administered, secure 'the common people' far more freedoms than those administered in England.

In the story above about the fire in Istanbul, Campbell rethought what the sixteenth-century Austrian diplomat Ogier Ghiselin de Busbecq reported in his *Itinera Constantinopolitanum et Amasianum* (1581). Busbecq recorded that Ottoman soldiers were often pleased when seeing houses burn in the Ottoman capital. Even some soldiers set people's houses on fire because the 'ruining' of 'the contiguous houses' allow them to 'plunder both', the houses that were set on fire and the nearby houses 'pluck[ed] down' (du Busbecq 1744: 73). Campbell clearly was not interested in confirming Busbecq's point that those who were employed to protect people were the real oppressors. Indeed, Campbell's reforming concerns encouraged him to rewrite Busbecq's story: people's properties in the Ottoman capital, as he mentioned, were protected by the laws of the Qur'an and the grand religious authority in the empire, the *Mufti*. In rethinking Busbecq's report about the fire in Istanbul, Campbell critiqued the British Parliament, but he did not go too far; that is, he did not critique the king or even call for rebellion against the government. What Campbell aimed to do here is to reconcile the people and their government in an age when many in Britain feared the tidal waves of revolutions which had already arrived on the shores of America and France.

Religious Toleration

In the same year in which Catholics and Protestants were involved in daily conflicts in Ireland, Campbell published his travel account in which the gravity of the matter of toleration in Christian Europe was examined. Campbell reimagined the landscape of toleration in Europe by referring to an Islamic context that he did not necessarily know much about. Yet the little knowledge he gathered about Muslims while travelling among them allowed him to rethink popular prejudices against religious minorities in late eighteenth-century Europe. J. G. A. Pocock wrote about the rise of an enlightened intellectual culture in Europe in which 'dispute was to be replaced by conversation, inspiration by opinion, doctrine by polite manners, and the warlike worlds of universal monarchy, wars of religion, feudal disorder and the wars of ancient virtue, by a European republic of trading states' (Pocock 1999: II, 169). This modern culture of civility celebrated by Pococke, however, did not completely brush off the religious tensions historians often associate with a pre-Enlightenment age.[28] 'In the eighteenth century, English Papists were deemed suspect in wartime', Colin Haydon remarkably wrote, 'but so were the Huguenots in France, and the Jews in the Habsburg empire; and the anti-Papist panics in 1745, and the subsequent violence, strongly resemble the *Grand Peur* in France in 1789 and the ensuing attacks on châteaux' (Haydon 2013: 59). In Britain, anti-Catholic riots, known as the Gordon Riots, proved that toleration was a fragile idea in a culture priding itself on being open to religious dissent in comparison to neighbouring Catholic states.[29]

In the 1790s, a decade in Britain known for the fear of a French invasion and an Irish rebellion, the British state was prepared to negotiate Catholic emancipation. In 1792 and 1793, the Parliament passed two Acts allowing the relief of the Roman Catholics. 'By the first, Papists might practise at the bar, though they were not entitled to be made King's Counsel', wrote the army officer and conservative MP Henry Jervis-White-Jervis in 1868, and 'Protestant barristers might have Papist wives, and solicitors were no longer required to educate their children as Protestants' (Jervis 1868: 248). The second Act, Jervis added, allowed 'Roman Catholics' to 'hold property, vote at elections, hold minor civil and military offices'; further, they 'were no longer bound to attend the parish church under a penalty' (Jervis 1868: 248). After the passing of these laws, Catholics, Haydon wrote, 'could enjoy a place in polite society that was largely unimaginable fifty years earlier' (Jervis 1868: 62). However, even after the Parliament passed the Relief Act, Jervis wrote, the Orange Society of the county of Armagh (a Protestant fraternity formed to maintain the Protestant ascendancy in Ireland) was involved in 'barbarous practices' against Irish Catholics (Jervis 1868: 255). 'It sufficed for a man to profess the Roman Catholic religion', Jervis continued, 'to have his dwelling burnt over his head, and himself, with his family, banished out of the county. Nearly half of the inhabitants of the country of Armagh had been thus expatriated' (Jervis 1868: 255). While the British state was prepared to grant political relief to Catholics, anti-popery sentiments remained central to religious, social, political and intellectual life in Britain.[30]

While travelling in the Ottoman Empire, Campbell did not find a perfect environment for toleration. But he was also aware that such an environment does not exist in Europe. 'The very first principle ingrafted in the minds of the Mahomedan children', Campbell noted,

> [...]is a high contempt of all religions but their own; and from the minute babies are capable of distinguishing, they are taught to call Christians by the name of Ghiaour, or Infidel: this grows up in their manhood so strong in them, that they will follow a Christian through the streets, and even justle against him with contempt, crying, Ghiaour! Ghiaour! or Infidel! Infidel! — Men of dignity and rank, indeed, will treat Christians with courtesy but as soon as they are gone out of hearing, will call them Dog! This is monstrous! (Campbell 1795: 21)

Campbell was surprised that the men of rank in Islamic societies behave in such a 'monstrous' way against Christians. However, the most prejudiced group, as the passage above indicated, were not the men of high social status and Ottoman officials but the common people – that is, the masses – whose prejudices passed from father to child.[31]

While Muslims were not a perfect model of toleration, Campbell emphasised, it was apparent that minorities in the Ottoman Empire lived under a government which required them to pay poll tax but also protected them and their private property. Such a system is not perfect but better than that of Europe. 'But let us recollect', he wrote, 'how a Turk would be treated in Spain or Portugal, and we shall see that inhuman bigotry may be found in a greater degree among Christians than even Mahomedans' (Campbell

1795: 21). In Portugal and Spain, Campbell added, 'the people of rank [...] would very conscientiously consign them to the Inquisition, where the pious Fathers of the Church would very piously consign them to the flames and cooly go to the Alter, and pray to God to damn them hereafter to all eternity' (Campbell 1795: 21). Campbell here might have in mind the persecution of Muslims by the Catholics in Spain after their empire in the West fell in the fifteenth century. But he little cared to historicise his argument. Indeed, what mattered for Campbell was the idea that the issue of toleration was one of global reach. Campbell's observation of the tension around toleration in Muslim societies taught him that Europeans often boast about their enlightenment, yet they have not been able to root out religious prejudices among them. For Campbell, if the observer of the period compares the religious prejudices of Muslims with those of Christians, he will discover that 'the balance is in favour of the Turks' (Campbell 1795: 21). 'The exercise of all religions is free', he added, 'and at Constantinople (we are told) Monks dress in their habits, and are allowed at funeral processions to elevate the Cross, which is more than the English tyranny allowed the Roman Catholics in Ireland to do, till very lately' (Campbell 1795: 32). Although Islam treats apostasy with severe punishment, Campbell found, the clergy, unlike their peers in Christian Europe, do not question the internal beliefs of their flock; they only care about the external appearance, not the inward soul of the believer: 'if they keep up a decent semblance of the forms of their religion, no intrusive inquiry is made into their real faith' (Campbell 1795: 32). 'Mahomet' praised the idea of converting '[u]nbelievers', Campbell concluded, but Muslims 'never fail to consider any renegado, or person who becomes a convert, with contempt, if not dislike' (Campbell 1795: 32). The detractors of Islam in Enlightenment Europe, most famously Henry Prideaux, spoke of the persecution of Christians in Muslim land and popularised the idea in England that Islam gained its converts by the violent means, a trope that kept circulating in print for most parts of the eighteenth century.[32] Campbell clearly disagreed with this view despite that he had little to say about the *millet* system in the Ottoman Empire which protected the people of the book – as Christians and Jews were known – and allowed them to freely practice their faiths as soon as they paid their taxes and acknowledged the superiority of Islam.[33]

Indeed, Campbell little studied the historical, political and jurisprudential contexts around Islamic attitudes and laws impacting the lives of Christian and Jewish minorities. He mostly aimed to remind his European readers to stop indulging in the idea that prejudices only exist in foreign land, far away from home. Campbell, like many deists in eighteenth-century Europe, used Islam as a prop to expand the space of toleration in the eighteenth-century British public sphere in which one finds many voices critiquing the established church.[34] Rather than repeating the negative tropes about Islam propounded by the likes of Prideaux who never travelled in the Muslim world, Campbell offered a positive image about the toleration of religious minorities in the Ottoman world. In doing so, he quoted extensively from Alexander Russell's *The Natural History of Aleppo*, a book written by a Briton who lived and worked in the Levant for many years. Russell, relying on his personal observations and also on his previous readings, explained the theological and economic contexts that defined Muslim attitudes to minorities: Christians and Jews.[35] For Russell, the basis of the disagreement between Muslims and Christians was theological: Muslims, as unitarians, as their reading of the Qur'an taught him, do not believe in the idea of the Trinity; for 'the Mahommedans are very apt to charge Christianity with idolatry, and a tendency towards polytheism' (Russell 1794: I, 213). But a theological difference is not the only context which shaped the religious tension between Muslims and non-Muslims in the Ottoman Empire. Referring to one important contributor to the republic of Arabic letters in Enlightenment Europe, that is, to Yusuf ibn Siman as-Simani, the composer of *Bibliotheca Orientalis Clementino-Vaticana* (1719–1728), Russell recalled how Islamic law demands that local Christians pay a certain amount of money (a poll-tax) in return for securing protection; the failure to pay could lead to imprisonment. While Russell investigated the topic of religious toleration by relying on previous readings, he also used his personal experience in Aleppo to support his claims. 'About the time that the capitation tax is due', he noted, 'numbers of the inferior artisans are daily met with in the streets, in their way to jail; and the gate of the Mohassil's prison is crowded by women bringing victuals to their relations, who are there confined on account of the tax' (Russell 1794: II, 42). However, contrary to what local Christians often complain about Muslim 'tyranny' and regardless that 'the Turks of similar rank are equal sufferers', once the tax is paid Christians and Jews are free to practise their religion (Russell 1794: II, 42). Therefore, '[n]otwithstanding the contemptuous light in which the Turks view all other religions, they permit liberty of conscience in their dominions, and tolerate the public exercise of the Christian and Jewish religions, with their respective rites and ceremonies' (Russell 1794: I, 214).

While Russell was more versed than Campbell with Islamic laws and Arabic scholarship about the subject of religious toleration in the Ottoman Empire, both agreed on the superiority of the culture of toleration among Muslims compared to what they had in Europe. Unlike Russell, however, Campbell used the idea of Islamic toleration of Christians as a beating rod against the clergy and the common people who defied the Papists Act of 1778. Indeed, Campbell travelled in Syria one year after the Gordon Riots (1780), a popular protest, took place in the streets of London because of the government's decision to grant Catholics some religious, legal and educational rights. Responding to this mass mobilisation efforts in Britain, Campbell mostly blamed the common people and the religious classes for being intolerant of other religions. He pointed to the intolerance of 'people of rank' in Portugal and Spain and at the 'English tyranny' in Ireland, but this is where his critique ended. While radical voices of his age, like Mirabeau in France, Thomas Paine in Britain and George Washington in America, critiqued the practice of toleration because it placed the power to grant and revoke political and religious rights in the hands of non-elected rulers, Campbell, a loyalist and a member of the Scottish aristocracy, had blamed religious prejudices on the clerical classes and the common people in Europe rather than the governments.[36]

Coffeehouse Radicalism

During the eighteenth century, as we saw in Chapters three and four, it was a common practice among travel writers to report about the great hospitality they enjoyed in the company of their countrymen who mainly resided abroad as consuls and merchants. Such an example of British sociability abroad indicates the extent to which travelling, and reporting travels, was part of what Jeremy Black called 'the national impact of the experience of travel', that is, the sense of patriotism which Britons in foreign countries felt when encountering fellow Britons (Black 2018: 168). In Aleppo, however, Campbell was aware of Laurence Sterne's advice for English travellers which appeared in his *A Sentimental Journey through France and Italy*: 'an Englishman does not travel to see Englishmen' (Sterne 1768: I, 34). Like Yorick in *A Sentimental Journey*, Campbell, a Scotsman, often avoided the company of other Britons in Aleppo. He rather enjoyed the company of Europeans; he mostly socialised with the French community even though his country was in a state of war with France, what the historian Jeremy Black called Britain's 'principal other' during the eighteenth century (Black 2018: 153). Campbell preferred to stay in Aleppo in the house of a French merchant, a man of 'politeness and hospitality' (51).[37] In a period in which francophobia dominated British culture, Campbell showed how in the Ottoman city of Aleppo he felt free to socialise with the French.[38] Campbell's new French friend spoke Arabic fluently and was sympathetic to local traditions in the Ottoman Empire. He often took Campbell for walks across the city. The bond between Campbell and the Frenchman in Aleppo was a transformative experience.

Campbell's friendship with the Frenchman alludes to an Enlightenment-era intellectual culture in which it was sociability rather than narrow nationalism and sectarianism that was mostly seen as a source of improvement for the individual. To that end, the Frenchman served as a moral and political mentor for the young Campbell in Aleppo. In the company of his French friend, Campbell went through not only a moral transformation but also a political one which involved an excursion into a space in Aleppo which escaped the notice of almost all travellers studied in this book. Coffeehouses in Aleppo, the physician Alexander Russell wrote in 1756, 'naturally attract the notice of a stranger, more than any of the objects he meets with in rambling over the city' (Russell 1794: I, 23). In the coffeehouse, a place mostly frequented by people of lower-class backgrounds, the traveller finds an 'amusing' and 'an interesting scene' (Ibid., I, 23). European travellers find a vibrant culture in the Aleppo coffeehouse, as John Griffiths who passed through Aleppo on his way to India in 1785 noted, where artists (satirists and storytellers) often perform acts aiming to pass critiques on what they considered the moral degeneration of their society. But, Griffiths added, coffeehouse artists and moralists in Aleppo often steer away from politics. Unlike what one expects to find in England, as Griffiths added, no serious political and social debates and arguments exist in the Aleppo coffeehouse.[39] 'Detaching these indecorous sallies of the puppet, Kara Guze', a Punch-like character, Griffiths recalled,

> [...] appears sometimes as a useful satyrist, and holds out to public derision the follies of individuals, or to public scorn and detection their vices. Unfortunately the peccadillos of authority are sheltered from his attacks by the fear of the bastinado; and Kara Guze seldom ventures to hint at the infamous conduct of a Cadee [judge] until his removal from power, and consequent flight from the city, ensures the safety of the satirist. (Griffiths 1805: 337)

Griffiths, like many literary and philosophical voices of the age who wrote about the absence of serious public sphere in the Ottoman Empire, considered Muslims 'unfree' and suggested that 'only fear compels them to act [...]' (Bevilacqua 2018: 171).

Like Griffiths, Campbell was fascinated with the Aleppo coffeehouse. 'Come hither', says the Frenchman, Campbell's friend, 'come into this coffee-house, here is something going forward that may amuse you' (Campbell 1795: 60). But, unlike Griffiths, however, Campbell did not lash out at the lack of serious political culture in the Ottoman Empire. Indeed, Campbell, in writing about the political culture of the Ottoman Empire, responded to the dominant views in Europe in which Ottoman and Arab cultures were seen as unwelcoming to free speech and public debates which resemble those that took place in what Jürgen Habermas called the European 'public sphere' (coffeehouses and literary and scientific clubs).[40] Campbell found that artists in the Ottoman coffeehouse often critique the corruption of judges and government officials. The idea of criticising the corruption of the judges and government, Campbell recalled, was an important characteristic of the coffeehouse.[41] '[M]alversation in office, public delinquency, and all those Crimes of the great', Campbell wrote,

> [...] which with us are cognizable by no tribunal but that of the public press, are not altogether so exempt from the lash and exposure of the satirist in Turkey, as the want of that great palladium of Freedom would dispose us to believe; and that, incredible as it may appear, the magistrates are held up to ridicule in public exhibition, satirised with all the extravagant vulgarity of coarse humour and unpolished wit, and exposed with all the bitter exaggerations of envenomed genius. (Campbell 1795: 66)

Campbell published his account in a period in which the British government, before and after the Two Acts in 1795, was acting ruthlessly in its efforts to suppress political dissent. In this politically charged climate, radical voices and dissenters gathered in coffeehouses which many late eighteenth-century British loyalists viewed as spaces of political radicalism.[42] Campbell offered his reader a different story of the coffeehouse, one in which government is not necessarily immune to criticism but also one in which people do not call for radical political changes. To that end, the Aleppo coffeehouse in his narrative appeared as a political space in which critics call for reforms rather than revolution.[43] 'C'est vrai, Monsieur!', said the Frenchman to Campbell, '[...]in Turkey criticism is the honest spontaneous issue of the heart, and with us is a trade, where sometimes lucre, sometimes vanity, but oftener than both, envy and malice direct the decision, and dispose to cavil and censure' (Campbell 1795: 64–65). In Ottoman coffeehouses, as Campbell learned from his French companion, criticisms of the government are genuine and spontaneous but also controlled and disciplined; they express what Adam Smith called 'social virtues'; however, those in Europe show excessive passions, what Smith called 'unsocial virtues' (Smith 1761: 51–60). The division of sentimental labour in the statement above was meant to show the difference between Ottoman and British political cultures, but it also showed how the discourse of sentimentalism widely popular in late eighteenth-century British culture was utilised by conservative writers and reformers like Campbell for purposes of negotiating the political tension between the government and its critics. For Campbell, the critique in the English press lacked spontaneity in the 'trade': he accused it of being full of 'vanity', 'envy' and 'malice'.

For Campbell and his French friend, the visit to the Ottoman coffeehouse improved their knowledge of Ottoman political culture. But it also allowed them to reflect on the political tensions in Europe between the radicals and the loyalists. Such a reflection took place in another coffeehouse where they attended a shadow play, which, as Donald Quataert postulates, 'was perhaps the most popular entertainment in Ottoman Times' (Quataert 2005: 161). The story of the shadow-show focused on the corruption of the Ottoman justice system. It tells an anecdote about a divorced man who wanted to remarry his ex-wife. The law in Islam, as the story goes, required that she marry and divorce another man before marrying her first husband. The new marriage took place; the woman and the new husband fell in love. The ex-husband went mad. He bribed the judge who changed the law, thus divorcing the woman from her new husband. 'Kara-ghuse (Punch) however, takes the defendant aside, and in a dialogue, which my friend assured me was pointed, witty, and bitterly satirical', Campbell wrote,

> develops to him the whole system of magisterial injustice, advises him to bribe the Bashaw, and, declaring his zeal for all young people fond of amorous enjoyment (which he is at some pains to enlarge upon to the excess of indelicacy), offers him the aid of his purse. The advice is followed; the bribe is accepted; the Cadi's decree is reversed, and himself disgraced, and the mob at once hustle him and bear the Hullah [new husband] home to his bride with clamours of joy. (Campbell 1795: 72)

In the passage above, the judges, government and the 'mob' were seen as corrupt. Not even 'Kara-ghuse' whom Campbell and his French friend compared with the press in Britain was immune to such culture of corruption. 'In England', the Frenchman told Campbell, 'you do not want him; every man there is a KARA-GHUSE, and every newspaper is a puppet show' (Campbell 1795: 73). Campbell agreed with the Frenchman but added a comment that would not necessarily go well with the defenders of radical freedoms during the period: 'we complain sadly of want of liberty' (Campbell 1795: 73). In his *The English Press in the Eighteenth Century*, Jeremy Black recalls how the 'newspaper agenda in the 1790s' in Britain was influenced by 'an external factor, the example and encouragement of French political, social and religious radicalism' (Black 1987: 269). Many radical commentators of the period argued against the corruption of the elites, members of the government and the aristocracy but 'these grievances', Black adds, 'usually entailed the reform of institutions and the reformation of morality, rather than any substantive change of the hierarchical social system' (Black 1987: 270). Campbell was aware of the late eighteenth-century political and social debate in Europe over corruption and censure. Yet he was not sympathetic to calls for radical change which he associated with 'the mob' and the press.

Campbell was aware of the need for reforms in the political system, but he was anxious about late eighteenth-century calls for radical change. 'Liberty is like money', the Frenchman reminded Campbell, 'the more we have of it, the more covetous we grow' (74). This is a striking image because it shows how the Enlightenment conception of improvement, as Adam Smith's *The Wealth of Nations* (1776) showed, which considered *laissez-faire* and pursuit of wealth as essential requirements for achieving a stable and prosperous society, was used by late eighteenth-century radicals for purposes of changing the political order: the idea of changing the established order (that is, instituting a new government which expands and protects labourers' rights, produces progressive taxation system, support the poor and fund universal education) constitutes an essential step for any society to move towards stability, equality, prosperity and happiness.[44] 'If universal peace, harmony, civilization and commerce are ever to be the happy lot of man', wrote the radical Thomas Paine in *Rights of Man*, 'it cannot be accomplished but by a revolution in the present system of governments' (Paine 1792: 4). The problem with this approach, as the conservative critics in Britain pointed out, is that when people show a zeal for changing the established political order, they end up losing the freedoms they gained throughout history. As one polemicist in 1795 put it, 'In the fervour of their zeal for liberty, they [the London Corresponding Society] may crucify the God they adore' (*Remarks* 1795: 24). In agreeing with the conservative rhetoric of the Frenchman in Aleppo ('Very true, Monsieur'), Campbell disagreed with Paine's call for radical change (Campbell 1795: 74). 'The English complaining of the want of liberty', the Frenchman said to Campbell, 'reminds me of the coffee-house orator's story of Cassem, who, wallowing in wealth, lost it all in the wild pursuit of more. I hope however that they never will, like him, lose their stock in vain endeavours to increase it' (Campbell 1795: 74). Using a French voice to critique the radicals in Britain, Campbell reminded his readers that changing the established political order is not only anathema to stability but also prosperity.

Emancipation of Slaves

In the world of Islam, the British traveller often looks for what he wants to see. To that end, the debate in England around political radicalism influenced Campbell's rambling curiosity while travelling along the overland routes to India. Campbell was not only interested in the political culture of the Ottoman Empire. He was also fascinated with Ottoman attitudes to slavery. The culture of slavery in the Ottoman Empire figured in Campbell's narrative as a vehicle for addressing political and moral concerns during the period of British involvements in the slave trade.[45] Campbell wrote his travel narrative during the period in which many slaves in Western colonies began to mobilise for emancipation. In St Domingue (between 1791 and 1804), slaves began to adopt the emancipatory ideals of the French Revolution, mobilising against the European plantation system which mainly depended on economic exploitation.[46] Such a development, as David Turley in his *The Culture of English Antislavery (1780-1860)* noted, 'was [in Britain] widely perceived as a disaster arising out of French revolutionary principles which at the same time threatened to destroy Britain's West Indian empire' (Turley 1991: 168). In the British colony on the Island of St Vincent, slaves and the colonists clashed in the Black Caribs wars (1769–1773 and 1795–1797). At home in Britain, Parliament debated the topic throughout the 1790s, with many members opposing the trade and arguing for the necessity of abolishing it.[47] In the English print scene, as David Turley showed, many opponents of slavery (authors like Joseph Priestly, Richard Price and Anna Lalita Barbauld) published accounts in which they adopted an 'antislavery' rhetoric reflecting the 'radical political temper' of the period (Turley 1991: 152). 'With growing anxiety in the early 1790s in Britain about the radical turn of the French Revolution', Turley added, 'opponents began to characterize antislavery even more negatively. Hostile opinions represented the movement as alien and extreme, revolutionary rather than improving' (Turley 1991: 183). The triumph of the American and the French revolutions, however, gave encouragement in Britain to radical voices calling for alternatives to oligarchy and corruption and, in this turbulent political climate, the rise of dissenting voices in the country, including those of the Church of England, as Robin Blackburn argued, who moved abolitionism 'to the centre of British political life' (Blackburn 1988: 138).[48] While the topic of slavery in England became a battlefield in the debate between the radicals and the conservatives, Campbell, drawing on the British tradition of praising the system of slavery in the Ottoman world, found in the treatment of slaves in the Levant what allowed him to intervene in such a heated debate in the 1790s. Campbell used the language of sentimentalism, one widely popularised among radical writers during the period, in order to show how, in William Blake's phrasing, 'pity is become a trade' (Blake 1988: 55).

While travelling along the overland routes between Aleppo and Basra, Campbell, imitating Yorick in Sterne's *Sentimental Journey*, decided to disguise his true British identity in the hope to find some moral enlightenment, a lesson to be communicated to his reader, while interacting with the people. He accepted to pass as a slave for his Tatar guide, Hassan Artaz, a man he hired in Aleppo to be his companion across the Syrian deserts.[49] Such a performance angered one British traveller who visited the region in 1797.[50] 'Some have attempted to travel under the character of the Tartar's servants' which is 'too degrading for the character of an Englishman', wrote John Jackson (Jackson 1799: xii). Jackson missed the point which Campbell tried to make while disguising himself as a slave in the Syrian deserts. The role reversal in Campbell's narrative meant to convey a lesson to the British public about the inhumanity of those benefitting from slavery.

While doing so, Campbell drew on the British traditions of sentimentalism popularised by Adam Smith which, as Lynn Festa put is, relies 'upon an eclipsing of identity, a transfer of persons in which one leaves oneself behind and tries to take someone else's part' (Festa 2006: 28). The idea of sympathising with slaves, however, does not entirely allow the traveller 'to take someone else' part' because what mainly concerned Campbell in this role-reversal act was his country's involvement in slavery. 'When young slaves, male of female, are bought by a Turk', Campbell wrote of what he saw en route to India,

> [...] they seem to be introduced into the family rather in the condition of an adopted child; they receive the same education, perform nearly the same offices, and are bound to no greater marks of respect than their master's own children – and in fact feel none of the galling circumstances of a state of servility; the very worst treatment they ever receive is to be put on a footing with the menial domestics, or ordered to the same duty as a valet or a page. It often happens, on the other hand, that they are married into the family, and very frequently promoted to high offices in the State. If they adopt the Religion of their masters,

> it is always spontaneously; and even to slaves taken in war, no compulsion is used to make them change their Faith. (Campbell 1795: 39)

The preceding passage is extracted from Alexander Russell's *The Natural History of Aleppo*, which makes complex arguments about the traditions of slavery in the Ottoman Empire. Russell focused on the global circulation of the trade, the financial benefits of slave traders, and the religious and legal framework organising the power relation between slaves and their owners.[51] Campbell, however, made no serious efforts to engage with the topic of slavery in Ottoman land: he did not examine any historical and geographical context of slavery in the region, and little was provided in his text about the sources of wealth among merchants in the slave markets of grand Ottoman cities like Aleppo, Cairo and Istanbul.[52] Campbell recalled what Russell mentioned about the humane treatment of slaves among Muslims, but he said nothing about what Russell mentioned about the white male and female slaves, 'the children of Christians' brought from Georgia and Circassia into Ottoman markets in the Levant (a subject that concerned many European writers during the seventeenth and eighteenth centuries), because, as we shall see later, Campbell was mostly concerned about the experience of black slaves in the Western hemisphere.[53]

Campbell recalled how the Ottomans enlist slaves in their households and promote them to higher positions in the state, but he did not mention how these slaves who held high office (Ali Bey in Egypt and Ahmed Pasha Al-Jazzar in Palestine were two prominent examples during the period) were often prepared to shake up the political hierarchy in the empire.[54] The French writer Constantin Volney, who visited Syria in 1782, reported how As'ad Pasha Al-Azm, the governor of Damascus, was 'betrayed by his Mamlouk (slave) and smothered in the bath' (Volney 1788: II, 382). Alexander Jardine, a British military man who visited Morocco in 1771, was surprised to discover that 'blacks' could reach higher status in the state: in Morocco, as Jardine observed, hierarchy is mostly based on religious rather than racial ground; in Britain and the colonies, he added, 'we see blacks only in the state of slavey, which produces always a distinct and familiar character' (Jardine 1788: I, 186). Blackness for Jardine was a political and social marker of inferiority which explains his surprise upon seeing 'blacks' holding higher offices in the Moroccan state. Indeed, such was the fascination of British travellers with the ability of slaves in the world of Islam to move up the political and social hierarchy that one eminent Briton during the period recalled how Prophet Muhammad started off as a slave before he was able to shake off his bondage and set up a huge empire.[55]

Campbell, as an aristocrat, was not keen on investigating the complex political machinations and power relations which allowed slaves in the Ottoman Empire to capture the highest offices of state.[56] Nor was he interested in confirming what Sir James Porter, his favourite writer about the Ottoman political system, asserted about an egalitarian Muslim political culture in which a man's ability rather than his birth decides what rank in life he reaches: 'Birth does not recommend to great office in Tukey; merit and abilities may exalt the cottager to the highest offices of the empire' (Porter 1768: I, 57). Campbell did not agree with Porter. He rather explained the reason why slaves reach a higher office of state by referring to the humanity and morality of their masters rather than their individual talents. This shows that whereas some travellers like Porter spoke of the relationship between the master and slave in the Islamic world as one of abilities, duties and even rights, Campbell preferred to view it as one of moral, sentimental and patriarchal bond.[57]

The problem here is one of politics but also of agency. For Campbell slaves in the Ottoman Empire can improve their status not because they were able to do so but because of the humanity of their masters. The idea of viewing slavery from the point of the view of the moralist and sentimentalist has another aim besides that of mystifying contemporary abolitionist calls for linking slavery to a discourse of rights. During the Enlightenment, slaves in British-Atlantic plantations, Justin Roberts noted, were essential in the improvement project aiming to extract profits from cultivating lands. Many planters sometimes cared to improve 'the conditions of slavery', Roberts added, but 'When there was a conflict between improving the conditions of life among slaves and increasing labour demands to extract more profits it was usually the former that gave away' (Roberts 2013: 28–29). Campbell was opposed to such a vision in the modern world in which humans were measured by their economic worth. 'Great God! —What a horrible though! —what an indelible stigma! that a Legislator shall, in the cold blood of commerce, make a calculation of the probable profit upon human lives – put commercial expediency in the balance against murder – and make convenience an excuse for crime!', wrote Campbell (114). In the Islamic world, however, as Campbell found, the culture of slavery was not rooted in a utilitarian discourse in which humans' worth was measured by their productivity. Rather the relationship between the master and the slave was based on a patriarchal bond, what may be called a sentimental rather than economic and racial hierarchy.

Campbell got the idea that the relationship between the master and slave in the Ottoman world was one of sentimental rather than economic bond from Edward Ives's *Travels from Persia to England* (1773) in which 'the Turks' appeared as opposed to 'cruelty in this respect, that should a master treat a slave with too great severity, his neighbours would not fail to reproach him, bidding him to reflect, that the slave is of the human species as well as himself, and shrewdly propose to him this interesting question, *How would you like to be served, in the same circumstances?*' (Ives 1773: 285). Both Ives and Campbell drew on British traditions of praising the humanity of slavery in the Ottoman Empire; it was primarily seen as a corrective to the European classical conception of slaves as chattels and personal possessions. The only difference between Campbell and Ives, however, was that Ives, in the 1750s, critiqued the economic exploitation of slaves in European colonies, principally those of the Dutch, whereas Campbell, in the 1790s, openly critiqued British exploitation of slaves in the Atlantic world. 'A Briton! – Hold! Have I not been uttering a most severe satire upon the British nation?', sobbed Campbell. 'Yes! Imputing to me a virtue which they want is the worst kind of satire'; therefore, 'Britons deserve the lash of satire [...] a worse lash: for the traffic in human bodies still stands a bloody brand of infamy on her great National Councils' (Campbell 1795: 113).

Nothing in the sentimental plea above indicates that Campbell supported contemporary radical voices during the period calling for the abolition of slavery: rather Campbell mostly aimed to raise awareness about the immorality of the trade.[58] Such a satire was not irrelevant to Campbell's anti-radical, conservative politics. If Campbell flirted with the idea of reforming the institution of slavery, it is not because of the damage it does to the slaves themselves. Rather it was because of the damage it does to the reputation of Britons in the eyes of their neighbours and competitors. 'But shall Britons, generous Britons', he added,

> whose boastful claim precedence of the world in freedom, humanity and justice-shall they look on and see inferior nations spurning from them with horror the debasing traffic; and stimulated by avarice, or misled by a wicked policy, retain the blot that other States have wiped away and live at once the curse of one part, and the scorn of the rest of mankind? (Campbell 1795: 114)

Campbell's commentary on 'the inferior nations' who managed to legislate against slavery refers to the Slave Trade Act (March 1794) in North America. It also refers to the ruling which abolished slavery in the French colonies in February 1794. While Campbell praised American and French decisions to ban slavery, he mentioned nothing about the political and intellectual context of the period in which Enlightenment ideals of equality and liberty informed radical political calls for 'universal manhood suffrage'.[59] Campbell used the same discourse of sentimentalism that many dissenting voices in Britain such as Joseph Priestly, Richard Price and William Wilberforce used in their attack against the trade.[60] In so doing, however, he mainly cared about the image of Britons in the eyes of others rather than about the suffering of slaves in British colonies. Campbell's was not an ideologically driven position: after all, he, though he was not involved in the slave trade, benefitted from Britain's imperial expansion, an expansion at the heart of which, to recall Sir Josiah Child, was the idea that expanding trade requires exchanging almost everything profitable the British lay their hands on.[61] Campbell's weak opposition to slavery was reflected in the fact that in subsequent editions and abridgements of his book (between 1796 and 1807) the texts critiquing his country's involvement in slave trade were axed. Campbell's critiques of slavery were removed from the new editions of his book published after the Coercion Act (1795), that is, in a period in which antislavery activism and publications were banned and accused of being sympathetic to French revolutionary and republican ideals.[62]

Conclusion

The key to understanding Campbell's views of Islam and Muslims begins with understanding the changing political scene in late eighteenth-century Britain and Europe. Donald Campbell, a Highlander of rank and status, wrote his travel book in a period in which conservative writers in Britain like Edmund Burke feared political and social change and actively sought to revive what Raymond Williams in *Culture and Society: 1780-1950* called 'the terms and accents' from the previous, classical, pre-commercial age of public spirit and virtue in order to ward off the danger of modern excesses and corruption (Williams 1960: 3).[63] The critique of conserving past traditions, which figured in the question posed by Mary Wollstonecraft in her *An Historical and Moral View of the Origin and*

Progress of the French Revolution and the Effects It Has Produced in Europe (1794), 'What then is to hinder man, at each epoch of civilization, from making a stand, and new modelling the materials, that have been hastily thrown into a rude mass, which time alone consolidated and rendered venerable?' was what mainly interested Campbell in his travel account (Wollstonecraft 1794: 15). Campbell's active engagement with defending the traditions of the past against the emerging calls for change, however, reflected a deep sense of loss. Campbell knew full well that old political and social traditions were no longer able to resist or push back against the deluge of change in late eighteenth-century Europe. Yet Campbell found in the idea of writing a travel narrative an opportunity to rethink the tension between radicalism and conservatism. He was the kind of traveller who showed how, to quote Vicesimus Knox's advice for travellers in 1782, 'If anything occurs injurious to the morals or political principles of one's own country, it ought to be either totally suppressed or represented with concomitant censure' (Knox 1787: I, 116). Such legitimation of censure was popular in conservative circles in Britain, but it also exercised Campbell's mind: it encouraged him to use Islam and the political culture of the Ottoman Empire to reflect on the moral, social and political conditions of Britain in the 1790s. And in so doing, he rethought the traditions of cultural differentiation inherent in European traditions of Orientalism. To that end, Campbell was keen on posing himself in his narrative as a man of Enlightenment cosmopolitanism.[64] But while Campbell's cosmopolitanism allowed him to rethink previous hostile attitudes to Islam and the Ottoman Empire, his knowledge of the region and the religion was limited. Indeed, Campbell assimilated Islamic moral and political traditions into the British political and moral experience. Thus, the Qur'an became the constitution of the Muslims, Prophet Muhammad a wise legislator and slaves obedient servants to their humane masters. It will become clear to the British reader well-versed in the political controversies of the period that all the tropes about Islam and Muslims in Campbell's narrative embed a political tension of late eighteenth-century Britain rather than the Ottoman Empire.

Still, Campbell did not essentialise the Muslims whom he encountered and socialised with; he did not see them as being part of an ontological frame of developmentalism that the Scottish Enlightenment philosophers had popularised throughout the century. Rather they figured in his account as the people whose cultural and political traditions offered a European traveller an opportunity to reflect on the corruption of modern Britons. In rethinking the prejudices in Europe about Arabs and Muslims, however, Campbell lent a dissenting voice which emphasised the danger and chaos of pursuing radical change in Europe although he did not deny the importance of reforms. For Campbell, Islam and Muslims were the material that helped him to reflect on the meaning of development in modern times. Campbell in 1795 offered a positive view on Islam, but such a view was dropped from all the editions and abridgements of his book after 1795.[65] In a period in which Britain's influence and power in the Ottoman Empire expanded on the eve of Napoleon Bonaparte's invasion of Egypt and Syria in 1799, Campbell's text kept appearing in print though without the positive views about Islam held in the 1795 edition. A change in the appreciation of Islamic cultures in the British travel writing scene was the result of new ways of understanding the idea of improvement in Britain. Improvement changed from being one of inclusion into what James

Morris Blaut called colonial 'diffusionism': an Enlightenment conception of improvement rooted in the idea of human diversity morphed into Romantic idealism, whose proponents measured the economic, political, and moral conditions of foreign nations and cultures against European standards of progress.[66]

Notes

1 Taylor, *Travels from England to India,* Vol II, 335.

2 Nigel Leask wrote about this blurring of boundaries between fiction and truth in many eighteenth-century travel books, arguing that 'the demotion of travel writing from the philosophical discourse to the realm of *belles-lettres*' was extremely *à la mode* during the period, *Curiosity and Aesthetics of Travel Writing: 1770–1840: From an Antique Land* (Oxford: Oxford University Press, 2002), 29. As early as 1754, *The Monthly Review* ridiculed travellers included scenes of fantasy and adventures in their accounts: those who wrote 'rencounters, shipwreck, and amors (most of which never happened to some travellers till they turned authors', *The Monthly Review of Literary Journal* (London: Printed for R. Griffiths, 1754), XI, 198. The part of Campbell's account which narrates his travels and adventures in India included many sentimental descriptions of his experience of being a captive in Haider Ali's prison. The Portuguese vessel which he joined in Goa was shipwrecked on its way to Madras. In 1782, Campbell was captured near the coast of Madras by Haider Ali's soldiers.

3 Major Sir Duncan Campbell, *Records of Clan Campbell in the Military Service of the East India Company 1600–1858* (New York; London: Longman: 1925), 93.

4 For a good account on the political alliances between clan Campbell and the British state, see John Tweed's *The House of Argyll And the Collateral Branches of the Clan Campbell from the Year 420 to the Present Time* (Glasgow: Houlston & Son, 1871). Sir Archibald Campbell (1682–1761), was the fourth Duke of Argyll. He was an avid supporter of the act of Union between England and Scotland. In 1711, as Tweeds notes, 'he was made Justice-General of Scotland; in 1711 he was called to the Privy Council, and in 1714, upon the accession of George the First, he was nominated Lord Register of Scotland. Though he had given up all command in the army, yet, at the breaking out of the Rebellion in 1715, he took to the field in defence of the House of Hanover, and was of signal service to the cause', 68.

5 Henry Lee, *History of the Campbell family* (New York: R.L Polk and Company, 1920), 134–137.

6 Upon the termination of his service in 1784, Campbell was awarded 'an annuity of £200' as an acknowledgement of 'the eminent Services' in the East India Company, *Records of Clan Campbell,* 97.

7 See chapter seven in Paul Keen's *Literature, Commerce and the Spectacle for Modernity* (Cambridge: Cambridge University Press, 2012). A good account on the political controversies of the period is Janet Todd's introduction to Mary Wollstonecraft's *A Vindication of the Rights of Women, A Vindication of the Rights of Men* and *An Historical and Moral View of the Origin and Progress of the French Revolution* (Oxford: Oxford University Press, 1993).

8 For almost all critics who traced the connection between outward colonial projects and inward bourgeoise culture, eighteenth-century sentimentalism was an apt mode of representing cross-cultural encounters. See Lynn Festa, *Sentimental Figures of Empire in Eighteenth-Century Britain and France* (Baltimore: John Hopkins University Press, 2006), 2.

9 Andrew Rudd notes: 'Sentimental literature was addressed to a modern readership and, in portraying scenarios that were rooted in modern life, aspired to be an instrument of moral edification', *Sympathy and India in British Literature 1770–1830* (New York: Palgrave, 2011), 7. *The British Critic, A New Review* in 1795 mentioned how Campbell was 'a man of [...] not a little delicacy of sentiment' who 'appears in the character, not of a philosopher, but that of an affectionate and fond parent, pouring forth all his mind to his son' (London: 1795), 112; 116.

10 On the eighteenth-century radical conception of improvement in Europe, see Jonathan's Israel's *Radical Enlightenment: Philosophy and the Making of Modernity* 1650–1750 (Oxford: Oxford University Press, 2001); *Revolutionary Ideas: An Intellectual History of the French Revolution from The Rights of Man to Robespierre* (Princeton: Princeton University Press, 2015). See the collections

of essay *Enlightenment and Religion: Rational Dissent in Eighteenth-Century Britain*, ed. Knud Haakonssen (Cambridge: Cambridge University Press, 1996).

11 Many studies examined the battle of ideas between radicals and conservatives during the period, but a few contributions in the field stand out: H. T. Dickenson, *The Politics of the People in Eighteenth-Century Britain* (London: Macmillan, 1994); The collection of essays in *The French Revolution and British Popular Politics*, ed. Mark Philip (Cambridge: Cambridge University Press, 1991); J.R. Dinwiddy, *Radicalism and Reform in Britain, 1780–1850* (London: The Hambeldon Press, 1992). Frank M. Turner, 'Introduction' in Edmund Burke's *Reflections on the Revolution in France*, ed. Frank M. Turner (New Haven: Yale University Press, 2003), xiv.

12 On how Islam and 'Mahomet' became useful material in the pamphlet wars between orthodox and dissenting writers in Britain, see the first and second chapters in Garcia's *Islam and the English Enlightenment.*

13 Peter W. Walker's 'Tolerating Protestants: Anti-Popery, Anti-Puritanism and Religious Toleration in Britain, 1776–1829' in *Against Popery: Britain, Empire and Anti-Catholicism,* ed. Evan Haefeli (Charlottesville and London: The University of Virginia Press, 2020), 257–288; see page 278.

14 Stuart Andrews, *Unitarian Radicalism: Political Rhetoric, 1770–1814* (Basingstoke: Palgrave, 2003), 85–94.

15 British defenders of the established political and religious order in Europe often accused French revolutionists and their radical supporters in Britain of being the acolytes of 'Mahomet'; they rejected Christian beliefs and ritualistic methods of worship and instead advocated a new religion rooted in the oneness of the deity, 'The Supreme Being'. This critique of 'Mahomet' and his radical supporters in Europe appeared in Francis Pages' *Secret History of the French Revolution*, 2 vols (London: Printed for T. N Longman, 1797), I, 154. On the debate in Europe about how Islam was a subject of fascination for many radicals in France in the wake of the French Revolution, see Ian Coller's *Muslims and Citizen: Islam, Politics and the French Revolution* (New Haven and London: Yale University Press, 2020).

16 For example, in *Socinianism Unmasked: In Four Letters to the Lay-Members of the Church of Ayr,* the Scottish scholar and pastor John Jamison associated prominent philosophers in Europe (David Hume, Henry St John, 1st Viscount Bolingbroke and Voltaire) with atheism and suggested that these men would prefer the 'Koran' over the Bible. In flirting with the idea that dissenters in Europe considered the Qur'an as superior to the Bible, Jamison responded to the Socinians in Scotland who doubted the divinity of Christ and poured 'contempt on the scripture'; *Socinianism unmasked* (Edinburgh, 1787), 133.

17 George Sale whose translation of the Qur'an appeared in 1734 took it that 'The Koran being the Mohammedans rule of faith and practise [...]', 68.

18 John V. Tolan, *Saracens: Islam in Medieval European Imagination* (New York: Columbia University Press, 2002), 137.

19 Historians of the late eighteenth-century Ottoman Empire might note that Campbell's choice of words about the Qur'an being the constitution of the Ottoman state is troubling. The eighteenth-century Ottoman Empire never declared that the Qur'an was its constitution. Rather, in a late eighteenth-century period known for the high aspirations among Ottoman officials, most notably Sultan Selim III, for secular reforms, a religious law known as *Sharia* was still considered the main law or *Kanun* of the state. The *Sharia* law here was God's law which Muslims need to abide by in every aspect of their lives. The first secular turn in the Ottoman Empire was the writing of the constitution in 1876; the constitution appeared in a period in which European powers, Britain and France, increasingly pressurised the Ottoman officials to seek reforms in the law and the machinery of the state. See Cemil Kocak's 'Transforming Through Constitution: Young Ottoman and the Kanun-i-Esasi of 1876' in *Dimensions of Transformation in the Ottoman Empire from the Late Medieval Age to Modernity*, ed. Seyfi Kenan and Selcuk Askin Somel (Leiden: Brill, 2021), 399–440.

20 Campbell saw the Qur'an as the constitution of the Ottoman state in a period in which radical aspirations for writing new laws advocating freedom and liberty for ordinary people were soaring high in Britain and the rest of the Western world: the Americans gained independence from England and then wrote their own constitution (1787) and in the same year in which the American constitution was ratified, that is in 1789, the French abolished their monarchy and introduced a republican government.

21 Edward Gibbon, *The History of the Decline and Fall of the Roman Empire* (London, 1788), Vol 6, 372. William Robertson, *The History of the Reign of the Emperor Charles V*, 5 vols (London, 1769), Vol 1, 391.

22 The image of a ruler with a sword was common trope in British writings about Muslim political leaders. One book, a play by James Miller titled *Mahomet the impostor : A tragedy. Taken from the manager's book, at the Theatre Royal, Drury-Lane* appeared in print in 1790 in London. The title page of the play is preceded by a cover image of 'Mahomet' standing firm and angry with a sword ready to be unsheathed for a quick strike.

23 On the origin and value of Wilkes' political radicalism during the period, Peter D.G. Thomas' *John Wilkes: A Friend to Liberty* (Oxford: Clarendon Press, 1996). On the culture of radicalism in Britain during the last decades of the eighteenth century in which Wilkes was an effective operator, see Anthony Page's *John Jebb and the Enlightenment Origin of British Radicalism* (Westport: Praeger Publishers, 2003), 259.

24 A good discussion on this topic can be pursued in Justin du Rivage's *Revolution Against Empire: Taxes, Politics, and the Origins of American Independence* (New Haven and London: Yale University Press, 2017).

25 According to John Barrell, ' in 1795 the government succeeded in passing, against widespread opposition, the 'two bills' which enlarged the definition of high treason, increased the penalty for seditious libel, and deprived the London Corresponding Society of what had become its most potent weapon, the open air mass-meeting', *The Spirit of Despotism: Invasion of Privacy in the 1790s* (Oxford: Oxford University Press, 2006), 4. On parliamentary measure against 'seditious writings' and freedom of speech, see chapter seven in Eric J. Evans, *William Pitt The Younger* (London: Routledge, 1999).

26 This quote is from Steve Poole's 'Not Precedents to Be Followed, But Examples to be Weighed: John Thelwall and the Jacobin Sense of the Past' in *John Thelwall: Radical Romantic and Acquitted Felon* (2009; Abingdon: Routledge, 2016), 170.

27 In 1755, Francoise Baron de Tott was in Constantinople. He visited the city after he was appointed a secretary to the French ambassador. In his account about the great fire in the city, Tott mentioned the story about the people's refusal to sell their properties to the government which had set out to tackle the problem of fires in the city by expanding public roads. Tott did not mention that the clergy defended the people against the government. He did not confirm the point which Campbell made that the Muslim clergy were defenders of people's properties. Rather he explained the reason why the Sultan failed to secure the concession of the people to sell their properties by referring to the lack of trust between the people and their rulers. See his *Memoires of Baron De Tott.* [...] *of The Manners and Customs of the Turks and Tartars*, Vol 1, 51.

28 Jeremy Black, *Natural and Necessary Enemies* (London: Duckworth, 1986), 161. The inhabitants of Toulouse, as Voltaire in his treatise on toleration wrote, in 1763 were still celebrating 'with procession and fireworks' the massacre of 'four thousand heretical citizens two hundred years ago', *Toleration and Other Essays by Voltaire*, Trans. Joseph McCabe (London and New York: G. P Putnam's Sons, 1912), 4.

29 See the introduction to Ian Haywood and John Seed's *The Gordon Riots: Politics, Culture and Insurrection in Late Eighteenth-Century Britain* (Cambridge: Cambridge University Press, 2012), 2.

30 For a wider analysis of the thorny issue of Catholic emancipation in late eighteenth and early nineteenth-century Britain, see Peter W. Walker's 'Tolerating Protestants: Anti-Popery, Anti-Puritanism and Religious Toleration in Britain, 1776–1829', 257–288. On the history of British anti-Catholic sentiments, see Antonia Fraser's *The King and the Catholics: England, Ireland, and the Fight for Religious Freedom, 1780–1829* (New York: Knopf Doubleday Publishing, 2018).

31 Campbell was not different from European travellers of upper-class backgrounds who did not hesitate to show their readers how the most tolerant and cosmopolitan people one could find in Muslim societies would be those from the upper classes, landowners, rich merchants and powerful rulers. Lord Charlemont's conversations with the rich and ruling classes of Istanbul in the 1740s clearly show this. See the chapter titled 'A meeting with A Sensible Turk' in *The Travels of Lord Charlemont in Greece and Turkey*, 176–183. See also the great admiration Miss Tully (the sister-in-law of the British ambassador at the court of Tripoli between 1783–1796) showed in her description of the polite and refined character of Sidy Hamet, the

eldest son of Ali Pasha Karamanli, who ruled Libya between 1754–1793, *Narrative of Ten Years' Residence at Tripoli in Africa* (London: Printed for Henry Colburn, 1816), 253.

32 As Henry Prideaux wrote: 'And to this purpose was it that he so often inculcated it into them that his doctrine was to be propagated by the Sword, and that all would receive the Faith which he preached, must fight for it', *The true nature of imposture fully display'd in the life of Mahomet; with a Discourse annex'd for the vindicating of Christianity from this charge; offered to the consideration of the deists of the present age* (London: Printed for William Rogers, 1698), 52.

33 Denis Lacorne, *The Limits of Tolerance: Enlightenment Values and Religious Fanaticism* (New York: Columbia University Press, 2019), 77.

34 A good account on how Islam were viewed by many in Enlightenment Europe as a rational and tolerant region in comparison to a superstitious Christianity is Nabil Matar's introduction to *Henry Stubbe and the Beginning of Islam: The Origin and Progress of Mahometanism* (New York: Columbia University Press, 2014). See also James R. Jacobs's *Henry Stubbe, Radical Protestantism and the Early Enlightenment* (Cambridge: Cambridge University Press, 1983).

35 Yusuf ibn Siman as-Simani, known in Europe as Giuseppe Simone Assemani, was born on 27 August 1687 in Hasroun, Mount Lebanon. When very young he was sent to the Marionite College in Rome and was transferred thence to the Vatican Library. After he was appointed librarian of the Vatican library, he began to work on his *Bibliotheca Orientalis Clementino-Vaticana in qua manuscriptos codices Syriacos, Arabicos, Persicos, Turcicos, Hebraicos, Samaritanos, Armenicos, Aethiopicos, Graecos, Aegyptiacos, Ibericos, et Malabaricos, jussu et munificentia Clementis XI Pontificis Maximi ex Oriente conquisitos, comparatos, et Bibliotecae Vaticanae addictos Recensuit, digessit, et genuina scripta a spuriis secrevit, addita singulorum auctorum vita, Joseph Simonius Assemanus, Syrus Maronita* (Rome, 1719–1728), 9 vols folio.

36 Lacorne, *The Limits of Tolerance*, 3–4.

37 Black, *Geographies of an Imperial Power*, 169.

38 Ibid., 169.

39 Indeed, in European writings about the Middle East, this dichotomy concerning the coffeehouse, being the space of pleasure rather than reason, goes back to the early modern period. Some early modern European travel accounts about the Ottoman Empire, as Markman Ellis showed, posited the Ottoman coffeehouse as a space of conviviality but also one which encourages irreligious pleasures, *The Coffee-House: A Cultural History* (London: Phoenix, 2011). George Sandys, who visited the Levant in 1610, was fascinated with the culture of conviviality and coffee-drinking in the coffeehouse. Yet he noted the permissive sexual culture in the Ottoman coffeehouse. The owners of coffeehouses, he noted, keep 'beautiful boys, who serve as stales to procure them customers', *A Relation of a Journey*, 66. As Islam was often described in early modern European accounts as a religion of the flesh, such an image of an 'un-Christian' pleasure that exists in a Muslim coffeehouse would not strike the early modern reader as a being rather odd.

40 On coffeehouse culture in Enlightenment Europe, see for instance Jürgen Habermas, *The Structural Trans- formation of the Public Sphere: An Inquiry into a Category of Bourgeois Society*, trans. Thomas Burger (Cambridge: MIT Press, 1989); on the radical correspondence societies and coffeehouses, see E. P. Thompson, *The Making of the English Working Class* (London: Victor Gollanz, 1963); on free-thinking print culture and coffeehouses, see for instance Robert Darnton, *Literary Underground in the Old Regime* (Cambridge: Harvard University Press, 1982); Jon Mee, *Dangerous Enthusiasm: William Blake and the Culture of Radicalism in the 1790s* (Oxford, UK: Clarendon, 1992); and Kevin Gilmartin, *Print Politics: The Press and Radical Opposition in Early Nineteenth- Century Britain* (New York: Cambridge University Press, 1996). On urbanity, commercialism and politeness in the coffeehouse in England, see Lawrence Klein's 'Coffee-House Civility, 1660–1714: An Aspect of Pos-Courtly Culture in England', *Huntington Library Quarterly* 59:1 (1996), 30–51.

41 The corruption of Ottoman judges often fascinated eighteenth-century British travellers in the Ottoman Empire. In their different ways, British travellers often used their observations of Ottoman legal practices to critique the legal and political system in Europe. One such example appeared in the traveller diary of Lord Charlemont who critiqued the corruption of Ottoman judges but also admired the speedy processes in the Ottoman legal system. See *The Travels of Lord Charlemont in Greece and Turkey*, 213–216.

42 Jon Mee, Print, *Publicity, and Popular Radicalism in the 1790s: The Laurel of Liberty* (Cambridge: Cambridge University Press, 2016), 48–49.

43 While the English coffeehouses were, in the first half of the eighteenth century, associated with the rise of bourgeoise culture of civility and politeness, wrote Trevor Harvey Levere and Gerard L'Estrange, '[i]t was in the latter half of the eighteenth century that some coffeehouses began to be associated with radical learnings. Joseph Priestly, before his association with the Coffeehouse Society, had been a member of a club that met at St Paul's Coffee House in St Paul's Churchyard. Other members of that club included Benjamin Franklin, who was in England acting for the government of Philadelphia, and Richard Price, a mathematician and Unitarian minister whose essay of 1789 on the French Revolution was to provoke Edmund Paine's Reflections on the Revolution in France (1790)', *Discussing Chemistry and Steam: The Minutes of a Coffee House Philosophical Society, 1780–1789* (Oxford: Oxford University Press, 2002), 3.

44 Gregory Claeys, *Thomas Paine: Social and Political Thought* (London: Unwin Hyman, 1989), 99. On the distinction between conservative and liberal views of economics and politics, see the chapter on the difference between the conservative Edmund Burke and the radical Thomas Paine in Yuval Levin's *The Great Debate: Edmund Burke, Thomas Paine and the Birth of Right and Left* (New York: Basic Books, 2014); see chapter four. See also the introduction to Collins' *Commerce and Manners.*

45 Despite the plethora of studies on the traditions of slavery in the Ottoman and English imperial spheres, there is still a gap about connected histories, tropes and perceptions in British and Ottoman traditions of slavery. On how the traditions of slavery in eighteenth-century Britain dominated the discourse of sentimentalism, see Lynn Festa, *Sentimental Figures of Empire in Eighteenth-Century Britain and France* (Baltimore: John Hopkins University Press, 2006); Markman Ellis, *The Politics of Sensibility* (Cambridge: Cambridge University Press, 1996); Brycchan Carey, *British Abolitionism and the Rhetoric of Sensibility: Writing, Sentiment and Slavery 1760–1807* (London: Palgrave, 2005). On the tradition of slavery in the Ottoman Empire, see Y. Hakan Erdem, *Slavery in the Ottoman Empire and its Demise 1800–1909* (Basingstoke: Palgrave, 1996); Madeline C. Zilfi, *Women and Slavery in the Late Ottoman Empire* (Cambridge: Cambridge University Press, 2010); Ehud Rafael Toledano, *Slavery and Abolition in the Ottoman Middle East* (Seattle: University of Washington Press, 1998); Nur Sobers-Khan, 'Slavery in the Early-Modern Ottoman Empire' in *The Cambridge World History of Slavery*, Vol II, ed. Craig Perry, David Eltis, Stanley L. Engerman, and David Richardson (Cornwall: TJ Books Limited, 2021).

46 See Doris L Garraway's 'Black Athena: Universal History, Colonisation, and the African Origin of Civilisation in Post-Revolutionary Haitian Writing' in *Enlightened Colonialism Civilization Narratives and Imperial Politics in the Age of Reason*, ed. Damien Tricoire (New York: Palgrave, 2017).

47 William O. Blake, *The History of Slavery and the Slave Trade, Ancient and Modern* (Ohio: H. Miller, 1861), 189.

48 See the introduction to J.R Oldfield's *Popular Politics and British Anti-Slavery: The Mobilisation of Public Opinion Against Slave Trade 1787–1807* (London: Routledge, 1998).

49 It is remarkable that Campbell chose to represent the Tatar guide as a brilliant horseman who delivers travellers and dispatches across Ottoman cities. But he also, deliberately, I suggest, presented him as a trader in slaves. During the eighteenth century, the common trope in British writings about the traditions of slavery in the Ottoman Empire was that the Crimean 'Turks', commonly known at the time as 'Tartars', were constantly attacking Christian villages in eastern and central Europe to supply slaves for the markets of Istanbul, Cairo and Aleppo. See Aaron Hill's *A Full and Just Account of the Present State of the Ottoman Empire*, 88.

50 John Jackson wrote: 'Some have attempted', he wrote, 'to travel under the character of the Tartar's servants[…].; but the Author considers this as too degrading for the character of an Englishman', *Journey from India Towards England,* xii.

51 Alexander Russell, *The Natural History of Aleppo*, Vol I, 217–221.

52 Russel recalled how the upper classes in Istanbul, 'bought' white slaves 'from Georgia and Circassia' (218). He further mentioned that 'if they [slaves] happen to distinguish themselves by their talents and application, they are almost certain of being one time or other emancipated', Vol I, 217.

53 Russell, whose account Campbell knew well, mentioned how 'The white slaves are purchased on the frontiers of Georgia, by certain merchants who make a trade of it, and by whom they

are transported to different parts of the Empire, but chiefly to Constantinople: some are bought every year to Aleppo, directly from Erzroon', Vol I, 218. In *The Fair Syrian* (1787), Robert Bage wrote about how an English woman, Honoria Warren whose father was a merchant in Syria, and another Georgian slave, Amina, were captured and sold as slaves in the markets of Aleppo. Bage never travelled in Syria. Bage, however, unlike Russell who mentioned how merchants protect their white slaves 'from violation', showed how slaves, mainly white women, were often preyed upon by cruel and primitive Muslim men. For Bage, Muslims' cruelty towards their white female slaves is part of their religion. '[T]hat horrid bear, Mahomet, with his lock-up houses for women', Honoria Warren's interlocutor Lady Bembridge recalled, 'is my aversion', *The Fair Syrian: A Novel* (Dublin, 1787), vol II. 31. Another account that touched on the tradition of enslaving white females among Ottoman elites appeared in the letters of Miss Tully, the sister of the English ambassador to Tripoli, Richard Tully, who lived in Libya between 1783 and 1793: see her *Narrative of a Ten-Year Residence at Tripoli in Africa* (London, 1818), 54–55; 73–76. The theme of 'Turks' capturing 'fair' Christians triggered the imagination of late eighteenth-century British dramatists: see Hannah Cowley's popular play *A Day in Turkey or the Russian Slaves: A Comedy* (London, 1792). In European writings about slavery in the Ottoman Empire, white slaves never appeared as labourers or engaged with any kind of drudgery, unlike black servants who worked in elite households. They were mostly men who were able to make it to the top jobs in the empire or women who enjoyed the privilege of being loved and looked after by rich and powerful Ottoman men. This observation was also made by Diane Robinson Dunn in her 'French and English Orientalisms and the Study of Slavery and Abolition in North Africa and the Middle East: What are the Connections?' in *Slavery in the Islamic World: Its Characteristics and Commonality* (New York: Palgrave, 2019), 57. On how white Georgian and Circassian slaves rose to power in Ottoman-Arab land throughout the eighteenth century, see Longrigg, 163–186.

54 Ali Bey ruled Egypt between 1768 and 1773. According to Sauveur Lusignan, a Greek traveller and merchant, Ali was born in Abkhazia as 'Joseph [...]in the year 1728 and nothing remarkable happened to him till he was thirteen years old, when being on a hunting party in a neighbouring wood, with some companions of his own age, they fell into the hands of a band of men, who make it their business to maraud in Circassia, Mingrelia, and Georgia, and to steal children, in order to steal them into other parts', *A History of the Revolt of Ali Bey, Against the Ottoman Porte* (London, 1784), 70. Also Ahmad Pasha Al-Jazzar Pasha, known as the butcher, was a Bosnian slave. As Andrew James McGrego wrote, 'Ahmad has sold himself into slavery as a youth and eventually found himself in Cairo, where he was trained as a Mamluk and served his master as an assassin', *A Military History of Modern Egypt: From the Ottoman Conquest to the Ramadan War* (Westport and London: Praeger Security International, 2006), 40.

55 Nathan Alcock, *The Rise of Mahomet Accounted for on Natural and Civil Principles* (London, 1796), 17–18.

56 Malcolm Yapp states that 'of twelve Ottoman grand viziers in the period 1785–1808 at least five were by origin the slaves of pashas', *The Making of the Modern Near East 1792–1923* (London: Routledge, 1987), 3. See also Longrigg, 165 and Ives, 285.

57 The traveller in the Levant, William George Browne, a contemporary of Campbell, mentioned in his travel account how the master is legally compelled to sell his slave in case the later feels 'discontented with his master' and 'the child of a female slave begotten by her master, is *ipso facto* free, and a slave may authorize a free person to purchase his emancipation', *Travels in Africa, Egypt and Syria*, 48–49.

58 Carey, 41.

59 In 1791, Anna Letittia Barbauld published a poem defending the abolition of slavery and critiquing the spread of luxury in commercial British, *An Epistle to William Wilberforce, EsQ* (London, 1791). Other literary voices appeared in the 1790s. Robert Southey and William Coleridge were also critics of the excessiveness and cruelty which the expansion of commercial culture ushered into Britain. A good analysis on these two romantic writers' views on commercialism and slave trade is Carl Bolton's first chapter in his *Writing the Empire: Robert Southey and Romantic Colonialism* (London: Pickering& Chatto, 2007). See also Ian Blackburn, *The Overthrow of Colonial Slavery 1776–1848* (London: Verso, 1988), 139.

60 A good account on the connection during the period between sentimentalism, dissent and anti-slavery rhetoric is *Christine Levecq's Slavery and Sentiment: The Politics of Feeling in Black Atlantic Antislavery Writing, 1770–850* (New Hampshire: University of New Hampshire Press, 2012).

61 Josiah Child, *A New Discourse of Trade* (London, 1698).

62 Blackburn, 147.

63 On the controversy surrounding the political radicalism of the period , see Marilyn Butler's *Jane Austen and the War of Ideas* (Oxford: Oxford University Press, 1987).

64 Campbell's travel book appeared in the same year in which Emmanuel Kant published his political pamphlet *Towards Perpetual Peace* in which he argued for the practice of cosmopolitan political rights based on 'the relations among civil persons to each other', as Seyla Benhabib wrote, 'as well as to organised political entity in global civil society', *Another Cosmopolitanism* (Oxford: Oxford University Press, 2006), 21. For Kant, as Pauline Kleingeld showed, 'cosmopolitanism is an attitude taken up in acting: an attitude of recognition, respect, openness, interest, beneficence, and concern toward other human individuals, cultures, and peoples as members of one global community', *Kant and Cosmopolitanism: The Philosophical Ideal of World Citizenship* (Cambridge: Cambridge University Press, 2012), 1. This attitude was also reflected in Campbell's travel account, particularly in the part of the narrative in which he critiqued prejudiced European representations of Islam and Prophet Muhammad.

65 All the subsequent editions and abridgements of Campbell's narrative that appeared in England after 1795 removed the parts in the 1795 edition which revealed positive views about Islam and the Ottoman Empire. These editions also removed the views which critiqued European slave trading practices. The following title appeared in Britain between 1796 and 1801: *A Narrative of Extraordinary Adventures and Sufferings by Shipwreck & Imprisonment of Donald Campbell, EsQ. Of BARBRECK with The Singular Humours of His Tartar Guide, Hassan Artaz Comprising The Occurrence of Four Years and Five Days, Overland Journey To India* (This book appeared in at least in four editions between 1796 and 1801). Another title appeared in 1807: *Shipwreck and Captivity of Captain Donald on Leaving Goa for Madras, May 21 1782[...] Interspersed with Several Curious Anecdotes.* As the titles of these abridgements indicate, Captain Campbell's travel and career in the East had less to do with improving the morals and manners of British readers – as we saw in the chapter – than to offer them sensationally entertaining accounts of British heroism in the East. These titles appeared in several editions and sold an enormous amount of copies.

66 Blaut, *The Colonizer's Model of the World.*

CONCLUSION
TRAVELS OF MIRZA ABU TALEB KHAN IN ASIA, AFRICA AND EUROPE DURING THE YEARS 1799, 1800, 1801, 1802 AND 1803: AN ISLAMIC RESPONSE TO ENLIGHTENMENT IMPROVEMENT

He who knows others is wise;
He who knows himself is enlightened.

—*Laozi* (Sixth century BC)

Mirza Abu Taleb Khan was born in 1752 in Lucknow to a family with Persian and Turkish roots. His father served as an assistant to Mohammed Culy Khan, the nephew of Abul Mansur Khan, better known as Safdar Jung who served as the nawab of Oudh (now Awadh) in the Mogul court between 1739 and 1754. Abu Taleb rose to be the *Aumildar* (tax collector) of Etawah and several other districts under the government of Asaf-ad-Daula (1748–1797), the nawab of Oudh. But after Asaf-ad-Daula died, Abu Taleb's life in Oudeh radically changed. The new nawab, Hyder Beg Khan, turned against him because of an old rivalry between him and Abu Taleb. In this new political development in Oudh, Abu Taleb found himself unemployed and unable to provide for his family: 'all my dependents and adherents, seeing my distress, left me, and even some of my children [...] abandoned me. I was quite overcome with grief and despondency' (Khan 1810: I, 5).[1] At this point in his life, he tried to find patronage and employment in the East India Company (EIC), relying on his friendship with influential British officials such as Lord Cornwallis and Sir John Shore. But they did nothing for him apart from floating the idea that the EIC might offer him a position as a Persian and Arabic instructor to its civil servants.

His Scottish friend David Richardson, an officer in the EIC, convinced him to travel to Europe and offered to bear all the costs of the journey. Abu Taleb accepted the offer. On his way to Britain in 1799, he stopped at Cape Town in South Africa and visited Dublin and Cork before reaching London where he stayed until June 1802. On the way back, Abu Taleb visited Paris, Genoa, Istanbul, Diarbekar, Mosul, Baghdad and Basra where he joined an EIC ship departing for India. He wrote a travel account about his journey to Europe by sea and back to India overland. The Persian manuscript was circulated originally among his friends and acquaintances upon his return to India in 1803. It was presented to Joseph Taylor, a captain in the Bengal Artillery, and it finally reached Charles Stewart, professor of Oriental Languages at Haileybury College, who translated it into English. This translation was published in 1810 as *Travels of Mirza Abu Taleb Khan in Asia, Africa, and Europe, During the Years 1799, 1800, 1801, 1802, and 1803, Written by Himself* and reissued in 1814, with translations into French and German. The book was the first travel account of Europe published by a Muslim of Southeast Asian origin.[2]

The early nineteenth-century reader versed in the genre of travel writing would note that Abu Talib's travel book shared one important trope with the British travel books written about India and the Levant. Abu Taleb shared with Carmichael, Parsons, Ives, Abbott, Irwin and Campbell – the travellers studied in this book – the idea that travelling and writing one's travel experiences are essentially improving exercises. As he wrote of the improving objective of writing his travel account, the idea of describing the 'curiosities' and 'wonders' of foreign travels and giving an account of 'the manners and customs of various nations' little known to the people of Asia 'would afford a gratifying banquet to his countrymen' (Khan 1810: I, 4). He often recalled in his travel book how he socialised with European and Muslim elites on cities and routes between India and Europe, showing how these social opportunities enabled him to reflect on the political and religious conditions of his nation. To that end, he shared with the travel writers and travellers which this book examined another important trope: that is, the idea that the more a nation encourages material improvement, the closer they it is to becoming civilised. In Europe, Abu Taleb was intrigued with the prospects of seeing improved land, enclosed gardens and prosperous manufacturing towns. He admired European commercial, scientific, agricultural, medical and artistic improvements to the extent that he encouraged his co-religionists in Asia to learn from Europeans. 'Many of the customs, inventions, sciences, and ordinances of Europe', he wrote, 'the good effects of which are apparent in those countries might with great advantage be imitated by Mohammedans' (Khan 1810: I, xxxv).

Nevertheless, Abu Taleb was aware that much of the wealth that enabled Europeans to show great improvements in sciences, arts, medicine and the art of government was collected in the context of relinquishing older virtues. 'The first and greatest defect I observed in the English', he wrote, 'is their want of faith in religion, and their great inclination to philosophy (atheism)' (Khan 1810: II, 28). Upon expressing his admiration of the many 'curiosities' he saw in the British Museum, Abu Taleb regretted that 'all Nature has been ransacked to procure them' (Ibid., I, 194-5). Abu Taleb admired European progress. Yet he was aware of the complex moral dilemma surrounding it. He had no doubt that Britons managed to improve their material conditions. But there is another view of England in his account, one rooted in war, pillage, violence and ecological disasters. 'By means of their navy', which is the 'principal source of their wealth', Abu Taleb wrote, 'they can at all times send an army to invade their enemy's country' (Khan 1810: I, 225).

Abu Taleb's response to modern Europe is indicative of the wider impact of European ideas of progress on the elite and reformers of Islamic cultures. His praise of European improvements in scientific, mechanical and industrial fields resembles that of Rifa'a al-Tahtawi, an Egyptian reformer who went to France in 1826 with the hope of learning about Europeans.[3] Al-Tahtawi's journey was funded by Muhammad Ali (1770–1849), the ruler of Egypt who led a reforming project aiming to modernise the army, agriculture and government and hoped to benefit from the European experience in these fields. But, unlike al-Tahtawi, Abu Taleb was not the kind of Muslim traveller who, as Daniel Newman argued, thought about the rise of Europe in binary terms: that is, European progress meant the defeat of Islam. For Newman, the travel account of the Egyptian cleric, first published in 1834 under the title *Takhlis al Ibriz fi Talkhis Bariz* (The extraction of gold or an overview of Paris), showed fascinations with European technical progress but also revealed painful critiques of the moral laxity of Europeans: these critiques were 'a way of compensating for the feelings of inferiority regarding the technologically and scientifically advanced Europe', Newman wrote (Newman 2004: 89).

Newman's analysis of the global reach of modernity was one of 'collision' between Islam and Europe, an idea which found mention in Christopher de Bellaigue's *The Islamic Enlightenment: The Struggle Between Faith and Reason, 1798 to Modern Times* (2017), in which modernity appeared as a European gift to the world that Muslims have 'to concede that only by adopting Western practices and technologies could they avoid political and economic oblivion' (Bellaigue 2017: xix). The attitude that Abu Taleb showed in his travel account towards European progress rather belongs to the strand of global modernity studied by Marshal Hodgson in his *The Venture of Islam* (1974), one in which 'Most temperaments and most facets of experience that are to be found in major tradition can be found in corresponding traditions elsewhere' (Hodgson 1974: I, 36). Rethinking the discourse of diffusion and collision in European studies of Islamic cultures, Hodgson argues that Europeans had no monopoly on definitions of modernity. De Bellaigue, however, found that the effort in Islamic cultures to modernise – that is, using European educational and political methods rooted in sciences and reason – was nothing more than a form of 'conceding' to the West and a 'collision of Western and Islamic civilisations that accompanied Napoleon's invasion of Egypt in 1798' (Bellaigue 2017: xxvii).

Bellaigue's position, however, is not new in the Western scholarship about what Bernard Lewis called 'the Muslim discovery of Europe'.[4] It harks back to the time when Abu Taleb's book appeared in the English press. In the preface to the first edition of *Travels of Mirza Abu Taleb Khan*, Stewart called Abu Taleb 'an intelligent foreigner' (Khan 1810: vi). Europeans are accustomed to reading travel books written by Europeans about Asians, but Abu Taleb, he added, reversed the trend. Steward gave a positive gloss on this reversal when he assured his reader that Abu Taleb is a different 'Asiatic': he is a man of 'liberal curiosity' (Khan 1810: I, vi). Upon its appearance in print, the *Travels* received mixed reviews, but one idea that was shared among commentators was that the writer is not typically an 'Asiatic' or Muslim: that is, his observations of the manners, traditions and values of Europeans did not include what Europeans are accustomed to reading in satirical books in which Eastern characters, such as the Chinese philosopher in Oliver Goldsmith's *Citizens of the World* (1762) and the Persian nobles Uzbek and Reza in Montesquieu's *Lettres Persanes* (1721), offered emotionally charged critiques of European culture. As *The Monthly Review* put it in 1811, Abu Taleb Khan did not offer 'exaggerated descriptions' of Europe (1810: 387). Abu Taleb, according to the *Monthly Review*, did not write in the manners of an Oriental overtly taken aback by European progress because his close connections with Britons in India and Europe meant that his first-hand experience of them taught him about their virtues and vices. As *the Monthly Review* put it, 'we may deem ourselves fortunate that we have now an opportunity to trace the real, though in some instances not very vivid, impressions which our various systems, avocations, etc. have upon the mind of an Asiatic [...]' (1810: 387). *The Critical Review* (1811), further, praised the disenchanted and 'real' style in Abu Taleb's book, attributing its credible reporting to the traveller's familiarity with European culture. 'His object appears to exhibit a plain, unvarnished account of what he saw and heard; and though inflation of style is ascribed to the Asiatics, there is no trace of this defect in the prose of Abu Taleb' (1810: 38). *The British Critic* stated that some might doubt the authenticity of the travels but given that the translator of Abu Taleb's account, Stewart, is widely respected in England, the book should be considered as an authentic account with an amusing and instructive commentary on European cultures and manners. *The British Critic* in 1811 called Abu Taleb 'an enlightened foreigner' because his comments on the vices of the English showed 'great originality of thinking' (1810: 274). His enlightenment was also shown in the book when it appears that he kept his 'habits' and 'prejudices' as 'remote and opposite as possible': that is, Abu Taleb commented on the character of the English as an enlightened man – not as a Muslim or Persian – who did not let his religious views get in the way of appreciating European culture (1810: 274). As these comments on Abu Taleb's book show, an enlightened man cannot be Muslim.

Abu Taleb's book has been studied by many scholars of cross-cultural encounters, almost all of whom concluded that he was not uncritically admiring of European cultures and manners. None of them, however, cared to examine the impact of his Islamic background on the way he approached modernity. Two lines of thought appeared in the scholarship about Abu Taleb's book: some postcolonial scholars associated the book with the idea of co-opting British views in which Asian cultures appeared inferior to those of the Europeans.[5] Other scholars, however, found in his book moments of resistance and what Claire Chambers called 'reverse Orientalism', a form of writing back to Western colonial discourse (Chambers 2015: 35). Despite their cooperation with colonisers, Indian travellers like Abu Taleb, Michael Fisher argues, remained 'staunch advocates of their own religions and customs' (Fisher 2004: 106).[6] Influenced by latest developments in the scholarship about global history, recent scholars situated Abu Taleb's book in a historical context of encounters between global elites from different cultures, which, as Humberto Garcia has recently shown, complicates polarising views of history that purge 'polycentric modernity from a historical teleology in which past multivalent possibilities are denied and made tributary to future nations and empires' (Garcia 2020: 7). Garcia, setting out to demonstrate the polycentricity of modernity, showed how a noble Persian's encounters with men and women who belong to similar class backgrounds in Britain transform, 'consolidate' and 'constrain shared cosmopolitanism, resulting at times of communicative breakdown' (Garcia 2020: 7). Garcia's notion of global cosmopolitanism is useful for viewing modernity as a polycentric phenomenon to which East and West contributed in their own unique ways. But his approach, as well as a postcolonial one mentioned earlier, does not offer a convincing argument on how a Muslim traveller belongs to a culture in which the link between the Self and the Sacred has not yet been broken.

In his journey, Abu Taleb, thus, had set out to reconcile a spiritual experience with a secular one. Although Abu Taleb was an admirer of Europeans' material progress, he was a critic of the impact of material advances on religion and morality. In Europe, Abu Taleb not only enjoyed the fruits of material advance: the culture of conviviality, cosmopolitanism and prosperity, but he was also committed to Islamic religious and cultural traditions. In Europe, he often expressed concerns over the lack of ablution facilities for Muslims. In London, Abu Taleb debated with an English bishop the message of Prophet Muhammad. He suggested that the Prophet was sent by God for all religions, including Christianity. The Bishop of London disagreed and expressed apprehension over the possibility that Abu Taleb came to England to convert Christians to Islam. In England, Abu Taleb reported that he was often called 'a Persian Prince' and referred to his native Bengal while comparing the manners of people in England with those in India. But his reflections on the geography, religion, culture and morals of Britons were rooted in an Islamic context. Even his 'Ode to London', a poem he wrote about his indulgence in earthly pleasures such as drinking, partying and flirting with women, serves to illustrate his Islamic frame of reference: in the poem, he recalled the Qur'anic trees of paradise 'Toba' (*Ṭūbā*) and 'Sudreh' (*Sidrat al-Muntaha*), referring to the fourteenth-century *Divan* of the Persian poet Hafiz in which trees of paradise (*Ṭūbā* and *Sidrat al-Muntaha*) do not shade Man endlessly: all pleasures are transient except those in the presence of God (I, 179).[7] Clare Chambers has perceptively argued that Abu Taleb's 'cultural referent is almost always Indian' (Chambers 2015: 33). But as these references show, Abu Taleb, albeit being an admirer of European modernity, was rooted in Islamic culture in which Sufi poetic tradition often used references to earthly pleasures as tools of allegorising the pleasure of connecting with the Creator.[8]

Abu Taleb was at home among his European friends, but his Islamic background shaped his understanding of European culture and geography. He used the term 'Sea of Roum' referring to the Mediterranean as a 'sea' that 'bounds Europe to the South' (1810: II, 70). In her *Byzantium Viewed by the Arabs* (2004), historian Nadia Maria El-Cheikh argues that the word 'Rum' in the early Islamic historiography refers to the Byzantines who ruled regions situated on the eastern Mediterranean coast in the period before the Arabs conquered Syria and Egypt in the seventh century. El-Cheikh further suggests that the Qur'anic verse of '*Rum*' offers a favourable view of the Byzantine victory over the Persians in the early years of the seventh century: the Byzantines are 'the people of the Book' and thus monotheistic, whereas the Persians are 'pagans' and thus polytheistic (EL Cheikh 2004: 29). Seen in this context, Abu Taleb's reference to Europe's maritime border with Islam (the sea of 'Roum') was rooted in a religious tradition which associated 'Rum' with Christianity.

None of the commentaries on Abu Taleb's book, including those recently published, examined the extent to which his celebrations and critique of Europe's culture of progress were played out in his views on Islamic habits of visiting Shia shrines and Sufi mystic tombs in Baghdad, Najaf and Karbala on the way back to India. In Najaf and Karbala, Abu Taleb visited the shrines Ali Bin Abi Taleb and his two sons, Hassan and Hussein, showing allegiance to his roots in Shia Islam. In Baghdad, he visited the tombs of Ibn Mansour Al-Hallaj (857–922) and Shihab Al Deen Al Suhrawardi (1145–1234), two Persian mystics and Sufi poets who expressed dissenting theological views based on the unity between Man and God, which led to their executions.[9] For both these mystics, whose work shaped Abu Taleb's views of man's role on earth, enlightenment requires a spiritual experience in which 'Divine Reality resides at the centre of our being', an experience which involves relinquishing worldly pleasures and seeking 'Truth' (*Haqq*) in the path of God.[10] In their poems, as Sir William Jones's essay on Sufi poetry stated, one encounters many allusions to earthly pleasures, but these metaphors allegorised a religious experience involving a loss of the Self in the love of the Divine.[11]

Such a Sufi experience tantalised Abu Taleb. In Karbala, he recalled, he met his aunt Kubelai Khatun 'who in the consequence of the misfortune of our family and my quitting home, had retired from the world and come to end her days in the sacred territory' (1810: II, 323–324). Retirement from the world was something that Abu Taleb struggled with: he enjoyed his wine and earthly comforts such as attending banquets, staying in luxurious places and socialising with women; yet he was always carrying a Sufi yearning for relinquishing earthly pleasures. Hence the spiritual burning that Abu Taleb felt while visiting the tomb of Ali in Najaf. 'Upon entering the holy shrine, I was so impressed with religious awe, that, although, supported by four of our attendants, I trembled like an aspen leaf, and it was with the utmost difficulty I could perform the prescribed ceremony' (1810: II, 346). This experience in a sacred space in the Shia tradition of Islam resembles the modern British experience of the sublime, one in which one feels overtaken by emotions, an experience which reminds humans of a spiritual lack intensifying in the midst of living in an environment drenched with luxuries, pleasures and wealth. Middle-class Englishmen of his generation would have rushed to mountains in the Alps and Wales to address this spiritual lack. For a Muslim of a respectable class background whose modern experience does not differ from his peers in the West, a visit to mosques and shrines meant that there was a spiritual gap caused by modern obsessions with material progress.

In the same sacred space, Abu Taleb found a bedouin whose clothes were dirty, and his bodily features were languid and yet 'was so much affected by his faith and sincerity that tears trickled from his eyes' (1810: II, 347). This Arab man connected with his faith in a simple manner: all he did was call upon Imam Ali in the shrine and immediately tears gushed down his face. Such a religious experience which paid little attention to religious ceremonies moved Abu Taleb. 'After observing him attentively, and reflecting on his sincerity and purity of heart, and on my own unworthiness, I was convinced that his own vows were more deserving of acceptance than mine and envied him his zeal and happiness' (1810: II, 347).

Abu Taleb's account of the regions he visited and people he encountered, whether in Europe or outside Europe, whether Muslims or Christians, as this short conclusion argues, was a response to modernity by a man rooted in the Islamic traditions and yet was conscious of the fact that the past glory of Islam was overshadowed in modern times by a rationalist culture that emphasises progress over traditions, reason over religion and individualism over virtue. Abu Taleb was a modern man. He socialised with Shia and Sunni Muslims in Mesopotamia, moving beyond narrow sectarian prejudices. He doubted the efficacy of organised religious practices even in a sacred space for Shia

Muslims. But Abu Taleb's unique response to modernity shows that he was not prepared to sever the link with the Sacred. In Europe, happiness for Abu Taleb meant living in a technologically advanced country in which land is improved, the law is kept separate from religious institutions and labour is encouraged. In a mosque in Mesopotamia, however, happiness meant moving beyond earthly pleasures.

European travellers, through their interactions with Arabs and Muslims, were uneasy about the moral ills caused by material progress, as the chapters in this book showed. But they were not prepared to escape the moral ills of modern life by a yearning for the Sacred. Abu Taleb was uneasy about public worship, as the previous example shows, but the idea that he discovered his unworthiness in a holy place indicates that he was not prepared to accept the radical Enlightenment conception of improvement: that is, the idea that man can be the cause of his own happiness without the need for the comfort of a deity. Abu Taleb in his travel account rather sought to walk the middle path between religious obscurantism and free-thinking materialism.

One major argument in this book is that the Enlightenment dogma and critique of material improvements were better rehearsed in the context of cross-cultural encounters in which Britons discovered the benefits and challenges of modernity while interacting with Arab and Islamic cultures. But this short conclusion makes another point which supplements the major argument in this book: celebrations and critiques of the Enlightenment idea of improvement did not take place only in Europe but also in the Islamic world, a point which raises this question: To what extent major ideas and tropes that scholars associate with the European Enlightenment affected both European and Muslim writers? Abu Taleb's book testifies to the fact that Enlightenment touched minds within the Islamic world. 'The affairs of this transitory world', wrote Abu Taleb, 'are intimately connected with each other' (1810: II, 69). Enlightenment fascinations with improvement emerged in the Islamic world, but with the publication of Abu Taleb's book in England, we note a profound Islamic response to the Enlightenment that celebrated material advance but without severing the link with the Divine.[12] Abu Taleb's attempt to reconcile materialism and religion, however, fell on deaf ears in Europe: hence the absence of commentaries on Abu Taleb's religious experience along the overland routes to India in all European reviews and studies of his book.

Notes

1 For biographical details about Abu Taleb, see Claire Chambers' *Britain Through Muslim Eyes: Literary Representations 1780-1988* (Basingstoke: Palgrave, 2015), 32–40.

2 Nigel Leask, 'Travelling the other way' *The Travels of Mirza Abu Taleb Khan* (1810) and Romantic Orientalism' *in Romantic Orientalism of British India*, Michael J. Franklin (Abingdon: Routledge, 2005), 2020.

3 An excellent account of al-Tahtawi's travel and encounters in Europe is Roxanne L. Euben's *Journeys to the Other Shore: Muslim and Western Travelers in Search of Knowledge* (Princeton: Princeton University Press, 2006). See chapter four.

4 The idea in Bellaigue's book that Muslims started to show curiosity about European cultures only in the period after European Empires started to dominate their regions is derived from Bernard Lewis's *The Muslim Discovery of Europe* (London and New York: W.W Norton, 2001).

5 Ronald Robinson, 'Non-European Foundations of European Imperialism: Sketch for a Theory of Collaboration', in Roger Owen and Bob Sutcliffe (eds), *Studies in the Theory of*

Imperialism, London: Longman, 1972, 117–42. See also Amrit Sen's 'The Persian Prince in London': Autoethnography and Positionality in Travels of Mirza Abu Taleb Khan', *Asiatic* 2:1 (2008), 58–68.

6 On claiming Abu Taleb for India, see Tabish Khair, 'A Multiplicity of Mirrors: Europe and Modernity in Travel Writing from Asia and Africa', *Indian Literature* 52: 6 (2008), 211–222. On the idea of reverse Orientalism in Abu Taleb's book, see Chambers, 35–36. On these moments of resistance in Abu Taleb's book, see Kate Teltscher's 'The Shampooing Surgeon and the Persian Prince: Two Indians in Early Nineteenth-century Britain', *Interventions* 2:3 (2000), 409–423. Hamid Dabashi claimed Abu Taleb for Persia; see chapter two in his *Reversing the Colonial Gaze: Persian Travelers Abroad* (Cambridge: Cambridge University Press, 2020).

7 Hafiz, *The Divan Written in the Fourteenth Century*, 3 vols, trans., Henry Wilberforce Clarke (Kolkata, 1891), Vol I, 196.

8 The term 'Sufism' is derived from the Arabic word *'suf'* which means wool. Early Sufis wore long woollen garbs, a reminder that early prophets and patriarchs wore rough material. The reference here is to the idea of refusing to wear clothes made of silk, that is, an opposition to indulging in earthly pleasures. See Seyyed Hosssein Nasr, *The Garden of Truth: The Vision and Promise of Sufism: Islam's Mystical Tradition* (New York: Harper One, 2007).

9 For biographical details about these two poets, see John Renard's *The A to Z of Sufism* (The Scarecrow Press, Lanham, 2009), 101–102; 230–231. On Al-Hallaj's Sufi thought, see Nasr, 174–175. On Al-Suhrawardi's philosophy of light, see Faris Hajamaideen, 'Ilm and the Human Body: Al-Suhrawardī's Concept of the Illuminated Temple', in *Ilm: Science, Religion and Art in Islam*, ed. Samer Akkach (Adelaide: University of Adelaide Press, 2019), 125–138.

10 Nasr, 175.

11 William Jones, *The Works Sir William Jones in Six Volumes* (London, 1799), Vol I, 458.

12 To that end, the fact that Abu Taleb's book was widely praised in the English press indicates that his attitudes to life and his Islamic response to modernity found a receptive audience in Britain which complicates what Michael Fisher argues that Britons in the East India Company employed literate and elite Indians; that is, they used their service 'while not necessarily accepting their cultural values', *Counterflows to Colonialism: Indian Travellers and Settlers in Britain 1600-1875* (New Delhi: Permanent Black, 2004).

UNPUBLISHED MANUSCRIPTS

IOR/R/15/1/4, ff 8v-9. The British Library, India Office Records and Private Papers.
IOR/L/MAR/C/570, ff 12-55. The British Library, India Office Records and Private Papers.
IOR/L/MAR/C/570, ff 56-84. The British Library, India Office Records and Private Papers.
IOR/L/PS/12/3773. The British Library, India Office Records and Private Papers.
IOR/G/29/11. The British Library, India Office Records and Private Papers.
IOR/L/MAR/C/570. The British Library, India Office Records and Private Papers.
IOR/L/PS/12/3773. The British Library, India Office Records and Private Papers.
IOR/F/4/747/20396. The British Library, India Office Records and Private Papers.
IOR/L/PS/5/345. The British Library, India Office Records and Private Papers.
IOR/R/15/1/4, f 21. Vol. 4. The British Library, India Office Records and Private Papers.
IOR/L/PS/20/C227. The British Library, India Office Records and Private Papers.
IOR/R/15/1/1, f 35v-1. The British Library, India Office Records and Private Papers.
IOR/R/15/1/4, ff 26v-27. The British Library, India Office Records and Private Papers.
IOR/1/63 ff, 21-22v. The British Library, India Office Records and Private Papers.
Letter to Clive From Edward Ives. The British Library, Ms G 37/67/4, November 1773.

REFERENCE LIST

Abbot, Henry. *A Journey on a Trip From Aleppo to Bussora*. Kolkata: from the Press of Joseph Cooper, 1789.

———. "Henry Abbott Papers". Mss Eur B412: 1764–1802. The British Library.

Abbott, James. *Prometheus Daughter*. London: Smith, Elder and Co., 1861.

———. *Narrative of a Journey From Heraut to Khiva, Moscow, and St. Petersburg*, 2 Vols. London: W. M. H Allen, 1843.

———. *The T'Hakoorine: Tale of Mandoo*. London: James Madden, 1841.

Abbott, Keith Edward. *A Complete History of the Arabs From the Birth of Mohammed to the Reduction of Baghdad*, 3 Vols. London, 1761.

———. "Notes of a Tour in Armenia in 1837." *The Journal of the Royal Geographical Society of London* 12 (1842): 207–2020.

Adam, Percy. *Travellers and Travel Liars 1660–1800*. New York: Dover Publication, 1980.

Adler, Judith. "Origins of Sightseeing." *Annals of Tourism Research* 16 (1989): 7–29.

Adorno, Theodore, and Max Horkheimer. *The Dialectic of the Enlightenment*. Edited by Gunzelin Schmid Noerr. Translated by Edmund Jephcott. Stanford: Stanford University Press, 2002.

Ahmed, Sara. *Strange Encounters: Embodied Others in Post-Coloniality*. Abingdon: Routledge, 2000.

Ahnert, Thomas, and Susan Manning. "Introduction." In *Character, Self and Sociability in the Scottish Enlightenment*. New York: Macmillan, 2016.

Aitchison, Charles Umpherston. *A Collection of Treaties, Engagements and Sanads Relating to India and Neighbouring Countries*, 11 Vols. Kolkata: Office of the Superintendent of Government Printing, 1892.

Aksan, Virginia. *Ottomans and Europeans*. Istanbul: Isis Press, 2004.

Alborn, Timothy. "King Solomon's Gold: Ophir in an Age of Empire." *Journal of Victorian Culture* 20, no. 4 (2015): 491–508.

Alcock, Nathan. *The Rise of Mahomet Accounted for on Natural and Civil Principles*. London, 1796.

Alexander, Isabella. "Copyright and the Circulation of Geographical Knowledge in Eighteenth-Century Britain." In *Forms, Formats and the Circulation of Knowledge: British Printscape's Innovations, 1688–1832*, edited by Louisiane Ferlier and Benedicte Miyamoto. Leiden: Brill, 2020, 87–111.

Al-Halak, Ahmad Bin Budairi. *Hawadith Dimashq Al Yawmiah (The Daily Incidents of Damascus)*. Cairo: Al-Jam'iyya al-Misriyya, 1959.

Amin, Abdul Amir. *British Interests in the Persian Gulf*. Leiden: Brill, 1967.

Alpini, Prosper. *De plantis Aegypti liber*. Venice, 1592.

Anonymous. *The Modern Part of the Universal History Compiled From Original Writers' By the Authors of the Antients Which Will Perfect the Work, and Render It a Complete Body of History From the Earliest Account of Time, to the Present*. London: Printed for T. Osborne, 1765.

Annual Biography and Obituary for the Year 1818. London: Printed for Longman, Hurst, Press, Orme, and Brown, Paternstoer-Row, 1818, Vol. II, 321–337.

Anon. *An Account for Several Workhouses for Employing the Maintaining the Poor*. London: Printed and Sold for Joseph Downing, 1725.

———. *An Account of the Work-Houses in Great Britain, in the Year M, DCC, XXXII*. London, 1786.

———. *Letters to the Ladies on the Preservation of Health and Beauty by a Physician*. London: Printed for Robinson and Roberts, 1770.

Ariel, Avraham, and Nora Ariel Berger. *Plotting the Globe: Stories of Meridians, Parallels and the International Date Line*. Westport: Praeger, 2006.

Arvamudan, Sirnivas. *Enlightenment Orientalism: Resisting the Rise of the Novel*. Chicago: Chicago University Press, 2012.

Atia, Nadia. "A Relic of Its Own Past: Mesopotamia in British Imagination: 1900–14." *Memory Studies* 2, no. 3 (2010): 232–241.

Assad, Talal. *Secular Translations: Nation-State, Modern Self and Calculative Reason*. New York: Columbia University Press, 2018.

Ayalon, Yaron. *Natural Disasters in the Ottoman Empire: Plague, Famine and Other Misfortunes*. Cambridge: Cambridge University Press, 2015.

Baack, Lawrence J. *Undying Curiosity: Carsten Niebuhr and the Royal Danish Expedition to Arabia (1761–1767)*. Stuttgart: Franz Steiner Verlag, 2014.

Bage, Robert. *The Fair Syrian: A Novel*, 2 Vols. Dublin, 1787.

Baldwin, George. "A Journey From Constantinople to Aleppo." In *Observations on the Passage to India Through Egypt*. London: Printed for W. Faden, 1785, 97–158.

———. *Political Reflections Relating to Egypt*. London:Printed for H. Baldwin and Son; New Bridge Street, 1801.

Barbauld, Anna Letittia. *An Epistle to William Wilberforce, EsQ.* London, 1791.

Barbir, Karl. *Ottoman Rule in Damascus 1708–1757*. Princeton: Princeton University Press, 1980.

Barczewski, Stephanie. "Is Britishness always British? Country Houses, Travels and the Cosmopolitan Identity of the British Elite in the Eighteenth Century." In *The British Abroad Since the Eighteenth Century. Vol I: Travellers and Tourists*, edited by Martin Farr and Xavier Guégan. New York: Palgrave Macmillan, 2013, 38–55.

Baridon, Michel. "Ruins as a Mental Construct." *The Journal of Garden History* 5 (1985): 84–96.

Barker, John. *Syria and Egypt Under the Last Five Sultans of Turkey*, 2 Vols. London: Samuel Tinsley, 1876.

Barnett, S. J. *The Enlightenment and Religion: The Myths of Modernity*. Manchester: Manchester University Press, 2003.

Barrell, John. *The Idea of Landscape and the Sense of Place 1730–1840: An Approach to the Poetry of John Clare*. Cambridge: Cambridge University Press, 1972.

———. *The Dark Side of the Landscape: The English Poor in English Painting 1730–1840*. Cambridge: Cambridge University Press, 1980.

———. "The Dark Side of the Landscape." In *Value: Art: Politics: Criticism, Meaning and Interpretation After Postmodernism*, edited by Jonathan Harris. Liverpool: Liverpool University Press, 2007, 23–62.

———. *The Spirit of Despotism: Invasion of Privacy in the 1790s*. Oxford: Oxford University Press, 2006.

Beaufoy, Henry. *Proceedings of the Association for Promoting the Discovery of the Interior Parts of Africa*. London: printed by C. Macrae, Printer to the Association, 1790.

Beawes, William. "A Journey From Aleppo to Basra in 1745." In *The Desert Route to India: Being the Journals of Four Travellers by the Great Desert Caravan Route Between Aleppo and Basra 1745–1751*, edited by Douglass Carruthers. London: Hakluyt Society, 1928, 1–40.

Bell, Gertrude. *Amurath to Amurath*. London: William Heinemann, 1911.

———. *Palace and Mosque at Ukhaidir: A Study in Early Mohammadan Architecture*. Oxford: The Clarendon Press, 1914.

Bellaigue, Christopher de. *The Islamic Enlightenment: The Struggle Between Faith and Reason 1798 to Modern Times*. London and New York: Liveright, 2017.

Bellamy, Liz. 1998. *Commerce, Morality and the Eighteenth-Century Novel*. Cambridge: Cambridge University Press, 1998.

Benhabib, Seyla. *Another Cosmopolitanism.* Oxford: Oxford University Press, 2006.

Berlin, Isaiah. "The Counter Enlightenment." In *Against the Current: Essays in the History of Ideas*, edited by Henry Hardy. Princeton and Oxford: Princeton University Press, 2013.

Berry, Christopher. *The Social Theory of the Scottish Enlightenment.* Edinburgh: Edinburgh University Press, 1997.

Bevilacqua, Alexander. *The Republic of Arabic Letters: Islam and the European Enlightenment.* Cambridge, MA: Belknap Press, 2018.

Bhattacharya, Sudip. *The Strange Case of Lord Pigot.* Cambridge: Cambridge Scholars, 2013.

Biddulph, William. *The Travels of Certaine Englishmen into Africa, Asia, Troy, Bythinia, Thracia and to the Blacke Sea.* London: Printed by Th. Haveland, 1609.

Black, Jeremy. *Geographies of an Imperial Power: The British World 1688–1815.* Indiana: Indiana University Press, 2018.

———. "Gibbon and International Relations." In *Edward Gibbon Empire*, edited by Rosamond Mcktitterick, and Ronald Quinault. Cambridge: Cambridge University Press, 1997.

———. *Natural and Necessary Enemies.* London: Duckworth, 1986.

———. *The English Press in the Eighteenth Century.* London & Sydney: Croom Helm, 1987.

Blackburn, Ian. *The Overthrow of Colonial Slavery 1776–1848.* London: Verso, 1988.

Blake, William. *The Complete Poetry and Propose of William Blake.* Edited by David Erdman. New York: Anchor Books, 1988.

Blake, William O. *The History of Slavery and the Slave Trade, Ancient and Modern.* Ohio: H. Miller, 1861.

Blaut, James. *The Colonizer's Model of the World: Geographical Diffusionism and Eurocentric History.* New York and London: The Guilford Press, 1993.

Blunt, Lady Anne. *The Bedouin Tribes of the Euphrates.* New York: Harper & Brothers, 1879.

Bodman, Herbert I. *Political Factions in Aleppo, 1760–1826.* Chapel Hill: The University of North Carolina Press, 1963.

Bohls, Elizabeth. "Picturesque Travel: The Aesthetic and Politics of Landscape". In *The Routledge Companion to Travel Writing*, edited by Carl Thompson. London and New York: Routledge, 2016, 246–257.

Bohls, Elizabeth and Ian Duncan. *Travel Writing 1700–1830: An Anthology.* Oxford: Oxford University Press, 2005.

Bolingbroke, Henry St John. *Letters on the Study and Use of History*, 2 Vols. London, 1752.

Bolton, Carl. *Writing the Empire: Robert Southey and Romantic Colonialism.* London: Pickering & Chatto, 2007.

Bolts, William. *Considerations on Indian Affairs.* London: Printed for J. Almon, 1772.

Boogert, Maurits van den. *Aleppo Observed: Ottoman Syria Through the Eyes of Two Scottish Doctors, Alexander and Patrick Russell.* Oxford: Oxford University Press, 2010.

———. "Freemasonry in Eighteenth-Century Izmir? A Critical Analysis of Alexander Drummond's Travels." In *Ottoman Izmir: Studies in Honour of Alexander de Groot*, edited by Maurits van den Boogert. Leiden: Nederlands Institut voor Het Nabije Oosten, 2007, 103–121.

Bowen, H. V. *The Business of Empire: The East India Company and Imperial Britain, 1756–1833.* Cambridge: Cambridge University Press, 2006.

Bowles, John. *The Real Grounds of the Present War with France.* London: Printed for J. Debrett, 1794.

Bown, Stephen R. *Scurvy: How a Surgeon, a Mariner, and a Gentlemen Solved the Greatest Medical Mystery of the Age of Sail.* London: St Martin Publishing, 2005.

Bredin, Miles. *The Pale Abyssinian: The Life of James Bruce, African Explorer and Adventurer.* London: Harper Press, 2012.

Broadie, Alexander. *The Idea of Commercial Society in the Scottish Enlightenment.* Edinburgh: Edinburgh University Press, 2013.

———. *The Scottish Enlightenment.* Edinburgh: Edinburgh University Press, 2007.

Browne, William George. *Travels in Africa, Egypt, and Syria.* London: Printed for T. Cadell, 1806.

Bruce, James. *Travels to Discover the Source of the Nile*, 6 Vols. Dublin, 1791.

Bryant, G. J. *The Emergence of British Power in India 1600–1784*. Suffolk: Boydell Press, 2013.

Brydges, Harford Jones. *An Account of the Transactions of His Majesty's Mission to the Court of Persia*, 2 Vols. London, 1834.

———. *The Dynasty of the Kajars*. London: John Bohn, 1833.

Bryson, Gladys. *Man and Society: The Scottish Inquiry of the Eighteenth Century*. Princeton: Princeton University Press, 1945.

Buckingham, James Silk. *Travels in Mesopotamia Including a Journey from Aleppo to Baghdad*, 2 vols. London: Henry Colburn, 1827.

Burckhardt, John Lewis. *Travels in Syria and the Holy Land*. London: J. Murray, 1822.

Burke, Edmund. *A Philosophical Inquiry into the Origin of Our Ideas of the Sublime and Beautiful*. London: Printed for R. and J. Dodsley, 1757.

———. *Reflection on the Revolution of France*. London, 1790.

———. *Speech of Edmund Burke on American Taxation, April 19, 1774*. London:Printed for J. Dodsley, 1775.

———. *The Works of the Right Honourable Edmund Burke*. London: Henry G. Bohn, 1885, Vol. IV.

———. *Works and Correspondence of the Right Honourable Edmund Burke*. 8 vols. London: Francis & John Rivington, 1852.

Burns, Emily. "The Old World Anew: The Atlantic as a Liminal Site of Expectation." In *Framing the Ocean, 1700 to the Present: Envisaging the Sea as Social Space*, edited by Tricia Cusack. Abingdon: Routledge, 2016 [2014], 37–54.

Burridge, Geoff. *British Diplomacy in Turkey, 1583 to the Present: A Study in the Evolution of a Resident Embassy*. Leiden: Martinus Nijhoff Publishers, 2009.

Bury, J. B. *The Idea of Progress*. New York: Dover, 1932.

Busbecq, Ogier Ghiselin de. *Travels into Turkey Containing the Most Accurate Account of the Turks*. London, 1744.

Butler, Marilyn. *Jane Austen and the War of Ideas*. Oxford: Oxford University Press, 1987.

Buzard, James. "The Grand Tour and After (1660–1840)." In *The Cambridge Companion to Travel Writing*, edited by Peter Hulme and Tim Youngs. Cambridge: Cambridge University Press, 2002, 37–52.

Byrne, James M. *Religion and the Enlightenment: From Descartes to Kant*. Kentucky: Westminster John Knox Press, 1997.

Caesar, Fredrick. *The Voyage and trauaile of M. Caesar Frederick, Merchant of Venice, into the East Indies*. London: Printed by Richard Iones and Edward White, 1588.

———. *Viaggio di M. Cesare de Fedrici, nell' India orientale*. Venice: Apresso Andrea Muschio, 1587.

Caird, Edward. *The Critical Philosophy of Kant*, 1898.

Caldwell, Robert. *A Political and General History of the District of Tinnevelly in the Presidency of Madras*. Chennai, 1881.

Campbell, Donald. *A Journey Overland to India Partly by A Route Never Gone Before by a European*. London: Printed for Cullen and Company, 1795.

———. *A Letter to the Marquis of Lorn on the Present Times*. London: Printed for J. Chavasse, 1798.

Campbell, Duncan. *Records of Clan Campbell in the Military Service of the East India Company 1600–1858*. London and New York: Longman, 1925.

Campbell, Frederick William. *A Letter to Mrs. Campbell of Barbreck, Containing an Account of the Campbells of Barbreck from the First Ancestor to the Present Time*. Ipswich: Printed By R. Deck, Cornhill, 1830.

Cannon, John. *Aristocratic Century*. Cambridge: Cambridge University Press, 1984.

Canton, James. *From Cairo to Baghdad*. London: Bloomsbury, 2011.

Capper, James. *Observations on the Passage to India Through Egypt, and Across the Great Desert With Occasional Remarks on the Adjacent Countries, and Also Sketches of the Different Routes*. London, 1783.

Carey, Brycchan. *British Abolitionism and the Rhetoric of Sensibility: Writing, Sentiment and Slavery 1760–1807.* London: Palgrave, 2005.

Careri, Giovanni Francesco Gemelli. *A Voyage Round the World: In Six Parts, viz. I. Of Turky, II. Of Persia, III. Of India, IV. Of China, V. of the Philippine-Islands, VI. Of New-Spain / by John Francis Gemelli Careri ; written originally in Italian, translated into English* S.l. : s.n., 17--?. See Giovanni Francesco Gemelli Careri, *A Voyage Round the World: In Six Parts* (London, 1700), 150.

Carlyle, Thomas. *Collected Works*, 30 Vols. London: Chapman and Hall, 1869.

Carmichael, John. "Appendix: A Journey From Aleppo to Busserah, Over the Desert." In *A Voyage to the East Indies Containing Authentic Accounts of the Mogul Government*, 2 Vols. London: Printed for S. Hooper, 1772, Vol. I, 1–53.

Carré, Barthélemy. *The Travels of the Abbe Carré in India and the Near East, 1672–1674*, 3 Vols. Translated by Lady Fawcett. London: The Hakluyt Society, 1947.

———. *Voyage des Indes orientales.* Paris: Chez La Veuve de Claude Barbin, 1699.

Carruthers, Douglas. "Introduction." In *The Desert Route to India: Being the Journal of Four Travellers by the Great Desert Caravan Route Between Aleppo and Basra 1745–1751*, edited by Douglass Carruthers. London: Hakluyt Society, 1929.

Cartwright, John. *The Preachers Travels: Wherein is Set Down a True Journall to the Confines of the East Indies.* London: Printed by William Stansby, 1611.

Caulfield, James. *The Travels of Charlemont in Greece and Turkey, 1749.* Edited by William Bedell Stanford and E. J. Finopolus. London: A. G. Levntis Foundation, 1984.

Celik, Semih. "Coping With Famine in Ottoman Anatolia, 1650–1850." In *An Economic History of Famine Resilience*, edited by Jessica Dijkman and Bas van Leeuwen. Abingdon: Routledge, 2020, 52–73.

Certeau, Michel de. *The Practice of Everyday Life.* Translated by Steven Rendall. Los Angeles and London: The University of California Press, 1984.

Chakrabarti, Pratik. *Medicine and Empire 1600–1960.* London: Palgrave, 2014.

Chambers, Claire. *Britain Through Muslim Eyes: Literary Representations 1780–1988.* Basingstoke: Palgrave, 2015.

Chambers, William. *Plans, Elevations, Sections and Perspective Views of the Gardens and Buildings at Kew in Surrey.* London: Printed for J. Haberkorn, 1763.

Chardin, Jean. "The Travels of John Chardin Through Mingrelia and Georgia and Persia." In *The World Displayed or a Curious Collection of Voyages and Travels.* London, 1760, Vol. XVI, 1–37.

Chatterjee, Partha. *The Black Hole of Empire: History of a Global Practice of Power.* Princeton: Princeton University Press, 2012.

Chaudhuri, K. N. *The Trading World of Asia and the English East India Company 1660–1760.* Cambridge: Cambridge University Press, 1779.

———. *Trade and Civilisation in the Indian Ocean: An Economic History from the Rise of Islam to 1750.* Cambridge: Cambridge University Press, 1985.

Chesney, Francis Rawdon. *Narrative of the Euphrates Expedition: Carried on by Order of the British Government in 1835, 1836 and 1837.* London, 1868.

———. *The Expedition for the Survey of the Rivers Euphrates and Tigris.* Carried on by Order of the British Government in the Years 1835, 1836, 1837, 2 Vols. London: Longman, Brown, Green, and Longmans, 1850.

Child, Josiah. *A New Discourse of Trade.* London, 1698.

Christians and Jews in the Ottoman Empire: The Functioning of a Plural Society, 2 Vols. Edited by Benjamin Braude and Bernard Russell. New York: Holmes and Meier, 1982.

Claeys, Gregory. *Thomas Paine: Social and Political Thought.* London: Unwin Hyman, 1989.

Clark, John. *Observations on the Diseases in Long Voyages in Hot Countries.* London, 1775.

Clark, Terence. "Iraq." In *British Missions Around the Gulf: 1575–2005: Iran, Iraq, Kuwait and Oman.* Folkstone: Global Oriental, 2008, 81–168.

Clifford, James. 1997. *Routes: Travel and Translation in the Late Twentieth Century.* Massachusetts: Harvard University Press.

Coats. A. W. "The Relief of Poverty, Attitudes to Labour, and Economic change in England 1660–1782." *International Review of Social History* 21, no. 1 (1976): 98–115.

Cokayne, George Edward . *Complete Baronetage: Volume V.* Exeter, 1906.

Colbert, Benjamin. *Shelley's Eye: Travel Writing and Aesthetic Vision.* London: Ashgate, 2005.

Colley, Linda. *Colley's Britons: Forging the Nation 1707–1837.* New Haven, CT: Yale University Press, 1993.

Collins, Gregory M. *Commerce and Manners in Edmund Burke's Political Economy.* Cambridge: Cambridge University Press, 2020.

Coote, Eyre. "Diary of a Journey With Sir Eyre Coote From Bussora to Aleppo in 1780, From the Original MS." *The Journal of the Royal Geographical Society of London* 30 (1860): 98–211.

Cope, Captain. *A New History of the East Indies.* London, 1754.

Cope, Thomas D. "Some Contacts of Benjamin Franklin With Mason, Dixon and Their Work." *Proceedings of the American Philosophical Society* 95 (1951): 232–238.

Copies of Papers Relative to the Restoration of the King of Tanjore, 2 Vols. London, 1772.

Copley, Stephen. "Commerce, Conversation and Politeness in the Early Eighteenth-Century Periodical." *The Journal of Eighteenth-Century Studies* 18 (1995): 63–77.

———. *Literature and the Social Order in Eighteenth-Century England.* Edited by Stephen Copley. London and New York: Routledge, 2020 [1984].

Coutu, Joan. *Then and Now: Collecting and Classicism in Eighteenth-Century England.* Montreal: McGill-Queens University Press, 2015.

Cowley, Hannah. *A Day in Turkey or the Russian Slaves: A Comedy.* London, 1792.

Craciun, Adriana, and Mary Terrall. "Introduction." In *Curious Encounters: Voyage Collecting and Making Knowledge in the Long Eighteenth Century*, edited by Adriana Craciun and Mary Terrall. Toronto: The University of Toronto, 2019.

Crosbie, Barry. *Irish Imperial Networks: Migration, Social Communication and Exchange in Nineteenth-Century India.* Cambridge: Cambridge University Press, 2011.

Cudworth, Erika, and Stephen Hobden. "Civilisation and the Domination of the Animal." *Millennium* 3 (2014): 746–766.

Curzon, George Nathaniel. *Persia and the Persian Question*, 2 Vols. London: Longman, Green and Co., 1892.

D' Arvieux, Chevalier. *The Chevalier D'Arvieux's Travels in Arabia the Desert; Written by Himself and Publish'd by Mr. De la Roque.* London: B. Barker and C. King, and J. Brown, 1718.

Dabashi, Hamid. *Reversing the Colonial Gaze: Persian Travelers Abroad.* Cambridge: Cambridge University Press, 2020.

Dallaway, James. *Constantinople: Ancient and Modern.* London: Printed by T. Binsley, 1797.

Dalrymple, William. *The Anarchy.* London: Bloomsbury, 2020.

Dalton, Richard. *Antiquities and Views in Greece and Egypt With Manners and Customs of the Inhabitants From Drawings Made on the Spot, A.D. 1749.* London: Printed for Thomas King and Henry Chapman, 1791.

———. *Remarks on Prints Intended to Be Published, Relative to the Manners, Customs &c of the Present Inhabitants of Egypt.* London: Printed by John Rivington, 1781.

Dandini, Girolamo. *A Voyage to Mount Libanus wherein is an account of the customs, manners, &c. of the Turks.* London: Printed by J. Orme for A. Roper, 1698.

Darnton, Robert. *Literary Underground in the Old Regime.* Cambridge: Harvard University Press, 1982.

———. *The Business of Enlightenment: A Publishing History of the Encyclopédie, 1775–1800.* Massachusetts: The Belknap Press, 1979.

Davidson, Jenny. *Hypocrisy and the Politics of Politeness: Manners and Morals From Locke to Austen.* Cambridge: Cambridge University Press, 2004.

Davis, Ralph. *Aleppo and the Devonshire Square: English Traders in the Levant in the Eighteenth Century.* London: MacMillan, 1967.

Day, Matthew. "'Honour to Our Nation': Nationalism. The Principal Navigation and Travel Collections in the Long Eighteenth Century." In *Richard Hakluyt and Travel Writing in Early Modern Europe*, edited by Daniel Carey and Clare Jowitt. Abingdon: Routledge, 2016 [2012], 77–86.

Debord, Guy. *The Society of the Spectacle*. Translated by Ken Knabb. Berkeley: The Bureau of the Public Secret, 2014 [1967].

Defoe, Daniel. *A Plan of the English Commerce*. London: Printed for Charles Rivington, 1728.

———. *The Complete English Gentleman*. Edited by Karl Daniel Bülbring. London, 1890.

Della Valle, Pietro. *The Travels of Sig. Pietro Della Valle*. London: Printed for J. Macock, 1665.

———. *Viaggi di Pietro della Valle il Pellegrino*. Rome: Appresso Vitale Mascardi, 1650.

Delumeau, Jean. *History of Paradise: The Garden of Eden in Myth and Tradition*. New York: Continuum, 1995.

Derek, Gregory. "Scripting Egypt: Orientalism and the Cultures of Travel." In *Rites of Passage: Reading Travel Writings*, edited by Derek Gregory and James Duncan. London: Routledge, 1999.

Dew, Nicholas. *Orientalism in Louis XIV's France*. Oxford: Oxford University Press, 2018.

Dickenson, H. T. *The Politics of the People in Eighteenth-Century Britain*. London: Macmillan, 1994.

Dictionary of National Biography. Edited by Sidney Lee. New York: Macmillan and Co, 1892.

Dinwiddy, J. R. *Radicalism and Reform in Britain, 1780–1850*. London: The Hambeldon Press, 1992.

Dirks, Nicholas. *The Scandal of Empire: India and the Creation of Modern Britain*. Massachusetts and London: Harvard University Press, 2006.

Discorides, Pedanius. *De Materia Medica*. Johannesburg: Osbaldeston, 2000.

Doddridge, Philip. *The Guilt and Doom of Capernaum, Seriously Recommended to the Consideration of the Inhabitants of London*. London, 1750.

Dodson, Michael D. *Orientalism, Empire, and National Culture: India, 1770–1880*. New York: Palgrave, 2007.

Dorner, Zachary. *Merchants of Medicines: The Commerce and Coercion of Health in Britain's Long Eighteenth Century*. Chicago: Chicago University Press, 2020.

Douwes, Dick, and Norman N. Lewis. "Taxation and Agriculture in the District of Hama, 1800–1831." In *The Syrian Land in the 18th and 19th Century*, edited by Thomas Philips. Stuttgart: Steiner, 1992, 268–271.

Dow, Alexander. *The History of Hindostan*. London: Printed for T. Becket and P. A De Hondt in the Strand, 1772.

Downs, Jim. *Maladies of Empire: How Colonialism, Slavery, and War Transformed Medicine*. Cambridge, MA: Belknap Press, 2021.

Drummond, Alexander. *Travels Through Different Cities of Germany, Italy and Greece and Several Parts of Asia*. London: Printed for W. Strahan, 1754.

Duffy, Cian. *The Landscape of the Sublime, 1700–1830: Classic Ground*. New York and London: Palgrave, 2013.

Dunbar, James. 1780. *Essays on the History of Mankind in Rude and Cultivated Ages*. London:Printed for W. Strahan; T. Cadell on the Strand and J. Balfour.

Dunn, Diane Robinson. "French and English Orientalisms and the Study of Slavery and Abolition in North Africa and the Middle East: What Are the Connections?" In *Slavery in the Islamic World: Its Characteristics and Commonality*, edited by Mary Ann Fay. New York: Palgrave, 2019, 51–74.

Dwyer, John. *Virtuous Discourse: Sensibility and Community in Late Eighteenth-Century Scotland*. Edinburgh: John Donald Publishers, 1987.

Eacott, Jonathan. *Selling Empire: India and the Making of Britain and America 1630–1830*. Virginia: The University of North Carolina Press, 2016.

Eagleton, Terry. *Culture and the Death of God*. New Haven and London: Yale University Press, 2014.

Earle, Peter. *The Making of the English Middle Class.* Berkeley: The University of California Press, 1989.

Eden, Frederick Morton. *The State of the Poor, or an History of the Labouring Classes in England.* London: Printed J. Davis, 1779.

Egmond, Johan van Ægidius, and Johannes Heyman. *Travels Through Part of Europe, Asia Minor, the Islands of the Archipelago.* London, 1759.

Elaine, James. "Sarah, Hagar, and Their Interpreters." In *Women's Bible Commentary*, edited by Carol A. Newsom, Sharon H. Ringe, and Jacqueline E. Lapsley, 1992. Louisville: Westminster John Knox Press, 2012.

El-Cheikh, Nadia Maria. *Byzantium Viewed by the Arabs.* Massachusetts and London: Harvard University Press, 2004.

Eldem, Edhem. "French Trade and Commercial Policy in the Levant in the Eighteenth-Century." *Oriente Moderno* 1 (1999): 27–47.

Eleana, Baird, and Christian Ionescu. *Eighteenth-Century Thing Theory in a Global Context.* London: Ashgate, 2013.

Eliot, Eliot. "Directions For Passing Over the Desert From Busserah, By the Way of Bagdad, Mosul, Orfa and Aleppo." In *The Desert Route to India: Being the Journal of Four Travellers by the Great Desert Caravan Route Between Aleppo and Basra 1745–1751*, edited by Douglass Carruthers. London: Hakluyt Society, 1928.

Ellis, Markman. *The Coffee-House: A Cultural History.* London: Phoenix, 2011.

———. *The Politics of Sensibility.* Cambridge: Cambridge University Press, 1996.

Ellison, James. *George Sandys: Travel, Colonialism, and Tolerance in the Seventeenth Century.* Cambridge: D. S Brewer, 2000.

Emberley, Julia. "Gertrude Lowthian Bell in Mesopotamia." In *Writing Travel and Empire: Colonial Narratives of Other Cultures*, edited by Peter Hulme and Russell McDougall. London: I. B. Tauris, 2009, 119–146.

Emin, Joseph. *The Life and Adventures of Joseph Emin*, 2 Vols. London: Printed in the Year, 1792.

Enlightenment and Religion: Rational Dissent in Eighteenth-Century Britain. Edited by Knud Haakonssen. Cambridge: Cambridge University Press, 1996.

Erdem, Y. Hakan. *Slavery in the Ottoman Empire and Its Demise 1800–1909.* Basingstoke: Palgrave, 1996.

Erikson, Emily. *Between Monopoly and Free Trade: The East India Company 1600–1757.* Princeton: Princeton University Press, 2014.

Eton, William. *A Survey of the Turkish Empire.* London:Printed for T. Cadell and W. Davies in the Strand, 1798.

Euben, Roxanne L. *Journeys to the Other Shore: Muslim and Western Travelers in Search of Knowledge.* Princeton: Princeton University Press, 2006.

Evans, Eric J. *William Pitt the Younger.* London: Routledge, 1999.

Evers. Samuel. 1784. *A Journal Kept on a Journey From Bassora to Baghdad Over the Little Desert.* London.

Fabian, Johannes. *Time and Other: How Anthropology Makes Its Objects.* New York: Columbia University Press, 1983.

Falck, Nikolai Detlef. *The Seaman's Medical Instructor.* London, 1774.

Faroqhi, Suraiya. *Subjects of the Sultan: Culture and Daily Life in the Ottoman Empire.* London & New York, 1995.

Fattah, Hala Mundhir. *The Politics of Regional Trade in Iraq, Arabia, and the Gulf, 1745–1900.* New York: New York State University Press, 1997.

Fay, Eliza. *The Original Letters From India of Mrs Eliza Fay.* Kolkata: Thacker, Spink & Co., 1908.

Ferguson, Adam. *An Essay on the History of Civil Society.* Dublin: Printed by Boulter Grierson, 1776.

Ferri, Sabrina. *Ruins Past: Modernity in Italy, 1744–1836.* Oxford: Voltaire Foundation, 2015.

Festa, Lynn. *Sentimental Figures of Empire in Eighteenth-Century Britain and France.* Baltimore: John Hopkins University Press, 2006.

Figres, Pascal. *French Revolutionaries in the Ottoman Empire, 1792–1789.* Oxford: Oxford University Press, 2017.

Finn, James. *Stirring Times or Records From Jerusalem Consular Chronicles of 1853–156.* London: C. Kegan Paul and Co., 1878, Vol. I.

Finn, Margot, and Kate Smith. "Introduction." In *The East India Company at Home, 1757–1857,* edited by Margot Finn and Kate Smith. London: UCL Press, 2018.

Finnegan, Richard. *English Explorers in the East 1738–1745: The Travels of Thomas Shaw, Charles Perry and Richard Pococke.* Leiden: Brill, 2019.

Fisher, Michael. *Counterflows to Colonialism: Indian Travellers and Settlers in Britain 1600–1875.* New Delhi: Permanent Black, 2004.

Floor, Willem. "Dutch Relations With the Persian Gulf." In *The Persian Gulf in History,* edited by Lawrence G. Potter. New York: Palgrave, 2009, 235–260.

Forster, Robert. *A Collection of the Most Celebrated Voyages & Travels, IV.* Newcastle: Mackenzie and Dent, 1818.

Fothergill, John Read. *An Essay on the Character of the Late Alexander Russell.* London, 1770.

Foucault, Michael. "What is Enlightenment." In *The Foucault Reader,* edited by Paul Rabinow. New York: Pantheon Book, 1984, 32–50.

Fowler, George. *Turkey or a History of the Origin, Progress and Decline.* London: T.H. Rees, 1854.

Francklin, William. "Accessing India: Orientalism, Anti-Indianism and the Rhetoric of Jones and Burke." In *Romanticism and Colonialism: Writing and Empire, 1780–1830,* edited by Tim Fulford and Peter J. Kitson. Cambridge: Cambridge University Press, 1998, 84–676.

———. *Observations Made on a Tour From Bengal to Persia.* Kolkata, 1788.

Franklin, Michael J. *Orientalist Jones: Sir William Jones, Poet, Lawyer and Linguist.* Oxford: Oxford University Press, 2011.

Franklin, William. *The Loves of Cámarúpa and Cámalatà: An Ancient Indian Tale: Elucidating the Customs and Manners of Orientals.* London, 1793.

Frazer, James. *The History of Nadir Shah Formerly Called Thamas Kuli Khan, Present Emperor of Persia.* London: Printed by W. Strahan for the Author, 1742.

Fullarton, William. *A View of the English Interests in India.* London: Printed for T. Cadell, 1787.

Galen. *Method of Medicine, 5–9.* Translated by Ian Johnston and G. H. R. Horsley. Massachusetts: Harvard University Press, 2011.

Garcia, Humberto. *Islam and the English Enlightenment 1670–1840.* Baltimore: The John Hopkins University Press, 2012.

———. *England Re-Oriented: How Central and South Asian Travelers Imagined the West, 1750–1857.* Cambridge: Cambridge University Press, 2020.

Garraway, Doris L. "Black Athena: Universal History, Colonisation, and the African Origin of Civilisation in Post-Revolutionary Haitian Writing." In *Enlightened Colonialism Civilization Narratives and Imperial Politics in the Age of Reason,* edited by Damien Tricoire. New York: Palgrave, 2017.

Garret, Aaron. 2003. "Anthropology: "the Original" of Human Nature." In *The Cambridge Companion to the Scottish Enlightenment,* edited by Alexander Broadie. Cambridge: Cambridge University Press, 79–93.

Gay, Peter. *The Enlightenment: An Interpretation: The Rise of Modern Paganism.* New York: Knopf, 1966.

———. *The Enlightenment: An Interpretation: Science of Freedom.* New York: Knopf, 1969.

Gibbon, Edward. *The History of the Decline and Fall of the Roman Empire,* 5 Vols. London, 1788.

Gillespie, Michael Allen. *The Theological Origin of Modernity.* Chicago: The University of Chicago Press, 2008.

Gilmartin, Kevin. *Print Politics: The Press and Radical Opposition in Early Nineteenth-Century Britain.* New York: Cambridge University Press, 1996.

Gilroy, Paul. 1993. *The Black Atlantic: Modernity and Double Consciousness.* London: Verso, 1993.

Ginio, Eyal. "Living on the Margins of Charity: Coping With Poverty in an Ottoman Provincial City." In *Poverty and Charity in Middle Eastern Contexts*, edited by Michael Bonner, Mine Ener, and Amy Singer. New York: State University of New York Press, 2003, 165–184.

Gipling, William. *Three Essays on Picturesque Beauty or Picturesque Travels*. London: Printed for Blamire, 1792.

Global Gifts and the Material Culture of Diplomacy in Early Modern Eurasia. Edited by Zoltan Biederman, Anne Gerristen, and Giorgio Riello. Cambridge: Cambridge University Press, 2018.

Gocek, Fatma Muge. *Rise of the Bourgeoisie, Demise of Empire: Ottoman Westernization and Social Change*. Oxford: Oxford University Press, 1996.

Goodman, Dena. *The Republic of Letters: A Cultural History of the French Enlightenment*. Ithaca and London: Cornell University Press, 1994.

Godwin, William. *An Inquiry Concerning Political Justice and Its Influence on General Virtue and Happiness*, 2 vols. London: Printed for G.G. J and J. Robinson, 1793.

Gotllieb, Eva, and Juliet Shields. "Introduction." In *Representing Place in British Literature and Culture, 1660–1830*, edited by Eva Gotllieb and Juliet Shields. Abingdon: Routledge, 2013.

Grant, Christina Phelps. *The Syrian Desert: Caravan, Travel and Exploration*. London: A. & C. Black Ltd, 1937.

Gray, John. *Enlightenment's Wake Politics and Culture at the Close of the Modern Age*. London: Routledge, 1995.

———. *Black Mass: Apocalyptic Religion and the Death of Utopia*. London: Allen Lane, 2007.

Greaves, Rose. "Iranian Relations With the European Trading Companies, to 1798." In *The Cambridge History of Iran: From Nadir Shah to the Islamic Republic*, edited by Peter Avery, Gavin Hambly, and Charles Melville. Cambridge: Cambridge University Press, 1991.

Gregory, Derek. "Scripting Egypt: Orientalism and the Cultures of Travel." In *Rites of Passage: Reading Travel Writings*, edited by Derek Gregory and James Duncan. London: Routledge, 1999.

Grehan, James. "Smoking and "Early Modern" Sociability: The Great Tobacco Debate in the Ottoman Middle East (Seventeenth to Eighteenth Centuries)." *The American Historical Review* 5 (2006): 1352–1377.

Griffiths, John. *Travels in Europe, Asia Minor and Arabia*. London: Printed for T. Cadell, 1805.

Grose, Henry. *A Voyage to the East Indies With Observations on Various Parts There*. London: Printed for S. Hooper, 1757.

———. *A Voyage to the East Indies Containing Authentic Accounts of the Mogul Government*, 2 Vols. London: Printed for S. Hooper, 1772.

Grosrichard, Alain. *The Sultan Court: European Fantasies of the East*. London: Verso, 1998.

Gust Onni. *Unhomely Empire: Whiteness and Belonging, 1760–1830*. London: Bloomsbury, 2021.

Guthrie, William. *A General History of the World*, 12 Vols. London: J. Newbury, 1764.

———. *A New System of Modern Geography*, 3 Vols. Philadelphia, 1795.

Habermas, Jürgen. *The Structural Transformation of the Public Sphere: An Inquiry into a Category of Bourgeois Society*. Translated by Thomas Burger. Cambridge: MIT Press, 1989.

Habesci, Elias. *The Partition of the Dominion of the Pope Preceded By That of the Ottoman Empire*. Kolkata: From the Press of Joseph Cooper, 1790.

———. *The Present State of the Ottoman Empire*. London: Printed for R. Baldwin, 1784.

Hachicho, Mohamed Ali. "English Travel Books About the Arab Near East in the Eighteenth Century." *Die Welt Des Islam* 9, no. 1 (Brill, 1964): 1–206.

Hafiz. *The Divan Written in the Fourteenth Century*, 3 Vols. Translated by Henry Wilberforce Clarke. Kolkata, 1891.

Hajamaideen, Faris. "Ilm and the Human Body: Al-Suhrawardī's Concept of the Illuminated Temple." In *Ilm: Science, Religion and Art in Islam*, edited by Samer Akkach. Adelaide: University of Adelaide Press, 2019.

Ḥajarī, Hiāl. *British Travel Writing on Oman: Orientalism Reappraised*. Bern: Peter Lang, 2006.

Hakluyt, Richard. *The Principal Navigations, Voyages, Traffiques, and Discoveries of the English Nation*. London: Imprinted at London by George Bishop, Ralph Newberie, and Robert Barker, 1599, Vol. II.

Hall, Stuart. *The Fateful Triangle: Race, Ethnicity, Nation.* Edited by Kobena Mercer. Massachusetts: Harvard University Press, 2017.

Hamilton, Alastair. "Introduction." In *Johann Michael Wansleben's Travels in the Levant, 1671–1674*, edited by Alastair Hamilton. Leiden: Brill, 2018.

———. "The English Interests in the Arabic-Speaking Christians." In *The 'Arabick' Interest of the Natural Philosophers in Seventeenth-Century England*, edited by G. A. Russell. Leiden: Brill, 1994, 30–53.

Hamilton, Alexander. *A New Account of the East Indies From the Years 1688–1723*, 2 Vols. London: Printed for A. Bettersworth and C. Hitch, 1739.

Hammond, Barbara, and J. L. Hammond. *The Village Labourer 1760–1832: A Study in the Government of England Before the Reform Bill.* London: Longmans, Green and Co., 1920.

Han, Geoff, Karen Dabrowska, and Tina Townsend-Greaves. *Iraq: Ancient Sites & Iraqi Kurdistan.* Guilford: Bradt Travel Guides Ltd, 2015 [2002].

Hanaway, Jonas. *An Historical Account of the British Trade Over the Caspian Sea . . . To Which Are Added, the Revolutions of Persia During the Present Century*, 4 Vols. London: Sold by Mr Dodsley, 1753.

Harrison, Robert. *Britain in the Middle East, 1619–1917.* London: Bloomsbury, 2016.

Haslam, Fiona. *From Hogarth to Rowlandson: Medicine in Art in Eighteenth-Century Britain.* Liverpool: Liverpool University Press, 1996.

Hasselquist, Frederick. *Voyages and Travels in the Levant.* London: Printed for L. Davis and C. Reymers, 1766.

Hastings, Warren. *The Letters of Warren Hastings to His Wife.* Edited by Sydney C. Grier. Edinburgh: Blackwood and Sons, 1905.

Hathaway, Jane. *The Arab Lands Under Ottoman Rule, 1516–1800.* London: Routledge, 2013.

Haydon, Colin. "Eighteenth-Century English Anti-Catholicism: Contexts, Continuity and Diminution". In *Protestant-Catholic Conflict from the Reformation to the 21st Century*, edited by John Wolffe. Basingstoke: Palgrave, 2013, 46–70.

Hayden, Judy A. "Intersections and Cross-Fertilization." In *Travel Narratives, the New Science, and Literary Discourse 1569–1750.* Farnham: Ashgate, 2012.

Hayley, William. *Memoirs of the Life and Writings of William Hayley, the Friend and Biographer of Cowper*, 2 Vols. London, 1823.

Haynes, James. *Travels in Several Parts of Turkey, Egypt and the Holy Land.* London, 1774.

Haynes, Rosalynn. "Travel Writing and the Desert." In *The Cambridge History of Travel Writing*, edited by Tim Youngs and Nandini Das. Cambridge: Cambridge University Press, 2020.

Haywood, Ian, and John Seed. *The Gordon Riots: Politics, Culture and Insurrection in Late Eighteenth-Century Britain.* Cambridge: Cambridge University Press, 2012.

Henry, Pierre François. *Route de l'Inde, ou Description geographique de l'Egypte, la Syrie, l'Arabie.* Paris, 1799.

Heron, Robert. *Travels Through Arabia and Other Countries in the East.* Edinburgh: Printed for R. Morrison and Son, 1792.

Hervey, Fredric. *The Naval History of Great Britain: From the Earliest Times to the Rising of Parliament in 1779*, 5 Vols. London: Printed by William Adlrad, 1779.

Heude, William. *A Voyage Up the Persian Gulf and a Journey Overland From India to England in 1817.* London: Longman and Hurst, 1819.

Hill, Aaron. *A Full Account of the Present State of the Ottoman Empire in All Its Branches With the Government, and Policy, Religion, Customs and Way of Living of the Turks, in General, Faithfully Related From a Serious Observation, Taken in Many Years Travels Though Those Countries.* London: Printed for the Author, 1709.

Hill, John. *The History of Materia Medica.* London:Printed for T. Longman, 1751.

Hodgson, Marshall. *The Venture of Islam: Conscience and History in a World Civilisation.* Chicago: The University of Chicago Press, 1974.

Homberg, Eva Johanna. "The Middle East". In *The Routledge Companion to Travel Writing*, edited by Carl Thompson. Abingdon: Routledge, 2016, 372–383.

Höpfl, H. M. "From Savage to Scotsman: Conjectural History in the Scottish Enlightenment." *The Journal of British Studies* 17 (1978): 19–40.

Hoskins, H. L. *British Routes to India*. London: Frank & Cass, 1966.

Howel, Thomas, and James Capper. *Voyage en retour de l'Inde, par terre, et par une route en partie inconnue jusqu'ici, par Thomas Howel; suivi d'Observations sur le passage dans l'Inde par l'Egypte et le grand désert, par James Capper*. Paris, 1796.

Howell, Georgian. *Queen of the Desert: The Extraordinary Life of Gertrude Bell*. London: Macmillan, 2006.

Howell, James. *Instructions for forreine Travell*. London: Printed by T. B., 1642.

Hudson, Geoffrey L. *British Military and Naval Medicine*. Amsterdam: Rodopi, 2007.

Hull, Richard. "Extract of Letters From the Chief Merchants of Gambia, to the Royal African Company, Relating to the Gum-Trade." In *Travels into the Inland Parts of Africa*. London: Printed by Edward Cave, 1738, 18–19.

Hull, Samuel. *The Fluctuating Condition of Human Life: And the Absolute Necessity of a Preparation for the Eternal World*. London, 1750.

Hulme, Peter. *Colonial Encounters: Europe and the Native Caribbean, 1492–1797*. London: Routledge, 1986.

Hume, David. *A Treatise on Human Nature*, 2 Vols. London: Longman and Green, 1878.

———. *Essays and Treatises on Several Subjects*, 4 Vols. London, 1753.

———. *Philosophical Essays Concerning Human Understanding*. London: Printed for A, Miller, 1748.

Hunt, Lynn. *Inventing Human Rights*. New York: W.W. Norton, 2007.

Hunter, Robert. "The Overland Routes to India." In *The Scots Magazine*. Edinburgh: 1798. Vol. VX, 879–881.

Iggers, Georg G. "The Idea of Progress in Historiography and Social Thought Since the Enlightenment." In *Progress and Its Discontents*, edited by Gabriel A. Almond, Marvin Chodorow, and Roy Harvey Pearce. Berkley, Los Angeles and London: University of California Press, 1985.

Inalcik, Halil, Suraya Faroqhi, and Donald Quataert. *An Economic and Social History of the Ottoman Empire 1300–1914*, 2 Vols. Cambridge: Cambridge University Press, 2004.

Innes, Jonna. "Managing the Metropolis: London's Social Problems and Their Control, c. 1660–1830." In *Two Capitals: London and Dublin 1500–1840*, edited by Peter Clark and Raymond Gillespie. Oxford: Proceedings of the British Academy, 2001, Vol. 107, 35–79.

Irving, Sarah. *Natural Science and the Origins of the British Empire*. Abingdon: Routledge, 2016 [2008].

Irwin, Eyles. "Letter 9 Eyles Irwin in London to the Court asking to be allowed his expenses for travelling overland from India.8 Jul 1778". OR/E/1/63 ff. 21–22v, The British Library.

———. *A Series of Adventures in the Course of a Voyage Up to the Red Sea, on the Coast of Arabia and Egypt and of a Route Through the Deserts o Thebais, Hitherto Unknown to the European Traveller in the Year M.DCC.LXXVII in Letters to a Lady*. London: Printed for J. Dodsley, Pall-Mall, 1780.

———. *A Series of Adventures in the Course of a Voyage Up the Red-Sea, on the Coasts of Arabia and Egypt*, 2 Vols. London: Printed for J. Dodsley, 1787.

———. *An Epistle to the Right Honourable George Lord Pigot*. London: Printed for J. Dodsley, in Pall-Mall, 1780.

———. *Bedouins: Or, Arabs of the Desert: A Comic Opera in Three Acts*. Dublin: J. Archer, 1802.

———. *Bedukha or the Self-Devoted: An Indian Pastoral*. London: Printed for J. Dodsley, in Pall-Mall, 1776.

———. *Begebenheiten einer Reise auf dem rothen Meer, auf der arabis*. Leipzig: Weidmanns Erben und Reich, 1781.

———. *Buonaparte in Egypt or, An Appendix into the Enquiry Into His Supposed Expedition to the East*. London: Printed for G. Nicol, Pall Mall, 1798.

———. *Eastern Eclogues Written During a Tour Through Arabia, Egypt, and Other Parts of Asia and Africa in the Year M.DCC. LXXVII*. London: Printed for J. Dodsley, Pall-Mall, 1780.

———. "Epitaph." In *The Poetical Register and Repository for Fugitive Poetry for 1810–1811*. London: Printed for F. C. and J. Rivington, 2006.

———. "Eyles Irwin to Bishop Percy." In *Illustrations of the Literary History of the Eighteenth Century*, edited by John Bowyer Nichols. London: Printed for J. B Nichols and Sons, 1858, Vol III.

———. *Nilus; An Elegy Occasioned by the Victory of Admiral Nelson Over the French Fleet on August 1, 1789.* London: Printed for W. Blumer and Co, 1798.

———. *Occasional Epistles Written During a Journey From London to Busrah, in the Gulf of Persia in the Year 1780 and 1781 to William Hayley, ESQ.* London: Printed for J. Dodsley, in Pall Mall, 1783.

———. *Ode to Robert Brooke, Occasioned by the Death of Hyder Ally.* London: Printed for J. Dodsley, 1784.

———. *The Failure of the French Crusade or the Advantages to Be Derived by Great Britain From the Restoration of Egypt to the Turks.* London: Printed by W. Blumer and Co, 1799.

———. *Voyage de l'Inde en Europe par l'Égypte, par M. Irwin.* Paris: Chez Fuchs, 1793.

———. *Voyage a la Mer Rouge, sur les cotes de l'Arabie, en Egypte, et dans les déserts de la Thébaide: Suivi d'un autre de Venice à Bassorali.* Paris: Chez Briand, 1792.

Irwin, Robert. *The Arabian Nights: A Companion.* London: I.B. Tauris, 2000.

Israel, Jonathan. *Radical Enlightenment: Philosophy and the Making of Modernity 1650–1750.* Oxford: Oxford University Press, 2001.

———. *Revolutionary Ideas: An Intellectual History of the French Revolution From the Rights of Man to Robespierre.* Princeton: Princeton University Press, 2015.

———. *The Revolution of the Mind: Radical Enlightenment and the Intellectual Origin of Modern Democracy.* Princeton and Oxford: Princeton University Press, 2010.

Ives, Edward. *A Voyage From England to India.* London: Printed for Edward and Charles Dilly, 1773.

Jackson, John. *Journey From India Towards England, in the Year 1797.* London, 1799.

Jacobs, James R. *Henry Stubbe, Radical Protestantism and the Early Enlightenment.* Cambridge: Cambridge University Press, 1983.

Jamison, John. *Socinianism Unmasked: In Four Letters to the Lay-Members of the Church of Ayr.* Edinburgh, 1787.

Jardine, Alexander. *Letters From Barbary, France, Spain, Portugal, &c,* 2 Vols. London: Printed for T. Cadell, 1788.

———. *Reflections on the Commerce of the Mediterranean.* London: Printed for W. Clarke and Sons, 1804.

Jarvis, Robin. *Romantic Poets as Travel Readers in Romantic Poetry and Transatlantic Travel: Expeditions and Tours in North America, 1760–1840.* Farnham: Ashgate, 2012.

Jeffrey, David Lyle. *A Dictionary of Biblical Tradition in English Literature.* Michigan: Wm. B. Eerdmans Publishing Co., 1992.

Jervis, H. J. W. *Ireland Under British Rule.* London: Chapman and Hall, 1868.

Johnson, Samuel. *A Dictionary of the English Language.* London: W. Strahan, 1773.

———. *A Dictionary of the English Language,* 2 Vols. London, 1755.

———. *A Dictionary of the English Language: In Which the Words Are Deduced From Their Originals and Explained in Their Different Meanings.* London: Printed for J. Knapton; C. Hitch and L. Hawes; A. Miller; R. and J. Dodsley and M. and T. Longman, 1756.

———. "Boerhaave." In *The Works of Samuel Johnson,* 11 Vols. London: Printed for J. Buckland, 1787, Vol. IV, 329–357.

———. *The Patriot Addressed to the Electors of Great Britain.* London: Printed for T. Cadell, 1774.

———. *The Works of Samuel Johnson,* 6 Vols. Edited by Robert Lynam. London: Printed for George Cowie and Co., 1825, Vol. II, 663–665.

Johnson, Sarah. "Missionary Positions: Romantic European Polynesia From Cook to Stevenson." In *Travel Writing in the Nineteenth Century,* edited by Tim Youngs. London: Anthem Press, 2006, 179–200.

Jones, William. *Grammar of the Persian Language.* London: Printed by W. and J. Richardson, 1771.

———. *Poems Consisting Chiefly of Translations From the Asiatick Languages.* Oxford: The Clarendon Press, 1772.

———. *The History of the Life of Nader Shah, King of Persia: Extracted From an Eastern Manuscript, Which Was Translated into French by Order of His Majesty the King of Denmark.* London: Printed by J. Richardson, 1773.

———. *The Works of Sir William Jones*, 6 Vols. London: Printed for G. G. and J. Robinson, 1799.

Joseph, Fruchtl. *Our Enlightened Barbarian Modernity and the Project of a Critical Theory of Culture*. Amsterdam: Vossiuspers UvA, 2007.

Kames, Lord. *Sketches of the History of Man*, 4 Vols. Dublin: Printed for James Williams, 1774.

Kant, Immanuel. "Idea for a Universal History From a Cosmopolitan Point of View." In *On History*, edited by Lewis White Beck. New York: Bobb-Merrill, 1963.

———. *Kant's Idea for a Universal History With a Cosmopolitan Aim: A Critical Guide*. Edited by Amelie Oksenberg and James Schmidt. Cambridge: Cambridge University Press, 2009.

———. "An Answer to the Question: What is Enlightenment?". In *What is Enlightenment? Eighteenth-Century Answers and Twentieth-Century Questions*, edited by James Schmidt. California: The University of California Press, 1996, 58–64.

Keen, Paul. *Literature, Commerce and the Spectacle for Modernity*. Cambridge: Cambridge University Press, 2012.

Keirstead, Christopher M. "Travel and Poetry." In *The Cambridge History of Travel Writing*, edited by Tim Youngs and Nandini Das. Cambridge: Cambridge University Press, 2020.

Kent, Eddy. *Corporate Character: Representing Imperial Power in British India, 1786–1901*. Toronto: The University of Toronto Press, 2014.

Khair, Tabish. "A Multiplicity of Mirrors: Europe and Modernity in Travel Writing From Asia and Africa." *Indian Literature* 52, no. 6 (2008): 211–222.

Khan, Abu Taleb. *The Travels of Abu Taleb Khan*, 2 Vols. London: Longman, 1810.

Khan, Nur Sobers. "Slavery in the Early-Modern Ottoman Empire." In *The Cambridge World History of Slavery*, edited by Craig Perry, David Eltis, Stanley L. Engerman, and David Richardson. Cornwall: TJ Books Limited, 2021, Vol. II.

Kia, Mehrdad. *The Persian Empire: A Historical Encyclopedia*. Santa Barbara: ABC-CLIO, LLC, 2016.

Kinsley, Zoë. *Women Writing the Home Tour, 1682–1812*. London: Routledge, 2013.

Klein, Laurence. "Coffee-House Civility, 1660–1714: An Aspect of Pos-Courtly Culture in England." *Huntington Library Quarterly* 59, no. 1 (1996): 30–51.

———. *Shaftesbury and the Culture of Politeness*. Cambridge: Cambridge University Press, 1994.

Kleingeld, Pauline. *Kant and Cosmopolitanism: The Philosophical Ideal of World Citizenship*. Cambridge: Cambridge University Press, 2012.

Knight, Henry H. *John Wesley: Optimist of Grace*. Oregon: Cascade Books, 2018.

Knox, Vicesimus. *Essays: Moral and Literary*, 2 vols. London: Charles Dilly, 1787.

Kocak, Cemil. "Transforming Through Constitution: Young Ottoman and the Kanun-i-Esasi of 1876." In *Dimensions of Transformation in the Ottoman Empire From the Late Medieval Age to Modernity*, edited by Seyfi Kenan and Selcuk Askin Somel. Leiden: Brill, 2021, 399–440.

Kramnick, Issac. *Bolingbroke and His Circle: The Politics of Nostalgia in the Age of Walpole*. Cambridge, MA: Harvard University Press, 1968.

———. *Republicanism and Bourgeois Radicalism: Political Ideology in Late Eighteenth-Century England and America*. Ithaca and London: Cornell University Press, 1990.

Kuehn, Julia. *Female Poetics of Empire: From Eliot to Woolf*. London: Routledge, 2014.

Kuhn, Michael F. *Finding Hagar: God's Pursuit of a Runaway*. Carlisle: Langham Global Library, 2019.

Kumar, Krishan. *The Idea of Englishness: English Culture, National Identity and Social Thought*. London: Ashgate, 2005.

Lacorne, Denis. *The Limits of Tolerance: Enlightenment Values and Religious Fanaticism*. New York: Columbia University Press, 2019.

Laidlaw, Christine. *The British in the Levant: Trade and Perceptions of the Ottoman Empire in the Eighteenth Century*. London: I.B. Tauris, 2010.

Lake, Andrew. *The First Protestants in the Arab World: The Contribution to Christian Mission of the English Aleppo Chaplains 1597–1782*. Melbourne School of Theology, PhD Thesis, 2015.

Lamb, Jonathan. *Preserving the Self in the South Seas, 1680–1840*. Chicago: University of Chicago Press, 2001.

Landen, Perceval. "Basra and the Shatt-Ul-Arab." *Journal of the Royal Society of Arts* 63, no. 3257 (1915): 505–519.

Landry, Donna. *Noble Brutes: How Eastern Horses Transformed English Culture*. Baltimore: The John Hopkins University Press, 2009.

Lane, William. *An Account of the Customs and Manners of the Modern Egyptians*, 2 vols. London: Charles Knight & Co., 1836.

Lange, Christian. *Paradise and Hell in Islamic Traditions*. Cambridge: Cambridge University Press, 2016.

Langford, Paul. *A Polite and Commercial People: England 1727–1783*. Oxford: Oxford University Press, 1989.

Larpent, George. *Turkey: Its History and Progress*, 2 Vols. London: Hurst and Blackett Publishers, 1854.

Leask, Nigel. *Curiosity and Aesthetics of Travel Writing: 1770–1840: From an Antique Land*. Oxford: Oxford University Press, 2002.

———. *Robert Burns and Pastoral: Poetry and Improvement in Late Eighteenth-Century Scotland*. Oxford: Oxford University Press, 2010.

———. "Romanticism and the Wider World: Poetry, Travel Literature and Empire." In *The Cambridge History of English Romantic Literature*, edited by James Chandler. Cambridge: Cambridge University Press, 2009, 271–292.

———. *Stepping Westward: Writing the Highland Tour 1720–1830*. Oxford: Oxford University Press, 2020.

———. "'Travelling the Other Way' The Travels of Mirza Abu Taleb Khan (1810) and Romantic Orientalism." In *Romantic Orientalism of British India*, edited by Michael J. Franklin. Abingdon: Routledge, 2005.

Le Cat, Claude-Nicolas. "An Account of Hydro-Enterocele, Appearing Like Hydro-Farcocele and Ending in the Death of the Patient. In a Letter to Charles Morton." In *The Philosophical Transactions for the Year 1767*. London, 1768, Vol. LVII, 293–296.

Lee, Henry. *History of the Campbell Family*. New York: R.L. Polk and Company, 1920.

Lee, Sidney. *Dictionary of National Biography*. New York: Macmillan and Co, 1892.

Lees, Lynn Hollen. *The Solidarities of Strangers: The English Poor Laws and the People, 1700–1948*. Cambridge: Cambridge University Press, 1998.

Lehman, William C. *John Millar of Glasgow 1735–1801: His Life and Thought and His Contributions to Sociological Analysis*. Cambridge: Cambridge University Press, 1960.

Lent, Jeremy. *The Patterning Instinct: A Cultural History of Humanity's Search for Meaning*. New York: Prometheus Book, 2017.

Lessing, Gotthold Ephraim. *Nathan the Wise: A Philosophical Drama From the German*. London:Printed for J. Fielding, 1781.

L'Estrange, Gerard, and Trevor Harvey Levere. *Discussing Chemistry and Steam: The Minutes of a Coffee House Philosophical Society, 1780–1789*. Oxford: Oxford University Press, 2002.

Levin, Yuval. *The Great Debate: Edmund Burke, Thomas Paine and the Birth of Right and Left*. New York: Basic Books, 2014.

Lewis, Bernard. "Gibbon on Muhammad." *Daedalus* 105, no. 3 (1976): 89–101.

———. *The Muslim Discovery of Europe*. London and New York: W.W. Norton, 2001.

Lind, James. *A Treatise of the Scurvy*. Edinburgh: Printed for Sands, Murray and Cochran, 1753.

———. *An Essay, on the Most Effectual Means, of Preserving the Health of Seamen, in the Royal Navy*. London: A. Millar, 1757.

———. "Mr Ives' Curious Observations Made in a Journey From India to Europe by Land." In *An Essay on Disease Incidental to Europeans in Hot Climates*. London: Printed for T. Becket, 1768, 97–106.

Lloyd Genevieve. *Enlightenment Shadows*. Oxford: Oxford University Press, 2013.

Locke, John. *An Essay Concerning Human Understanding*. London: Printed for T. Tegg and Son, 1836 [1689].

Lockhart, Laurence. *Nadir Shah: A Critical Study Based Upon Contemporary Sources*. London: Luzac & Co, 1938.

———. "Nadir Shah's Campaigns in Oman, 1737–1744." *Bulletin of the School of Oriental Studies* 8, no. 1 (1835): 157–171.

Lomas, Michael-Ledger, and David Grange. "Introduction." In *Cities of God: The Bible and Archaeology in Nineteenth-Century Britain*, edited by Michael Ledger-Lomas and David Gange. Cambridge: Cambridge University Press, 2013.

Longrigg, Stephen Hemsley. *Four Centuries of Modern Iraq*. Oxford: The Clarendon Press, 1925.

Lorimer, John Gordon. *Gazetteer of the Persian Gulf, Oman and Central Arabia*, 2 Vols. Kolkata: Superintendent Government Printing, 1915.

Losonsky, Michael. *Enlightenment and Action From Descartes to Kant: Passionate Thought*. Cambridge: Cambridge University Press, 2003.

Lovejoy, Arthur O. *The Great Chain of Being*, 1936. Massachusetts: Harvard University Press, 2001.

Lowe, Lisa. *Critical Terrains: British and French Orientalisms*. Ithaca and London: Cornell University Press, 1991.

Lusignan, Sauveur. *A History of the Revolt of Ali Bey, Against the Ottoman Porte*. London, 1784.

Macfarlane, Alan. *The Riddle of the Modern World: Of Liberty, Wealth and Equality*. New York: Palgrave, 2000.

MacGregor, Arthur. *Curiosity and Enlightenment: Collectors and Collections From the Sixteenth to the Nineteenth Century*. London: Yale University Press, 2007.

Macintyre, Alasdair. *After Virtue: A Study in Moral Theory*. Indiana: The University of Notre Dame Press, 2007 [1981].

MacLean, Gerald. *The Rise of Oriental Travel: English Visitors to the Ottoman Empire, 1580–1722*. New York: Palgrave, 2004.

Magnusson, Andrew D. "A History of Violence? Islam, English Orientalism and the Bombay Riot of 1851." In *Britain in the Islamic World: Imperial and Post-Imperial Connections*, edited by Justin Quinn Olmstead. New York: Palgrave, 2019.

Majeed, Javed. *Ungoverned Imaginings: James Mill's the History of British India and Orientalism*. London: Clarendon Press, 1992.

Makdisi, Saree, and Felicity Nussbaum. "Introduction." In *The Arabian Nights in Historical Context Between East and West*. Oxford: Oxford University Press, 2008.

Malhotra, Ashok. *Making British Indian Fictions: 1772–1823*. New York: Palgrave, 2012.

Mandeville, Bernard. *The Fable of the Bees, Or Private Vices, Public Benefits*. London: Printed for Edmund Parker, 1723.

Mariti, Abbe. *Travels Through Cyprus, Syria and Palestine*, 2 Vols. Dublin, 1792.

Marriott, John. *The Other Empire: Metropolis, India and Progress in the Colonial Imagination*. Manchester: Manchester University Press, 2003.

Marozzi, Justin Baghdad: *City of Peace, City of Blood*. London: Penguin, 2014.

Marriot, John. *The Other Empire: Metropolis, India and Progress in the Colonial Imagination*. Manchester: Manchester University Press, 2009.

Marshall, P. J. *Problems of Empire: Britain and India 1757–1813*. London: Allen and Unwin, 1968.

———. *The Making and Unmaking of Empires: Britain, India and America 1750–1783*. Oxford: Oxford University Press, 2005.

Masters, Bruce. "Aleppo: The Ottoman Empire's Caravan City." In *The Ottoman City Between East and West: Aleppo, Izmir and Istanbul*, edited by Eldem Edhem, Daniel Goffman, and Bruce Masters. Cambridge: Cambridge University Press, 1991.

———. *Christians and Jews in the Ottoman Arab World: The Roots of Sectarianism*. Cambridge: Cambridge University Press, 2001.

———. *The Arabs of the Ottoman Empire, 1516–1918*. Cambridge: Cambridge University Press, 2013.

———. "The Millet Wars in Aleppo, 1726–1821: An Ottoman Perspective." In *Aleppo and its Hinterland in the Ottoman Period*, edited by Stefan Winter and Mafalda Ade. Amsterdam: Brill, 2019, 130–151.

Matar, Nabil. *Henry Stubbe and the Beginning of Islam: The Origin and Progress of Mahometanism.* New York: Columbia University Press, 2014.

Mathar, James. *Pashas: Traders and Travellers in the Islamic World.* New Haven, CT: Yale University Press, 2009.

Mattson, Ingrid. "Status-Based Definitions of Need in Early Islamic *Zakat* and Maintenance Laws." In *Poverty and Charity in Middle Eastern Contexts,* edited by Michael Bonner, Mine Ener, and Amy Singer. New York: State University of New York Press, 2003.

Maundrell, Henry. *A Journey From Aleppo to Jerusalem.* Oxford: Printed at the Theatre, 1703.

Maxwell, Donald. *A Dweller in Mesopotamia, Being the Adventures of an Official Artist in the Garden of Eden.* London: John Lane, 1921.

McGrego, Andrew James. *A Military History of Modern Egypt: From the Ottoman Conquest to the Ramadan War.* Westport and London: Praeger Security International, 2006.

McMahon, Darrin. *Enemies of the Enlightenment: The French Counter-Enlightenment and the Making of Modernity.* Oxford: Oxford University Press, 2002.

Medical Observations and Inquiries. London, 1758.

Mee, Catherine. *Interpersonal Encounters in Contemporary Travel Writing.* London: Anthem Press, 2014.

Mee, Jon. *Dangerous Enthusiasm: William Blake and the Culture of Radicalism in the 1790s.* Oxford, UK: Clarendon, 1992.

Meek, Ronald. *Social Science and the Ignoble Savage.* Cambridge: Cambridge University Press, 1976.

Melman, Billie. *Empires of Antiquities: Modernity and the Rediscovery of the Ancient Near East 1914–1950.* Oxford: Oxford University Press, 2020.

———. *The Culture of History: English Uses of the Past 1800–1953.* Oxford: Oxford University Press, 2006.

———. "The Middle East/Arabia: "The Cradle of Islam"." In *The Cambridge Companion to Travel Writing,* edited by Peter Hulme and Tim Young. Cambridge: Cambridge University Press, 2002, 105–119.

———. *Women's Orients: English Women and the Middle East, 1781–1918.* Basingstoke: Macmillan, 1992.

Millar, John. *The Origin of the Distinction of Ranks or an Inquiry into the Circumstances Which Give Rise to Influence and Authority in the Different Members of Society.* Dublin: Printed by T. Ewing, 1771.

Miller, James. *Botanicum Officinale: Or a Compendious Herbal: Giving an Account of All Such Plants as Are Now Used in the Practice of Physics.* London, 1722.

———. *Mahomet the Impostor: A Tragedy. Taken From the Manager's Book, at the Theatre Royal, Drury-Lane.* London, 1790.

Mills, Sara. *Discourse of Difference: An Analysis of Women Travel Writing and Colonialism.* London: Routledge, 1991.

Mills, Simon. *A Commerce of Knowledge: Trade, Religion, and Scholarship Between England and the Ottoman Empire 1600–1760.* Oxford: Oxford University Press, 2020.

———. "The English Chaplains at Aleppo: Exploration and Scholarship Between England and the Ottoman Empire, 1620–1760." *Bulletin for the Council for British Research in the Levant* 6, no. 1 (2011): 13–20.

Milner, Thomas. *The Ottoman Empire: The Sultans, the Territory, and the People.* London: The Religious Tract Society, 1799.

Minchinger, Ethan L. *The First of Modern Ottomans: The Intellectual History of Ahmed Vasif.* Cambridge: Cambridge University Press, 2017.

Moltchanova, Anna, and Susannah Ottaway. "Right and Reciprocity in the Political and Philosophical Discourse of Eighteenth-Century England." In *The Culture of the Gift in Eighteenth-Century England,* edited by Linda Zionkowski and Cynthia Klekar. New York: Palgrave, 2009, 25–36.

Momigliano, Arnaldo. "Ancient History and the Antiquarian." *Journal of the Warburg and Courtauld Institutes* 13 (1950): 285–315.

Montagu, Mary. *Letters of the Right Honourable Lady M-y W-y M-e; written during her Travels in Europe, Asia, and Africa,* 4 vols. London: Printed for B. Dodd and T. Reily, 1771.

Montesquieu, Charles-Louis de Secondat. *The Spirit of the Laws.* Edited by Anne M. Cohler, Basia C. Miller, and Harold S. Stone. Cambridge: Cambridge University Press, 1998.

Moore, Wendy. *The Knife Man: Blood, Blood Snatching and the Birth of Modern Surgery.* New York: Broadway Books, 2005.

Morgann, Maurice. *In Considerations on the Present Internal and External Condition of France.* London: J. Debrett, 1794.

Morton, Charles. *An Extract From the Journals of the Royal Society Respecting a Letter Addressed to the Society by a Member of the House of Jesuits at Pekin in China.* London: W. Bowyer and J. Nichols, 1770.

Mulholland, James. *Sounding Imperial: Poetic Voice and the Politics of Empire, 1730–1820.* Baltimore: The John Hopkins University Press, 2013.

Nalbandian, Louise. *The Armenian Revolutionary Movement.* Berkeley: University of California Press, 1963.

Nash, Geoffrey. *From Empire to Orient: Travellers in the Middle East 1830–1926.* London: IB Tauris, 2005.

Nasr, Seyyed Hosssein. *The Garden of Truth: The Vision and Promise of Sufism: Islam's Mystical Tradition.* New York: Harper One, 2007.

Nechtman, Tillman. "A Jewel in the Crown: Indian Wealth in Domestic Britain in the Late Eighteenth Century." *Eighteenth Century Studies* 1 (2007): 71–86.

———. *Nabobs: Empire and Identity in Eighteenth-Century Britain.* Cambridge: Cambridge University Press, 2010.

Newman, Daniel. *An Imam in Paris: Account of a Stay in France by an Egyptian Cleric (1826–1831).* London: Saqi, 2004.

Nicholas, Rogers. "Policing the Poor in Eighteenth-Century London: The Vagrancy Laws and their Administration." *Histoire sociale-Social History* 24 (1991): 127–147.

Niebuhr, Carsten. *Reisebeschreibung nach Arabien.* Kopenhagen: Gedrluckt bey N. Moeller, 1774.

———. *Travels Through Arabia and other Countries in the East.* Translated by Robert Heron, 2 Vols. Edinburgh: Printed for R. Morison, 1792.

———. *Voyage en Arabie et en d'autres pays circonvoisins*, 2 Vols. Amsterdam: S.J. Baalde, 1776.

Nohara, Shinji. *Commerce and Strangers in Adam Smith.* Singapore: Springer, 2018.

Norden, Fredric. *Voyage d'egypte et de nubie.* Copenhagen, 1755.

North, Dudley. *The Lives of the Right Hon. Francis North, Baron Guilford; the Hon. Sir Dudley North and the Hon. and Rev. Dr John North*, 3 Vols. London, 1890.

Norton, David Fate, and Mary Norton. *The David Hume Library.* Edinburgh: Edinburgh Bibliographical Society, 1996.

O'Brien, Karen. *Women and Enlightenment in Eighteenth-Century Britain.* Cambridge: Cambridge University Press, 2009.

O'Flaherty, Niall. *Utilitarianism in the Age of the Enlightenment.* Cambridge: Cambridge University Press, 2019.

Ockley, Simon. *The History of the Saracens.* Chicago: 2 Vols. Cambridge: Printed for the sole benefit of Mrs. Anne Ockley, 1557.

Ogilvie, Brian. *The Science of Describing: Natural History in Renaissance Europe.* Chicago: The University of Chicago Press, 2006.

Oldfield, J. R. *Popular Politics and British Anti-Slavery: The Mobilisation of Public Opinion Against Slave Trade 1787–1807.* London: Routledge, 1998.

Ooghe, Bart. "The Rediscovery of Babylonia: European Travellers and the Development of Knowledge on Lower Mesopotamia, Sixteenth to Early Nineteenth Century." *Journal of the Royal Asiatic Society* 17, no. 3 (2007): 231–52.

Oliver, Susan. *Walter Scott and the Greening of Scotland: Emergent Ecologies of a Nation.* Cambridge: Cambridge University Press, 2021.

Oliphant, Patrick. "An Account of the Epidemick Disease Most Frequent at Gambroon, by the Late Dr Oliphant and Communicated to Dr Fothergill, by J. Hardcastle, Surgeon in the Hon. East- India Company's Service." In *Medical Observations and Inquiries.* London: Printed for William Johnston, 1557, Vol. I.

O'Loughlin, Katrina. *Women Writing and Travel in the Eighteenth Century*. Cambridge: Cambridge University Press, 2018.

O'Quinn, Daniel. *Engaging the Ottoman Empire: Vexed Mediations, 1690–1815*. Pennsylvania: The University of Pennsylvania Press, 2019.

Ousley, William. *Oriental Collections Consisting of Original Essays and Dissertations, Translations and Miscellaneous Papers*. London: Printed for Cadell and Davis, 1797–1798, 2 Vols.

———. *The Oriental Geography of Ebn Haukal, an Arabian Traveller of the Tenth Century*. London: Printed at the Oriental Press, 1800.

Outram, Dorinda. *Panorama of the Enlightenment*. Oxford: Oxford University Press, 2006.

Özkoray, Hayri Gökşin. "Poverty, Law and Labour in the Ottoman Empire." In *The Routledge History of Poverty 1400–1800*, edited by David Hitchcock and Julia McClure. Abingdon and New York: Routledge, 2021, 309–321.

Oz-Salzberger, Fania. "Introduction." In *An Essay on the History of Civil Society*, edited by Fania Oz-Salzberger. Cambridge: Cambridge University Press, 1995.

Pagden, Anthony. *The Enlightenment: And Why It Still Matters*. Oxford: Oxford University Press, 2013.

Paine, Thomas. *Rights of Man, Part the Second Combining Principle and Practice*. London: Printed for J.S Jordan, 1792.

Pagès, François. *Travels Round the World, in the Years 1767, 1768, 1769, 1770, 1771 by Monsieur de Pagès, in 1791*, 3 Vols. London: Printed for J. Murray, 1791.

———. *Voyages autour du monde et vers les deux pôles, par terre et par mer, pendant les années 1767 à 1776*. Paris, 1782.

Palmeri, Frank. *State of Nature, Stages of Society: Enlightenment Conjectural History and Modern Social Discourse*. Columbia: Columbia University Press, 2015.

Pande, Ishita. *Medicine, Race and Liberalism in British Bengal: Symptoms of Empire*. New York: Routledge, 2010.

Parsons, Abraham. *Travels in Asia and Africa Including a Journey From Scanderoon to Aleppo, and Over the Desert to Baghdad and Bussora*. London: Printed for Longman, Hurst, Rees and Ormt, Paternoster-Bow, 1808.

Paton, Andrew Archibald. *The Modern Syrians: Or, the Native Society in Damascus, Aleppo, and The Mountains of the Druses From Notes Made in Those Parts During the Years 1841-2-3. By an Oriental Student*. London, 1844.

Patrick Russell. *A Treatise of the Plague*, 2 Vols. London: Printed for G. G. and Robinson, 1791.

Pearson, Richard. *Observations on the Nutritive Properties of Gum Arabic*. London, 1818.

Perry, Jonathan. *Promised Lands: The British and the Ottoman Middle East*. Princeton: Princeton University Press, 2022.

Philips, Jim, and Philip Lawson. "Our Execrable Banditti: Perceptions of Nabobs in Mid-Eighteenth Century Britain." *Albion: A Quarterly Journal Concerned With British Studies* 16, no. 3 (1984): 225–241.

Philips, Mark Salber. *Society and Sentiment: Genres of Historical Writing in Britain, 1740–1820*. Princeton: Princeton University Press, 2000.

Philipson, Nicholas. *Adam Smith: An Enlightened Life*. London: Penguin, 2010.

Pickford, Susan. "The Page as Private/Public Space in Mariana Starke's Travel Writings on Italy." In *Travel Writing, Form and Empire*, edited by Julia Kuehn and Paul Smethurst. London: Routledge, 2009.

Pinto, V. de Sola. "Sir William Jones and English Literature." *Bulletin of the School of Oriental and African Studies, University of London* 11, no. 4 (1946): 686–694.

Pittock, Murray G. H. *Enlightenment in a Smart City: Edinburgh's Civic Development, 1660–1750*. Edinburgh: Edinburgh University Press, 2019.

———. "Historiography." In *The Cambridge Companion to the Scottish Enlightenment*, edited by Alexander Broadie. Cambridge: Cambridge University Press, 2003, 258–279.

Pitts, Jennifer. "The Global Enlightenment in Historical Thought". In *A Companion to Global Historical Thought*, edited by Prasenjit Duara, Viren Murthy, and Andrew Sartori. Chichester: Wiley Blackwell, 2014.

———. *A Turn to Empire: A Rise of Imperial Liberalism in Britain and France*. Princeton and Oxford: Princeton University Press, 2005.

Plaisted, Bartholomew. *A Journal From Calcutta in Bengal, by Sea, to Busserah*. London: T. Kinnersly, 1758.

Pocock, J. G. A. *Barbarism and Religion: The Enlightenments of Edward Gibbon 1737–1746*. Cambridge: Cambridge University Press, 1999, Vol. I.

———. *Barbarism and Religion: Narratives of Civil Government*. Cambridge: Cambridge University Press, 1999, Vol. II.

Pococke, Richard. *A Description of the East and Some Other Countries: Observations on Egypt*. London: Printed for the Author by W. Bowyer, 1743, Vol. I.

———. *A Description of the East and Some Other Countries: Observations on Palestine or the Holy Land, Syria, Mesopotamia, Cyprus and Candia*. London: Printed for the Author by W. Bowyer, 1745, Vol. II.

Polanyi, Karl. *The Great Transformation*. New York: Farrar and Rinehart, Inc, 1944.

Poole, Steve. "Not Precedents to Be Followed, But Examples to be Weighed: John Thelwall and the Jacobin Sense of the Past." In *John Thelwall: Radical Romantic and Acquitted Felon*, edited by Steve Poole. Abingdon: Routledge, 2009, 161–174.

Porter, Dorothy and Roy Porter. *Patient's Progress: Doctors and Doctoring in Eighteenth-Century England*, Stanford and California: Stanford University Press, 1989.

Porter, James. *Observations on the Religion, Law, Government, Manners of the Turks*, 2 Vols. London: Printed for J. Nourse, 1768.

Porter, Roy. *The Creation of the Modern World: The Untold Story of the British Enlightenment*. New York: W.W Norton, 2000.

———. *Disease, Medicine and Society in England, 1550–1860*. Cambridge: Cambridge University Press, 1995.

Poynter, J. R. *Society and Pauperism: English Ideas on Poor Relief, 1795–1834*. London, 1969.

Prasad, Ishwari. *India in the Eighteenth Century*. Allahabad: Chugh Publications, 1973.

Prasad, Ram Chandra. *Early English Travellers in India*. New Delhi: Motilal, 1965.

Pratt, Mary Louise. *Imperial Eyes: Travel Writing and Transculturation*. London: Routledge, 1992.

Prideaux, Humphrey. *A Letter to Deists*. London: Printed for Edward Castle, 1696.

———. *The Old and New Testaments Connected in the History of Jews and Neighbouring Nations*, 2 Vols. New York, 1842.

———. *The True Nature of Imposture Fully Display'd in the Life of Mahomet; With a Discourse Annex'd for the Vindicating of Christianity From This Charge; Offered to the Consideration of the Deists of the Present Age*. London: Printed for William Rogers, 1698.

Pritchard, Earl H. "The Instructions of the East India Company to Lord Macartney on His Embassy to China and His Reports to the Company, 1792–4. Part I: Instructions From the Company." *Journal of the Royal Asiatic Society of Great Britain and Ireland* 2 (1938): 201–230.

Purchas, Samuel. *Purchas His Pilgrimage or Relations of the World*. London: Printed by William Stansby, 1626.

Quataert, Donald. *The Ottoman Empire, 1700–1922*. Cambridge: Cambridge University Press, 2005.

Rafeq, Abdul-Karim. "The Poor in Ottoman Damascus: A Socioeconomic and Political Study." In *Pauvreté et richesse dans le monde musulman méditerranéen*. Paris: Maisonneuve et Larose, 2003, 217–226.

Raikes, Charles. *Notes on the Revolt in the North-Western Provinces of India*. London: Longman, Brown, Green, Longmans and Roberts, 1858.

Ramsey, Allan. *The Poems of Allan Ramsey*, 2 Vols. Glasgow: Printed for Chapman, 1797.

Rasmussen, Dennis C. "Does "Bettering Our Condition" Really Make Us Better Off? Adam Smith on Progress and Happiness." *The American Political Science Review* 100, no. 3 (2006): 309–318.

———. *The Pragmatic Enlightenment.* Cambridge: Cambridge University Press, 2014.

Rauwolff, Leonhart. "Itinerary into the Eastern Countries." In *A Collection of Curious Travels and Voyages*, edited by John Ray. London: Printed for S. Smith, 1693.

Raynal, Guillaume Thomas Francois. *A Philosophical and Political History of the Settlements and Trade of the Europeans in the East and West Indies*, 4 Vols. Dublin: Printed for Exshaw, 1779.

Remarks. *Upon the Principles and Views of the London Corresponding Society.* London: Printed for J. Debrett, 1795.

Renard, John. *The A to Z of Sufism.* Lanham: The Scarecrow Press, 2009

Rennell, James. "On the Rate of Travelling, as Performed by Camels and its Applications, as a scale to the Purpose of Geography." *Philosophical Transactions of the Royal Society* 18 (1791): 129–145.

Reynold, Joshua. *The Works of Joshua Reynolds*, 2 Vols. London: Printed for T. Cadell, 1801.

Rich, Claudius James. *A Narrative of Residence in Koordistan*, 2 Vols. London, 1836.

———. *Memoir on the Ruins of Babylon.* London: Longman, 1818.

Richmond, Herbert William. *The Navy in the War of 1739–48.* Cambridge: Cambridge University Press, 1920.

Roberts, Justine. *Slavery and the Enlightenment in the British Atlantic, 1750–1807.* Cambridge: Cambridge University Press, 2013.

Robertson, John. *The Case for the Enlightenment: Scotland and Naples 1680–1760.* Cambridge: Cambridge University Press, 2005.

———. *The Enlightenment: A Very Short Introduction.* Oxford: Oxford University Press, 2015.

Robertson, William. *The History of the Reign of the Emperor Charles V*, 5 Vols. London, 1769.

Robins, Nick. *The Corporation That Changed the World: How the East India Company Shaped the Modern Multinational*. London: Pluto Press, 2006.

Robson, Laura. *The Politics of Mass Violence in the Middle East.* Oxford: Oxford University Press, 2020.

Roddis, Louis H. *James Lind: Founder of Nautical Medicine.* New York: Henry Schuman, 1950.

Rooke, Henry. *Travels to the Coast of Arabia Felix and from Thence by the Red Sea and Egypt to Europe.* London: Printed for R. Blamire, 1783.

Rosenblatt, Helena. "Rousseau: The Anti-Cosmopolitan." *Daedalus* 137, no. 3 (2008): 59–67.

Roque, Jean de La. *A Voyage to Arabia the Happy: By the Way of the Eastern Ocean, and the Streights of the Red Sea Performed by the French for the First Time A.D. 1798, 1709, 1710.* London: Printed for G. Strahan at the Golden-Ball over against the Royal Exchange and R. Williamson near Grey's-Inn Gate, Holborn, 1730.

Rousseau, Jean Jacques. *On the Social Contract: With Geneva Manuscript and Political Economy.* Translated by Roger D. Masters and Judith R. Masters. New York: St. Martin's Press, 1978.

Rowley, William. *A Treatise on Putrid, Malignant, Infectious Fevers.* London: Printed by J. Barfield, Wardour Street, 1804.

Rowse, Alfred Leslie. *The Expansion of Elizabethan England.* New York: St Martin's Press, 1955.

Roy, Rohan Deb. *Malarial Subjects: Empire, Medicine and Nonhumans in British India, 1820–1909.* Cambridge: Cambridge University Press, 2017.

Rudd, Andrew. *Sympathy and India in British Literature 1770–1830.* New York: Palgrave, 2011.

Russell, Alexander. *The Natural History of Aleppo: A Description of the City, and the Principal Natural Productions in Its Neighbourhood. Together With an Account of the Climate, Inhabitants, and Diseases; Particularly the Plague*, 2 Vols. London: Printed for G.G and J. Robinson, 1794.

———. *The Natural History of Aleppo and the Parts Adjacent.* London: Printed for A. Miller, 1756.

Rycaut, Paul. *The Present State of the Ottoman Empire.* London: Printed by T. N for John Starkey, 1682.

Ryley, J. Horton. *Ralph Fitch: England's Pioneer to India and Burma, His Companions and Contemporaries, His Remarkable Narrative Told in His Own Words.* London: T. Fisher Unwin, 1899.

Said, Edward. *Orientalism.* London: Penguin, 2003.

Saggs, H. W. F. *People of the Past: Babylonians.* Berkeley: University of California Press, 2000.

Said, Rosemarie J. *George Baldwin and British Interests in Egypt 1775 to 1798.* PhD Thesis, SOAS University of London, 1968.

Sakhnini, Mohammad. "Eighteenth-Century European Medical Encounters With the Ottoman Levant." *Tarih Dergisi - Turkish Journal of History* 73 (2021): 77–101.

Saldanha, Jerome Antony. *Précis of Turkish Arabia Affairs 1801–1905.* Simla: Government Central Press, 1906.

Sale, George. *The Koran, Commonly Called the Alcoran of Mohammed.* London, 1734.

Sandys, George. *A Relation of a Journey Began Anno Dom 1610.* London: Printed for W. Barrett, 1615.

Santayana, George. "The Philosophy of Travel." *The Virginia Quarterly Review* 1 (1964): 1–10.

Scafi, Alessandro. *Mapping Paradise: A History of Heaven on Earth.* Chicago: University of Chicago, 2006.

———. "Mapping Eden: Cartographies of the Earthly Paradise." In *Mappings*, edited by Denis Cosgrove. London: Reaktion Books, 1999, 50–70.

Schurer, Norbert. "John Henry Grose." In *Christian-Muslims Relations: A Bibliographical History*, edited by David Thomas and John Chestworth. Leiden: Brill, 2019, Vol. 13, 600–606.

Scott, Richard. "Letter on the Passage Over the Isthmus of Suez and Project of a New Route to India, 1780." East India Company, the Board of Control, the India Office, or other British Government Department, IOR/L/MAR/C/570, ff 56–84.

Scrivener, Michael. *The Cosmopolitan Ideal.* London: Pickering and Chatto, 2007.

Sebastiani, Silvia. *The Scottish Enlightenment: Race, Gender and the Limit of Progress.* New York: Palgrave, 2013.

Sellin, Christine Petra. *Fractured Families and Rebel Maidservants: The Biblical Hagar in Seventeenth-Century Dutch Art and Literature*, 2006.

Sen, Amrit. ""The Persian Prince in London": Autoethnography and Positionality in Travels of Mirza Abu Taleb Khan." *Asiatic* 2, no. 1 (2008): 58–68.

Seymour, Michael. "Babylon." In *Cities of God: The Bible and Archaeology in Nineteenth Century Britain*, edited by David Gange and Michael Ledger-Lomas. Cambridge: Cambridge University Press, 2013.

Shalev, Zur. *Sacred Words and Worlds: Geography, Religion and Scholarship, 1550–1700.* Leiden: Brill, 2012.

———. "The Travel Notebook of John Greaves." In *The Republic of Letters and the Levant*, edited by Alastair Hamilton, Maurits H. Van Den Boogert, and Bart Westerweel. Leiden: Brill, 2005, 77–102.

Sharkey, Heather J. *The History of Muslims, Christians and Jews in the Middle East.* Cambridge: Cambridge University Press, 2017.

Shaw, Stanford. *Between Old and New: The Ottoman Empire Under Selim HI, 1789–1808.* Cambridge, MA: Harvard University Press, 1971.

———. *History of the Ottoman Empire and Modern Turkey.* Cambridge: Cambridge University Press, 1967.

Sheehan, Jonathan. *The Enlightenment Bible: Translation, Scholarship, Culture.* Princeton: Princeton University Press, 2005.

Shefer, Miri. "Charity and Hospitality: Hospitals in the Ottoman Empire in the Early Modern Period." In *Poverty and Charity in Middle Eastern Contexts*, edited by Michael Bonner, Mine Ener, and Amy Singer. New York: State University of New York Press, 2003.

Sher, Richard. *The Enlightenment and the Book: Scottish Authors and Their Publishers in Eighteenth-Century Britain, Ireland and America.* Chicago: The University of Chicago Press, 2006.

Sheridan, Thomas. *A Plan Of Education for the Noble Youth Nobility and Gentry of Great Britain Most Humbly Addressed to the Father of His People.* London, 1969.

Sherlock, Thomas. *A Letter to the Clergy and People of London and Westminster on Occasion of the Late Earthquake.* London, 1750.

Shirley, Anthony. *Sir Anthony Shirly, His Relations of His Travels into Persia.* London: N. Butler & Bagfet, 1613.

Short, Thomas. *Discourses on Tea, Sugar, Milk, Made-Wine, Spirits, Punch, Tobacco.* London, 1750.

Shoshan, Boaz. "Social Life and Popular Culture in the Arabian Nights." In *The Arabian Nights Encyclopedie.* California: ABC-CLIO, 2004.

Sicily, Diodorus. *Diodorus of Sicily.* Translated by C. H Oldfather, 10 Vols. London: William Heinemann LTD, 1946.

Sikka, Sonia. *Herder on Humanity and Cultural Difference.* Cambridge: Cambridge University Press, 2011.

Singer, Amy. *Charity in Islamic Societies.* Cambridge: Cambridge University Press, 2008.

Siskin, Clifford, and William Warner. "This is Enlightenment: Invitation in the Form of an Argument." In *This is Enlightenment,* edited by Clifford Siskin and William Warner. Chicago: Chicago University Press, 2010.

Skinner, Quentin. *Visions and Politics: Renaissance Virtues.* Cambridge: Cambridge University Press, 2002.

Smethurst, Paul. *Travel Writing and the Natural World, 1768–1840.* Basingstoke: Palgrave, 2012.

Smith, Adam. *The Theory of Moral Sentiments.* London: Printed for A. Miller, 1761.

———. *An Inquiry into the Nature and Causes of the Wealth of Nations,* 2 Vols. London, 1776.

———. *Lectures on Jurisprudence.* Edited by R. L. Meek, D. D. Rapahel, and P. G. Stein. Reprint. Indianapolis: Library Classics, 1982.

Smith, Vanessa. *Intimate Strangers: Friendship, Exchange and Pacific Encounters.* Cambridge: Cambridge University Press, 2010.

———. *Tobias Smollett put it in his Travels Through France and Italy,* 2 Vols. London: Printed for R. Baldwin, 1778.

Sonnini, Charles. *Travels in Upper and Lower Egypt.* London: Printed for J. Debrett, 1800.

Sorkin, David. *The Religious Enlightenment: Protestants, Jews, and Catholics From London to Vienna.* Princeton and Oxford: Princeton University Press, 2008.

Stammers, Tom. *The Purchas of the Past: Collecting Culture in Post-Revolutionary Paris 1790–1890.* Cambridge: Cambridge University Press, 2020.

Stewart, Dugald. "Account of the Life and Writings of Adam Smith." In *The Theory of Moral Sentiments.* London: Henry G. Bohn, 1853.

Sterne, Laurence. *A Sentimental Journey through France and Italy,* 2 vols. London: T. Becket and P.A De Hondt, 1768.

Stirling, James Hutchinson. *The Secret of Hegel.* London: Longman and Green, 1856.

Strahan, W. *A New and General Biographical Dictionary.* London: Printed for, 1784, Vol VI, 477–478.

Struys, John. *The Voyages and Travels of John Struys Through Italy, Greece, Muscovy, Media, Persia.* London: Printed for Abel Swalle, 1684.

Sullivan, Richard. *Philosophical Rhapsodies: Fragments of Akbur of Betlis,* 3 Vols. London, 1784.

Suranyi, Anna. *The Genius of the English Nation: Travel Writing and National Identity in Early Modern England.* Newark: University of Delaware Press, 2008.

Sweet, Rosemary. *Antiquaries: The Discovery of the Past in Eighteenth-Century Britain.* London: Hambledon and London, 2004.

Swinton, John. "Description of Two Parthian Coins, Never Hitherto Published. By the Rev. John Swinton, B. D. F. R. S. Member of the Academy degli Apatisti at Florence, and of the Etruscan Academy of Cortona in Tuscany, in a Letter to Charles Morton, M.D. Sec. R. SPhil." *Transactions of the Royal Society.* London, 1766, Vol. 56, 296–301.

———. "Description of a Meteor Seen at Oxford, October 12, 1766. In a Letter to Charles Morton, M. D. Sec. R. S. From the Rev. John Swinton, B. D. F. R. S. Member of the Academy Degli Apatisti at Florence, and of the Etruscan Academy of Cortona in Tuscany." *Philosophical Transactions.* London, 1767, Vol. 57, 108–110.

———. "Interpretation of the Inscription on a Punic coin. In a letter to Charles Morton, M. D. Sec. R. S. From the Rev. John Swinton, B. D. F. R. S." *Philosophical Transactions of the Royal Society*. London, 1768, Vol. 58, 235–245.

Sykes, Percy Molesworth. *The History of Persia*, 2 Vols. London: Macmillan and Co, Limited, 1915.

Talbot, Michael. *British-Ottoman Relations, 1661–1807: Commerce and Diplomatic Practice in Eighteenth-Century Istanbul*. Woodbridge: Boydell & Brewer, 2017.

———. "Gifts of Time: Watches and Clocks in British-Ottoman Diplomacy, 1693–1803." *Jahrbuch für Europäische Geschichte* 17 (2016): 55–79.

———. "Petitions of the Supplicant Ambassador: British Commercial Representations to the Ottoman State in the Eighteenth Century." *Osmanli Arastirmalari/The Journal of Ottoman Studies* 46 (2015): 163–191.

Tavernier, Jean-Baptiste. *Collections of Travels Through Turkey into Persia and the East Indies*, 2 Vols. London: Printed for Moses Pitt, 1684.

———. *The Six Voyages of John Baptista Tavernier*. London: Printed for R. L and M. P, 1678.

Taylor, Barbara. "Feminists Versus Gallant: Sexual Manners and Morals in Enlightenment Britain." In *Women, Gender and Enlightenment*, edited by Sarah Knott and Barbara Taylor. Basingstoke: Palgrave, 2005.

Taylor, John. *Travels From England to India, in the Year 1789, by the Way of the Tyrol, Venice, Scandaroon, Aleppo, and Over the Great desart to Bussora*, 2 Vols. London, 1799.

Teixeira, Pedro. *Relaciones de Pedro Teixeira d'el origen, descendencia y succession de los Reyes de Persia*. Antwerp: Hieronymus Verdussen, 1610.

———. *The Travels of Pedro Teixeira With His "Kings of Harmuz."* Translated by William Sinclair. London: Printed for the Hakluyt Society, 192.

Teltscher, Kate. "The Shampooing Surgeon and the Persian Prince: Two Indians in Early Nineteenth-Century Britain." *Interventions* 2, no. 3 (2000): 409–423.

The Analytical Review or History of Literature, Domestic and Foreign, Vol. XXII. London: Printed for J. Johnson, 1796.

The Annual Biography and Obituary. "Eyles Irwin, EsQ. M. R. I. A." London: Printed for Longman, Hurst, Rees, 1818, Vol. II, 221–236.

The Annual Register: Or a View of the History, Politics and Literature For the Year 1780. London:Printed for J. Dodsley, 1781, 54–57.

The British Critic. London: Printed for F. and C. Rivington, 1802, Vol. XX, 403.

The Critical Review: Or Annals of Literature, Vol. 4. London:Printed for R. Baldwin, 1758, 318–324.

The Critical Review or Annals of Literature, Vol. 7. London: Printed for Hamilton, 1759, 504–512.

The Critical Review or Annals of Literature, Vol. 8. London: Printed for A Hamilton, 1793, 91–92.

The Critical Review of Annals of Literature. London: Printed for A. Hamilton, 1780, 405–412.

The Critical Review or Annals of Literature. London: Printed for S. Hamilton, 1799.

The Dutch and English East India Companies: Diplomacy, Trade and Violence in Early Modern Asia, edited by Adam Clulow and Tristan Mostert. Amsterdam: The University of Amsterdam Press, 2019.

The Eclectic Review. Vol IV, Part II. London: Printed for Longman, 1808.

The Enlightenment World, edited by Martin Fitzpatrick, Peter Jones, Christa Knellwolf, and Iain McCalman. Abingdon and New York, 2004.

The European Magazine and the London Review. "Memoires of Eyles Irwin." London: Printed for J. Sewell, 1789, Vol. XV, 179–182.

The Gentleman's Magazine and Historical Chronicle in the Year MDCCXCII. Vol LXII. London: Printed for John Nichols, 1792.

The Global Eighteenth Century, edited by Felicity Nussbaum. Maryland: The John Hopkins University Press, 2003.

The London Review: Conducted by Richard Cumberland, Vol. II. London: Printed for Samuel Tipper, 1809, 363–372.

The Modern Part of the Universal History Compiled From Original Writers' By the Authors of the Antients which will Perfect the Work, and Render it a Complete Body of History From the Earliest Account of Time, to the Present. London: Printed for T. Osborne, 1765, Vol. XLIII.

The Modern Part of The Universal History Compiled From Original Writers. London: Printed for C. Bathhurst, 1783, Vol XXXVI.

The Monthly Review of Literary Journal, Vol. VI. London: Printed for R. Griffiths, 1791, 547–555.

The Monthly Review or Literary Journal by Several Hands. Vol. XVII. London: Printed for R. Griffiths, 1757.

The Monthly Review or Literary Journal, Vol. LIII. London: Printed for R. Griffiths, 1776.

The Monthly Review or Literary Journal. London:Printed for R. Griffiths, 1792, Vol. VII, 525–528.

The Monthly Review or Literary Journal. London:Printed for R. Griffiths, 1780, Vol. LXIII, 401–409.

The Monthly Review or Literary Journal. London:Printed for R. Griffiths, 1788, 518–520.

The Monthly Review or Literary Journal. London:Printed for R. Griffiths, 1779, Vol. IX.

The Monthly Review or Literary Journal by Several Hands. Vol XVII. London:Printed for R. Griffiths, 1757, 89–96.

The Monthly Review or Literary Journal. Vol. LXI. London: Sold by Becket and Porter, 1810, 286–299.

The Monumental Inscriptions in the Church and Churchyard of S. Mary, Lewisham, edited by Herbert Charles Kirby and Leland Lewis Duncan. Lee: Printed by Charles Forth, 1889.

The Naval Chronicle From July to December 1799, 38 Vols. London, 1799, Vol. II.

The Parliamentary Register or History of the Proceedings and Debates of the House of Commons, Vol. XXXIV. London: J. Debrett, 1793.

The Pedigree Register, edited by George Sherwood. London: Published by the Editor, 1913–1916.

The Philosophical Transactions of the Royal Society of London, Vol X From 1750 to 1755. London, 1809.

The Poetical Register. London, 1814.

The Proceedings of the Association Promoting the Discover of the Interior Parts of Africa. London: Printed by C. Macrae, 1790.

The Teaching and Learning of Arabic in Early-Modern Europe, edited by Jan Loop, Alastair Hamilton, and Charles Burnett. Leiden: Brill, 2007.

Thevenot, Jean de. *The Travels of Monsieur De Thevenot Into The Levant: In Three Parts.* London: Printed for H. Clark for H. Faithorne, 1687.

Tidrick, Kathryn. *Heart Beguiling Arabia: The English Romance with Arabia.* London: I. B Tauris, 1989.

Thomas, Keith. *In Pursuit of Civility: Manners and Civilisations in Early Modern England.* Massachusetts: Brandeis University Press, 2018.

Thomas, Nicholas. *Entangled Objects: Exchange, Material Culture and Colonialism in the Pacific.* Massachusetts: Harvard University Press, 1991.

Thompson, Carl. *Travel Writing.* London: Routledge, 2011.

Thompson, Charles. *Travels Through Turkey in Asia*, 2 Vols. London, 1767.

Thompson, E. P. *The Making of the English Working Class.* London: Victor Gollanz, 1963.

———. *Customs in Common: Studies in Traditional Popular Culture.* London: Penguin Books, 1991.

Thompson, John L. *Writing the Wrongs: Women of the Old Testament Among Biblical Commentators From Philo Through the Reformation.* Oxford: Oxford University Press, 2001.

Tobias, Smollett. *The Adventures of Roderick Random*, Vol. 2. London: Printed for J. Osborne, 1748.

Todd, Janet. "Introduction." In *A Vindication of the Rights of Women, a Vindication of the Rights of Men and an Historical and Moral View of the Origin and Progress of the French Revolution.* Oxford: Oxford University Press, 1993.

Tolan, John V. *Saracens: Islam in Medieval European Imagination.* New York: Columbia University Press, 2002.

Toledano, Ehud Rafael. *Slavery and Abolition in the Ottoman Middle East.* Seattle: University of Washington Press, 1998.

Tott, François Baron de. *Memoires of the Baron de Tott*, 3 Vols. Dublin, 1785.

Tournefort, Joseph Pitton de. *A Voyage into the Levant*, 2 Vols. London: Printed for D. Browne, 1718.

———. *Materia Medica, or a Description of Simple Medicines Generally Used in Physic.* London: Printed by J. H. for Andrew Bell, 1708.

Troelenberg, Eva-Maria. ""...That We Trusted Not to Arab Notions of Archaeology": Reading the Grand Narrative Against the Grain." In *Antiquarianisms: Contact, Conflict, Comparison*, edited by Benjamin Anderson and Felipe Rojas. Oxbow: Oxford, 2017, 161–183.

Tudela, Benjamin. *The Itinerary of Rabbi Benjamin of Tudela.* Translated by A. Asher, 2 Vols. London and Berlin: A. Asher & Co., 1840.

Tully, Miss. *Narrative of a Ten-Year Residence at Tripoli in Africa.* London, 1818.

Turgot on Progress: Sociology and Economics: A Philosophical Review of the Successive Advances of the Human Mind, edited by Ronald L. Meek. New York: Cambridge University Press, 1973.

Turley, David. *The Culture of English Anti-Slavery.* London: Routledge, 1991.

Turner, Frank M. "Introduction." In *Edmund Burke's Reflections on the Revolution in France*, edited by Frank M. Turner. New Haven: Yale University Press, 2003.

Turner, Katherine. *British Travel Writers in Europe, 1750–1800: Authorship, Gender and National Identity.* London: Ashgate, 2001.

Tweed, John. *The House of Argyll and the Collateral Branches of the Clan Campbell From the Year 420 to the Present Time.* Glasgow: Houlston & Son, 1871.

Urquhart, David. *The Spirit of the East: Illustrated in a Journal of Travels*, 2 Vols. London: Henry Colburn, 1838.

Varthema, Lodvico di. *The Travels of Ludovico di Varthema.* London: The Hakluyt Society, 1863.

Vernon, Francis. *Voyages and Travels of a Sea Officer.* London: Printed for the Author, 1792.

Verzeau, Father. "A Letter of Father Verzeau Superior General of the Missioners of the Society of Jesus in Syria to F. Fleuriau of the Same Society." In *Edifying and Curious Letters of Some Missions of the Society of Jesus From Foreign Missions.* Printed in the Year 1709, Vol. 2, 1–62.

Viviès, Jean. *English Travel Narratives in the Eighteenth Century: Exploring Genres.* Aldershot: Ashgate, 2002.

Vlami, Despina. *Trading With the Ottomans: The Levant Company in the Middle East.* London: I. B. Tauris, 2015.

Volney, Constantine. *Travels Through Syria and Egypt*, 2 Vols. London, 1788.

Voltaire. *Toleration and Other Essays by Voltaire.* Translated by Joseph McCabe. London and New York: G. P. Putnam's Sons, 1912.

Walter, Benjamin. *Illuminations.* New York: Harcourt, 2007.

Watt, James. *British Orientalisms 1759–1835.* Cambridge: Cambridge University Press, 2019.

Weitzman, Steven. *Solomon: The Lure of Wisdom.* New Haven: Yale University Press, 2011.

White, Daniel. *Early Romanticism and Religious Dissent.* Cambridge: Cambridge University Press, 2006.

White, William. *Observations on the Use of Dr. James's Powder.* London, 1774.

Whitelocke, Bulstrode. *A Journal of the Swedish Ambassy: In the Years MDCLIII and MDCLIV*, 2 Vols. London, 1772.

Wilford, Francis. "On Mount Caucasus". In *Asiatick Researches or Transactions of the Society Instituted in Bengal*, Vol VI. London: Printed by Bunney and Gold, 1801, 455–539.

Willcocks, William. "Mesopotamia: Past, Present, and Future." *The Geographical Journal* 35, no. 1 (1910): 1–15.

———. *Egyptian Irrigation.* London: E. & F. N. Spon, 1889.

———. *The Irrigation of Mesopotamia.* London: E. & F. N. Spon, 1911.

Williams, Bernard. *Ethics and the Limit of Philosophy.* Massachusetts: Harvard University Press, 1985.

Williams, Raymond. *Culture & Society 1780–1950.* New York: Anchor Books, 1960.

———. *Keywords: A Vocabulary of Culture and Society.* Oxford: Oxford University Press, 2015 [1976].

———. *Marxism and Literature.* Oxford: Oxford University Press, 1977.

Wilson, Arnold Talbot. *A Précis of the Relations of the British Government with the Tribes and Shaikhs of Arabistan.* Kolkata: Superintendent Government Printing, 1912.

———. "A Periplus of the Arabia Gulf." *The Geographical Journal* 69, no. 3 (1927): 235–255.

———. *The Persian Gulf: An Historical Sketch from the Earliest Times to the Beginning of the Twentieth Century.* Oxford: The Clarendon Press, 1928.

Wilson, Curtis. *The Cambridge History of Science*, Vol. IV. Edited by Roy Porter. Cambridge: Cambridge University Press, 2008, 328–353.

Wilson, Kathleen, and Wilson Kathleen (Eds.). *A New Imperial History: Culture, Identity and Modernity in Britain and the Empire, 1600–1840.* Cambridge: Cambridge University Press, 2004.

Wilson, Kathleen. "Citizenship, empire and modernity in the English provinces, 1720–90". In *Cultures of Empire: Colonizers in Britain and the Empire in the Nineteenth and Twentieth Centuries*, edited by Kathrine Hall. New York: Routledge, 2000, 157–186.

———. *The Island Race: Englishness, Empire and Gender in the Eighteenth Century.* New York: Routledge, 2003.

Wilson, Philip K. *Surgery, Skin and Syphilis: Daniel Turner (1667–1741).* Amsterdam: Rodopi, 1999.

Withers, Charles W. J. *Placing the Enlightenment: Thinking Geographically About the Age of Reason.* Chicago: The University of Chicago Press, 2007.

Wittman, William. *Travels in Turkey, Asia Minor and Syria.* London, 1803.

Wold, Atle L. *Scotland and the French Revolutionary War, 1792–1802.* Edinburgh: Edinburgh University Press, 2015.

Wolloch, Nathaniel. *History and Nature in the Enlightenment.* London: Routledge, 2016.

Wood, Alfred C. A. *History of the Levant Company.* Oxford: Oxford University Press, 1935.

Wood, Mark. "Captain Mark Wood's Narrative of His Overland Journey, 1779–1780." The British Library, India Office Records and Private Papers: IOR/L/MAR/C/570, ff 12–55.

Wood, Robert. *An Essay on the Original Genius and Writing of Homer.* London: Printed for H. Hughs, 1775.

———. *The Ruins of Palmyra Otherwise Tadmor in the Desart.* London, 1753.

Woodman, Thomas M. *Politeness and Poetry in the Age of Pope.* London and Toronto: Associated University Press, 1989.

Wollstonecraft, Mary. *An Historical and Moral View of the Origin and Progress of the French Revolution and the Effects It Has Produced in Europe.* London: J. Johnson, 1794.

Womak, Peter. *Improvement and Romance: Constructing the Myth of the Highlands.* Basingstoke: Macmillan, 1989.

Wraxall, Nathaniel William. *The History of France.* London, 1814.

Wulf, Andrea. *Chasing Venus: The Race to Measure the Heavens.* New York: Alfred A. Knopf, 2012.

Yapp, Malcolm. *The Making of the Modern Near East 1792–1923.* London: Routledge, 1987.

Yeldiz, Aysel. *Crisis and Rebellion in the Ottoman Empire: The Downfall of a Sultan in the Age of Revolution.* London: I.B. Tauris, 2017.

Young, Arthur. *Political Essays Concerning the Present State of the British Empire.* London: W. Strahan and T. Cadell, 1772.

Zarinebaf, Fariba. *Mediterranean Encounters: Trade and Pluralism in Early Modern Galata.* California: University of California Press, 2018.

Zilfi, Madeline C. *Women and Slavery in the Late Ottoman Empire.* Cambridge: Cambridge University Press, 2010.

Zoller, Olga. "Crossing Borders: The Pioneering Role of the Architect-Engineer Giovanni Battista Borra Between Piedmont and Britain." In *Turin and the British in the Age of the Grand Tour*, edited by Paola Bianchi and Karin Wolfe. Cambridge: Cambridge University Press, 2017, 263–281.

INDEX

www.ingramcontent.com/pod-product-compliance
Lightning Source LLC
LaVergne TN
LVHW090617090826
845264LV00022B/104
* 9 7 8 1 8 0 1 3 6 0 5 1 7 *